Forbes®

RICHEST PEOPLE

Forbes®
RICHEST PEOPLE

The Forbes® Annual Profile of the World's Wealthiest Men and Women

EDITED AND WITH AN INTRODUCTION BY
JONATHAN T. DAVIS

JOHN WILEY & SONS, INC.

NEW YORK • CHICHESTER • WEINHEIM • BRISBANE • SINGAPORE • TORONTO

ISBN 0471-17751-2 (paper)

Printed in the United States of America

10 9 8 7 6 5 4 3 2 1

Contents

Introduction

Let me tell you about the very rich. They are different from you and me.

     —F. Scott Fitzgerald

Yes, they have more money.

     —Ernest Hemingway

Who are the rich, and just how much money do they have? Each year, the editors of *Forbes* magazine seek fresh answers to these questions and publish their findings in a series of articles known in-house as the "rich lists," covering the wealthiest people in America, the world's billionaires, the highest-paid CEOs, and the top-earning athletes and entertainers.

In Forbes *Richest People,* these lists are, for the first time, published together in a single volume. Nowhere else will you be able to find so complete an accounting of other people's money, not even in the legendary IRS databanks, which focus on income as opposed to wealth and whose figures are, in any event, supplied by the subjects themselves.

By far the best known of the rich lists is the Forbes 400, a directory of America's wealthiest individuals and families. This list was the brainchild of the late Malcolm Forbes, who had an unerring sense of how to combine serious business with serious fun.

At first the editors of *Forbes* had some misgivings about counting other people's money in so public a manner. "We were aware from the start that many people would regard such a list as an invasion of privacy and a magnet for unwelcome attention," Jim Michaels, *Forbes* top editor and a legend in business journalism, wrote at the time.

Nonetheless, Michaels and his staff forged ahead. Now, a decade and a half later, the most indignant complaints come not from people who feel their privacy has been invaded but from those who feel their fortunes have been underestimated or that they have been unfairly omitted from the list altogether.

Perhaps the late Mr. Forbes realized something that had escaped the rest of us: the secrecy that surrounds great wealth is, historically, a modern invention. For most of Western history, being wealthy meant owning land; great fortunes were, literally, a matter of public record. With the rise of capitalism came forms of wealth whose ownership would not necessarily be on public display; secrecy in such matters became possible. Once governments figured out how to tax such wealth and the income it generates, the desire for secrecy became acute.

Counting someone else's money isn't easy, nor is it an exact science. Do the editors at *Forbes* miss anyone? I suppose some errors and omissions are inevitable in so large a task. Several years ago, before I became involved with the *Forbes* lists, I was at a dinner party at a friend's home in Locust Valley and the conversation turned to the newly published Forbes 400. One guest chuckled that *Forbes* had missed old Charley So-and-so, who lived two driveways down. Now, maybe the folks in Locust Valley knew something that the editors at *Forbes* had overlooked. My guess, however, is that unless Charley kept his fortune in specie and hid it in a windowless bunker, à la Scrooge McDuck, the editors at *Forbes* had probably weighed it and found it wanting.

Critics of American capitalism often begin their criticism with an incantation that starts, "The rich get richer. . . ." The Forbes 400 gives us a chance to test this thesis. Looking at the Forbes 400 lists published during the Reagan years, which many of us remember quite fondly, it is undeniably true that the average net worth of people on the list increased more than threefold.

But that statistic doesn't tell the real story. Let me quote Jim Michaels again: "Happily for the economy, constant turmoil characterized the Forbes 400 during the 1980s. Of the 400 richest Americans in 1982, only 171 remained on the list in 1991. Most of the 230-odd dropoffs were pushed off by newcomers. Mark this: Only 160, 40% of the Forbes 400, simply inherited their wealth."

Between 1991 and 1996 we can observe the same phenomena occurring again. The numbers got larger—the median net worth on the 1991 list would put someone near the bottom of today's list—but the names kept changing. The rich are getting richer, but they're different rich.

The Forbes 400 is the best known of the rich lists, but it wasn't the first. In 1971 *Forbes* ran its first survey of Chief Executive Officer compensation. The highest-paid CEO in the nation that year was Harold Geneen of International Telephone & Telegraph, who pulled down a bit more than three-quarters of a million dollars. Even if we adjust that figure for inflation, we don't begin to approach the $66 million dollars earned this year by list-topper Lawrence Cross of Green Tree Financial, and we're a far cry from the near quarter of a billion dollars that Walt Disney's Michael Eisner has earned in the last five years.

In the article accompanying the 1971 list, *Forbes* observed that "the corporate boss is usually well off, but he's rarely rich." Well, things change. By 1991, the CEO list was headed by Time Warner's Steve Ross, who made $78 million; even the CEO who was number 25 on the list pulled down $6.5 million, far more than poor Mr. Geneen earned twenty years earlier.

The 800 Highest-Paid CEOs list finally lets the man at the top know what every worker on the assembly line knows: how much his colleagues are making. Perhaps a CEO could gather such data himself from SEC filings, but then he wouldn't have the time to run his company.

In 1987, the editors of *Forbes* offered readers two new lists: foreign billionaires and the world's highest-paid entertainers.

Forbes and its competitor *Fortune* were both preparing lists of foreign billionaires at about the same time. Those of us who follow such things were eager to see how the lists would compare. The results turned out to be substantially different, because *Forbes* counted only capitalist fortunes. No kings or queens or sultans or dictators were added to pad the list. Their wealth is of a different nature and should rightly be measured with a different yardstick. Eventually, *Fortune* abandoned its effort to count foreign billionaires, ceding this field to *Forbes*.

By 1991, *Forbes* counted 274 billionaires worldwide; today, there are 447. The biggest surprise isn't the sheer increase in the number of people whose wealth is best expressed in scientific notation; after all, some part of the increase must be attributed to inflation or simply better counting by the editors. The shock is from the change in the geographic distribution. While the number of Japanese billionaires stagnated at 41, the roster of billionaires in Asia excluding Japan and in Latin America grew explosively. Colombia, for example, which in earlier years had appeared on the list only as the domicile of the lords of the cocaine cartels, is now represented by three legitimate fortunes.

Later in 1987 *Forbes* published The Top 40, a list of the world's 40 highest-paid entertainers, led by Bill Cosby. Either he or Michael Jackson was in the number one position each year until 1991, when both were displaced by the appropriately named New Kids On The Block. Cosby fell to number two, while Jackson was pushed all the way down to number five by a singer named Madonna and a talk show host named Oprah Winfrey.

Oprah had rounded out the bottom of the entertainers list in 1987; today she sits in the number one spot. Bill Gates take note: this year, Oprah is at the bottom of the Forbes 400; ten years from today, who knows? Perhaps David Letterman (number 37 on this year's Top 40) is right: someday Oprah will have *all* the money.

Building on the success of the top entertainers list, in 1990 *Forbes* added The Super 40, a list of the world's highest-paid athletes. Number one in 1990: Mike Tyson. Number one this year: Mike Tyson. Of course, while he was on another list, one maintained by the State of Ohio, he didn't appear on the Forbes Super 40 at all.

As the editor of this book and its companion volume, Forbes *Top Companies,* I feel obliged to point out that the real work on this project was done by the writers and editors whose by-lines appear in these pages. In addition, it is hard to imagine any of the lists coming into existence without the guiding hand of Jim Michaels, whom I have quoted previously. I would like to thank Greg Zorthian, Fred Maynor, Laura Santry, Ann Mintz and, especially, Barbara Strauch at Forbes, as well as Myles Thompson, Jacqueline Urinyi, and Janice Weisner at Wiley, for the contributions they have made to the development and publication of these books.

A final note, for readers who wonder if they are alone in their fantasies of appearing, one day, on one of these lists:

Shortly after I started work on this project, I received a telephone call from a friend with whom I'd lost touch, a fellow who is what used to be called a man-about-town—custom-made suits, multiple club memberships, the type of man who keeps a dinner jacket at the office, just in case. He suggested that I meet him at one of his clubs for lunch.

After a pleasant meal, he cleared his throat and said, "I understand you're editing a book that will include the Forbes 400."

"Yes, I am." I was only slightly surprised that he would have learned such a fact so quickly.

"Do you have control over what goes into the book?"

"My contract states that *Forbes* has final approval over the contents of . . ."

"That's not what I'm asking," he interrupted. "As a practical matter, are you the last person to see the manuscript before it goes to the publisher."

I thought about that for a second or two and answered cautiously.

"Yes, in a practical sense, I am."

He took a deep breath, the sort of deep breath a man might take before making a marriage proposal. Then he just blurted out, "Can you put me on the list?"

"Are you craz—"

"I don't care if I'm number 400. Or if that would be too obvious, hide me a little higher up. I'd even settle for being in the article about people who nearly made the list, but didn't."

His name doesn't appear on any of the lists this year, but the sort of person who has the audacity to make such a request just may be the sort of person who one day will earn a place in a future edition of this book.

The World's 10 Richest People

1. **William Henry Gates III** $18,000,000,000
   Microsoft's stock rose over 40% in the last year—boosting Gates' net worth by $5.1 billion. That's on top of a $4.7 billion increase the year before.

2. **Warren Buffett** $15,300,000,000
   His calling Berkshire Hathaway an overvalued stock hasn't scared away investors. Up 43% in the last year, Berkshire's rise has boosted his net worth by $4.6 billion.

3. **Paul Sacher** $13,100,000,000
   Although he's stepped down from the Roche board, this Swiss is still believed to preside over his family's interests in the pharmaceutical giant.

4. **Lee Shau Kee** $12,700,000,000
   Shares of his Henderson Land Development Co. have risen over sevenfold in six years. Now he's spun off his China projects into a new company, Henderson China.

5. **Tsai Wan-lin** $12,200,000,000
   The stock of his Cathay Life Insurance rose 50% in April after Morgan Stanley announced it was considering adding Taiwan to three of its global stock indexes.

6. **Li Ka-shing** $10,600,000,000
   After making billions in Hong Kong real estate, he's now investing in container ports, power plants and other projects in China.

7. **Yoshiaki Tsutsumi** $9,200,000,000
   This magnate used to be the world's richest individual, but falling Japanese property prices have taken their toll.

8. **Paul G. Allen** $7,500,000,000
   His smartest move was holding on to most of his stock in Microsoft after a scary encounter with Hodgkin's disease prompted him to leave the company in 1983.

9. **Kenneth R. Thomson** $7,400,000,000
   He's taking his Thomson Corp. into the front ranks of electronic publishers.

10. **Tan Yu** $7,000,000,000
    Holdings in his property portfolio stretch from the Philippines, Taiwan and China to San Francisco, Las Vegas and Houston.

EDITED BY GRAHAM BUTTON, COMPILED JULY 1996

Foreign Billionaires

EDITED BY GRAHAM BUTTON

Reported by Hiroko Asami, Riva Atlas, Natasha Bacigalupo, Justin Doebele,
Kerry A. Dolan, David S. Fondiller, Kambiz Foroohar, Carleen Hawn,
Stephen S. Johnson, Sumi Kawakami, Philippe Mao, Kazumi Miyazawa,
Taro Ohata, Juliette Rossant, Cristina von Zeppelin, Esther Wachs Book,
Caroline Waxler, Neil Weinberg and Soo Young Yoon

Additional research by Cynthia Crystal, Velma Van Voris and Mei Chi Chin

It's Asia's turn. *Forbes'* 1996 roster of the world's wealthiest people includes 82 non-Japanese Asians plus 41 Japanese. Thus, today Asia, largely a backward area at the end of World War II, is home to more than one in four of the world's great fortunes—those worth $1 billion or more. Five of the world's ten richest people are Asians. Of the ten superrich only three are U.S. citizens.

Great fortunes are made in times of rapid social, technological and economic change by those who grasp the meaning of the change early on. That's why the big fortunes matter. They spring up like plants after a spring rain wherever economies come to life and there is solid economic progress.

Primarily as a reflection of Wall Street's continuing boom, together with the changes wrought by the computer revolution, the number of billion-dollar fortunes in the U.S. climbed by 20, to 149, in the past year. The U.S. is thus still home to a third of the world's great fortunes, though Asia is gaining. The value of Bill Gates' Microsoft holdings increased by $5.1 billion to reach $18 billion. Gates is typical in a way: Many of the new U.S. fortunes are built on computer and communication technologies. In Asia, however, much of the big new money comes from such businesses as property development, energy and natural resources. In this respect, Asia mirrors the U.S. of a few decades back.

Europe? Overall the picture is fairly bleak: Witness some of Europe's double-digit unemployment rates. But there are areas of opportunity, too—witness the growing fortunes in the pharmaceutical, retailing and financial services industries.

Latin America? After a rough patch brought on by Mexico's financial crisis last year, the region is bouncing back. There are now 15 Mexicans we identify as billionaires—a gain over last year but still well below the 1994 figure of 24.

But keep your eye on Asia. The big surprise here is Southeast Asia—the ASEAN countries. Almost primitive in an economic sense 30 years ago, countries like Thailand and Indonesia are fast integrating into the global economy. As opposed to Europe and the U.S., Asia has this going for it: a high savings rate. Countries with high savings rates are less dependent on foreign capital and the vagaries of the exchange markets—such as sank the Mexican economic boom. By reinvesting internally generated capital, they can raise productivity at a fast rate—which is exactly what is happening. As an investor, you'll want to be part of this Asian boom, but don't expect a smooth ride. China is still a riddle, and the local markets are relatively thin and extremely volatile.

SHIFTING WEALTH		
	1991	1996
Total billionaires of which:	274	447
United States	96	149
Europe	81	110
Japan	41	41
Asia excluding Japan	27	82
Latin America	8	39
Other	21	26

FOREIGN BILLIONAIRES

Name/country/*industry*

$5 BILLION AND UP

Albrecht, Karl and Theo/Germany/*retailing*
Berlusconi, Silvio/Italy/*media, diversified*
Bettencourt, Liliane/France/*cosmetics*
Bin Mahfouz, Mohamed Salim and family/
  Saudi Arabia/*bank, invest*
Cheng Yu-tung/Hong Kong/*real estate*
Chung Ju-yung and family/Korea/*diversified*
Ermírio de Moraes, Antonio and family/
  Brazil/*diversified*
Haefner, Walter/Switzerland/*automobiles, software*
Haniel family/Germany/*diversified*
Kuok, Robert/Malaysia/*diversified*
Kwek Leng Beng and family/Singapore/*diversified*
Kwok brothers/Hong Kong/*real estate*
Lee Shau Kee/Hong Kong/*real estate*
Li Ka-shing and family/Hong Kong/*diversified*
Merck family/Germany/*pharmaceuticals, chemicals*
Mulliez, Gerard and family/France/*retailing, mail order*
Ng, Teng Fong and Robert/Hong Kong/*real estate*
Otto, Michael and family/Germany/*retailing*
Quandt, Johanna, Susanne and Stefan/
  Germany/*automobiles*
Rausing, Hans and Gad/Scandinavia/*packaging*
Sacher, Paul Hoffman and Oeri family/Switzerland/*pharmaceuticals*
Slim Helú, Carlos and family/Mexico/*diversified*
Takei, Yasuo and family/Japan/*consumer finance*
Yu Tan/Philippines/*real estate*
Thomson, Kenneth R./Canada/*media, retailing, real estate*
Tsai Wan-lin and family/Taiwan/*insurance, financial services*
Tsutsumi, Yoshiaki/Japan/*real estate*
Widjaja, Eka Tjipta/Indonesia/*diversified*
Wonowidjojo family/Indonesia/*tobacco*

Name/country/*industry*

$2 BILLION AND UP

Agnelli, Giovanni and family/Italy/*automobiles*
Al-Kharafi, Jassim and family/Kuwait/*construction, banking*
Al-Rajhi family/Saudi Arabia/*banking*
Angelini, Anacleto and family/Chile/*diversified*
Arison, Ted/Israel/*Carnival Corp.*
Azcárraga Milmo, Emilio and family/
  Mexico/*media*
Beisheim, Otto/Germany/*retailing*
Bertarelli, Fabio/Switzerland/*pharmaceuticals*
Benetton, Luciano and family/Italy/*clothing*
Birla family/India/*diversified*
Boehringer family/Germany/*pharmaceuticals*
Botin family/Spain/*banking*
Bouriez, Philippe and family/France/*retailing*
Bozano, Julio Rafael de Aragao/Brazil/*financial services, diversified*
Brenninkmeijer family/Netherlands/*retailing*
Bronfman, Charles/Canada/*beverages, spirits*
Brost family/Germany/*media, investments*
Chearavanont, Dhanin and family/Thailand/*diversified*
Chey Jong-hyon and family/Korea/*diversified*
Ciputra and family/Indonesia/*real estate*
Defforey, Denis and family/France/*retailing*
Del Vecchio, Leonardo/Italy/*eyewear*
Dumas, Jean-Louis and family/France/*Hermes*
Engelhorn, Curt and family/Germany/*pharmaceuticals, health care*
Fentener van Vlissingen family/Netherlands/*energy, retail*
Ferrero, Michele and family/Italy/*confectionery*
Flick, Friedrich Karl Jr./Germany/*investments*
Fok, Henry Ying-tung/Hong Kong/*casinos, real estate*
Funke family/Germany/*media, investments*
Gerling, Rolf/Germany/*insurance*

FOREIGN BILLIONAIRES *(CONT.)*

Name/country/*industry*

$2 BILLION AND UP *(continued)*

Gokongwei, John Jr./Philippines/*diversified*
Gotianun, Andrew/Philippines/*real estate*
Hariri, Rafic/Lebanon/*construction, banking*
Haub, Erivan/Germany/*retailing*
Heineken, Alfred/Netherlands/*beer*
Henkel family/Germany/*chemicals*
Herz, Günter and family/Germany/*consumer products*
Ho, Stanley/Hong Kong/*casinos, hotels, transportation*
Hopp, Dietmar and family/Germany/*software*
Irving family/Canada/*diversified*
Ito, Masatoshi and family/Japan/*retailing*
Iwasaki family/Japan/*real estate, hotels*
Itoyama, Eitaro and family/Japan/*golf courses, resorts*
Jameel family/Saudi Arabia/*auto distribution, real estate*
Jinnai, Ryoichi and family/Japan/*consumer finance*
Kadoorie, Michael and family/Hong Kong/*utilities, hotels*
Khoo Teck Puat/Singapore/*hotels, banking*
Kim Woo-choong/Korea/*diversified*
Kinoshita Kyosuke and family/Japan/*consumer finance*
Kipp, Karl-Heinz/Germany/*real estate*
Kirch, Leo/Germany/*media*
Koc, Vehbi and family/Turkey/*diversified*
Koo Cha-kyung and family/Korea/*diversified*
Koo, Jeffrey and family/Taiwan/*banking*
Kristiansen, Kjeld Kirk and family/Scandinavia/*Lego*
Lamsam, Banyong and family/Thailand/*banking*
Landolt family/Switzerland/*pharmaceuticals, financial services*
Latsis, John/Greece/*shipping, investments*
Lee family/Singapore/*banking, plantations*

Name/country/*industry*

$2 BILLION AND UP *(continued)*

Lee Kun-hee and family/Korea/*diversified*
Lemos family/Greece/*shipping, investments*
Liem Sioe Liong and family/Indonesia/*diversified*
Lim Goh Tong/Malaysia/*diversified*
Livanos family/Greece/*shipping, investments*
Luksic, Andronico and family/Chile/*diversified*
Marinho, Roberto/Brazil/*media*
Matsuda, Kazuo and family/Japan/*finance*
Moller, Maersk McKinney and family/Scandinavia/*shipping*
Mori, Minoru and Akira and family/Japan/*real estate*
Morita Akio and family/Japan/*Sony, real estate, food*
Nambu, Yasuyuki and family/Japan/*temp agencies, retailing*
Niarchos family/Greece/*shipping, investments*
Oetker, Rudolf and family/Germany/*food*
Ohga, Masahiro and family/Japan/*publishing*
Olayan, Suliman S./Saudi Arabia/*diversified*
Oppenheimer family/South Africa/*mining*
Otsuka, Akihiko and family/Japan/*pharmaceuticals, health drinks*
Pangestu, Prajogo/Indonesia/*lumber*
Peralta, Alejo and family/Mexico/*industry, telecommunications*
Perez Companc family/Argentina/*diversified*
Porsche family/Germany/*automobiles*
Quek Leng Chan and family/Malaysia/*diversified*
Rocca, Roberto and family/Argentina/*diversified*
Rothschild family/U.K./France/*banking, wine*
Sabanci, Sakip and family/Turkey/*diversified*
Sainsbury, David and family/U.K./*supermarkets*
Saji, Keizo and family/Japan/*food, beverages*
Sampoerna, Putera and family/Indonesia/*tobacco*
Schickedanz family/Germany/*retailing*

FOREIGN BILLIONAIRES *(CONT.)*

Name/country/*industry*

$2 BILLION AND UP *(continued)*

Schmidheiny, Stephan/Switzerland/*investments*
Schmidheiny, Thomas/Switzerland/*construction materials*
Schmidt-Ruthenbeck family/Germany/*retailing*
Schorghuber, Stefan/Germany/*beer, real estate*
Schwarz, Dieter/Germany/*retailing*
Servier, Jacques/France/*diversified*
Seydoux/Schlumberger families/France/*pharmaceuticals*
Shin Kyuk-ho/Korea/*diversified*
Shinawatra, Thaksin and family/Thailand/*telecommunications*
Shino, Rinji/Japan/*real estate*
Son, Masayoshi/Japan/*software, publishing, trade shows*
Sophonpanich, Chatri and family/Thailand/*banking*
Sutanto, Djuhar and family/Indonesia/*diversified*
Swire brothers/Hong Kong/*diversified*
Sy, Henry and family/Philippines/*shopping malls*
Tan, Lucio/Philippines/*tobacco, airlines*
Tiong Hiew King and family/Malaysia/*lumber*
Ty, George and family/Philippines/*banking*
Verspieren/Decoster family/France/*electrical fittings, insurance*
Villar, Manuel and family/Philippines/*housing*
von Finck, Wilhelm and August/Germany/*investments*
von Oppenheim, Alfred and family/Germany/*banking*
von Siemens family/Germany/*electronics, heavy industry*
Wang, Nina/Hong Kong/*real estate*
Wang, Yue-Che (Y.C.) and family/Taiwan/*plastics, electronics*
Wertheimer, Alain and family/France/*luxury goods*

Name/country/*industry*

$2 BILLION AND UP *(continued)*

Weston, Garry and family/U.K./*food*
Woo, Peter and family/Hong Kong/*diversified*
Wu, Eugene and family/Taiwan/*insurance*
Yamaguchi, Hisakichi/Japan/*packaging*
Yaw Teck-seng and family/Malaysia/*lumber*
Yoshimoto, Goroemon and family/Japan/*real estate*
Zobel de Ayala, Jamie and family/Philippines/*real estate, diversified*

$1 BILLION AND UP

Ahmad, Yahaya/Malaysia/*automobiles*
Al-Sulaiman, Abdul Aziz/Saudi Arabia/*cement, investments*
Ambani family/India/*textiles, energy*
Andrade, Roberto and Gabriel/Brazil/*construction*
André, Georges and family/Switzerland/*commodities trading*
Aramburuzabala family/Mexico/*beer*
Arango, Jeronimo/Mexico/*retail*
Ardila Lulle, Carlos/Colombia/*soft drinks, diversified*
Asavabhokhin, Boonsong and family/Thailand/*housing*
Autrey family/Mexico/*steel, distribution*
Bailleres, Alberto/Mexico/*mining, diversified*
Bemberg family/Argentina/*beer, investments*
Bencharongkul, Boonchai and family/Thailand/*telecomm*
Bhirombhakdi, Piya and family/Thailand/*beer*
Bosch family/Germany/*auto parts*
Branson, Richard/U.K./*diversified*
Brescia family/Peru/*diversified*
Busujima, Kunio/Japan/*pachinko machines*
Camargo family/Brazil/*construction*
Chang Yung-fa/Taiwan/*shipping, aviation*
Chao, K.P. and family/Hong Kong/*textiles*

FOREIGN BILLIONAIRES *(CONT.)*

Name/country/*industry*

$1 BILLION AND UP *(continued)*

Chen, Din Hwa/Hong Kong/*real estate*
Cisneros family/Venezuela/*diversified*
Conle family/Germany/*travel services*
Dassault, Serge and family/France/*aerospace, electronics*
David-Weill, Michel and family/France/*banking*
DeGroote, Michael G./Canada/*diversified*
Diehl, Karl and family/Germany/*mechanical engineering, defense*
Diniz, Abílio and family/Brazil/*retailing*
Dorrance, John T. III/Ireland/*Campbell Soup*
Ebner, Martin/Switzerland/*investments*
Eisenberg, Shoul/Israel/*diversified*
Feffer, Leon and family/Brazil/*diversified*
Freudenberg family/Germany/*auto parts, textiles*
Fujita, Den/Japan/*fast food*
Fukutake, Soichiro and family/Japan/*cram schools*
Garcia, Luiz Alberto and family/Brazil/*telecomm, diversified*
Garza Lagüera, Eugenio and family/Mexico/*banking, beverages*
Garza Sada, Bernardo and family/Mexico/*diversified*
González Barrera, Roberto/Mexico/*food, banking*
Goulandris family/Greece/*shipping, investments*
Halim Saad/Malaysia/*diversified*
Halley, Paul-Louis and family/France/*retailing*
Hartono, R. Budi and family/Indonesia/*tobacco*
Hector, Hans-Werner/Germany/*software*
Hilti, Martin and family/Liechtenstein/*construction tools*
Huang Shi-hui/Taiwan/*automobiles, motorcycles, banking*
Inamori, Kazuo/Japan/*electronics*
Isono family/Japan/*food, spirits*
Jacobs, Klaus/Switzerland/*chocolate, investments*
Jahr family/Germany/*publishing*

Name/country/*industry*

$1 BILLION AND UP *(continued)*

Juffali family/Saudi Arabia/*diversified*
Kamel, Saleh Abdullah/Saudi Arabia/*banking, diversified*
Kamprad, Ingvar/Scandinavia/*furniture, retailing*
Kanoo, Ahmed Ali and family/Bahrain/*trading, shipping, invest*
Karnasuta, Chaijudh and family/Thailand/*construction*
Kim Suk-won and family/Korea/*diversified*
Knauf family/Germany/*construction materials*
Koplowitz sisters/Spain/*construction*
Krishnan, T. Ananda/Malaysia/*diversified*
Larragoiti family/Brazil/*insurance*
Larrea, Jorge/Mexico/*mining*
Lee Hon Chiu and family/Hong Kong/*real estate*
Leibbrand family/Germany/*retailing, real estate*
Leophairatana, Prachai and family/Thailand/*petrochemicals*
Liebherr family/Switzerland/*construction equipment*
Lo Ying Shek and family/Hong Kong/*real estate*
Lopez, Eugenio and family/Philippines/*diversified*
Louis-Dreyfus family/France/*commodities trading, diversified*
Mabuchi, Kenichi and family/Japan/*minimotors*
Mann, Hugo and family/Germany/*retailing*
Mantegazza, Sergio/Switzerland/*travel services*
March family/Spain/*diversified*
Matte family/Chile/*banking, paper*
Mendoza, Lorenzo and family/Venezuela/*beer*
Merckle, Adolf/Germany/*pharmaceuticals, cement*
Mittal, Lakshmi and family/India/*steel*
Miyomoto, Masafumi and family/Japan/*videogame software*
Mohn, Reinhard and family/Germany/*media*
Moores family/U.K./*retailing*
Murata, Junichi and family/Japan/*machinery*
Nakajima, Kenkichi/Japan/*pachinko*

FOREIGN BILLIONAIRES *(CONT.)*

Name/country/*industry*

$1 BILLION AND UP *(continued)*

Noboa family/Ecuador/*bananas, diversified*

Nursalim, Sjamsul and family/Indonesia/*diversified*

Odebrecht, Norberto and family/Brazil/*construction*

Ofer, Sammy and Yehuda/Israel/*shipping, real estate*

Osano, Masakuni and family/Japan/*real estate, hotels, transport*

Oshima, Kenshin/Japan/*finance*

Otani family/Japan/*hotels*

Packer, Kerry/Australia/*media*

Persson, Stefan and family/Scandinavia/*retailing*

Peugeot family/France/*automobiles*

Plattner, Hasso/Germany/*software*

Ramli, Tajudin/Malaysia/*telecommunications, airlines*

Ratanarak, Krit and family/Thailand/*banking, cement*

Reimann family/Germany/*chemicals, consumer products*

Riady, Mochtar and family/Indonesia/*real estate, financial services*

Röchling family/Germany/*steel, engineering, defense*

Romo Garza, Alfonso/Mexico/*tobacco, vegetable seeds, investments*

Rossi di Montelera family/Italy/*spirits, wine*

Rupert, Anton and family/South Africa/*tobacco, media*

Saba Raffoul, Isaac and family/Mexico/*diversified*

Safra, Edmond and brothers/Lebanon/*banking*

Sahenk, Ayhan and family/Turkey/*banking, construction*

Said, José and Jaime/Chile/*beverages, banking*

Name/country/*industry*

$1 BILLION AND UP *(continued)*

Salinas Pliego, Ricardo and family/Mexico/*retailing, media*

Santo Domingo, Julio and family/Colombia/*beer, diversified*

Sarmiento Angulo, Luis Carlos/Colombia/*diversified*

Schroder family/U.K./*banking*

Shaw, Run Run/Hong Kong/*media, real estate*

Shi Wen-long and family/Taiwan/*plastics*

Shiiki, Masakazu/Japan/*consumer finance*

Simon family/Germany/*beer*

Ströher family/Germany/*hair care*

Takei family/Japan/*hotels, real estate*

Takenaka, Renichi and family/Japan/*construction*

Teh Hong Piow/Malaysia/*banking*

Thyssen-Bornemisza, Hans Heinrich/Switzerland/*art, industry*

Toyoda family/Japan/*Toyota*

Tschira, Klaus and family/Germany/*software*

Uehara, Shoji and family/Japan/*pharmaceuticals, health drinks*

von Thurn and Taxis, Albert/Germany/*real estate, beer*

Wee Cho Yaw/Singapore/*banking*

Werhahn family/Germany/*construction materials*

Weston, Galen and family/Canada/*food*

Wong, George/Hong Kong/*real estate*

Würth, Reinhold and family/Germany/*fasteners, hardware*

Yamauchi, Hiroshi/Japan/*Nintendo*

Yeoh, Tiong-lay and family/Malaysia/*construction*

Yoshida, Tadahiro and family/Japan/*zippers, construction materials*

Zambrano, Lorenzo and family/Mexico/*cement*

The 800 Highest-Paid CEOs

A handful of chief executives were paid staggering amounts over the past five years. But the median five-year pay for 800 chief executives was just $6.9 million.

BY ERIC S. HARDY

Data compiled May, 1996.

It isn't easy to justify some of these astronomical pay packets given to chief executives.

Walt Disney Co.'s Michael Eisner tops Forbes' long-term compensation list for the third year in a row, earning $233 million in the last five years.

Green Tree Financial's chief executive, Lawrence Coss, earned $119 million in total compensation over the same period, $66 million in 1995 alone.

But it is well to put all this in perspective. The 25 top-paid chief executives for the past five years (see table of Best-paid executives: 1991–95) earned a total of nearly $425 million last year alone. More than half of this huge sum came from exercising stock options. In short, most of these outsize rewards were a by-product of a roaring bull market. It is hard for most shareholders to complain in a year when the stock market—measured by the S&P 500—rose 38% and added $1.8 trillion to their net worths.

Take Coss of Green Tree Financial. Over that same five-year period that he was pocketing well over $100 million, a $10,000 investment in Green Tree stock would have multiplied to $160,000. That's an average return of 74% a year, including reinvested dividends. Coss was an innovator. He made mortgages available to buyers of mobile homes, a class of buyers most lenders shirked. He proved they were good risks. In that innovation he made everyone better off: his customers, his shareholders, the economy and himself.

11

Then there's Jack Welch of General Electric. Welch took home $45 million in the past five years. In those years GE shareholders were made richer by $68 billion, and GE solidified its position as one of the world's best-managed corporate giants.

We won't try to justify what H.J. Heinz has paid the flamboyant Anthony O'Reilly since 1991. O'Reilly's total is $119 million, ranking him fourth in the top 25. But Heinz's results have been disappointing over the last several years. Earnings per share have risen an average 6.5% over the last five years. And during this period, Heinz stock has failed to keep pace with the S&P 500. Tony O'Reilly's ego and paycheck are bigger than his accomplishments.

What about Howard Solomon, chief executive of Forest Laboratories? Solomon's compensation totaled $79 million over the past five years, while his firm's stock rose an average 4% a year—about in line with returns for money market funds. Let's hear a big Bronx cheer for Howard Solomon.

And, to put it mildly, it was pretty poor public relations on the part of AT&T's board to award Robert Allen $6 million right on the heels of announcing the company was about to cut its payroll by 40,000 people through attrition and layoffs.

Perspective again. While the media and politicians wallowed in indignation over some of the bigger stock option packages, no one was looking at the whole picture. So let's look at it.

Forbes tracks 800 major U.S. corporations. What was the median pay packet for the chief executive of the 800?

Was it $10 million?

Was it $5 million? It was $1.5 million, including gains from exercising stock options. No one doubts that this is a nice living, but $1.5 million a year, taxed at the margin at well over 40%, is not a ticket to The Forbes Four Hundred. It is, in fact, about in line with the take-home of top earners in a whole range of professions: physicians, lawyers, fashion models, TV personalities and poets, Indian chiefs and professional gamblers. The corporate chief executive is, after all, a person who has risen to the top of his profession. A few of them will get rotten rich. Most of them will merely retire in comfort and leave their families relatively well off.

Helped along nicely by the bull market, there were lots of happy faces in executive suites last year: The median chief executive in this survey took home $1.5 million in total compensation, a 15% increase over 1994. The increase was well above the inflation rate, but if you want to look at the downside, it was a good deal less than the 38% increase in the stock market. Who was number one? For the second year in a row, Lawrence Coss of Green Tree Financial. Only $434,000 of Coss'

Don't ask us why, but chief executives without a college degree earned more money than those who own a sheepskin.

Best-paid executives: 1991-95

| Company/ chief executive | Stock owned market value ($mil) | 1995 COMPENSATION | | | | | 5-year total ($thou) | Unexercised vested options ($mil) | 5-year return |
		salary + bonus ($thou)	% change	other ($thou)	stock gains ($thou)	total ($thou)			
Walt Disney/ Michael D Eisner	184.1	8,775	9	7	—	8,782	232,746	238	17
Conseco/ Stephen C Hilbert	63.6	7,666	−21	17,130	—	24,796	231,651	26	40
Travelers Group/ Sanford I Weill	251.4	5,329	45	2,255	41,971	49,555	199,673	—	36
HJ Heinz/ Anthony J F O'Reilly	198.1	1,775	136	664	—	2,439	119,144	50	8
Green Tree Financial/ Lawrence M Coss	154.6	65,580	126	—	—	65,580	119,108	19	74
Forest Labs/ Howard Solomon	25.4	611	6	24	16,416	17,050	79,263	48	4
Gateway 2000/ Theodore W Waitt	1,195.6	839	−11	—	61,024	61,863	64,369	67	17[4]
Coca-Cola/ Roberto C Goizuet	672.4	4,880	12	1,640	6,566	13,086	59,585	65	27
DSC Communications/ James L Donald	24.2	919[5]	−38	5,981	12,488	19,388	55,857	28	47
Advanced Micro/ Walter J Sanders	4.6	3,006	−34	2,027	—	5,033	54,562	7	11
Colgate-Palmolive/ Reuben Mark	47.0	1,985	−16	2,325	11,567	15,877	54,522	31	18
Mirage/ Stephen A Wynn	438.2	3,750	0	4	—	3,755	49,539	134	29
Comcast/ Ralph J Roberts	190.3	800[1]	0	4,552	4,674	10,026	49,397	15	11
General Dynamics/ James R Mellor	20.2	2,420	7	2,178	—	4,598	46,481[3]	1	46
Leucadia National/ Ian M Cumming	246.8	795	−45	251	27,996	29,042	45,448	—	30
General Electric/ John F Welch Jr	34.7	5,250	21	3,431	5,316	13,997	45,401	35	21
Compaq Computer/ Eckhard Pfeiffer	0.1	3,625	2	1,250	12,493	17,368	42,459	40	13
Bear Stearns Cos/ James E Cayne	89.2	4,230	−45	4,774	913	9,917	42,026[2]	—	23
Parametric Tech/ Steven C Walske	44.6	800	10	5	5,390	6,195	41,644	12	67
Enron/ Kenneth L Lay	31.9	2,430	11	1,254	4,937	8,621	41,439	19	25
Merrill Lynch/ Daniel P Tully	32.1	5,144	6	1,511	—	6,654	39,483	53	31
American Intl Grp/ Maurice R Greenberg	944.1	4,150	11	7	6,834	10,991	38,613	24	17

(Continued)

Best-paid executives: 1991-95 *(Cont.)*

| Company/
chief executive | Stock owned
market value
($mil) | 1995 COMPENSATION | | | | | 5-year
total
($thou) | Unexercised
vested
options
($mil) | 5-year
return |
		salary + bonus ($thou)	% change	other ($thou)	stock gains ($thou)	total ($thou)			
Masco/ Richard A Manoogian	29.0	1,407[1]	17	4,201	—	5,608	38,013	—	7
Applied Materials/ James C Morgan	25.5	1,688	32	12	10,631	12,331	36,767	—	56
AutoZone/ Joseph R Hyde III	484.3	1,053	–9	6	—	1,058	36,458	—	34[4]

*Average annual total return as of Mar. 31.
[1]Prior-year data.
[2]Three-year total.
[3]Four-year total.
[4]Return is for less than five-year period.
[5]Received options or restricted stock in lieu of salary or bonus.

Compensation Trends

It is easier for a top executive to earn a great paycheck at a rapidly growing firm than at a well-established giant.

Company/chief executive	Total compensation ($thou)
Green Tree Financial/Lawrence M Coss	65,580
Gateway 2000/Theodore W Waitt	61,863
Travelers Group/Sanford I Weill	49,555
Leucadia National/Ian M Cumming	29,042
Conseco/Stephen C Hilbert	24,796
Amgen/Gordon M Binder	21,634
Health Systems Intl/Malik M Hasan	20,685
DSC Communications/James L Donald	19,388[1]
US Robotics/Casey G Cowell	18,586
Compaq Computer/Eckhard Pfeiffer	17,368

[1]Received options or restricted stock in lieu of portion of salary or bonus.

Wealthy today

The ten people listed in the table below own a total of $53 billion of their firms' stock.

Company/chief executive	5-year total compensation ($thou)	STOCK OWNED	
		%	market value ($mil)
Berkshire Hathaway/Warren E Buffett	500	43.22	16,770
Microsoft/William H Gates	1,852	23.92	14,949
Oracle/Lawrence J Ellison	20,703	22.68	4,603
NIKE/Philip H Knight	6,889	33.93	4,503
Viacom/Sumner M Redstone	NA	24.84	3,742
Turner Broadcasting/Robert E Turner	7,197	38.16	2,180
Estee Lauder Cos/Leonard A Lauder	NA	48.77	1,973
US Satellite Broad/Stanley E Hubbard	NA	51.28	1,715
Loews/Laurence A Tisch	2,892	15.75	1,383
Gateway 2000/Theodore W Waitt	64,369	44.63	1,196

NA: Not available.

Wealthier tomorrow?

Based on their unexercised stock options, the executives in the table below have a good shot at adding to their personal fortunes – provided that Wall Street cooperates.

Company/chief executive	Total compensation ($THOU)	5-year total compensation ($THOU)	MARKET VALUE ($MIL) stock owned	unexercised vested options
Walt Disney/ Michael D Eisner	8,782	232,746	184	238
HFS/Henry R Silverman	1,441	5,035[1]	6	176
HealthSouth/ Richard M Scrushy	7,388	29,283	12	136
Mirage/Stephen A Wynn	3,755	49,539	438	134
Amgen/Gordon M Binder	21,634	25,755	9	76
Computer Associates/ Charles B Wang	5,623	21,017	643	69
Intel/Andrew S Grove	8,448	20,607	59	67
Gateway 2000/ Theodore W Waitt	61,863	64,369	1,196	67
Coca-Cola/ Roberto C Goizueta	13,086	59,585	672	65
Oracle/Lawrence J Ellis	14,143	20,703	4,603	62

[1]Four-year total.

pay came from his base salary; the rest was a huge $65.1 million bonus in the form of nearly 2 million shares of Green Tree stock and cash. Coming in second was Theodore Waitt of Gateway 2000, the PC company. Waitt received most of his handsome compensation via a $61 million gain from exercising stock options.

Dragging the median figure down were chaps like Citizens Bancorp's Alfred Smith Jr., who took only a director's fee and car allowance totaling $27,000. Robert Levine of Cabletron Systems, Stanley Hubbard of U.S. Satellite Broadcasting and Warren Buffett of Berkshire Hathaway were satisfied with $100,000 or less in salary. As for Buffett, you can view his low pay rate as being a statement to the troops to keep costs down. He happens to be either the richest or second-richest man in the country.

About that median figure of $1.5 million: It was made up of $609,000 in salaries and $440,000 in bonuses. Two hundred seventy-three executives realized a total of $695 million from exercising stock options. Other compensation, including long-term incentive pay, car allowances, company contributions to 401(k) savings plans and insurance premiums, added $143,000.

Here's a twist: For some unascertainable reason, pay and educational level are inversely related. The median pay of the 58 chief executives who

The 800 Highest-Paid CEOs

Company/chief executive	Rank among 800 execs	in industry	Age	Birthplace	Education undergraduate	graduate
AEROSPACE & DEFENSE						
AlliedSignal/Lawrence A Bossidy	38	2	61	Pittsfield MA	Colgate U, BA '57	
Boeing/Philip M Condit	460	9	54	Berkeley CA	U of Cal Berkeley, BSME '63	Princeton, MS '65
General Dynamics/James R Mellor	111	4	66	Detroit MI	U of Michigan, BS '52	MS '53
Litton Industries/John M Leonis	474	11	62	Whittier CA	U of Arizona, BSEE '59	
Lockheed Martin/Norman R Augustine	33	1	60	Denver CO	Princeton, BSE '57	MSE '59

lack a college degree is $1.6 million, compared with $1.5 million for those executives with just an undergraduate degree. Could it be because the highest earners are entrepreneurs who were in too much of a hurry to waste time going to college? However, the 428 chief executives with a graduate degree did beat out their bachelor degree brethren by $55,000. Which undergraduate schools turned out the most chief executives? Harvard came in first with 23. Cornell and Princeton tied for second with 18. Stanford can claim 13.

There's a half-century age gap between the eldest and the youngest chief executive. The youngest is Michael Dell, 31, of Dell Computer Corp.; the eldest, Dillard Department Stores founder William Dillard Sr., 81. New York State was the birthplace of the most top execs (120), while second place goes to Illinois (59); 61 were born outside the U.S.

A few words about how the following statistics were compiled: Forbes counts the value of restricted stock shares that vested during the past fiscal year. We don't include stock grants that vest in the future. If the precise date of vesting is not disclosed in the proxy statement, we use the average of the high and low stock price during the year to calculate the value. The "stock gains" column gives the value of options that were exercised during the year less the purchase price of the shares.

TENURE (YRS)		COMPENSATION							STOCK OWNED		COMPANY DATA		
with firm	as CEO	salary	bonus	% change*	other	stock gains	total	5-year total	%	market value	sales	profits	5-year return
		($thou)				($thou)				($mil)	($mil)		
		$825	$1,000	17%	$1,336	—	$3,126	$16,768	0.05%	$7.2	$11,716	$393	24%
5	5	2,000	2,350	20	1,336	4,056	9,741	35,237	0.09	13.9	14,346	875	35
31	—[10]	559	374	NA	136	249	1,318[9]	NA	—[6]	0.6	19,515	393	16
15	3	670	1,750	7	2,178	—	4,598	46,481[4]	0.53	20.2	3,067	321	46
36	2	446	500	18	6	292[15]	1,244	2,971[5]	0.02	0.4	3,412	144	21
19	8	984	1,300	25	8,281	—	10,565	24,050	0.05	7.8	22,853	682	29

Rank is based on total compensation for latest fiscal year. **Market value** of CEO stock is based on Apr. 17 stock price and includes all classes of common. **Sales and profits** are as reported in The Forbes 500s Annual Directory issue. **Five-year return** is average annual total return as of Mar. 31. Sources of return data: Market Guide via OneSource Information Services; Bloomberg Financial Markets. *Percentage change is for combined salary and bonus. [1]Company founder. [2]Return is for less than five-year period. [3]Annualized salary. [4]Four-year total. [5]Three-year total. [6]Less than 0.01%. [7]Less than $100,000. [8]Prior-year data. [9]New CEO; compensation may be for another executive office. [10]New CEO; less than six months' service. [11]Director's fees only. [12]Includes shares indirectly held. [13]Paid to date. [14]Received options or restricted stock in lieu of portion of salary or bonus. [15]Includes value for Western Atlas' options exercised. NA: Not available.

(Continued)

The 800 Highest-Paid CEOs (Cont.)

Company/chief executive	RANK among 800 execs	in industry	Age	Birthplace	EDUCATION undergraduate	graduate
AEROSPACE & DEFENSE, *Cont.*						
McDonnell Douglas/Harry C Stonecipher	265	8	60	Scott County TN	Tennessee Tech, BS '60	
Northrop Grumman/Kent Kresa	168	6	58	New York NY	MIT, BS '59	MS '61
Raytheon/Dennis J Picard	91	3	63	Providence RI	Northeastern U, BSEE '62	
Sundstrand/Robert H Jenkins	461	10	53	Chicago IL	U of Wisc Madison, BS '66	
Textron/James F Hardymon	117	5	61	Maysville KY	U of Kentucky, BS '56	MS '58
United Technologies/George David	237	7	54	Bryn Mawr PA	Harvard, BA '65	U of Virginia, MBA '67
BUSINESS SERVICES & SUPPLIES						
Alco Standard/John E Stuart	179	6	52	Berkeley CA	Pace U NY, BS '80	MBA '80
Automatic Data/Josh S Weston	51	2	67	Brooklyn NY	CUNY City, BS '50	U of New Zealand, MA '52
Avery Dennison/Charles D Miller	316	10	68	Hartford CT	Johns Hopkins U, BA '49	
H&R Block/Richard H Brown	697	20	48	New Brunswick NJ	Ohio U, BS '69	
Browning-Ferris Inds/Bruce E Ranck	570	17	47	Canada	Michigan State U, BS '73	
Ceridian/Lawrence Perlman	469	15	58	St Paul MN	Carleton C, BA '60	Harvard, JD '63
Comdisco/Jack Slevin	589	18	59	East Orange NJ	Rutgers, BSCE '58	
Computer Sciences/Van B Honeycutt	760	23	51	Harrisburg VA	Franklin U, BBA '71	
Deluxe/John A Blanchard III	607	19	53	Laurel MS	Princeton, BA '65	MIT, MS '78
Equifax/Daniel W McGlaughlin	308	8	59	Erie PA	U of Cincinnati, BS '59	Case Western, PhD '66
First Data/Henry C Duques	740	21	52	Washington DC	George Washington U, BBA '65	MBA '69
WW Grainger/Richard L Keyser	434	13	53	Harrisburg PA	US Naval Acad, BS '64	Harvard, MBA '71

with firm	as CEO	salary	bonus	% change*	other	stock gains	total	5-year total	%	market value ($mil)	sales	profits	5-year return
		($thou)					($thou)				($mil)		
2	2	825	1,042	NA	294	—	2,161	NA	0.05	5.3	14,332	–416	52
21	6	730	1,000	12	1,396	—	3,126	10,698	0.43	12.4	6,818	252	22
41	5	1,000	870	2	2,725	820	5,415	20,031	0.14	16.9	11,716	793	23
1	1	650[3]	659	NA	9	—	1,318	NA	0.10	2.3	1,473	79	25
6	4	925	1,472	31	1,919	—	4,316	13,505	0.02	1.6	9,973	479	24
21	2	977	900	17	165	291	2,333	9,254[5]	0.05	7.2	22,624	750	22
		$650	$451	12%	$178	—	$1,415	$8,774	0.14%	$6.4	$3,114	$128	18%
11	3	850	850	21	1,080	151	2,931	5,553[5]	0.11	6.4	10,272	219	29
26	13	1,000	200	12	8	6,992	8,199	26,559	0.15	16.7	3,166	422	21
32	18	732	1,000	12	178	—	1,909	11,237	0.32	9.3	3,114	144	21
1	1	650[3]	NA	—	—	—	650	NA	0.04	1.7	1,528	95	10
26	1	500	500	NA	13	—	1,013[9]	NA	0.05	3.0	5,917	378	6
16	6	650	634	8	3	—	1,287	5,744	0.13	4.0	1,333	98	NA
21	2	400	401	0	6	145	952	NA	0.42	6.8	2,246	106	8
21	1	490	0	NA	3	—	493[9]	NA	0.06	2.5	4,100	133	26
1	1	500[3]	403	NA	2	—	905	NA	0.04	1.0	1,858	87	0
7	—[10]	377	143	NA	1,441	—	1,962[9]	NA	0.14	5.1	1,623	148	20
9	7	502	0	19	45	—	547	4,450	—[6]	—[7]	4,081	–84	32[2]
10	1	512	674	3	206	—	1,391	NA	—[6]	0.2	3,277	187	12

For footnotes 1–14 see page 17.

(Continued)

The 800 Highest-Paid CEOs (Cont.)

| | RANK | | | | EDUCATION | |
Company/chief executive	among 800 execs	in industry	Age	Birthplace	undergraduate	graduate
BUSINESS SERVICES & SUPPLIES, *Cont.*						
Kelly Services/Terence E Adderley	496	16	62	Detroit MI	U of Michigan, BBA '55	MBA '56
Manpower/Mitchell S Fromstein	110	4	68	Milwaukee WI	U of Wisc Madison, BBA '49	
Minn Mining & Mfg/Livio D DeSimone	248	7	59	Canada	McGill, BSCE '57	
Ogden/R Richard Ablon	435	14	46	New York NY	Boston U, BA '71	
Olsten/Frank N Liguori	32	1	49	New York NY	St Francis C NY, BBA '69	
Paychex/B Thomas Golisano[1]	756	22	54	Irondequoit NY		
PHH/Robert D Kunisch	311	9	54	Norwalk CT	NYU, BBA '63	
Pitney Bowes/Michael J Critelli	425	12	47	Newark NY	U of Wisc Madison, BA '70	Harvard, JD '74
Thermo Electron/George N Hatsopoulos[1]	416	11	69	Greece	MIT, BS '49	PhD '56
WMX Technologies/Dean L Buntrock[1]	141	5	64	Columbia SD	St Olaf C, BA '55	
Xerox/Paul A Allaire	73	3	57	Worcester MA	Worcester Polytech, BSEE '60	Carnegie-Mellon, MSIA '66
CAPITAL GOODS						
AGCO/Robert J Ratliff	417	18	64	Wichita KS	U of Maryland, BS '57	
American Standard/Emmanuel A Kampouris	121	2	61	Egypt	Oxford U, MA '57	
Case/Jean-Pierre Rosso	376	17	55	France	Ecole Poly Lausanne, BCE '64	U of Penn-Wharton, MBA '67
Caterpillar/Donald V Fites	199	6	62	Tippecanoe IN	Valparaiso U, BS '56	MIT, MS '71
Cooper Industries/H John Riley Jr	519	21	55	Syracuse NY	Syracuse U, BS '61	
Deere & Co/Hans W Becherer	239	10	61	Detroit MI	Trinity College CT, BA '57	Harvard, MBA '62
Dover/Thomas L Reece	282	13	53	Kalamazoo MI	Western Michigan U, BA '64	
Emerson Electric/Charles F Knight	278	12	60	Lake Forest IL	Cornell, BME '58	MBA '59

TENURE (YRS)		COMPENSATION							STOCK OWNED		COMPANY DATA		
with firm	as CEO	salary	bonus	% change*	other	stock gains	total	5-year total	%	market value ($mil)	sales	profits	5-year return
		($thou)					($thou)				($mil)		
38	29	650	241	−21	297	—	1,188	4,428	5.42	63.3	2,690	70	3
20	20	860	2,862	43	941	—	4,663	11,778	0.30	7.7	5,484	128	18[2]
39	5	904	367	9	764	233	2,268	10,134	0.03	8.2	13,460	976	11
25	6	800	400	−33	143	47	1,390	8,669	0.48	4.6	2,185	7	5
25	6	900	1,175	25	4,175	4,345	10,595	24,864	1.28	25.8	2,519	91	36
25	25	441	60	14	4	—	505	1,973	12.69	351.7	311	48	55
30	8	698	396	−10	665	182	1,941	5,990	0.46	4.4	2,304	78	18
17	—[10]	500	550	NA	332	33	1,415[9]	NA	0.04	2.6	3,555	583	16
40	40	450	500	10	7	487	1,444[8]	8,774	1.51	74.6	2,207	140	32
40	28	1,400	1,792	27	448	—	3,640	15,037	0.60	99.6	10,248	604	−3
30	5	858	3,308	26	429	1,795	6,391	17,561	0.05	7.0	16,611	−472	21
		$681	**$734**	**21%**	**$303**	—	**$2,084**	**$6,648**	**0.10%**	**$7.0**	**$4,865**	**$272**	**17%**
8	8	687	313	8	251	191	1,442	4,117	1.42	17.7	2,125	129	49[2]
31	7	600	1,200	24	2,388	—	4,188	10,034[5]	0.65	13.8	5,221	142	39[2]
2	2	639	700	NA	257	—	1,596	NA	0.05	1.6	4,937	346	77[2]
40	6	1,000	564	−1	502	627	2,694	7,253	0.03	4.1	16,072	1,136	25
34	1	541	250	NA	321	—	1,112	NA	0.08	3.2	4,886	281	−2
34	7	817	996	11	502	—	2,315	9,191	0.07	7.6	10,520	734	25
31	2	650	650	53	772	—	2,072	NA	0.10	5.5	3,746	278	20
23	23	900	1,100	1	96	—	2,096	19,960	0.34	59.5	10,294	935	16

For footnotes 1–14 see page 17.

(Continued)

The 800 Highest-Paid CEOs (Cont.)

	RANK among 800 execs	in industry	Age	Birthplace	EDUCATION undergraduate	graduate
Company/chief executive						
CAPITAL GOODS, Cont.						
General Electric/John F Welch Jr	18	1	60	Peabody MA	U of Massachusetts, BS '57	U of Illinois, PhD '60
Harnischfeger Inds/Jeffery T Grade	206	7	52	Chicago IL	Illinois Tech, BS '66	DePaul U, MBA '72
Honeywell/Michael R Bonsignore	226	9	55	Plattsburg NY	US Naval Acad, BSEE '63	
Hubbell/G Jackson Ratcliffe	528	23	60	Charleston WV	Duke U, AB '58	U of Virginia, JD '61
Illinois Tool Works/W James Farrell	606	24	54	Buffalo NY	U of Detroit, BEE '65	
Ingersoll-Rand/James E Perrella	277	11	60	Gloversville NY	Purdue U, BSME '60	MSIM '61
Nacco Industries/Alfred M Rankin Jr	306	15	54	Cleveland OH	Yale, BA '63	JD '66
Parker Hannifin/Duane E Collins	369	16	60	Holcombe WI	U of Wisc Madison, BSME '61	
Rockwell Intl/Donald R Beall	171	5	57	Beaumont CA	San Jose State U, BS '60	U of Pitts-burgh, MBA '61
Stanley Works/Richard H Ayers	524	22	53	Newton MA	MIT, BS '65	MS '65
Teledyne/William P Rutledge	422	19	54	Pittston PA	Lafayette C, BS '63	George Washing-ton U, MS '67
Tenneco/Dana G Mead	290	14	60	Cresco IA	US Military Acad, BS '57	MIT, PhD '67
Trinity Industries/W Ray Wallace	156	4	73	Shreveport LA	Louisiana Tech U, BS '44	
Tyco International/L Dennis Kozlowski	149	3	49	Irvington NJ	Seton Hall U, BA '68	
Westinghouse/Michael H Jordan	219	8	59	Kansas City MO	Yale, BSCE '57	Princeton, MSCE '59
York International/Robert N Pokelwaldt	488	20	59	N Tonawanda NY	SUNY Buffalo, BS '60	
CHEMICALS						
Air Prods & Chems/Harold A Wagner	444	19	60	Oakland CA	Stanford U, BSME '58	Harvard, MBA '63

TENURE (YRS)		COMPENSATION							STOCK OWNED		COMPANY DATA		
with firm	as CEO	salary	bonus	% change*	other	stock gains	total	5-year total	%	market value ($mil)	sales	profits	5-year return
		($thou)					($thou)				($mil)		
36	15	2,000	3,250	21	3,431	5,316	13,997	45,401	0.03	34.7	70,028	6,573	21
13	4	555	752	11	451	860	2,619	6,709	0.66	13.4	2,335	104	19
27	3	683	542	21	1,216	—	2,441	5,001[5]	0.10	6.5	6,731	334	16
22	8	500	550	16	48	—	1,098	6,587	0.57	12.3	1,143	122	11
31	1	317	370	NA	227	—	914[9]	NA	0.04	3.0	4,152	388	20
34	3	648	913	25	544	—	2,104	5,031[5]	0.08	3.4	5,729	270	14
7	5	664	1,098	12	218	—	1,979	6,360	3.26	17.7	2,205	66	8
35	3	680	659	26	28	266	1,634	3,393[5]	0.09	2.5	3,427	239	21
28	8	815	2,000	33	240	—	3,055	15,018	0.21	25.3	13,420	769	20
24	9	503	288	-17	312	—	1,102	5,102	0.13	3.5	2,624	59	13
10	5	710	715	35	—	8	1,434	4,952	0.02	0.3	2,568	162	8
4	2	957	800	-1	294	—	2,051	5,640[5]	0.04	3.6	8,899	735	10
50	38	1,000	2,000	22	315	—	3,315	15,573	2.21	30.3	2,474	109	17
21	4	1,000	1,000	26	1,492	—	3,492	11,366[4]	0.52	29.2	4,843	273	9
3	3	1,000	1,500	84	19	—	2,519	4,995[5]	—[6]	0.6	6,296	15	-5
13	5	542	667	-15	3	—	1,211	11,555	0.46	9.5	2,930	-96	16[2]
		$633	**$634**	**17%**	**$185**	—	**$1,612**	**$5,771**	**0.11%**	**$5.3**	**$3,146**	**$249**	**18%**
33	4	687	640	36	21	—	1,347	5,216	0.05	3.5	3,892	371	12

For footnotes 1–14 see page 17.

(Continued)

The 800 Highest-Paid CEOs *(Cont.)*

	RANK				EDUCATION	
Company/chief executive	among 800 execs	in industry	Age	Birthplace	undergraduate	graduate
CHEMICALS, *Cont.*						
Cabot/Samuel W Bodman	270	10	57	Chicago IL	Cornell, BS '61	MIT, PhD '64
Cytec Industries/Darryl D Fry	475	20	57	Canada	Nova Scotia Technical, BSCE '61	
Dow Chemical/William S Stavropoulos	186	4	57	Bridgehampton NY	Fordham U, BA '61	U of Washington, PhD '66
du Pont de Nemours/John A Krol	281	11	59	Gilbertville MA	Tufts U, BS '58	MS '59
Eastman Chemical/Earnest W Deavenport Jr	240	8	58	Macon MS	Mississippi State, BS '60	MIT, MS '85
FMC/Robert N Burt	423	17	58	Lakewood OH	Princeton, BS '59	Harvard, MBA '64
Georgia Gulf/Jerry R Satrum	562	24	51	Silverton OR	Oregon State U, BS '68	
BF Goodrich/John D Ong	207	5	62	Uhrichsville OH	Ohio State U, BA '54	Harvard, LLB '57
WR Grace/Albert J Costello	317	14	60	New York NY	Fordham U, BS '57	NYU, MS '64
Great Lakes Chemical/Robert B McDonald	592	26	59	Seattle WA	Yale, BSCE '58	U of Washington, MSCE '60
Hercules/Thomas L Gossage	287	13	62	Nashville TN	Georgia Tech, BS '56	MS '57
IMC Global/Wendell F Bueche	427	18	65	Flushing MI	U of Notre Dame, BSME '52	
Intl Flavors & Frags/Eugene P Grisanti	120	1	66	Buffalo NY	Boston U, LLB '53	Harvard, LLM '54
Lubrizol/William G Bares	551	22	54	Cleveland OH	Purdue U, BS '63	Case Western, MBA '69
Lyondell Petrochem/Bob G Gower	243	9	58	West Frankfort IL	Southern Illinois U, BA '58	U of Minnesota, PhD '63
Monsanto/Robert B Shapiro	136	2	57	New York NY	Harvard, BA '59	Columbia, JD '62
Morton International/S Jay Stewart	235	7	57	Pineville WV	U of Cincinnati, BSCE '61	West Virginia U, MBA '66
Nalco Chemical/Edward J Mooney	617	27	55	Omar WV	U of Texas Austin, BS '64	JD '67

TENURE (YRS) with firm	as CEO	salary ($thou)	bonus ($thou)	% change*	other ($thou)	stock gains ($thou)	total ($thou)	5-year total ($thou)	%	market value ($mil)	sales ($mil)	profits ($mil)	5-year return
9	8	646	800	34	679	—	2,125	5,771	1.49	30.9	1,845	181	33
35	5	450	485	4	309	—	1,244	3,828[4]	0.64	9.0	1,260	282	115[2]
29	1	627	650	NA	238	1,347	2,862[9]	NA	0.02	3.7	20,200	2,078	17
33	—[10]	702	1,040	NA	21	317	2,080[9]	NA	0.02	8.4	36,508	3,293	21
36	7	563	755	0	991	—	2,310	5,923	0.04	2.2	5,040	559	22[2]
23	5	725	634	16	60	—	1,419	8,280	0.23	5.7	4,510	216	15
11	5	470	550	17	11	—	1,031	3,372	2.92	39.8	1,082	187	18
35	17	750	782	9	185	899	2,616	9,861	0.66	13.8	2,409	118	21
1	1	900[3]	900	NA	107	—	1,907	NA	0.03	2.0	3,666	-326	25
28	2	609	325	55	8	—	942	NA	0.07	3.1	2,361	296	10
8	5	838	1,020	24	209	—	2,066	8,732	0.82	54.8	2,427	333	39
3	3	530	460	24	419	—	1,409	2,950[5]	0.09	2.2	2,360	164	12
36	11	850	425	10	2,914	—	4,189	18,471	0.20	10.2	1,439	249	16
33	—[10]	490	244	NA	33	291	1,058[9]	NA	0.17	2.9	1,664	152	5
33	8	698	649	7	952	—	2,299	10,287	0.11	2.6	4,936	389	13
17	1	685	1,236	31	1,036	775	3,731	NA	0.04	7.9	8,962	739	26
23	2	633	720	27	1,019	—	2,372	10,807[5]	0.10	5.3	3,475	326	20
27	2	490	298	17	92	—	881	2,851[5]	0.06	1.2	1,215	154	2

For footnotes 1–14 see page 17.

(Continued)

The 800 Highest-Paid CEOs *(Cont.)*

Company/chief executive	RANK among 800 execs	in industry	Age	Birthplace	EDUCATION undergraduate	graduate
CHEMICALS, *Cont.*						
Olin/Donald W Griffin	559	23	59	Evansville IN	U of Evansville, BSBA '61	
PPG Industries/Jerry E Dempsey	229	6	63	Landrum SC	Clemson U, BSME '54	Georgia State U, MBA '68
Praxair/H William Lichtenberger	286	12	60	Yugoslavia	U of Iowa, BA '57	SUNY Buffalo, MBA '62
Rohm & Haas/J Lawrence Wilson	373	15	60	Rosedale MS	Vanderbilt U, BE '58	Harvard, MBA '63
Sherwin-Williams/John G Breen	176	3	61	Cleveland OH	John Carroll U, BS '56	Case Western, MBA '61
Sigma-Aldrich/Carl T Cori	505	21	59	St Louis MO	U of Wisc Madison, BS '59	Washington U, PhD '69
Sterling Chemicals/J Virgil Waggoner[1]	633	29	68	Judsonia AK	Ouachita Baptist U, BS '48	U of Texas Austin, MS '50
Terra Industries/Burton M Joyce	587	25	54	Evanston IL	Miami U Ohio, BSBA '64	
Union Carbide/William H Joyce	379	16	60	Greensburg PA	Penn State U, BS '57	NYU, PhD '84
Witco/William R Toller	628	28	65	Fort Smith AR	U of Arkansas, BA '56	
COMPUTERS & COMMUNICATIONS						
Adobe Systems/John E Warnock	677	72	55	Salt Lake City UT	U of Utah, BS '61	PhD '69
Advanced Micro/Walter J Sanders III[1]	101	25	59	Chicago IL	U of Illinois, BSEE '58	
AirTouch Commun/Sam Ginn	291	41	59	St Clair AL	Auburn U, BS '59	
Alltel/Joe T Ford	356	49	58	Conway AR	U of Arkansas, BS '59	
Altera/Rodney Smith	636	65	56	England	Southampton College, BSEE '63	
America Online/Stephen Case[1]	185	34	36	Oahu HI	Williams C, BA '80	
Ameritech/Richard C Notebaert	195	35	48	Canada	U of Wisc Madison, BA '69	U of Wisc Milwaukee, MBA '83
AMP/William J Hudson Jr	440	55	62	Chicago IL	Cornell, BEE '56	

| TENURE (YRS) | | COMPENSATION | | | | | | | STOCK OWNED | | COMPANY DATA | | |
with firm	as CEO	salary	bonus ($thou)	% change*	other	stock gains	total	5-year total	%	market value ($mil)	sales	profits ($mil)	5-year return
35	—[10]	413	480	NA	72	80	1,044[9]	NA	0.05	1.1	3,150	140	20
3	3	641	1,440	5	43	310	2,434	5,454[5]	—[6]	0.9	7,058	768	18
37	4	627	1,000	27	165	275	2,066	5,435[4]	0.13	7.2	3,146	262	29[2]
31	8	616	210	8	611	175	1,612[14]	6,667	0.10	4.4	3,884	292	11
17	17	793	585	0	1,208	396	2,982	11,585	0.43	15.8	3,274	201	17
26	13	660	196	-3	301	—	1,157	6,139	0.29	8.0	960	132	10
10	10	325	507	101	10	—	842	2,238	7.39	50.9	981	144	16
10	5	485	375	-4	102	—	962	4,446	0.11	1.2	2,216	164	32
39	1	550	825	51	207	—	1,582	NA	0.16	10.2	5,888	925	51
12	6	650	0	36	25	188	863	5,436	0.12	2.2	1,985	104	18
		$502	**$452**	**17%**	**$24**	**$81**	**$1,875**	**$10,777**	**0.22%**	**$10.5**	**$2,430**	**$159**	**25%**
14	14	375	293	14	45	—	713	14,222	1.24	31.5	762	94	4
27	27	979	2,027	-34	2,027	—	5,033	54,562	0.20	4.6	2,430	301	11
36	8	650	571	10	115	713	2,049	7,495[4]	0.02	2.8	1,619	132	10[2]
37	9	650	585	0	486	—	1,721	8,164	0.27	16.2	3,110	355	13
13	13	325	493	19	17	—	834	2,638	1.76	36.0	402	87	44
11	3	200	0	24	4	2,679	2,884	7,203	0.25	10.5	713	4	133[2]
27	2	880	1,030	30	688	112	2,709	5,890[5]	—[6]	2.2	13,428	2,008	16
34	3	700	437	11	191	36	1,364	3,970[4]	0.03	3.1	5,227	427	12

For footnotes 1–14 see page 17.

(Continued)

25

The 800 Highest-Paid CEOs *(Cont.)*

Company/chief executive	RANK among 800 execs	in industry	Age	Birthplace	EDUCATION undergraduate	graduate
COMPUTERS & COMMUNICATIONS, *Cont.*						
Analog Devices/Ray Stata[1]	383	50	61	Coatesville PA	MIT, BSEE '57	MSEE '58
Anixter Intl/Rod F Dammeyer	147	32	55	Cleveland OH	Kent State U, BA '60	
Apple Computer/Gilbert F Amelio	575	60	53	New York NY	Georgia Tech, BS '65	PhD '68
Applied Materials/James C Morgan	23	7	57	Danville IL	Cornell, BS '62	MBA '63
Arrow Electronics/Stephen P Kaufman	300	42	54	Cambridge MA	MIT, BS '63	Harvard, MBA '65
Ascend Commun/Mory Ejabat	537	58	46	Iran	Cal St Northridge, BS '74	Pepperdine U, MBA '80
AST Research/Ian Diery	684	73	46	Australia		
AT&T/Robert E Allen	83	22	61	Joplin MO	Wabash C, BA '57	
Atmel/George Perlegos	777	84	46	Greece	San Jose State U, BSEE '72	Stanford U, MS '74
Avnet/Leon Machiz	334	46	71	Brooklyn NY		
Bay Networks/Andrew K Ludwick[1]	770	82	50	Dayton OH	Harvard, BA '67	MBA '69
Bell Atlantic/Raymond W Smith	262	39	58	Pittsburgh PA	Carnegie-Mellon, BS '59	U of Pittsburgh, MBA '67
BellSouth/John L Clendenin	108	27	62	El Paso TX	Northwestern U, BA '55	
BMC Software/Max P Watson Jr	201	36	50	New Orleans LA	Louisiana Tech U, BBA '68	
Cabletron Systems/S Robert Levine[1]	792	88	38	Worcester MA	U of Miami, BS '80	
Cascade Commun/Daniel E Smith	734	78	46	Nyack NY	Lehigh U, BA '71	Harvard, MBA '76
Cisco Systems/John T Chambers	47	12	46	Cleveland OH	West Virginia U, BS '71	Indiana U, MBA '76
Citizens Utilities/Leonard Tow	269	40	68	Brooklyn NY	CUNY Brooklyn, BA '50	Columbia, PhD '60
Compaq Computer/Eckhard Pfeiffer	10	4	54	Germany	Nuremberg Business, BA '63	SMU, MBA '83

TENURE (YRS)		COMPENSATION						STOCK OWNED		COMPANY DATA		
with firm	as CEO	salary	bonus ($thou)	% change*	other	stock gains	total ($thou)	5-year total	%	market value ($mil)	sales ($mil)	profits	5-year return

with firm	as CEO	salary	bonus	% change*	other	stock gains	total	5-year total	%	market value	sales	profits	5-year return
31	25	631	567	17	11	347	1,555	5,836	2.48	68.0	1,014	136	41
11	3	395	344	−43	662	2,144	3,546	12,939[5]	0.46	3.8	2,195	39	20
—[10]	—[10]	990[3]	NA	—	—	—	990	NA	—[6]	—[7]	11,378	167	−18
20	19	546	1,142	32	12	10,631	12,331	36,767	0.39	25.5	3,596	560	56
14	10	649	1,039	28	311	—	2,000	10,993	2.59	60.5	5,919	203	52
6	1	163	82	NA	5	831	1,080[8]	NA	0.92	53.3	150	31	519[2]
1	1	700[3]	NA	—	—	—	700	NA	—[6]	—[7]	2,348	−262	−29
39	8	1,153	1,524	−20	2,539	630	5,846	23,031	—[6]	9.1	79,609	139	15
11	11	242	162	5	—	—	404	1,600	8.31	257.7	634	114	49
44	7	1,000	660	33	151	—	1,811	7,134	0.14	3.1	4,798	172	12
11	11	270	170	−5	2	—	442	2,145	1.06	52.3	1,728	218	57[2]
37	7	842	1,000	14	342	—	2,185	12,036	0.03	8.5	13,430	1,862	9
41	12	509	1,047	6	2,943	303	4,801	13,323	0.02	6.9	17,886	1,564	12
11	6	240	512	−6	1,918	—	2,670	16,539	0.40	11.2	397	70	21
13	13	52	0	0	—	—	52	260	15.41	716.8	1,070	164	36
4	4	194	82	52	—	280	556	2,578[5]	0.29	10.3	135	25	323[2]
5	1	230	164	14	2	8,489	8,885	NA	0.11	26.5	2,668	634	98
6	6	1,210	0	−36	918	—	2,129	20,447	2.15[12]	53.6	1,069	160	9
13	5	1,125	2,500	2	1,250	12,493	17,368	42,459	—[6]	—[7]	14,755	789	13

For footnotes 1–14 see page 17.

(Continued)

The 800 Highest-Paid CEOs *(Cont.)*

Company/chief executive	RANK among 800 execs	RANK in industry	Age	Birthplace	EDUCATION undergraduate	EDUCATION graduate
COMPUTERS & COMMUNICATIONS, *Cont.*						
Computer Associates/Charles B Wang[1]	88	23	51	China	CUNY Queens, BS '67	
Dell Computer/Michael S Dell[1]	603	63	31	Houston TX		
Digital Equipment/Robert B Palmer	428	54	55	Gorman TX	Texas Tech U, BS '62	MS '65
DSC Communications/James L Donald	8	2	64	Carthage TX	SMU, BSIE '57	MSIE '65
EMC/Michael C Ruettgers	71	16	53	Muskogee OK	Idaho State, BBA '64	Harvard, MBA '67
FORE Systems/Eric Cooper	788	86	37	Brooklyn NY	Harvard, BA '80	U of Cal Berkeley, PhD '85
Frontier/Ronald L Bittner	404	52	54	Bethlehem PA	Muhlenberg C, BA '63	U of Rochester, MBA '78
Gateway 2000/Theodore W Waitt	2	1	33	Sioux City IA		
General Instrument/Richard S Friedland	645	67	45	Pittsfield MA	Ohio State U, BS '72	Seton Hall U, MBA '85
GTE/Charles R Lee	127	29	56	Pittsburgh PA	Cornell, BA '62	Harvard, MBA '64
Harris/Phillip W Farmer	310	43	57	Goldsboro NC	Duke U, BS '60	
Hewlett-Packard/Lewis E Platt	386	51	55	Johnson City NY	Cornell, BSME '64	U of Penn-Wharton, MBA '66
Informix/Phillip E White	72	17	53	Taylorville IL	Illinois Wesleyan U, BA '66	U of Illinois Urbana, MBA '68
Intel/Andrew S Grove	50	13	59	Hungary	CUNY City, BS '60	U of Cal Berkeley, PhD '63
IBM/Louis V Gerstner Jr	76	18	54	Mineola NY	Dartmouth, BA '63	Harvard, MBA '65
Intuit/William V Campbell	665	71	55	Homestead PA	Columbia, BBA '62	MA '64
Linear Technology/Robert H Swanson Jr[1]	541	59	57	Boston MA	Northeastern U, BS '63	

TENURE (YRS)		COMPENSATION							STOCK OWNED		COMPANY DATA		
with firm	as CEO	salary	bonus	% change*	other	stock gains	total	5-year total	%	market value ($mil)	sales	profits	5-year return
		($thou)			($thou)						($mil)		
20	20	1,000	4,585	–17	38	—	5,623	21,017	3.85	643.4	3,196	–109	66
12	12	375	443	128	103	—	921[8]	2,864	21.27	789.1	5,296	272	29
11	4	900	375	42	134	—	1,409	3,056[5]	0.01	1.1	14,440	431	–4
15	15	919	0	–38	5,981	12,488	19,388[14]	55,857	0.79	24.2	1,422	193	47
8	4	277	366	3	2	5,809	6,454	21,812[4]	0.16	8.0	1,921	327	68
6	6	133	63	4	5	—	201	NA	8.32	150.1	198	24	153[2]
33	4	575	660	63	266	—	1,501	4,366	0.09	4.4	2,144	145	22
11	11	573	266	–11	—	61,024	61,863	64,369	44.63	1,195.6	3,676	173	17[2]
18	1	590	214	NA	5	—	809[9]	NA	0.07	2.5	2,432	124	42[2]
13	4	898	1,404	15	1,358	368	4,027	13,099	0.01	4.3	19,957	2,538	13
14	1	442	408	NA	982	111	1,942[9]	NA	0.25	6.0	3,507	165	23
30	4	1,375	156	30	18	—	1,548	6,886[4]	0.04	18.1	33,503	2,621	32
7	7	422	400	20	4	5,598	6,424	23,940	—[6]	0.3	709	105	109
28	9	400	2,357	31	266	5,425	8,448	20,607	0.11	59.4	16,202	3,566	38
3	3	2,000	2,775	4	1,413	133	6,321	26,385[5]	0.02	14.0	71,940	4,178	3
2	2	357	388	NA	—	—	745	NA	—[6]	—[7]	490	–5	48[2]
15	15	227	680	21	24	139	1,070	3,345	0.35	8.2	328	113	56

For footnotes 1–14 see page 17.

(Continued)

The 800 Highest-Paid CEOs (Cont.)

Company/chief executive	RANK among 800 execs	in industry	Age	Birthplace	EDUCATION undergraduate	graduate
COMPUTERS & COMMUNICATIONS, *Cont.*						
LSI Logic/Wilfred J Corrigan[1]	119	28	58	England	Imperial C London, BSCE '61	
MCI Communication/Bert C Roberts Jr	173	33	53	Kansas City MO	Johns Hopkins U, BS '65	
Merisel/Dwight A Steffensen	—	—	53	Fresno CA	Stanford U, BS '65	
MFS Communication/James Q Crowe[1]	620	64	46	Camp Pendleton CA	Rensselaer, BSME '72	Pepperdine U, MBA '82
Micron Technology/Steven R Appleton	99	24	36	Covina CA	Boise State U, BBA '82	
Microsoft/William H Gates[1]	775	83	40	Seattle WA		
Molex/Frederick A Krehbiel	465	56	54	Hinsdale IL	Lake Forest C, BA '63	
Motorola/Gary L Tooker	28	8	56	Shelby OH	Arizona State, BSEE '62	
Natl Semiconductor/Richard M Beyer[15]	738	79	47	Brooklyn NY	Georgetown U, BS '74	Columbia, MBA '77
Netscape Commun/James L Barksdale	789	87	53	Jackson MS	U of Mississippi, BBA '65	
Nextel Commun/Daniel F Akerson	—	—	47	Oakland CA	US Naval Acad, BSE '70	London Sch Economics, MBA '78
Novell/Robert J Frankenberg	504	57	49	Chippewa Falls WI	San Jose State U, BS '74	
Nynex/Ivan G Seidenberg	257	38	49	New York NY	CUNY City, BS '72	Pace U NY, MBA '80
Oracle/Lawrence J Ellison[1]	17	6	51	New York NY		
Pacific Telesis/Philip J Quigley	341	48	53	San Francisco CA	Cal St Los Angeles, BS '67	
Paging Network/Glenn W Marschel	713	76	49		U of Missouri, BS	
PanAmSat/Frederick A Landman	656	70	48	Richmond VA	U of Oklahoma, BA '70	
Parametric Tech/Steven C Walske	81	21	43	Los Alamos NM	Princeton, BA '74	Harvard, MBA '78
PeopleSoft/David A Duffield[1]	784	85	55	Cleveland OH	Cornell, BSEE '62	MBA '64

| TENURE (YRS) | | COMPENSATION | | | | | | | STOCK OWNED | | COMPANY DATA | | |
| with firm | as CEO | salary | bonus | % change* | other | stock gains | total | 5-year total | % | market value ($mil) | sales | profits | 5-year return |
		($thou)					($thou)				($mil)		
15	15	601	730	17	51	2,847	4,229	9,558	4.92	196.1	1,268	238	41
24	4	890	1,300	25	830	—	3,020	11,462	0.08	15.1	15,265	548	19
4	—[10]	NA	NA	—	—	—	—	NA	—[6]	—[7]	5,802	-9	-4
10	5	373	500	52	—	—	873[8]	2,120[5]	—[6]	—[7]	583	-268	34[2]
13	2	450	1,240	57	57	3,438	5,184	NA	0.03	2.0	3,972	1,018	58
21	15	275	141	-9	—	—	416	1,852	23.92	14,948.7	7,419	1,838	34
31	8	403	562	106	187	152	1,304	3,654	12.85	424.8	1,337	139	19
34	3	990	1,030	2	1,822	7,046	10,888	19,286[5]	0.03	10.5	27,037	1,781	31
3	—[10]	301	225	NA	24	—	550[9]	NA	—[6]	—[7]	2,681	258	14
1	1	100	0	NA	—	—	100	NA	9.14	398.5	81	-3	NA
—[10]	—[10]	NA	NA	—	—	—	—	NA	—[6]	—[7]	178	-263	6[2]
2	2	504	309	NA	357	—	1,170	NA	0.01	0.5	1,986	320	1
27	1	640	845	104	709	50	2,244	NA	—[6]	2.2	13,407	1,070	13
19	19	1,100	2,243	39	—	10,800	14,143	20,703	22.68	4,602.5	3,777	519	73
29	2	646	662	43	462	—	1,770	NA	—[6]	0.2	9,042	1,048	8
—[10]	—[10]	600[3]	NA	NA	8	—	608	NA	—[6]	—[7]	646	-44	35[2]
12	2	500	275	29	—	—	775	NA	7.81	220.5	116	18	NA
9	9	300	500	10	5	5,390	6,195	41,644	0.92	44.6	441	91	67
9	9	200	127	11	8	—	334	1,334	31.29	835.3	228	29	82[2]

For footnotes 1–14 see page 17. [15]Office of the President jointly held with Ellen Hancock and Kirk Pond, which presently heads the company on an interim basis.

(Continued)

The 800 Highest-Paid CEOs *(Cont.)*

Company/chief executive	RANK among 800 execs	RANK in industry	Age	Birthplace	EDUCATION undergraduate	EDUCATION graduate
COMPUTERS & COMMUNICATIONS, *Cont.*						
Qualcomm/Irwin M Jacobs	12	5	62	New Bedford MA	Cornell, BEE '56	MIT, ScD '59
Quantum/Michael A Brown	590	61	37	Houston TX	Harvard, BA '80	Stanford U, MBA '84
Raychem/Richard A Kashnow	697	75	54	Worcester MA	Worcester Polytech, BS '63	Tufts U, PhD '68
Read-Rite/Cyril J Yansouni	45	11	53	Egypt	U of Louvain, BSEE '65	Stanford U, MSEE '67
SBC Communications/Edward E Whitacre Jr	106	26	54	Ennis TX	Texas Tech U, BSIE '64	
SCI Systems/Olin B King[1]	596	62	62	Sandersville GA	North Georgia C, BS '53	
Seagate Technology/Alan F Shugart[1]	80	20	65	Los Angeles CA	U of Redlands, BS '53	
Silicon Graphics/Edward R McCracken	415	53	52	Fairfield IA	Iowa State, BSEE '66	Stanford U, MBA '68
Solectron/Koichi Nishimura	653	69	57	Pasadena CA	San Jose State U, BSEE	Stanford U, PhD
So New Eng Telecom/Daniel J Miglio	717	77	55	Philadelphia PA	U of Penn-Wharton, BS '62	
Sprint/William T Esrey	204	37	56	Philadelphia PA	Denison U, BA '61	Harvard, MBA '64
StrataCom/Richard M Moley	42	10	57	England	Manchester U, BS '61	Stanford U, MSEE '68
Sun Microsystems/Scott G McNealy[1]	128	30	41	Columbus IN	Harvard, BA '76	Stanford U, MBA '80
Tandem Computers/Roel Pieper	693	74	39	Netherlands		Delft University, PhD
Tech Data/Steven A Raymund	648	68	40	Los Angeles CA	U of Oregon, BS '78	Georgetown U, MS '80
Tele & Data Systems/LeRoy T Carlson Jr	747	80	49	Chicago IL	Harvard, BA '68	MBA '71

Tenure (yrs) with firm	as CEO	salary	bonus	% change*	other	stock gains	total	5-year total	%	market value ($mil)	sales	profits	5-year return
		($thou)					($thou)				($mil)		
11	11	391	250	23	5	15,520	16,166	17,366	4.19	85.9	457	34	33[2]
12	1	349	470	NA	1	132	952[9]	NA	0.03	0.3	4,174	56	2
1	1	650[3]	NA	—	—	—	650	NA	—[6]	—[7]	1,602	64	21
5	5	500	520	76	—	8,001	9,021	17,821	0.24	2.3	1,083	147	8[2]
33	6	825	1,500	19	2,531	—	4,856	19,122	0.05	13.9	12,670	1,889	18
35	35	465	452	50	17	—	934	3,317	3.27	37.6	3,514	62	36
17	17	600	523	20	376	4,710	6,208	22,098	0.45	19.3	5,493	394	28
12	12	755	691	15	—	—	1,446	7,812	0.23	9.6	2,497	231	20
8	4	375	413	46	2	—	789	7,163[4]	0.10	2.1	2,435	98	60
34	3	404	176	–10	16	—	597	2,289[4]	0.01	0.4	1,839	169	9
16	11	938	541	–24	877	289	2,645	13,754	0.09	11.9	12,765	946	18
10	10	300	263	13	1	8,588	9,152	10,947[4]	3.06	87.3	332	53	116[2]
14	12	600	2,400	147	2	1,020	4,022	10,234	1.85	171.3	6,390	447	22
3	—[10]	337	0	NA	35	289	660[9]	NA	—[6]	—[7]	2,263	74	–8
15	10	400	400	29	5	—	805	3,730	9.71	65.4	3,087	22	41
22	10	390	115	13	21	—	526	2,389	1.75	50.2	954	104	7

For footnotes 1–14 see page 17.

(Continued)

The 800 Highest-Paid CEOs (Cont.)

Company/chief executive	Rank among 800 execs	Rank in industry	Age	Birthplace	Education undergraduate	Education graduate
COMPUTERS & COMMUNICATIONS, *Cont.*						
Tellabs/Michael J Birck[1]	324	44	58	Missoula MT	Purdue U, BSEE '60	NYU, MSEE '62
Teradyne/Alexander V d'Arbeloff[1]	137	31	68	France	MIT, BS '49	
Texas Instruments/Jerry R Junkins	30	9	58	Fort Madison IA	Iowa State, BS '59	SMU, MS '68
3Com/Eric A Benhamou	80	19	40	France		Stanford U, MS '77
360° Commun/Dennis E Foster	757	81	55	Fostoria OH	Findlay U, BA '67	Michigan State
U S West Commun/Solomon D Trujillo[15]	339	47	44	Cheyenne WY	U of Wyoming, BS '73	MBA '74
Unisys/James A Unruh	640	66	55	Goodrich ND	Jamestown C, BSBA '63	U of Denver, MBA '64
US Robotics/Casey G Cowell[1]	9	3	43	Detroit MI	U of Chicago, BA '75	
Varian Associates/J Tracy O'Rourke	63	15	61	Columbia SC	Auburn U, BS '56	
Western Digital/Charles A Haggerty	326	45	54	Rochester MN	U of St Thomas (Minn), BA '63	
WorldCom/Bernard J Ebbers	54	14	54	Canada	Mississippi C, BA '67	
Xilinx/Willem P Roelandts	—	—	51	Belgium	Rijks Hogere Technisc, BSEE '65	
CONSTRUCTION						
Centex/Laurence E Hirsch	634	8	50	New York NY	U of Pennsylvania, BS '68	Villanova, JD '71
Fluor/Leslie G McCraw	182	4	61	Sandy Springs SC	Clemson U, BSCE '56	
Foster Wheeler/Richard J Swift	457	7	51	Indianapolis IN	US Military Acad, BS '66	Fairleigh Dickinson U, MBA '76
Lafarge/Michel Rose	679	9	53	France	Ecole Mines Paris, BA '68	Intl Management Inst, MBA '77
Masco/Richard A Manoogian	89	2	59	Long Branch NJ	Yale, BA '58	

TENURE (YRS)		COMPENSATION							STOCK OWNED		COMPANY DATA		
with firm	as CEO	salary	bonus	% change*	other	stock gains	total	5-year total	%	market value ($mil)	sales	profits	5-year return
		($thou)				($thou)					($mil)		
21	21	341	150	−8	148	1,236	1,875	4,280	11.54	517.9	635	116	81
36	25	308	450	12	37	2,918	3,712	7,284	2.28	32.8	1,191	159	27
37	11	792	1,750	32	475	7,714	10,731	19,734	0.06	6.0	13,128	1,088	22
9	6	472	49	9	1	5,699	6,221	10,606	0.29	16.3	1,792	167	77
5	—[10]	249	164	NA	87	—	501	NA	—[6]	—[7]	834	−2	NA
22	1	343	300	NA	1,016	120	1,779	NA	—[6]	0.9	9,484	1,184	2
16	6	800	0	−34	18	—	818	6,967	0.20	2.2	6,202	−625	4
20	20	450	2,349	92	17	15,770	18,586	22,777	3.06	170.0	1,092	96	95[2]
6	6	744	1,493	35	2,152	2,528	6,918	16,673	0.24	3.8	1,581	144	18
4	3	600	536	21	35	703	1,874	NA	0.07	0.7	2,430	91	29
11	11	711	750	20	9	6,548	8,018[8]	11,224	4.30	318.4	3,640	268	49
—[10]	—[10]	NA	NA	—	—	—	—	NA	NA	—	520	87	35
		$575	$450	12%	$239	—	$1,339	$8,676	0.29%	$3.9	$2,927	$58	10%
11	8	515	275	−13	51	—	841	13,709	1.35	10.5	3,074	47	13
21	6	755	840	13	1,313	—	2,908	16,451	0.15	8.1	9,644	239	8
24	2	575	339	28	416	—	1,330	3,265[5]	0.04	0.6	3,042	29	9
26	4	450	247	10	14	—	710	2,325[4]	—[6]	—[7]	1,472	130	8
38	28	930	477	17	4,201	—	5,608[8]	38,013	0.65	29.0	2,927	−442	7

For footnotes 1–14 see page 17. [15]Overall CEO for US West is Richard D McCormick.

(Continued)

The 800 Highest-Paid CEOs *(Cont.)*

Company/chief executive	Rank among 800 execs	in industry	Age	Birthplace	Education undergraduate	graduate
CONSTRUCTION, *Cont.*						
Owens Corning/Glen H Hiner	86	1	61	Morgantown WV	West Virginia U, BSEE '57	
Pulte/Robert K Burgess	288	5	52	Canada	Michigan State U, BS '66	
Schuller/W Thomas Stephens	144	3	53	Crossett AR	U of Arkansas, BS '65	MS '66
Turner/Alfred T McNeill	749	11	59	Elizabeth NJ	Lehigh U, BS '58	
USG/William C Foote	686	10	45	Milwaukee WI	Williams C, BA '73	Harvard, MBA '77
Vulcan Materials/Herbert A Sklenar	450	6	64	Omaha NE	U of Nebraska Omaha, BS '52	Harvard, MBA '54
CONSUMER DURABLES						
Armstrong World Ind/George A Lorch	236	12	54	Glenridge NJ	Virginia Polytech, BS '63	
Black & Decker/Nolan D Archibald	116	6	52	Ogden UT	Weber State, BS '68	Harvard, MBA '70
Brunswick/Peter N Larson	105	3	57	Los Angeles CA	Oregon State U, BS '60	Seton Hall U, JD '72
Chrysler/Robert J Eaton	123	7	56	Buena Vista CO	U of Kansas, BSME '63	
Cooper Tire & Rubber/Patrick W Rooney	637	31	60	Findlay OH	U of Findlay, BS '58	
Cummins Engine/James A Henderson	335	19	61	South Bend IN	Princeton, AB '56	Harvard, MBA '63
Dana/Southwood J Morcott	187	9	58	Covington GA	Davidson C, BA '60	U of Michigan, MBA '63
Eaton/Stephen R Hardis	183	8	60	New York NY	Cornell, BA '56	Princeton, MPA '60
Echlin/Frederick J Mancheski	109	5	69	Stevens Point WI	U of Wisc Madison, BS '48	
Fleetwood Enterprise/John C Crean[1]	210	11	70	Bowden ND		
Ford Motor/Alex J Trotman	57	1	62	England	Michigan State U, MBA '72	
General Motors/John F Smith Jr	107	4	58	Worcester MA	U of Massachusetts, BBA '60	Boston U, MBA '65
Genuine Parts/Larry L Prince	542	27	57	Dyersburg TN		

| TENURE (YRS) | | COMPENSATION | | | | | | | STOCK OWNED | | COMPANY DATA | | |
with firm	as CEO	salary	bonus ($thou)	% change*	other	stock gains	total ($thou)	5-year total	%	market value ($mil)	sales	profits ($mil)	5-year return
4	4	840	1,400	23	3,480	—	5,720	11,679[4]	0.30	5.9	3,612	231	10
13	3	400	450	-19	2	1,214	2,065	7,514[4]	0.02	0.1	2,010	58	14
33	10	600	680	2	2,331	—	3,611	9,839	0.29	3.9	1,392	122	NA
38	7	438	0	-10	86	—	524	2,421	0.50	0.3	3,281	1	-8
12	—[10]	373	285	NA	35	—	694[9]	NA	0.06	0.6	2,444	-32	59
24	10	600	500	26	239	—	1,339	5,398	0.33	6.6	1,461	166	14
		$700	**$612**	**6%**	**$435**	**—**	**$2,047**	**$8,551**	**0.22%**	**$6.0**	**$4,714**	**$163**	**18%**
33	3	588	929	32	795	34	2,346	4,101[5]	0.25	5.2	2,085	123	19
11	10	839	810	5	2,081	799	4,528	11,429	0.18	5.8	4,766	255	26
1	1	800[3]	984	NA	3,117	—	4,900	NA	0.23	5.2	3,041	127	12
4	3	1,213	2,360	9	598	—	4,171	21,596[4]	0.03	7.2	53,195	2,121	38
40	2	403	374	21	47	—	824	NA	0.27	5.7	1,494	113	17
32	2	728	647	-3	435	—	1,809	NA	0.21	3.5	5,245	224	18
33	7	912	1,638	33	85	208	2,843	8,551	0.12	4.1	7,787	288	22
17	1	580	868	NA	970	483	2,901[9]	NA	0.07	3.2	6,822	399	20
33	27	625	600	12	1,705	1,848	4,779	10,659	1.11	23.0	2,911	150	27
46	46	111	1,207	-8	1,272	—	2,589	15,497	17.38	188.2	2,795	80	16
40	3	1,500	3,000	-40	3,130	—	7,630	20,731[5]	0.03	13.1	137,137	4,139	21
35	4	1,500	763	6	2,575	—	4,837	9,940[4]	0.01	10.0	168,829	6,933	10
38	6	465	547	5	2	54	1,068	4,670	0.07	4.0	5,262	309	15

For footnotes 1–14 see page 17.

(Continued)

The 800 Highest-Paid CEOs (Cont.)

Company/chief executive	Rank among 800 execs	in industry	Age	Birthplace	Education undergraduate	graduate
CONSUMER DURABLES, *Cont.*						
Goodyear/Samir F Gibara	521	26	57	Egypt	Cairo U, BBA '60	Harvard, MBA '65
Harley-Davidson/Richard F Teerlink	555	28	59	Chicago IL	Bradley U, BS '61	U of Chicago, MBA '76
ITT Industries/Travis Engen	189	10	51	Pasadena CA	MIT, BS '67	
Johnson Controls/James H Keyes	251	13	55	La Crosse WI	Marquette U, BS '62	North-western U, MBA '63
Lear Seating/Kenneth L Way	398	21	56	Detroit MI	Michigan State U, BS '61	MBA '71
Leggett & Platt/Harry M Cornell Jr	405	22	67	Dutch East Indies	U of Missouri, BS '50	
Maytag/Leonard A Hadley	292	16	61	Earlham IA	U of Iowa, BS '58	
Navistar Intl/John R Horne	580	30	58	Lansing IL	Purdue U, BSME '60	Bradley U, MSME '64
Newell Co/William P Sovey	493	25	62	Helen GA	Georgia Tech, BS '55	
Paccar/Charles M Pigott	272	14	67	Seattle WA	Stanford U, BS '51	
Premark Intl/Warren L Batts	472	24	63	Norfolk VA	Georgia Tech, BEE '61	Harvard, MBA '63
Rubbermaid/Wolfgang R Schmitt	284	15	52	Germany	Otterbein C, BA '66	
Shaw Industries/Robert E Shaw[1]	348	20	64	Cartersville GA		
Springs Industries/Walter Y Elisha	438	23	63	Gary IN	Wabash C, BA '54	Harvard, MBA '65
TRW/Joseph T Gorman	78	2	58	Rising Sun IN	Kent State U, BA '60	Yale, LLB '62
US Industries/David H Clarke	573	29	54	Long Branch NJ	Hobart C, BA '65	
Varity/Victor A Rice	330	18	55	England		
Whirlpool/David R Whitwam	293	17	54	Stanley WI	U of Wisc Madison, BS '67	

| TENURE (YRS) | | COMPENSATION | | | | | | | STOCK OWNED | | COMPANY DATA | | |
with firm	as CEO	salary	bonus	% change*	other	stock gains	total	5-year total	%	market value ($mil)	sales ($mil)	profits	5-year return
		($thou)				($thou)							
32	—[10]	464	387	NA	256	—	1,107[9]	NA	—[6]	0.5	13,166	611	36
15	7	486	500	-14	67	—	1,054	10,608	0.59	19.9	1,351	113	41
11	—[10]	700	612	NA	1,193	336	2,841[9]	NA	0.01	0.4	8,382	21	NA
30	8	731	599	3	363	569	2,262	7,979	0.31	9.1	8,659	202	25
30	8	585	900	11	25	—	1,510	6,024	0.33	5.3	4,714	94	31[2]
46	36	534	539	11	162	265	1,500	7,747	2.99	61.5	2,059	135	27
37	4	600	400	-6	1,047	—	2,047	5,198	0.15	3.0	3,040	-15	9
30	1	544	425	78	10	—	980	NA	0.22	1.2	6,358	163	-23
10	4	650	527	7	13	—	1,190	4,333[4]	0.22	9.0	2,498	223	13
40	28	980	693	18	442	—	2,115	8,305	4.33	80.4	4,848	253	12
16	10	750	370	-33	153	—	1,273	28,273	0.96	30.6	2,213	238	41
30	4	427	365	-25	1,277	—	2,070	7,267[4]	0.15	6.4	2,344	60	4
36	34	1,000	750	-14	5	—	1,755	8,823	5.31	88.3	2,870	64	13
16	15	650	412	-6	312	—	1,374	5,685	0.30	2.7	2,233	72	14
28	7	1,007	3,808	20	643	779	6,238	19,786	0.10	6.0	10,172	446	21
23	4	750[3]	187	NA	61	—	998	NA	0.99	11.3	2,262	-20	NA
26	16	780	882	25	195	—	1,857[8]	8,496	0.22	3.8	2,375	126	9
28	9	900	550	-38	595	—	2,045	21,919	0.25	10.7	8,347	209	16

For footnotes 1–14 see page 17.

(Continued)

The 800 Highest-Paid CEOs *(Cont.)*

Company/chief executive	RANK among 800 execs	in industry	Age	Birthplace	EDUCATION undergraduate	graduate
CONSUMER NONDURABLES						
Avon Products/James E Preston	309	12	63	Cleveland OH	Northwestern U, BS '55	
Burlington Industries/George W Henderson III	296	11	47	Atlanta GA	U of North Carolina, BA '70	Emory U, MBA '74
Clorox/G Craig Sullivan	395	14	56	Huntington NY	Boston C, BS '64	
Colgate-Palmolive/Reuben Mark	13	1	57	Jersey City NJ	Middlebury C, BA '60	Harvard, MBA '63
Dial/John W Teets	158	7	62	Elgin IL		
Duracell Intl/Charles R Perrin	525	17	50	Brooklyn NY	Trinity College CT, BA '67	Columbia, MBA '69
Eastman Kodak/George M C Fisher	77	4	55	Anna IL	U of Illinois, BS '62	Brown, PhD '66
Estee Lauder Cos/Leonard A Lauder	153	6	63	New York NY	U of Penn-Wharton, BS '64	
Fruit of the Loom/William Farley	516	16	53	Pawtucket RI	Bowdoin C, AB '64	Boston C, JD '69
Gillette/Alfred M Zeien	90	5	66	New York NY	Webb Institute, BS '52	
Hasbro/Alan G Hassenfeld	483	15	47	Providence RI	U of Pennsylvania, BA '70	
James River Corp Va/Miles L Marsh	588	20	48	South Africa	U of Cape Town, BS '70	North-western U, PhD '76
Kimberly-Clark/Wayne R Sanders	366	13	48	Chicago IL	Illinois Tech, BSCE '69	Marquette U, MBA '72
Liz Claiborne/Paul R Charron	212	8	53	Schenectady NY	U of Notre Dame, BA '64	Harvard, MBA '71
Mattel/John W Amerman	62	3	64	Newark NJ	Dartmouth, BA '53	MBA '54
NIKE/Philip H Knight[1]	263	10	58	Portland OR	U of Oregon, BA '59	Stanford U, MBA '62
Polaroid/Gary T DiCamillo	552	19	45	Niagara Falls NY	Rensselaer, BSChE '73	Harvard, MBA '75
Procter & Gamble/John E Pepper	256	9	57	Pottsville PA	Yale, BA '60	

TENURE (YRS)		COMPENSATION							STOCK OWNED		COMPANY DATA		
with firm	as CEO	salary ($thou)	bonus ($thou)	% change*	other ($thou)	stock gains ($thou)	total ($thou)	5-year total	%	market value ($mil)	sales ($mil)	profits ($mil)	5-year return
		$865	**$542**	**12%**	**$506**	**—**	**$2,019**	**$16,808**	**0.24%**	**$20.1**	**$3,575**	**$165**	**19%**
32	7	610	381	−6	962	—	1,953	16,808	0.11	6.3	4,492	257	19
22	1	475	605	30	939	—	2,019	NA	0.24	1.8	2,207	64	−3[2]
25	4	615	542	19	244	15,115	1,516	4,451[4]	0.07	2.7	2,079	210	21
33	12	985	1,000	−16	2,325	11,567	15,877	54,522	0.42	47.0	8,358	172	18
32	15	1,112	0	−53	1,103	1,051	3,266	21,596	0.86	22.9	3,575	1	21
11	2	535	532	31	35	—	1,102	NA	0.08	4.1	2,180	246	19[2]
2	2	2,000	2,282	12	2,005	—	6,287	17,777[5]	0.04	9.2	14,980	1,252	20
38	14	1,522	788	NA	1,080	—	3,390	NA	48.77	1,973.5	3,095	141	NA
20	11	950	0	−30	166	—	1,116	12,446	9.23	173.5	2,403	−227	15
28	5	1,125	1,300	21	177	2,922	5,524	22,611	0.16	35.2	6,795	824	24
26	7	928	220	2	79	—	1,226	12,606	3.44	109.4	2,858	156	19
1	1	800[3]	150	NA	7	—	957	NA	—[6]	—[7]	6,800	126	2
21	4	800	845	45	9	—	1,653	7,248	0.02	3.9	13,789	33	15
2	1	682	1,319	NA	585	—	2,586	NA	0.26	6.9	2,082	127	−3
16	9	1,042	916	10	5,012	—	6,970	30,600	0.28	20.1	3,639	358	32
32	32	865	788	84	526	—	2,178	6,889	33.93	4,502.6	5,961	510	30
—[10]	—[10]	550[3]	0	NA	506	—	1,056	NA	0.09	1.8	2,237	−140	14
33	1	910	51	NA	240	1,044	2,244[9]	NA	0.06	32.3	34,923	2,835	17

For footnotes 1–14 see page 17.

(Continued)

The 800 Highest-Paid CEOs *(Cont.)*

Company/chief executive	RANK among 800 execs	in industry	Age	Birthplace	EDUCATION undergraduate	graduate
CONSUMER NONDURABLES, *Cont.*						
Reebok International/Paul B Fireman	529	18	52	Cambridge MA		
Service Corp Intl/Robert L Waltrip[1]	34	2	65	Austin TX	U of Houston, BBA '54	
VF/Mackey J McDonald	608	21	49	Rome GA	Davidson C, BA '68	Georgia State U, MBA '73
ELECTRIC UTILITIES						
Allegheny Power/Klaus Bergman	658	37	64	Germany	Columbia, AB '53	LLB '55
American Electric/E Linn Draper Jr	470	15	54	Houston TX	Rice U, BA '64	Cornell, PhD '70
American Water Work/George W Johnstone	701	43	57	Buffalo NY	Penn State U, BS '60	
Baltimore G&E/Christian H Poindexter	642	35	57	Evansville IN	US Naval Acad, BS '60	Loyola U (IL), MBA '75
Boston Edison/Thomas J May	666	39	49	Hartford CT	Stonehill C, BS '69	Bentley C, MS '80
Carolina Power & Lt/Sherwood H Smith Jr	553	21	61	Jacksonville FL	U of North Carolina, AB '56	JD '60
Centerior Energy/Robert J Farling	779	55	59	Warren OH	Case Western, BSEE '58	MBA '65
Central & So West/E R Brooks	611	31	58	Slaton TX	Texas Tech U, BSEE '61	
Cinergy/James E Rogers	346	6	48	Birmingham AL	U of Kentucky, BBA '70	JD '74
CMS Energy/William T McCormick Jr	319	5	51	Washington DC	Cornell, BS '66	MIT, PhD '69
Consolidated Edison/Eugene R McGrath	557	22	54	New York NY	Manhattan C, BSME '63	Iona C, MBA '80
Dominion Resources/Thos E Capps	477	16	60	Wilmington NC	U of North Carolina, BA '58	JD '65
DPL/Peter H Forster	605	30	53	Germany	U of Wisc Madison, BS '64	Brooklyn Law School, JD '72
DQE/Wesley W von Schack	412	9	52	Wantagh NY	Fordham U, AB '65	Pace U NY, PhD '90
DTE Energy/John E Lobbia	695	42	54	Chicago IL	U of Detroit, BSEE '64	

with firm	as CEO	salary	bonus	% change*	other	stock gains	total	5-year total	%	market value ($mil)	sales	profits	5-year return
TENURE (YRS)		COMPENSATION							STOCK OWNED		COMPANY DATA		
		($thou)				($thou)					($mil)		
17	17	1,000	0	-50	97	—	1,097	9,261	13.68	288.6	3,481	165	4
34	34	822	1,919	34	4,745	2,941	10,428	32,838	0.46	26.2	1,652	184	27
13	—[10]	545	350	NA	10	—	905[9]	NA	0.03	0.9	5,062	157	19
		$535	**$232**	**11%**	**$113**	**—**	**$933**	**$3,444**	**0.03%**	**$0.8**	**$2,648**	**$240**	**12%**
24	11	515	188	16	64	—	766	3,109	—[6]	0.3	2,648	240	17
4	3	685	236	11	366	—	1,287	3,457[4]	0.01	0.7	5,670	530	15
30	4	446	0	7	195	—	641	2,085	0.11	1.4	803	92	19
29	3	537	247	19	32	—	816	2,516[4]	0.06	2.3	2,935	338	14
20	2	415	293	23	36	—	744	NA	0.03	0.3	1,629	112	13
31	16	630	360	22	64	—	1,054	4,112	0.07	3.5	3,007	373	16
37	4	360	0	0	22	—	382	1,838	0.03	0.4	2,516	221	-9
35	5	629	163	32	105	—	896	3,857	0.02	1.3	3,735	402	11
8	—[10]	535	322	NA	434	466	1,757[9]	NA	0.04	1.8	3,031	347	14
11	11	725	470	8	126	581	1,902[8]	5,909	0.15	3.6	3,890	204	3
33	6	660	273	11	119	—	1,052	4,500	—[6]	0.4	6,537	724	12
12	6	628	314	12	298	—	1,240	4,303	0.04	2.6	4,652	425	11
23	11	572	344	9	1	—	917	4,366	0.02	0.5	1,255	165	18
12	10	440	195	5	179	658	1,472	5,291	0.04	0.7	1,220	171	17
32	6	577	58	11	23	—	658	2,964	0.02	1.0	3,636	406	10

For footnotes 1–14 see page 17.

(Continued)

The 800 Highest-Paid CEOs *(Cont.)*

	RANK				EDUCATION	
Company/chief executive	among 800 execs	in industry	Age	Birthplace	undergraduate	graduate
ELECTRIC UTILITIES, *Cont.*						
Duke Power/William H Grigg	439	11	63	Shelby NC	Duke U, AB '54	LLB '58
Edison International/John E Bryson	387	8	52	New York NY	Stanford U, BA '65	Yale, JD '69
Enova/Stephen L Baum	690	40	55	Boston MA	Harvard, BA '63	U of Virginia, LLB '66
Entergy/Edwin Lupberger	275	4	59	Atlanta GA	Davidson C, AB '58	Emory U, MBA '63
Florida Progress/Jack B Critchfield	446	12	62	Rockwood PA	Slippery Rock U, BS '55	U of Pittsburgh, MA '60
FPL Group/James L Broadhead	208	2	60	New Rochelle NY	Cornell, BSME '58	Columbia, JD '63
General Public Utils/James R Leva	530	19	64	Boonton NJ	Fairleigh Dickinson U, BSEE '60	Seton Hall U, JD '80
Hawaiian Electric/Robert F Clarke	615	32	54	Oakland CA	U of Cal Berkeley, BA '65	MBA '66
Houston Industries/Don D Jordan	178	1	64	Corpus Christi TX	U of Texas Austin, BBA '54	S Texas Col of Law, JD '69
Illinova/Larry D Haab	711	45	58	Fairbury IL	Millikin U, BS '59	
Kansas City P&L/A Drue Jennings	720	48	49	Topeka KS	U of Kansas, BS '68	JD '72
Long Island Lighting/William J Catacosinos	714	47	66	New York NY	NYU, BS '51	PhD '62
MidAmerican Energy/Russell E Christiansen	691	41	61	Jefferson SD	South Dakota State, BS '59	
New England Electric/John W Rowe	582	26	51	Dodgeville WI	U of Wisc Madison, BS '67	JD '70
New York State E&G/James A Carrigg	750	52	63	Johnson City NY	Broome Comm, AAS '58	
Niagara Mohawk Pwr/William E Davis	754	53	54	Schenevus NY	US Naval Acad, BS '64	George Washington U, MSA '70
Nipsco Industries/Gary L Neale	454	13	56	Lead SD	U of Washington, BA '62	MBA '65

THE 800 HIGHEST-PAID CEOs 47

Tenure (yrs) with firm	as CEO	Compensation salary	bonus ($thou)	% change*	other	stock gains	total	5-year total ($thou)	Stock owned %	market value ($mil)	Company data sales	profits ($mil)	5-year return
33	2	637	313	43	416	—	1,366	3,037[5]	0.02	1.9	4,677	715	18
12	6	664	651	98	232	—	1,547	5,475	—[6]	0.2	8,405	739	4
11	—[10]	264	191	NA	208	—	663[9]	NA	0.04	1.0	1,871	234	8
17	10	700	568	41	843	—	2,112	6,452	0.05	2.8	6,274	485	9
13	6	590	383	4	374	—	1,346	4,703	0.03	0.9	3,056	239	12
7	7	824	700	5	1,092	—	2,616	10,164	0.08	6.4	5,592	553	15
44	4	585	333	6	174	—	1,092	3,797	—[6]	0.1	3,805	440	13
9	5	440	108	−16	18	317	883	3,285	0.04	0.4	1,296	78	8
40	19	885	907	12	1,145	—	2,937	11,545	0.05	2.9	3,680	1,124	11
31	5	472	77	11	65	—	614	2,467	0.01	0.3	1,641	152	13
22	8	403	132	5	57	—	592	2,453	0.03	0.5	886	123	15
17	12	588	0	1	15	—	603	2,721	—[6]	0.2	3,075	303	3
37	4	428	148	39	87	—	662	2,116[4]	0.02	0.3	1,724	131	6
7	7	538	427	23	14	—	979	3,674	0.03	0.8	2,272	205	14
38	8	472	46	18	2	—	521	2,262	0.02	0.3	2,010	197	5
6	3	491	0	7	19	—	509	1,818[4]	—[6]	—[7]	3,917	248	−10
7	3	460	286	8	586	—	1,332	3,026[4]	0.13	3.0	1,722	176	19

For footnotes 1–14 see page 17.

(Continued)

The 800 Highest-Paid CEOs *(Cont.)*

| | RANK | | | | EDUCATION | |
Company/chief executive	among 800 execs	in industry	Age	Birthplace	undergraduate	graduate
ELECTRIC UTILITIES, *Cont.*						
Northeast Utilities/Bernard M Fox	595	27	53	New York NY	Manhattan C, BSEE '63	Rensselaer, MSEE '64
No States Power/James J Howard	581	25	60	Pittsburgh PA	U of Pittsburgh, BBA '57	MIT, MS '70
Ohio Edison/Willard R Holland	663	38	60	Springfield TN	Rose-Hulman Tech, BS '65	MS '66
Oklahoma G&E/James G Harlow Jr	644	36	61	Oklahoma City OK	U of Oklahoma, BS '57	
Pacific G&E/Stanley T Skinner	466	14	58	Fort Smith AR	San Diego State U, BA '60	U of Cal Berkeley, JD '64
PacifiCorp/Frederick W Buckman	430	10	50	Kalamazoo MI	U of Michigan, BS '66	MIT, PhD '70
PECO Energy/Corbin A McNeill Jr	623	33	56	Santa Fe NM	US Naval Acad, BS '62	
Pinnacle West/Richard Snell	534	20	65	Phoenix AZ	Stanford U, BA '52	JD '54
Portland General/Ken L Harrison	598	29	53	Bakersfield CA	Oregon State U, BS '64	MS '66
Potomac Electric/Edward F Mitchell	569	23	64	Harrisonburg VA	U of Virginia, BSEE '56	George Washington U, MEA '60
PP&L Resources/William F Hecht	744	51	53	New York NY	Lehigh U, BS '64	MS '70
Public Service Colo/Wayne H Brunetti	761	54	53	Cleveland OH	U of Florida, BSBA '64	
Pub Svc Enterprise/E James Ferland	495	17	54	Boston MA	U of Maine, BS '64	U of New Haven, MBA '76
Puget Sound P&L/Richard R Sonstelie	741	50	51	Canada	US Military Acad, BS '66	Harvard, MBA '74
Scana/Lawrence M Gressette Jr	513	18	64	St Matthews SC	Clemson U, BS '54	U of S Carolina, LLB '59
Southern Co/Alfred W Dahlberg	347	7	55	Atlanta GA	Georgia State U, BBA '70	

TENURE (YRS)		COMPENSATION							STOCK OWNED		COMPANY DATA		
with firm	as CEO	salary	bonus	% change*	other	stock gains	total	5-year total	%	market value ($mil)	sales	profits	5-year return
		($thou)				($thou)					($mil)		
32	3	551	246	−6	138	—	935	2,749[5]	0.02	0.4	3,749	282	7
9	9	565	400	16	14	—	979	4,443	0.05	1.6	2,587	276	13
5	3	502	180	6	66	—	748	2,414[4]	—[6]	0.1	2,466	317	12
35	20	500	183	8	127	—	810	3,441	0.12	1.8	1,302	125	8
32	2	570	471	52	99	161	1,302	NA	—[6]	0.4	9,622	1,339	3
2	2	570	89	−18	742	—	1,400	NA	0.04	2.6	3,401	505	5
8	1	445	273	39	153	—	871	NA	—[6]	0.1	4,186	610	12
6	6	515	380	17	190	—	1,085	4,786	0.06	1.3	1,670	200	24
21	7	492	371	30	70	—	932	3,448	0.08	1.2	984	81	18
40	7	560	207	39	248	—	1,015	4,139	0.04	1.3	1,957	94	12
32	3	489	0	11	52	—	541	1,812[4]	0.01	0.4	2,752	323	9
2	—[10]	331	150	NA	7	—	488[9]	NA	—[6]	0.2	2,111	179	17
10	10	682	251	2	255	—	1,189	4,977	0.02	1.2	6,164	662	8
22	4	389	140	43	16	—	545	2,509	0.01	0.2	1,179	136	11
13	6	449	198	55	483	—	1,130	3,784	0.05	1.2	1,353	168	15
36	1	722	120	17	914	—	1,757	NA	—[6]	1.2	9,180	1,103	18

For footnotes 1–14 see page 17.

(Continued)

The 800 Highest-Paid CEOs (Cont.)

Company/chief executive	RANK among 800 execs	in industry	Age	Birthplace	EDUCATION undergraduate	graduate
ELECTRIC UTILITIES, *Cont.*						
Southwestern PS/Bill D Helton	726	49	57	Wheeler TX	Texas Tech U, BSEE '64	
TECO Energy/Timothy L Guzzle	574	24	59	Ottumwa IA	U of Oklahoma, BS '58	Texas Christian U, PhD '65
Texas Utilities/Erle A Nye	597	28	58	Fort Worth TX	Texas A&M, BSEE '59	SMU, JD '65
Unicom/James J O'Connor	259	3	59	Chicago IL	Col of the Holy Cross, BS '58	George-town U, LLB '63
Union Electric/Charles W Mueller	712	46	57	Belleville IL	St Louis U, BSEE '61	MBA '66
Western Resources/John E Hayes Jr	703	44	58	Kansas City MO	Rockhurst C, BS '59	
Wisconsin Energy/Richard A Abdoo	638	34	52	Port Huron MI	U of Dayton, BSEE '65	U of Detroit, MA '69
ENERGY						
Amerada Hess/John B Hess	323	12	42	Perth Amboy NJ	Harvard, BA '75	MBA '77
Amoco/H Laurance Fuller	344	14	57	Moline IL	Cornell, BSCE '61	DePaul U, JD '65
Anadarko Petroleum/Robert J Allison Jr	268	8	57	Evanston IL	U of Kansas, BS '60	
Ashland/John R Hall	539	30	63	Dallas TX	Vanderbilt U, BS '55	
Atlantic Richfield/Michael R Bowlin	363	16	53	Amarillo TX	U of North Texas, BBA '65	MBA '67
Baker Hughes/James D Woods	298	11	64	Falmouth KY	Cal St Fullerton, BA '67	
Burlington Resources/Bobby S Shackouls	577	33	45	Greenville MS	Mississippi State, BSCE '72	
Chevron/Kenneth T Derr	122	4	59	Wilkes-Barre PA	Cornell, BSME '59	MBA '60
Coastal/David A Arledge	549	32	51	El Dorado AR	U of Texas Austin, BA '65	LLB '68
Columbia Gas System/Oliver G Richard III	437	20	43	Lake Charles LA	Louisiana State U, BA '74	JD '77

with firm	as CEO	salary	bonus	% change*	other	stock gains	total	5-year total	%	market value ($mil)	sales	profits	5-year return
TENURE (YRS)		COMPENSATION							STOCK OWNED		COMPANY DATA		
		($thou)			($thou)						($mil)		
32	6	292	95	14	194	—	581	2,087	0.04	0.5	853	123	11
8	7	494	415	7	82	—	991	5,076	0.09	2.4	1,392	186	13
36	1	679	140	NA	113	—	933	NA	0.02	2.1	5,639	–139	11
33	16	827	827	31	550	—	2,204	6,084	0.01	0.8	6,910	660	–1
35	2	420	157	11	34	—	611	1,467[5]	—[6]	0.3	2,103	314	13
7	7	467	102	4	68	—	637	2,704	0.03	0.6	1,572	182	12
21	5	496	232	8	92	—	820	3,066	0.02	0.5	1,770	234	10
		$675	$377	10%	$196	—	$1,383	$7,059	0.09%	$4.0	$3,666	$128	8%
19	1	900	0	NA	976	—	1,876	NA	1.70	90.5	7,302	–394	5
35	5	875	763	–2	132	—	1,769	9,369	0.02	6.2	27,066	1,862	11
23	17	825	1,000	16	317	—	2,142	10,364	0.34	11.4	434	21	17
38	15	877	0	–46	127	75	1,079	6,772	0.11	2.9	11,495	76	8
27	2	836	670	14	166	—	1,672	NA	—[6]	1.4	15,819	1,376	4
41	9	787	769	10	202	249	2,006	9,526	0.24	9.8	2,725	128	4
3	—[10]	530	263	NA	196	—	989[9]	NA	—[6]	—[7]	873	–280	4
36	7	1,000	721	1	2,465	—	4,186	15,149	0.02	7.3	31,322	930	13
16	1	623	300	NA	136	—	1,059[9]	NA	0.02	0.8	10,448	270	6
1	1	528[13]	263	NA	593	—	1,383	NA	0.03	0.7	2,635	–432	1

For footnotes 1–14 see page 17.

(Continued)

The 800 Highest-Paid CEOs *(Cont.)*

	RANK				EDUCATION	
Company/chief executive	among 800 execs	in industry	Age	Birthplace	undergraduate	graduate
ENERGY, *Cont.*						
Consol Natural Gas/George A Davidson Jr	515	26	57	Pittsburgh PA	U of Pittsburgh, BS '60	
Diamond Shamrock/Roger R Hemminghaus	413	19	59	St Louis MO	Auburn U, BS '58	
Dresser Industries/William E Bradford	548	31	61	Dallas TX	Centenary C, BS '58	
Enron/Kenneth L Lay	49	1	54	Tyrone MO	U of Missouri, BA '64	U of Houston, PhD '70
Exxon/Lee R Raymond	74	2	57	Watertown SD	U of Wisc Madison, BS '60	U of Minnesota, PhD '63
Fina/Ron W Haddock	739	39	55	St Elmo IL	Purdue U, BS '63	
Halliburton/Dick Cheney	468	23	55	Lincoln NE	U of Wyoming, BA '65	MA '66
Kerr-McGee/Frank A McPherson	336	13	63	Stillwell OK	Oklahoma State U, BS '57	
Mapco/James E Barnes	631	36	62	Ponca City OK	Oklahoma State U, BS '57	
Mobil/Lucio A Noto	162	6	58	Brooklyn NY	U of Notre Dame, BS '58	Cornell, MBA '62
NGC/Charles L Watson	202	7	46	Great Lakes IL	Oklahoma State U, BS '72	
NorAm Energy/T Milton Honea	624	35	63	Fulton AR	U of Cal Berkeley, BS '55	Harvard, MBA '58
Occidental Petroleum/Ray R Irani	112	3	61	Lebanon	American U Beirut, BS '53	USC, PhD '57
Oryx Energy/Robert L Keiser	725	38	53	Mount Olive IL	U of Missouri, BS '65	
Pacific Enterprises/Willis B Wood Jr	463	22	61	Kansas City MO	U of Tulsa, BS '57	
Panhandle Eastern/Paul M Anderson	512	25	51	Richland WA	U of Washington, BSME '67	Stanford U, MBA '69
Pennzoil/James L Pate	535	29	60	Mt Sterling IL	Monmouth C, AB '63	Indiana U, MBA '64
Phillips Petroleum/W Wayne Allen	392	18	59	Fort Smith AR	Oklahoma State U, BSME '59	MSIE '69

with firm	as CEO	salary	bonus ($thou)	% change*	other	stock gains	total	5-year total ($thou)	%	market value ($mil)	sales	profits ($mil)	5-year return
TENURE (YRS)		**COMPENSATION**							**STOCK OWNED**		**COMPANY DATA**		
30	9	568	214	38	335	—	1,116	5,041	0.14	5.8	3,307	21	5
12	9	551	276	−1	490	142	1,458	5,830	0.33	3.0	2,937	47	8
26	1	546	316	NA	88	111	1,060[9]	NA	0.04	1.9	5,775	221	9
12	12	990	1,440	11	1,254	4,937	8,621	41,439	0.33	31.9	9,189	520	25
33	3	1,400	1,000	30	994	2,994	6,388	16,031[4]	—[6]	8.4	107,893	6,470	12
10	7	500	0	−19	49	—	549	2,806	0.05	0.7	3,607	104	8
1	1	1,000[3]	150	NA	143	—	1,293	NA	0.09	5.5	5,699	234	8
39	13	668	775	95	360	—	1,803	4,914	0.12	4.0	1,801	−31	12
13	12	795	0	10	48	—	843	12,930	0.67	10.9	3,152	75	5
34	2	833	675	16	1,038	653	3,199	8,705[5]	0.02	6.7	64,767	2,376	17
11	11	601	1,994	−29	70	—	2,664	11,397[4]	6.68	110.0	3,666	93	6[2]
12	3	195	345	8	327	—	868[14]	2,685[4]	0.29	3.7	2,965	66	−9
13	5	1,900	872	0	1,816	—	4,588	24,621	0.25	20.9	10,423	511	13
31	1	474	0	32	109	—	583[14]	NA	0.10	1.6	1,014	158	−15
35	4	641	603	16	64	—	1,308	5,123	0.03	0.7	2,343	185	−2
5	1	455	334	NA	335	6	1,130[9]	NA	0.02	0.9	4,968	304	21
20	6	657	0	−21	428	—	1,084	4,831	0.05	1.0	2,385	−305	−7
35	2	824	414	−22	78	216	1,532	4,540[5]	0.03	3.4	13,368	469	11

For footnotes 1–14 see page 17.

(Continued)

The 800 Highest-Paid CEOs (Cont.)

Company/chief executive	RANK among 800 execs	in industry	Age	Birthplace	EDUCATION undergraduate	graduate
ENERGY, *Cont.*						
Sonat/Ronald L Kuehn Jr	289	10	61	Queens NY	Fordham U, BA '57	LLB '64
Sun Co/Robert H Campbell	517	27	58	Pittsburgh PA	Princeton, BSCE '59	MIT, MBA '78
Texaco/Alfred C DeCrane Jr	155	5	64	Cleveland OH	U of Notre Dame, BA '53	George-town U, JD '59
Tosco/Thomas D O'Malley	283	9	54	New York NY	Manhattan C, BBA '63	
Ultramar/Jean Gaulin	618	34	53	Canada	U of Montreal, BS '67	
Unocal/Roger C Beach	500	24	59	Lincoln NE	Colo Sch Mines, BS '61	
USX-Marathon/Thomas J Usher	362	15	53	Reading PA	U of Pittsburgh, BS '64	PhD '71
UtiliCorp United/Richard C Green Jr	718	37	42	Kansas City MO	SMU, BSBA '76	
Valero Energy/William E Greehey	367	17	59	Fort Dodge IA	St Mary's U, BBA '60	
Western Atlas/Alton J Brann	452	21	54	Portland ME	U of Massachusetts, BA '69	
Williams Cos/Keith E Bailey	532	28	54	Kansas City MO	U of Missouri, BS '64	
ENTERTAINMENT & INFORMATION						
American Greetings/Morry Weiss	479	20	56	Czechoslovakia	Case Western, BA '61	
Comcast/Ralph J Roberts[1]	35	1	76	New York NY	U of Pennsylvania, BS '41	
Cox Communications/James O Robbins	659	26	53	Mount Kisco NY	U of Pennsylvania, BA '65	Harvard, MBA '70
Walt Disney/Michael D Eisner	48	2	54	New York NY	Denison U, BA '64	
RR Donnelley & Sons/John R Walter	98	7	49	Pittsburgh PA	Miami U Ohio, BS '69	
Dow Jones/Peter R Kann	329	14	53	Princeton NJ	Harvard, BA '64	
Dun & Bradstreet/Robert E Weissman	190	12	55	New Haven CT	Babson C, BS '64	
Gannett/John J Curley	140	8	57	Easton PA	Dickinson C, BA '60	Columbia MS '63
Gaylord Entertain/Earl W Wendell	584	23	68	Akron OH	Wooster, BBA '50	

TENURE (YRS)		COMPENSATION ($thou)							STOCK OWNED		COMPANY DATA		
with firm	as CEO	salary	bonus	% change*	other	stock gains	total	5-year total	%	market value ($mil)	sales	profits ($mil)	5-year return
26	12	710	419	2	441	483	2,052	7,688	0.19	6.2	1,990	193	16
36	5	699	377	78	40	—	1,116	4,120	0.05	1.1	8,370	227	3
37	3	978	863	21	529	976	3,346	10,772[4]	0.06	13.7	35,551	728	11
8	6	550	1,452	36	70	—	2,072	7,703	3.07	56.0	7,284	77	19
22	7	665	195	–16	20	—	879	4,027	0.12	1.5	2,714	48	25[2]
35	2	718	212	15	253	—	1,183[14]	NA	0.02	1.8	7,235	260	8
30	1	675[15]	900[15]	NA	98	—	1,673	NA	0.02	1.2	11,163	–83	–2
20	11	495	0	0	101	—	596	4,092	0.65	8.5	2,799	80	11
33	22	685	560	100	402	—	1,647	7,347	0.77	8.8	3,020	60	3
23	3	649	670	10	17	—	1,336	6,743[5]	—[6]	0.2	2,226	100	21[2]
23	2	572	250	49	14	256	1,092[14]	3,076[5]	0.20	10.4	2,856	1,318	30
		$800	**$525**	**4%**	**$266**	**—**	**$1,869**	**$12,651**	**0.38%**	**$14.9**	**$2,581**	**$138**	**12%**
35	8	500	470	0	266	—	1,236	11,994	1.06	21.7	1,958	113	9
34	33	800	0	0	4,552	4,674	10,026[8]	49,397	4.57	190.3	3,363	–38	11
13	2	528	227	4	6	—	761	NA	0.04[12]	2.4	1,328	101	33[2]
12	12	750	8,025	9	7	—	8,782	232,746	0.56	184.1	12,128	1,394	17
27	7	900	555	12	3,468	366	5,289	10,055	0.15	8.0	6,512	299	10
33	5	680	445	7	728	16	1,869	7,158	0.16	5.6	2,284	190	12
23	2	830	802	10	1,207	—	2,839	8,182[5]	0.07	7.3	5,415	321	10
26	10	800	850	6	806	1,195	3,651	12,975	0.15	13.5	4,007	477	14
46	5	654	286	6	33	—	973	5,362	0.05	1.2	707	108	22[2]

For footnotes 1–14 see page 17.   [15]Salary and bonus is paid by USX Corp. for services rendered to Marathon, Steel and Delhi.

(Continued)

The 800 Highest-Paid CEOs *(Cont.)*

Company/chief executive	RANK among 800 execs	in industry	Age	Birthplace	EDUCATION undergraduate	graduate
ENTERTAINMENT & INFORMATION, *Cont.*						
Harcourt General/Robert J Tarr Jr	53	3	52	Freeport NY	US Naval Acad, BS '66	Harvard, MBA '73
Interpublic Group/Philip H Geier Jr	349	16	61	Pontiac MI	Colgate U, BA '57	Columbia, MBA '58
King World Prods/Michael King	55	4	48	Summit NJ	Fairleigh Dickinson U, BA '71	
Knight-Ridder/P Anthony Ridder	508	21	55	Duluth MN	U of Michigan, BA '62	
McGraw-Hill Cos/Joseph L Dionne	150	9	62	Montgomery AL	Hofstra U, BA '55	Columbia, EdD '65
New York Times/Arthur Ochs Sulzberger	380	17	70	New York NY	Columbia, BA '51	
Omnicom Group/Bruce Crawford	92	5	67	W Bridgewater MA	U of Pennsylvania, BS '52	
Reader's Digest Assn/James P Schadt	332	15	57	Saginaw MI	Northwestern U, BA '60	
EW Scripps/Lawrence A Leser	397	19	61	Cincinnati OH	Xavier U, BS '57	
Tele-Com-Liberty/John C Malone[15]	621	24	55	Milford CT	Yale, BS '63	Johns Hopkins U, PhD '67
Tele-Com-TCI/John C Malone[15]	621	24	55	Milford CT	Yale, BS '63	Johns Hopkins U, PhD '67
Time Warner/Gerald M Levin	96	6	57	Philadelphia PA	Haverford C, BA '60	U of Pennsylvania, LLB '63
Times Mirror/Mark H Willes	384	18	54	Salt Lake City UT	Columbia, AB '63	PhD '67
Tribune/John W Madigan	177	11	58	Chicago IL	U of Michigan, BBA '58	MBA '59
Turner Broadcasting/Robert E Turner[1]	224	13	57	Cincinnati OH		
U S West Media/Charles M Lillis[17]	174	10	54	Overland Park KS	U of Washington, BA '68	U of Oregon, PhD '72

TENURE (YRS)		COMPENSATION							STOCK OWNED		COMPANY DATA		
with firm	as CEO	salary	bonus	% change*	other	stock gains	total	5-year total	%	market value ($mil)	sales	profits	5-year return
		($thou)					($thou)				($mil)		
20	4	1,500	1,125	7	183	5,291	8,099	21,257	0.47	15.1	3,013	171	20
21	16	965	550	15	115	122	1,752[8]	26,533	0.64	23.8	2,180	130	18
23	12	1,050	1,760	−14	4,237	768	7,815	36,178	5.50	84.9	589	133	7
34	1	603	195	−4	12	341	1,151	NA	0.13	4.4	2,752	167	9
30	13	850	678	−1	1,726	178	3,433	12,327	0.21	9.3	2,935	227	12
45	23	555	822	1	203	—	1,580	7,093	7.08	217.8	2,409	136	8
7	7	985	1,520	22	696	2,206	5,407	15,082	0.28	9.2	2,258	140	29
5	2	741	235	−8	870	—	1,846	NA	0.10	4.9	3,151	240	10
28	11	675	540	4	297	—	1,512	5,786	0.06	2.1	1,030	133	19
23	23	850[16]	0[16]	3	21	—	871	21,993	3.90	175.0	1,433	−25	NA
23	23	850[16]	0[16]	3	21	—	871	21,993	3.88	483.7	5,022	−24	10
24	4	1,050	4,000	0	261	—	5,311	30,247	0.09	14.7	8,067	−124	10
1	1	800[3]	525	NA	226	—	1,551	NA	0.06	2.3	3,448	−395	19
21	1	677	510	NA	36	1,757	2,979[9]	NA	0.48	19.4	2,245	278	12
33	33	945	596	10	916	—	2,457[8]	7,197	38.16	2,179.7	3,437	103	17
11	1	490	375	NA	1,520	634[18]	3,019	NA	0.01	0.9	2,374	145	NA

For footnotes 1–14 see page 17. [15]Overall CEO for Tele-Communications. [16]Salary and bonus is paid by Tele-Communications for services rendered to Liberty Media and TCI Group. [17]Overall CEO for U S West is Richard D McCormick. [18]Includes value for U S West Communications' options exercised.

(Continued)

The 800 Highest-Paid CEOs *(Cont.)*

Company/chief executive	among 800 execs	in industry	Age	Birthplace	undergraduate	graduate
	RANK				**EDUCATION**	
ENTERTAINMENT & INFORMATION, *Cont.*						
US Satellite Broad/Stanley E Hubbard	789	27	35	St Paul MN	U of Minnesota, BA '83	
Viacom/Sumner M Redstone	—	—	72	Boston MA	Harvard, BA '44	LLB '47
Washington Post/Donald E Graham	578	22	51	Baltimore MD	Harvard, BA '66	
FINANCIAL SERVICES						
Advanta/Alex W Hart	214	35	55	Meadville PA	Harvard, BA '62	
HF Ahmanson/Charles R Rinehart	213	34	49	San Francisco CA	U of San Francisco, BS '68	
Ambac/Phillip B Lassiter	196	32	52	Kansas City MO	NC State U, BS '64	
American Express/Harvey Golub	40	8	57	New York NY	NYU, BS '61	
AmSouth Bancorp/C Dowd Ritter	594	102	48	Birmingham AL	Birmingham-Southern C, BA '69	
Associated Banc-Cp/Harry B Conlon	700	125	61	Green Bay WI	U of Notre Dame, BS '57	U of Wisc Madison, LLB '64
Astoria Financial/George L Engelke Jr	419	65	57	Englewood NJ	Lehigh U, BS '60	
Banc One/John B McCoy	115	20	52	Columbus OH	Williams C, BA '65	Stanford U, MBA '67
Bancorp Hawaii/Lawrence M Johnson	441	72	55	Honolulu HI	U of Hawaii, BBA '63	
BancorpSouth/Aubrey Burns Patterson	372	55	53	Grenada MS	U of Mississippi, BBA '64	Michigan State U, MBA '69
Bank of Boston/Charles K Gifford	95	16	53	Providence RI	Princeton, BA '64	
Bank of New York/John Carter Bacot	94	15	63	Utica NY	Hamilton C, AB '55	Cornell, LLB '58
BankAmerica/David A Coulter	125	21	48	Pittsburgh PA	Carnegie-Mellon, BS '71	MS '71
Bankers Trust NY/Frank N Newman	320	49	54	Quincy MA	Harvard, BA '63	
BanPonce/Richard L Carrion	766	145	43	San Juan PR	U of Penn-Wharton, BS '75	MIT, MS '76

TENURE (YRS)		COMPENSATION							STOCK OWNED		COMPANY DATA		
with firm	as CEO	salary	bonus ($thou)	% change*	other	stock gains	total	5-year total ($thou)	%	market value ($mil)	sales	profits ($mil)	5-year return
21	—[10]	100	0	NA	—	—	100	NA	51.28	1,715.5	108	–91	NA
10	—[10]	NA	NA	—	—	—	—	NA	24.84[12]	3,742.1	11,689	223	11
25	5	400	0	0	585	—	985	3,032	16.04	505.3	1,719	190	8
		$525	**$349**	**12%**	**$105**	**—**	**$1,324**	**$5,704**	**0.33%**	**$6.4**	**$1,072**	**$135**	**25%**
2	1	495	228	NA	1,858	—	2,581	NA	0.60	12.8	782	137	63
7	3	760	851	25	974	—	2,585	5,620[5]	0.12	3.0	4,398	451	11
5	5	500	400	29	740	1,064	2,705	5,594[4]	0.12	2.1	304	168	21[2]
12	3	877	1,860	–4	4,244	2,303	9,284	22,640[4]	0.06	14.5	16,445	1,564	18
27	—[10]	460	400	NA	77	—	937[9]	NA	0.17	3.6	1,507	175	24
31	21	355	130	6	57	102	644	3,495	0.83	5.4	317	47	22
25	7	525	126	4	787	—	1,438	3,123[4]	1.72	9.3	444	45	30[2]
29	12	995	1,124	41	2,305	137	4,561	15,619	0.11	16.7	8,971	1,278	14
33	2	575	489	69	40	257	1,362	NA	0.33	4.7	1,043	122	11
24	4	330	134	–44	1,157	—	1,620	3,661[4]	0.33	1.7	284	36	26
29	1	708	1,500	NA	955	2,177	5,341[9]	NA	0.12	5.9	5,411	541	45
36	14	1,047	2,100	–9	1,751	446	5,344	15,926	0.23	20.6	5,327	914	34
20	—[10]	531	1,250	NA	2,258	—	4,039[9]	NA	0.04	11.3	20,386	2,664	20
1	—[10]	500[3]	1,165	NA	222	—	1,887	NA	0.01	0.7	8,309	215	17
20	3	350	75	15	37	—	462	1,162[5]	0.78	11.4	1,279	146	27

For footnotes 1–14 see page 17.

(Continued)

The 800 Highest-Paid CEOs *(Cont.)*

| | RANK | | | | EDUCATION | |
Company/chief executive	among 800 execs	in industry	Age	Birthplace	undergraduate	graduate
FINANCIAL SERVICES, *Cont.*						
Barnett Banks/Charles E Rice	138	24	60	Chattanooga TN	U of Miami, BBA '58	Rollins C, MBA '64
BayBanks/William M Crozier Jr	242	39	63	Brooklyn NY	Yale, BA '54	Harvard, MBA '63
Bear Stearns Cos/James E Cayne	36	6	62	Evanston IL		
Beneficial/Finn M W Caspersen	126	22	54	New York NY	Brown, AB '63	Harvard, LLB '66
Boatmen's Bancshs/Andrew B Craig III	365	54	65	Buffalo NY	Cornell, BA '55	
BOK Financial/Stanley A Lybarger	783	151	46	Kansas City KS	U of Kansas, BA '72	MBA '73
Cal Fed Bancorp/Edward G Harshfield	482	81	59	New York NY	Southeastern U, BBA '62	
CCB Financial/Ernest C Roessler	733	136	55	Pittsburgh PA	Dartmouth, BA '62	MBA '63
Center Financial/Robert J Narkis	687	120	62	Nashua NH	U of New Hampshire, BA '56	Yale, JD '61
Central Fidelity Bks/Lewis N Miller Jr	689	122	52	Philadelphia PA	Washington & Lee U, BA '66	U of Virginia, MBA '72
Centura Banks/Robert R Mauldin	702	126	61	China Grove NC	U of North Carolina, BS '59	
Charter One Finl/Charles John Koch	681	119	50	Baltimore MD	Lehigh U, BS '68	Loyola U (IL), MBA '71
Chase Manhattan/Walter V Shipley	84	14	60	Newark NJ	NYU, BS '61	
Citicorp/John S Reed	24	4	57	Chicago IL	MIT, BS '61	MS '65
Citizens Bncp/Alfred H Smith Jr	793	153	62	Washington DC		
Citizens Banking/Robert J Vitito	563	94	53	Saginaw MI	Michigan State U, BBA '65	
City National/Russell Goldsmith	764	143	46	Chicago IL	Harvard, BS '71	JD '75
CNB Bancshares/James J Giancola	787	152	47	New York NY	Harvard, BS '70	
Coast Savings Finl/Ray Martin	688	121	60	Nogales AZ		

TENURE (YRS) with firm	as CEO	salary ($thou)	bonus ($thou)	% change*	other ($thou)	stock gains ($thou)	total ($thou)	5-year total ($thou)	STOCK OWNED %	market value ($mil)	sales ($mil)	profits ($mil)	5-year return
31	17	835	935	4	1,209	714	3,693	12,693	0.17	9.7	3,680	533	26
32	22	600	390	15	823	487	2,300	6,765	0.35	6.8	1,019	137	47
27	3	200	4,030	−45	4,774	913	9,917	42,026[5]	3.19	89.2	4,383	371	23
24	20	1,102	0	5	1,469	1,457	4,028[14]	14,300	9.58	280.1	2,398	151	21
11	8	650	500	23	506	—	1,656	6,595	0.03	1.5	2,996	419	20
22	—[10]	275	60	NA	15	—	350[9]	NA	0.15	0.6	367	49	−2
3	3	550	650	44	32	—	1,232	2,327[5]	—[6]	—[7]	1,072	94	−17
8	3	348	143	32	20	52	562	1,421[5]	0.11	0.8	436	58	21
6	6	350	210	15	130	—	690	2,635	0.66	1.8	285	23	42
24	2	650	0	6	22	—	672	NA	0.24	3.2	851	105	25
27	3	375	181	18	83	—	639	2,114[4]	0.29	2.4	440	58	24
20	8	339	239	5	46	79	702	3,258	0.38	5.3	1,141	34	38
40	2	850	2,400	30	2,551	—	5,801	11,523[5]	0.04	13.3	26,220	2,970	37
31	12	1,300	3,000	1	4,016	3,760	12,076	25,184	0.08	27.7	31,690	3,464	43
33	9	17[11]	0	—	10	—	27	131	8.77	39.4	300	36	13
28	—[10]	241	113	NA	20	656	1,030[9]	NA	0.44	1.8	277	34	28
1	1	420[3]	48	NA	—	5	473	NA	12.25	74.3	252	49	0
4	—[10]	222	44	NA	6	—	273[9]	NA	0.09	0.5	320	36	18
37	12	500	0	0	173	—	673	3,005	0.14	0.8	671	33	52

For footnotes 1–14 see page 17.

(Continued)

The 800 Highest-Paid CEOs *(Cont.)*

Company/chief executive	RANK among 800 execs	in industry	Age	Birthplace	EDUCATION undergraduate	graduate
FINANCIAL SERVICES, *Cont.*						
Collective Bncp/Thomas H Hamilton	674	116	65	Egg Harbor City NJ	Rutgers, BS '53	
Colonial BancGroup/Robert E Lowder	544	92	54	Tuscaloosa AL	Auburn U, BBA '64	
Comerica/Eugene A Miller	377	57	58	Detroit MI	Detroit Tech, BBA '64	
Commerce Bancshs/David W Kemper	523	88	45	Kansas City MO	Harvard, BA '72	Stanford U, MBA '76
Commercial Federal/William A Fitzgerald	643	110	58	Omaha NE	Creighton U, BS '59	
Compass Bancshares/D Paul Jones Jr	765	144	53	Birmingham AL	U of Alabama, BS '64	NYU, JD '67
CoreStates Financial/Terrence A Larsen	345	52	49	Chicago IL	U of Dallas, BA '68	Texas A&M, PhD '71
Countrywide Credit/David S Loeb[1]	238	38	72	New York NY	NYU, BS '51	
Crestar Financial/Richard G Tilghman	307	46	55	Norfolk VA	U of Virginia, BA '63	
Cullen/Frost Bankers/Thomas C Frost	719	130	68	San Antonio TX	Washington & Lee U, BS '50	
Dauphin Deposit/Christopher R Jennings	755	141	52	New York NY	U of Pennsylvania, BA '65	U of Penn-Wharton, MBA '68
Dean Witter Discover/Philip J Purcell	148	27	52	Salt Lake City UT	U of Notre Dame, BBA '64	U of Chicago, MBA '67
Deposit Guaranty/Emerson B Robinson Jr	629	108	54	Centreville MS	Davidson C, BS '63	Harvard, MBA '67
Dime Bancorp/James M Large Jr	526	89	64	Philadelphia PA	Princeton, BSE '54	
Downey Financial/Stephen W Prough	752	140	51	Riverside CA	Colorado C, BS '66	
AG Edwards/Benjamin F Edwards III	402	62	64	St Louis MO	Princeton, BA '53	
Federal Home Loan/Leland C Brendsel	261	41	54	Sioux Falls SD	U of Colorado, BS '67	Northwestern U, PhD '73

TENURE (YRS)		COMPENSATION							STOCK OWNED		COMPANY DATA		
with firm	as CEO	salary	bonus ($thou)	% change*	other	stock gains	total ($thou)	5-year total	%	market value ($mil)	sales ($mil)	profits	5-year return
41	34	348	146	8	26	195	716	3,638	4.02	20.2	368	53	42
15	15	675	240	31	6	145	1,066	2,979	9.98	46.6	301	39	38
41	7	625	560	−4	41	364	1,589	6,804	0.13	6.7	3,113	413	23
18	10	509	210	6	11	374	1,104	4,909	1.30	17.2	764	108	20
41	21	373	193	14	104	142	810	3,448	1.14	6.2	500	49	60
18	5	450	0	−41	17	—	467	6,750	1.30	16.6	849	110	27
19	8	688	576	5	496	—	1,759	7,865	0.05	4.3	2,868	452	24
27	27	878	1,121	−35	328	—	2,327	15,132	1.94	37.5	1,285	196	31
29	11	605	545	17	83	737	1,970	5,998	0.18	4.4	1,525	180	33
46	25	270	150	5	173	—	593[8]	3,528	2.78	15.0	344	46	48
9	1	375	126	14	4	—	505	NA	0.04	0.3	435	66	16
18	14	725	2,800	10	5	—	3,530	18,777	0.10	9.1	7,934	856	21[2]
29	12	381	407	−5	70	—	858	4,360	0.45	4.0	495	73	34
7	7	675	377	56	49	—	1,101	3,644	0.09	1.1	1,423	62	20
2	2	396	102	NA	16	—	514	NA	0.24	0.9	339	21	14
40	30	387	926	22	189	—	1,501	6,393	1.02	15.6	1,341	154	15
14	9	865	394	−12	929	—	2,188	9,627	0.05	7.2	9,519	1,091	29

For footnotes 1–14 see page 17.

(Continued)

The 800 Highest-Paid CEOs *(Cont.)*

Company/chief executive	RANK among 800 execs	RANK in industry	Age	Birthplace	EDUCATION undergraduate	EDUCATION graduate
FINANCIAL SERVICES, *Cont.*						
Federal Natl Mort/James A Johnson	103	17	52	Benson MN	U of Minnesota, BA '65	Princeton, MA '68
Fidelity Federal Bank/Richard M Greenwood	722	131	48	Fargo ND	U of Idaho, BS '72	American Grad School, MS '73
Fifth Third Bancorp/George A Schaefer Jr	467	78	51	Cincinnati OH	US Military Acad, BS '67	Xavier U, MBA '74
Finova Group/Samuel L Eichenfield	169	29	58	New York NY	Amherst C, BA '60	
First American/Dennis C Bottorff	458	77	51	Clarksville IN	Vanderbilt U, BE '66	Northwestern U, MBA '68
First Bank System/John F Grundhofer	58	9	57	Los Angeles CA	Loyola U (IL), BA '60	USC, MBA '64
First Chicago NBD/Verne G Istock	274	43	55	Grosse Pointe MI	U of Michigan, BA '62	MBA '63
First Citizens Bcshs/Lewis R Holding	746	139	68	Smithfield NC	U of North Carolina, BS '50	Harvard, MBA '52
First Commerce/Ian Arnof	676	117	56	McCrory AR	Vanderbilt U, BA '61	Harvard, MBA '63
First Commercial/Barnett Grace	696	124	51	Batesville AK	SMU, BBA '66	JD '68
First Empire State/Robert G Wilmers	678	118	62	New York NY	Harvard, BA '56	
First Financial/John C Seramur	314	48	53	Milwaukee WI	Marquette U, BS '65	
First Hawaiian/Walter A Dods Jr	443	73	54	Honolulu HI	U of Hawaii, BBA '67	
First Natl Nebraska/F Phillips Giltner	619	106	71			
First of America Bk/Richard F Chormann	731	135	58	Adrian MI	Western Michigan U, BBA '59	
First Security/Spencer F Eccles	668	114	61	Ogden UT	U of Utah, BS '56	Columbia, MA '59
First Tennessee Natl/Ralph Horn	391	59	55	Corinth MS	Mississippi State, BS '63	

| TENURE (YRS) | | salary | bonus | % | other | stock gains | total | 5-year total | % | market value | sales | profits | 5-year |
with firm	as CEO	($thou)		change*						($mil)	($mil)		return
6	5	800	833	4	3,354	—	4,987	18,759	—[6]	3.0	22,249	2,156	26
4	4	439	150	49	—	—	589	1,410[5]	0.07	0.2	253	–69	NA
25	5	721	410	15	162	—	1,293	5,973	0.16	9.2	1,479	288	29
9	9	520	558	13	2,020	—	3,097	7,045[5]	0.48	6.9	782	98	28[2]
5	5	550	275	4	499	—	1,324	3,701	0.32	4.1	730	103	41
6	6	620	1,085	1	174	5,515	7,393	17,884	0.16	13.6	3,297	568	32
33	2	746	550	12	445	372	2,113	NA	0.06	7.6	10,681	1,150	14
43	39	529	0	–1	9	—	538	2,519	10.65	72.9	563	57	23
18	13	525	175	6	14	—	714	5,485	0.39	4.8	738	76	31
24	9	363	211	10	11	69	654	2,926	1.16	9.8	396	57	29
14	13	400	300	10	13	—	713	12,377	8.94	138.6	1,078	131	30
30	30	680	272	15	243	719	1,913	6,280	2.23	14.5	462	64	43
27	7	776	313	46	261	—	1,350	5,737	0.87	7.5	655	77	6
32	2	408	435	NA	35	—	878[8]	NA	2.59	36.9	829	82	42[2]
38	—[10]	454	44	NA	70	—	568[9]	NA	0.03	0.8	2,143	237	19
36	14	544	163	0	33	—	740	3,706	2.75	49.2	1,193	120	31
33	2	457	223	7	861	—	1,542	3,906[5]	0.50	10.2	1,319	165	36

For footnotes 1–14 see page 17.

(Continued)

The 800 Highest-Paid CEOs (Cont.)

| | RANK | | | | EDUCATION | |
| | among | in | | | | |
Company/chief executive	800 execs	industry	Age	Birthplace	undergraduate	graduate
FINANCIAL SERVICES, *Cont.*						
First Union/Edward E Crutchfield	113	18	54	Dearborn MI	Davidson C, BA '63	U of Pennsylvania, MBA '65
First USA/John C Tolleson	230	36	47	Ennis TX		
First Virginia Banks/Barry J Fitzpatrick	706	129	56	Washington DC	U of Notre Dame, BBA '62	American U, MBA '72
Firstar/Roger L Fitzsimonds	414	64	57	Milwaukee WI	U of Wisc Milwaukee, BBA '60	MBA '71
FirstFed Financial/William S Mortensen	767	146	63	Philadelphia PA	USC, BS '54	
FirstMerit/John R Cochran	727	133	53	Council Bluffs IA	U of Iowa, BS '66	
Fleet Finl Group/Terrence Murray	132	23	56	Woonsocket RI	Harvard, BA '62	
Franklin Resources/Charles B Johnson	649	111	63	Montclair NJ	Yale, BA '54	
Fulton Financial/Rufus A Fulton Jr	771	147	55	Dallas TX	Franklin & Marshall C, BA '66	
GATX/Ronald H Zech	585	99	52	Reedsburg WI	Valparaiso U, BSEE '65	U of Wisc Madison, MBA '67
Glendale Federal Bk/Stephen J Trafton	612	105	49	Mt Vernon WA	Washington State, BS '68	
Golden West Finl/Marion O Sandler[1, 15]	591	101	65	Biddeford ME	Wellesley C, BA '52	NYU, MBA '58
Great Western Finl/John F Maher	509	86	53	Berkeley CA	Menlo C, BS '65	U of Pennsylvania, MBA '67
Green Tree Financial/Lawrence M Coss[1]	1	1	57	Miller SD		
GreenPoint Financial/Thomas S Johnson	538	91	55	Racine WI	Trinity College CT, AB '62	Harvard, MBA '64
Hibernia/Stephen A Hansel	448	74	48	Long Branch NJ	Wesleyan C, BA '69	U of Virginia, MBA '71
Household Intl/William F Aldinger III	325	50	48	Brooklyn NY	CUNY Baruch, BBA '69	Brooklyn Law School, JD '75

with firm	as CEO	salary	bonus	% change*	other	stock gains	total	5-year total	%	market value ($mil)	sales	profits	5-year return
TENURE (YRS)		**COMPENSATION**						($thou)	**STOCK OWNED**		**COMPANY DATA**		
31	12	850	1,700	53	1,889	149	4,588	15,127	0.04	5.8	10,583	1,430	27
21	11	620	620	19	72	1,106	2,418	13,548	1.63	51.7	1,298	211	83[2]
27	1	350	156	52	49	67	623	NA	0.07	0.9	664	112	21
32	5	617	349	7	483	—	1,449	6,021	0.09	2.8	1,740	229	28
41	13	342	95	33	18	—	456	6,190	2.17	3.7	310	7	–4
1	1	333	140	NA	104	—	577	NA	0.34	3.5	485	26	25
34	14	992	1,900	21	964	—	3,856	12,574	0.09	9.8	7,875	610	25
39	25	519	260	5	20	—	798	3,340	19.87	878.8	857	280	27
30	3	361	21	18	54	—	436	1,346[5]	0.11	0.7	265	46	19
18	—[10]	400	247	NA	322	—	969[9]	NA	0.11	1.1	1,233	101	10
6	4	650	240	37	3	—	893	3,679[4]	—[6]	—[7]	1,134	56	–36
33	33	931	0	5	15	—	946	12,316	8.61	261.7	2,470	235	13
10	—[10]	650	303	NA	193	—	1,147[9]	NA	0.17	5.1	3,566	261	12
21	21	434	65,147	126	—	—	65,580	119,108	3.34	154.6	672	254	74
3	3	538	425	20	117	—	1,080	3,334[5]	0.59	8.8	732	108	20[2]
4	4	500	468	13	376	—	1,344	3,771[4]	0.12	1.5	615	124	15
2	2	700	893	NA	283	—	1,875	NA	0.02	1.4	5,144	453	29

For footnotes 1–14 see page 17. [15]Office jointly held with Herbert M Sandler.

(Continued)

The 800 Highest-Paid CEOs *(Cont.)*

Company/chief executive	RANK among 800 execs	in industry	Age	Birthplace	EDUCATION undergraduate	graduate
FINANCIAL SERVICES, *Cont.*						
Huntington Bancshs/Frank Wobst	431	69	62	Germany	U of Erlangen, BA '55	Rutgers, MBA '64
KeyCorp/Robert W Gillespie	254	40	52	Cleveland OH	Ohio Wesleyan U, BA '66	Case Western, MBA '68
Keystone Finl/Carl L Campbell	705	128	53	Sunbury PA	Susquehanna U, BS '65	
Lehman Bros Holding/Richard S Fuld Jr	146	26	50	New York NY	U of Colorado, BS '69	NYU, MBA '73
Long Island Bancorp/John J Conefry Jr	536	90	51	New York NY	Manhattan C, BS '67	
Magna Group/G Thomas Andes	432	70	53	Lincoln IL	Illinois State U, BS '65	
Marsh & McLennan/A J C Smith	209	33	62	Scotland		
Marshall & Ilsley/James B Wigdale	453	75	59	Milwaukee WI	Stanford U, BA '59	
MBIA/David H Elliott	161	28	54	Canaan CT	Yale, BA '64	Boston U, JD '67
MBNA/Alfred Lerner	399	60	63	New York NY	Columbia, BA '55	
Mellon Bank/Frank V Cahouet	64	11	63	Boston MA	Harvard, BA '54	U of Penn-Wharton, MBA '59
Mercantile Bancorp/Thomas H Jacobsen	352	53	56	Chicago IL	Lake Forest C, BS '63	U of Chicago, MBA '68
Mercantile Bkshs/H Furlong Baldwin	273	42	64	Baltimore MD	Princeton, AB '54	
Mercury Finance/John N Brincat	21	3	60	Brooklyn NY		
Merrill Lynch/Daniel P Tully	66	13	64	Queens NY	St John's U NY, BBA '53	
MGIC Investment/William H Lacy	191	31	51	Chicago IL	U of Wisc Milwaukee, BBA '68	
JP Morgan & Co/Douglas A Warner III	114	19	49	Cincinnati OH	Yale, BA '68	
Morgan Stanley/Richard B Fisher	26	5	59	Philadelphia PA	Princeton, BA '57	Harvard, MBA '62

| TENURE (YRS) | | COMPENSATION | | | | | | | STOCK OWNED | | COMPANY DATA | | |
| with firm | as CEO | salary | bonus | % change* | other | stock gains | total | 5-year total | % | market value ($mil) | sales | profits | 5-year return |
		($thou)					($thou)				($mil)		
22	15	808	400	−11	103	88	1,399	9,826	0.53	17.1	1,710	245	27
28	1	754	404	NA	517	571	2,247[9]	NA	0.07	6.1	6,054	789	23
24	14	330	129	−2	53	117	629	2,453	0.22	1.7	414	61	17
27	3	750	1,450	54	1,376	—	3,576	14,959[5]	0.19	5.1	14,281	301	26[2]
3	2	600	250	71	234	—	1,084	1,730[5]	0.38	2.7	366	45	53[2]
31	1	375	129	19	382	509	1,394[14]	NA	0.59	3.9	395	51	23
35	4	1,125	775	4	699	—	2,599	13,262[4]	0.27	17.9	3,770	403	5
34	4	550	275	6	510	—	1,335	5,532[4]	0.32	7.6	1,349	193	23
20	4	525	225	−16	214	2,246	3,210	8,749	0.05	1.4	462	271	18
13	5	1,505	0	44	—	—	1,505[14]	5,744	12.93	795.7	2,565	353	42
9	9	860	645	31	2,200	3,192	6,898	26,186	0.26	19.0	4,514	691	31
7	7	574	516	6	643	—	1,733	6,972	0.27	7.5	1,398	217	24
40	20	747	488	43	108	772	2,115	6,468	0.39	4.8	555	104	13
12	11	360	1,618	14	9	10,965	12,953	25,087	1.58	33.1	348	111	37
40	4	500	4,644	6	1,511	—	6,654	39,483	0.31	32.1	21,513	1,114	31
25	9	487	400	31	75	1,872	2,834	7,901	0.48	15.4	618	208	30[2]
28	1	592	1,816	23	682	1,497	4,586	NA	0.02	3.5	13,838	1,296	17
34	5	477	4,187	77	1,259	5,178	11,101[15]	34,973	2.42	175.5	10,797	609	22

For footnotes 1–14 see page 17. [15]Figures are for ten months ending 11/30/95.

(Continued)

The 800 Highest-Paid CEOs (Cont.)

Company/chief executive	RANK among 800 execs	in industry	Age	Birthplace	EDUCATION undergraduate	graduate
FINANCIAL SERVICES, Cont.						
National City/David A Daberko	455	76	50	Akron OH	Denison U, BA '67	Case Western, MBA '69
Natl Commerce Bncp/Thomas M Garrott	724	132	58	Memphis TN	Vanderbilt U, BS '59	U of Penn-Wharton, MBA '62
NationsBank/Hugh L McColl Jr	65	12	60	Bennettsville SC	U of North Carolina, BS '57	
North Fork Bancorp/John Adam Kanas	507	85	49	East Moriches NY	LIU, BA '68	
Northern Trust/William A Osborn	471	79	48	Argos IN	Northwestern U, BA '69	MBA '73
Norwest/Richard M Kovacevich	139	25	52	Enumclaw WA	Stanford U, BS '65	MS '66
Old Kent Financial/David J Wagner	480	80	42	Cincinnati OH	Indiana U, BA '75	MBA '76
Old National Bncp/John N Royse	782	150	62	Terre Haute IN	Amherst C, BA '56	
OnBancorp/Robert J Bennett	742	137	54	Fitchburg MA	Babson C, BS '63	U of Massachusetts, MBA '66
One Valley Bncp WV/J Holmes Morrison	743	138	55	New York NY	Washington & Lee U, AB '63	JD '66
PaineWebber Group/Donald B Marron	60	10	61	Goshen NY		
People's Bank/David E A Carson	492	84	61	England	U of Michigan, BBA '55	
PNC Bank/Thomas H O'Brien	305	45	59	Pittsburgh PA	U of Notre Dame, BS '58	Harvard, MBA '62
Provident Bncp/Allen L Davis	424	68	54	Dayton OH	U of Cincinnati, BBA '64	
Quick & Reilly Group/Leslie C Quick Jr[1]	232	37	70	Brooklyn NY	Widener U, BSBA '50	
RCSB Financial/Leonard S Simon	600	103	59	Passaic NJ	MIT, BS '58	Columbia, PhD '63
Regions Financial/J Stanley Mackin	375	56	63	Birmingham AL	Auburn U, BS '54	
Republic New York/Walter H Weiner	586	100	65	Brooklyn NY	U of Michigan, BA '52	JD '53

| TENURE (YRS) | | COMPENSATION | | | | | | | STOCK OWNED | | COMPANY DATA | | |
with firm	as CEO	salary	bonus	% change*	other	stock gains	total	5-year total	%	market value ($mil)	sales	profits	5-year return
		($thou)				($thou)					($mil)		
28	1	499	300	NA	328	204	1,332[9]	NA	0.04	3.2	3,450	465	21
13	3	334	242	16	9	—	585	1,606[5]	4.10	30.5	300	49	27
37	13	900	2,600	17	3,357	—	6,857	24,747	0.14	33.1	16,327	1,950	22
25	19	507	500	49	59	89	1,155	3,301	0.85	4.9	254	52	29
26	1	410	251	NA	522	99	1,282[9]	NA	0.13	4.0	1,782	220	19
10	3	820	2,187	4	667	—	3,674	20,718[4]	0.16	20.6	7,582	956	27
19	1	480	264	45	252	240	1,236	NA	0.14	2.4	1,096	142	24
11	1	292	0	38	59	—	351	NA	0.64	5.3	394	52	16
9	7	500	0	2	43	—	543	4,421	0.84	3.9	461	45	29
29	5	340	140	13	4	57	541	2,033	0.04	0.2	320	49	23
37	16	800	2,975	50	1,060	2,475	7,310	33,207	0.79	15.6	5,320	81	20
13	11	492	250	2	73	378	1,194	3,666	0.18	1.4	608	71	42
34	11	900	657	42	203	223	1,982	12,339	0.05	5.5	6,110	408	18
12	10	567	525	12	326	—	1,419	5,498	0.84	7.4	519	72	34
22	22	675	1,700	74	30	—	2,405	8,161	16.24	123.5	411	57	34
27	12	397	250	−9	134	149	930	3,147	0.51	1.6	321	38	23
30	6	600	553	31	320	132	1,605	8,625	0.33	8.5	1,177	173	19
16	16	208	755	−23	6	—	968	5,704	0.09	3.1	2,860	289	12

For footnotes 1–14 see page 17.

(Continued)

The 800 Highest-Paid CEOs (Cont.)

Company/chief executive	RANK among 800 execs	in industry	Age	Birthplace	EDUCATION undergraduate	graduate
FINANCIAL SERVICES, *Cont.*						
Riggs National/Joe L Allbritton	572	98	71	D'Lo MS	Baylor U, LLB '49	
Roosevelt Finl Group/Stanley J Bradshaw	704	127	38	Terre Haute IN	Indiana State U, BS '79	Butler U, MBA '84
St Paul Bancorp/Joseph C Scully[1]	436	71	55	Detroit MI	Loyola U (IL), BS '62	MBA '72
Sallie Mae/Lawrence A Hough	390	58	52	Janesville WI	Stanford U, BS '66	MIT, MS '72
Salomon/Robert E Denham	571	97	50	Dallas TX	U of Texas Austin, BA '66	Harvard, JD '71
Charles Schwab/Charles R Schwab[1]	39	7	58	Sacramento CA	Stanford U, BA '59	MBA '61
Signet Banking/Robert M Freeman	312	47	55	Richmond VA	U of Virginia, BS '63	
Southern National/John A Allison IV	669	115	47	Charlotte NC	U of North Carolina, BBA '71	Duke U, MBA '74
SouthTrust/Wallace D Malone Jr	485	82	59	Dothan AL	U of Alabama, BS '57	U of Pennsylvania, MBA '60
Sovereign Bancorp/Jay S Sidhu	694	123	44	India		Wilkes C, MBA '73
Standard Federal/Thomas R Ricketts	564	95	65	Detroit MI	U of Michigan, BBA '53	JD '56
Star Banc/Jerry A Grundhofer	401	61	51	Los Angeles CA	Loyola Marymount U, BA '67	
State Street Boston/Marshall N Carter	489	83	56	Newport News VA	US Military Acad, BSCE '62	George Washington U, MA '76
Sumitomo Bank Calif/Tsuneo Onda	781	149	55	Japan	Tokyo U, LLB '65	
Summit Bancorp/T Joseph Semrod	302	44	59	Oklahoma City OK	U of Oklahoma, BA '58	JD '63
SunTrust Banks/James B Williams	340	51	63	Sewanee TN	Emory U, AB '55	
Synovus Finl/James H Blanchard	520	87	54	Augusta GA	U of Georgia, BBA '63	LLB '65
TCF Financial/William A Cooper	420	66	52	Detroit MI	Wayne State U, BS '67	

with firm	as CEO	salary	bonus ($thou)	% change*	other	stock gains	total	5-year total ($thou)	%	market value ($mil)	sales	profits ($mil)	5-year return
TENURE (YRS)		**COMPENSATION**							**STOCK OWNED**		**COMPANY DATA**		
15	15	380	570	25	58	—	1,008	3,637	30.90	114.7	373	88	0
10	5	400	125	-10	10	98	633	3,475	0.64	5.1	622	45	51
33	14	372	154	-18	144	717	1,387	4,452	0.48	2.2	312	36	27
23	6	525	210	12	404	404	1,542	7,184	0.23	9.7	3,917	366	11
5	4	1,000	0	0	10	—	1,010	4,484[4]	0.02	1.0	8,933	457	8
22	18	800	8,606	187	25	—	9,431	22,286	20.03	774.7	1,777	173	55
25	7	555	440	-2	369	563	1,927[8]	7,481	0.26	3.6	1,145	134	54
25	7	406	192	4	139	—	737	3,110	0.07	1.8	1,775	178	24
37	15	695	460	17	67	—	1,222	7,814	1.46	34.5	1,693	199	32
10	7	195	460	6	5	—	660	3,857	1.71	8.5	519	56	39
40	22	992	0	6	35	—	1,027	7,167	0.12	1.5	991	120	37
3	3	625	781	9	98	—	1,504	3,591[5]	0.13	2.5	849	137	29
5	4	750	456	-1	5	—	1,210	6,829	0.01	0.4	2,446	247	19
31	1	358	0	NA	—	—	358	NA	0.01	—[7]	416	-107	3
15	15	708	559	16	515	214	1,995	7,232	0.21	8.2	1,720	243	32
41	6	700	302	4	769	—	1,771	7,609	0.46	36.2	3,740	566	24
26	26	475	356	41	280	—	1,112	3,954	0.62	16.0	957	115	30
11	11	600	615	41	223	—	1,438	7,323	2.07	24.5	740	62	42

For footnotes 1–14 see page 17.

(Continued)

The 800 Highest-Paid CEOs *(Cont.)*

| | RANK | | | | EDUCATION | |
Company/chief executive	among 800 execs	in industry	Age	Birthplace	undergraduate	graduate
FINANCIAL SERVICES, *Cont.*						
Travelers Group/Sanford I Weill	3	2	63	New York NY	Cornell, BA '55	
Trustmark/Frank R Day	662	112	58	Aberdeen MS	U of Mississippi, BA '53	
UMB Financial/R Crosby Kemper	664	113	69	Kansas City MO		
Union Planters/Benjamin W Rawlins Jr	609	104	58	Murfreesboro TN	Vanderbilt U, BA '61	Georgia State U, MBA '69
UnionBanCal/Kanetaka Yoshida	758	142	58	Japan	Tokyo U, LLB '62	
United Carolina Bcsh/E Rhone Sasser	730	134	59	Columbus NC	NC State U, BS '59	
US Bancorp/Gerry B Cameron	421	67	57	Grandview WA	Portland State U, BS '62	
Valley Natl Bancorp/Gerald H Lipkin	558	93	55	Passaic NJ	Rutgers, BA '63	NYU, MBA '66
Wachovia/Leslie M Baker Jr	409	63	54	Lovettsville VA	U of Richmond, BA '64	U of Virginia, MBA '69
Washington Federal/Guy C Pinkerton	780	148	61	Seattle WA	U of Washington, BA '59	
Washington Mutual/Kerry K Killinger	627	107	46	Des Moines IA	U of Iowa, BBA '70	MBA '71
Wells Fargo/Paul M Hazen	184	30	55	Lansing MI	U of Arizona, BA '63	U of Cal Berkeley, MBA '64
Wilmington Trust/Leonard W Quill	635	109	64	Wilmington DE	U of Delaware, BS '59	MBA '65
Zions Bancorp/Harris H Simmons	567	96	41	Salt Lake City UT	U of Utah, BA '77	Harvard, MBA '80
FOOD DISTRIBUTORS						
Albertson's/Gary G Michael	355	5	55	Laurel MT	U of Idaho, BS '62	
American Stores/Victor L Lund	197	3	48	Salt Lake City UT	U of Utah, BS '69	MBA '72
Circle K/John F Antioco	673	18	46	Brooklyn NY	New York Inst of Tech, BS '71	
Darden Restaurants/Joe R Lee	751	23	55	Blackshear GA		

TENURE (YRS)		COMPENSATION							STOCK OWNED		COMPANY DATA		
with firm	as CEO	salary ($thou)	bonus ($thou)	% change*	other ($thou)	stock gains ($thou)	total ($thou)	5-year total	%	market value ($mil)	sales ($mil)	profits ($mil)	5-year return
10	10	1,025	4,304	45	2,255	41,971	49,555	199,673	1.31	251.4	17,624	1,834	36
38	15	450	300	36	6	—	756	2,533	4.04	33.1	408	60	31
46	26	627	0	3	27	94	748	3,331	16.37	116.4	501	52	14
22	12	510	383	54	11	—	903	5,412	0.40	5.5	994	135	28
34	3	466	0	−4	34	—	500	1,402[5]	—[6]	0.2	1,550	207	NA
29	13	395	158	−13	16	—	569	2,866	0.48	2.5	331	44	25
40	2	700	630	75	105	—	1,435	2,982[5]	0.07	3.4	2,917	329	17
21	7	422	260	−6	143	223	1,048	4,244	0.35	3.6	338	63	28
27	2	596	387	8	305	198	1,487	3,523[5]	0.09	6.4	3,755	603	16
31	4	274	50	9	34	17	375	2,000[4]	1.10	10.1	371	78	10
20	6	510	288	15	66	—	864	6,425	0.74	14.8	1,625	191	31
26	1	813	2,000	42	82	—	2,894	NA	0.42	49.0	5,246	1,032	33
38	4	437	392	17	6	—	835	3,480[4]	0.41	4.5	505	90	14
15	5	355	170	10	104	389	1,018	3,029	3.67	36.8	517	81	35
		$526	$289	4%	$48	—	$1,203	$5,684	0.20%	$3.4	$4,594	$69	10%
30	5	694	315	3	109	606	1,724	7,888	0.10	9.2	12,585	465	11
19	4	750	307	−3	570	1,077	2,704	11,024	0.35	17.0	18,309	317	11
5	3	450	270	−47	3	—	723	NA	0.46	3.4	3,544	33	90[2]
29	1	439	0	NA	81	—	520	NA	0.15	3.2	3,200	58	NA

For footnotes 1–14 see page 17.

(Continued)

The 800 Highest-Paid CEOs *(Cont.)*

| | RANK | | | | EDUCATION | |
Company/chief executive	among 800 execs	in industry	Age	Birthplace	undergraduate	graduate
FOOD DISTRIBUTORS, *Cont.*						
Flagstar Cos/James B Adamson	267	4	48	Japan	Gonzaga U, BBA '71	
Fleming Cos/Robert E Stauth	723	21	51	Dodge City KS	Kansas State U, BS '66	
Food Lion/Tom E Smith	473	11	55	Salisbury NC	Catawba C, BA '64	
Giant Food/Pete L Manos	774	24	59	Washington DC	George Washington U, BS '56	MS '61
Grand Union/Joseph J McCaig	374	6	51	Brooklyn NY		
Great A&P Tea/James Wood	459	10	66	England	Loughborough C, CB '55	
Hannaford Bros/Hugh G Farrington	682	19	51	North Conway NH	Dartmouth, BA '67	U of New Hampshire, MA '68
Kroger/Joseph A Pichler	426	8	56	St Louis MO	U of Notre Dame, BA '61	U of Chicago, PhD '66
McDonald's/Michael R Quinlan	194	2	51	Chicago IL	Loyola U (IL), BS '67	MBA '70
Nash Finch/Alfred N Flaten	776	25	61	Edinburg ND	U of North Dakota, BS '57	
Penn Traffic/John T Dixon	778	26	56	Lucasville OH		
Richfood Holdings/Donald D Bennett	533	15	59	Jefferson City MO	Butler U, BS '59	Michigan State U, MS '61
Ruddick/John W Copeland	728	22	61	Durham NC	NC State U, BS '57	U of North Carolina, MBA '60
Safeway/Steven A Burd	442	9	46	Valley City ND	Carroll C, BS '71	U of Wisc Milwaukee, MA '73
Smith's Food & Drug/Jeffrey P Smith	491	14	46	Brigham City UT		
Southland/Clark J Matthews II	709	20	59	Arkansas City KS	SMU, BA '59	JD '61

TENURE (YRS)		COMPENSATION							STOCK OWNED		COMPANY DATA		
with firm	as CEO	salary	bonus ($thou)	% change*	other	stock gains	total	5-year total ($thou)	%	market value ($mil)	sales	profits ($mil)	5-year return
1	1	894[13]	0	NA	1,251	—	2,145	NA	0.15	0.2	2,571	−56	−31
19	3	588	0	−28	—	—	589	1,727[5]	0.10	0.5	17,502	42	−15
26	10	709	307	7	250	—	1,267	5,486	0.47	17.6	8,211	172	−11
35	—[10]	264	134	NA	29	—	427[9]	NA	0.08	1.5	3,861	102	6
35	7	502	123	−3	981	—	1,607	2,959[5]	NA	—	2,312	−156	NA
16	16	1,161	0	−2	157	—	1,318	18,278	0.03	0.4	10,101	57	−8
28	4	375	188	4	139	—	702	2,762[4]	0.49	5.8	2,568	70	9
16	6	447	614	−5	351	—	1,412	5,684	0.23	12.0	23,938	319	11
30	9	1,051	1,050	8	363	259	2,723	11,375	0.08	27.5	9,795	1,427	24
35	2	279	130	27	5	—	414	NA	0.20	0.4	2,889	17	1
39	1	400[3]	0	NA	—	—	400	NA	0.34	0.5	3,448	−44	−5
6	6	350	630	12	3	104	1,087	6,256	0.40	4.0	3,155	35	35
17	2	289	147	16	35	103	573	NA	0.18	1.1	2,092	39	17
4	3	650	706	7	—	—	1,356	4,575[4]	0.07	4.6	16,398	328	24
26	8	684	.516	−2	—	—	1,200[8]	5,866	11.72	71.2	3,084	−41	−9
31	5	410	197	7	11	—	617	3,016	0.04	0.5	5,825	168	8

For footnotes 1–14 see page 17.

(Continued)

The 800 Highest-Paid CEOs *(Cont.)*

	Rank				Education	
	among	in				
Company/chief executive	800 execs	industry	Age	Birthplace	undergraduate	graduate
FOOD DISTRIBUTORS, *Cont.*						
Stop & Shop Cos/Robert G Tobin	490	13	58	Rochester NY	Cornell, BS '60	
Supervalu/Michael W Wright	481	12	57	Minneapolis MN	U of Minnesota, BA '61	JD '63
Sysco/Bill M Lindig	410	7	59	Austin TX		
Vons Cos/Lawrence A Del Santo	561	16	62	Ross CA	U of San Francisco, BS '55	
Wendy's International/Gordon F Teter	172	1	52	Lawrence IN	Purdue U, BA '66	MS '68
Winn-Dixie Stores/A Dano Davis	657	17	50	New Rochelle NY		
FOOD DRINK & TOBACCO						
American Brands/Thomas C Hays	217	14	61	Chicago IL	Cal Tech, BS '57	Harvard, MBA '63
Anheuser-Busch Cos/August A Busch III	318	18	58	St Louis MO		
Archer Daniels/Dwayne O Andreas	143	10	78	Worthington MN		
Brown-Forman/Owsley Brown II	354	20	53	Louisville KY	Yale, BA '64	Stanford U, MBA '66
Campbell Soup/David W Johnson	25	3	63	Australia	U of Sydney, BE '54	U of Chicago, MBA '58
Chiquita Brands Intl/Carl H Lindner Jr	773	32	77	Dayton OH		
Coca-Cola/Roberto C Goizueta	19	1	64	Cuba	Yale, BS '53	
Coca-Cola Enterprise/Summerfield K Johnston Jr	31	4	63	Chattanooga TN		
ConAgra/Philip B Fletcher	97	7	62	Watertown NY	St Lawrence U, BS '54	MIT, MBA '70
CPC International/Charles R Shoemate	130	9	56	La Harpe IL	Western Illinois U, BS '62	U of Chicago, MBA '72
Dean Foods/Howard M Dean	385	22	58	Hinsdale IL	SMU, BBA '60	Northwestern U, MBA '61
Dole Food/David H Murdock	61	5	73	Kansas City MO		

| TENURE (YRS) | | COMPENSATION | | | | | | | STOCK OWNED | | COMPANY DATA | | |
with firm	as CEO	salary	bonus ($thou)	% change*	other	stock gains	total ($thou)	5-year total	%	market value ($mil)	sales ($mil)	profits	5-year return
36	2	452	746	33	8	—	1,206[8]	NA	0.21	3.4	4,116	69	25[2]
19	15	780	0	–47	448	6	1,234	7,890	0.31	6.9	16,530	161	6
26	1	563	483	18	439	—	1,485	NA	0.23	13.4	12,722	267	14
2	2	550	437	NA	47	—	1,035	NA	0.14	1.9	5,071	68	–1
9	1	571	963	58	5	1,504	3,043	NA	0.09	2.0	1,746	110	13
28	14	366	352	0	49	—	767	4,163	3.46	171.1	12,567	243	14
		$769	**$613**	**13%**	**$176**	**—**	**$2,126**	**$10,579**	**0.30%**	**$17.9**	**$5,930**	**$408**	**10%**
32	1	900	812	57	828	—	2,541	NA	0.06	4.2	5,905	543	4
39	21	995	616	–26	80	212	1,903	19,455	0.50	81.8	10,340	887	8
26	26	3,460	0	16	159	—	3,618	14,593	4.72	450.3	12,971	810	10
28	3	639	581	13	404	100	1,724	4,471[5]	15.05	402.9	1,520	157	13
6	6	917	1,288	22	9,399	—	11,604	21,515	0.17	25.1	7,581	746	12
12	12	269	0	–35	2	158	429	2,085	19.19[12]	144.3	2,566	17	–15
42	15	1,680	3,200	12	1,640	6,566	13,086	59,585	0.67	672.4	18,018	2,986	27
40	4	945	756	8	8,914	—	10,615	15,308	8.09	299.6	6,773	82	11
14	4	896	1,000	19	3,395	—	5,291	15,773[4]	0.23	21.5	24,651	533	9
34	6	766	600	14	2,545	—	3,911	11,543	0.07	7.2	8,431	512	14
41	9	524	336	2	14	677	1,551	5,380	0.88	8.2	2,765	62	–1
14	11	700	788	49	—	5,738	7,225	11,344	22.65	533.2	3,804	120	6

For footnotes 1–14 see page 17.

(Continued)

The 800 Highest-Paid CEOs *(Cont.)*

	RANK				EDUCATION	
	among	in				
Company/chief executive	800 execs	industry	Age	Birthplace	undergraduate	graduate
FOOD DRINK & TOBACCO, *Cont.*						
General Mills/Stephen W Sanger	736	31	50	Cincinnati OH	DePauw U, BA '68	U of Michigan, MBA '70
HJ Heinz/Anthony J F O'Reilly	227	15	60	Ireland	U of Dublin, BCL '58	U of Bradford UK, PhD '80
Hershey Foods/Kenneth L Wolfe	304	17	57	Lebanon PA	Yale, BA '61	U of Penn-Wharton, MBA '67
Hormel Foods/Joel W Johnson	579	27	52	Staten Island NY	Hamilton C, AB '65	Harvard, MBA '67
IBP/Robert L Peterson	70	6	63	Hartington NE		
Intl Multifoods/Anthony Luiso	699	30	52	Italy	Iona C, BA '67	U of Chicago, MBA '82
Kellogg/Arnold G Langbo	124	8	59	Canada		
Loews/Laurence A Tisch[15]	602	28	73	Brooklyn NY	NYU, BS '42	U of Pennsylvania, MA '43
PepsiCo/Roger A Enrico	22	2	51	Chisholm MN	Babson C, BA '65	
Philip Morris Cos/Geoffrey C Bible	203	12	58	Australia	Inst of Chartered Acc, BA	
Pioneer Hi-Bred Intl/Charles S Johnson	566	26	58	Belmond IA	Iowa State, BA '65	
Quaker Oats/William D Smithburg	494	24	57	Chicago IL	DePaul U, BS '60	Northwestern U, MBA '61
Ralston Purina/William P Stiritz	211	13	61	Jasper AR	Northwestern U, BS '59	St Louis U, MA '68
RJR Nabisco/Steven F Goldstone	353	19	50	New York NY	U of Pennsylvania, BA '67	NYU, JD '70
Sara Lee/John H Bryan	250	16	59	West Point MS	Rhodes C, BA '58	
Tyson Foods/Leland E Tollett	522	25	59	Nashville AR	U of Arkansas, BSA '58	MSA '59

| TENURE (YRS) | | COMPENSATION | | | | | | | STOCK OWNED | | COMPANY DATA | | |
| with firm | as CEO | salary | bonus | % change* | other | stock gains | total | 5-year total | % | market value ($mil) | sales | profits | 5-year return |
		($thou)					($thou)				($mil)		
22	1	473	0	NA	79	—	552[9]	NA	0.02	1.8	5,262	386	7
27	17	646	1,129	136	664	—	2,439	119,144	1.63	198.1	8,997	648	8
29	2	570	508	20	473	437	1,989	4,467[5]	0.09	4.8	3,691	282	15
5	3	345	618	−2	17	—	980	2,828[5]	0.02	0.4	3,040	106	6
35	16	1,000	5,278	29	176	—	6,455	22,216	0.13	2.8	12,668	280	21
9	7	380	265	70	5	—	650[14]	3,004	0.47	1.6	2,412	30	−4
40	4	880	765	11	10	2,393	4,048[14]	12,315	0.04	6.1	7,004	490	13
37	36	862	0	43	60	—	922	2,892	15.75	1,382.7	17,219	1,766	9
25	—[10]	772	785	NA	117	11,274	12,946[9]	NA	0.01	5.1	30,421	1,606	15
20	2	1,125	1,350	32	180	—	2,655	NA	0.02	14.3	53,139	5,478	10
31	1	475	248	NA	300	—	1,023[9]	NA	0.06	2.5	1,555	182	30
30	15	855	0	−39	175	159	1,189	23,810	0.94	41.8	5,954	724	7
32	15	900	1,071	49	616	—	2,587	9,813	1.07	69.3	5,804	285	8
—[10]	—[10]	1,100[3]	610	NA	21	—	1,731	NA	—[6]	0.5	16,008	627	−11
37	21	922	1,118	30	224	—	2,263	31,146	0.27	40.7	18,335	856	13
37	5	600	0	−49	56	449	1,105	5,186	1.43	46.0	5,732	210	4

For footnotes 1–14 see page 17. [15]Office jointly held with Preston R Tisch.

(Continued)

The 800 Highest-Paid CEOs *(Cont.)*

| | RANK | | | | EDUCATION | |
Company/chief executive	among 800 execs	in industry	Age	Birthplace	undergraduate	graduate
FOOD DRINK & TOBACCO, *Cont.*						
Universal/Henry H Harrell	660	29	56	Richmond VA	Washington & Lee U, AB '61	
UST Inc/Vincent A Gierer Jr	198	11	48	New York NY	Iona C, BBA '69	
Whitman/Bruce S Chelberg	406	23	61	Chicago IL	U of Illinois, BS '56	LLB '58
Wm Wrigley Jr/William Wrigley	370	21	63	Chicago IL	Yale, BA '54	
FOREST PRODUCTS & PACKAGING						
Ball/George A Sissel	593	17	59	Chicago IL	U of Colorado, BSEE '58	U of Minnesota, JD '66
Boise Cascade/George J Harad	364	9	52	Newark NJ	Franklin & Marshall C, BA '65	Harvard, MBA '71
Bowater/Arnold M Nemirow	543	15	53	Hartford CT	Harvard, AB '66	U of Michigan, JD '69
Champion Intl/Andrew C Sigler	20	1	64	Brooklyn NY	Dartmouth, AB '53	MBA '56
Consolidated Papers/Patrick F Brennan	675	20	64	New York NY	Fordham U, BA '57	
Crown Cork & Seal/William J Avery	327	7	55	Chicago IL	U of Chicago, BS '68	
Gaylord Container/Marvin A Pomerantz[1]	188	2	65	Des Moines IA	U of Iowa, BSC '52	
Georgia-Pacific/Alston D Correll	223	3	55	Brunswick GA	U of Georgia, BS '63	U of Maine, MS '67
International Paper/John T Dillon	403	11	57	Newcomb NY	U of Hartford, BA '65	Columbia, MBA '71
Jefferson Smurfit/James E Terrill	396	10	62	Twin Falls ID	U of Idaho, BS '59	
Louisiana-Pacific/Mark A Suwyn	715	21	53	Denver CO	Hope C, BA '64	Washington State, PhD '67
Mead/Steven C Mason	249	5	60	Canada	MIT, BS '57	
Owens-Illinois/Joseph H Lemieux	357	8	65	Providence RI	Bryant C, BS '57	
Rayonier/Ronald M Gross	456	13	63	Cleveland OH	Ohio State U, BA '55	Harvard, MBA '60

TENURE (YRS) with firm	as CEO	COMPENSATION salary ($thou)	bonus ($thou)	% change*	other ($thou)	stock gains ($thou)	total ($thou)	5-year total ($thou)	STOCK OWNED %	market value ($mil)	COMPANY DATA sales ($mil)	profits ($mil)	5-year return
30	8	444	202	−2	91	21	758	3,602	0.32	2.7	3,525	44	16
18	2	613	2,072	11	9	—	2,694	7,477[5]	0.18	10.7	1,300	430	11
14	4	629	575	4	293	—	1,497	8,320	0.23	5.9	2,947	134	20
40	35	475	428	1	730	—	1,632	7,283	17.79	1,149.5	1,755	224	26
		$623	**$587**	**26%**	**$105**	**—**	**$1,501**	**$6,784**	**0.09%**	**$3.0**	**$3,874**	**$281**	**12%**
26	2	440	391	25	105	—	937	NA	0.10	0.9	2,592	−19	9
25	2	672	839	71	64	95	1,670	NA	0.02	0.5	5,074	352	13
2	1	492	573	NA	2	—	1,067	NA	—[6]	—[7]	2,001	258	11
40	22	1,000	2,530	131	142	9,385	13,057	19,073	0.05	2.6	6,972	772	12
33	3	523	185	47	7	—	715	1,632[5]	0.04	0.9	1,579	229	10
37	7	700	207	−8	5	963	1,874	7,206	0.09	5.3	5,054	75	17
10	10	600	0	0	2,241	—	2,841	5,818	8.31	52.3	1,064	142	23
8	3	962	1,300	48	211	—	2,473	12,123[4]	0.11	7.1	14,292	1,018	13
31	—[10]	490	600	NA	130	281	1,501[9]	NA	0.08	9.7	19,797	1,153	8
25	2	800	624	53	90	—	1,514	NA	—[6]	—[7]	4,093	247	−12[2]
—[10]	—[10]	600[3]	NA	—	—	—	600	NA	0.14	3.6	2,843	−52	21
39	4	635	875	12	630	125	2,265	6,417	0.14	4.2	5,179	350	15
39	6	540	620	−6	552	—	1,712	7,833	0.16	3.0	3,790	169	7[2]
18	15	471	390	4	22	447	1,330	2,868[5]	0.33	3.6	1,260	142	7[2]

For footnotes 1–14 see page 17.

(Continued)

The 800 Highest-Paid CEOs (Cont.)

Company/chief executive	RANK among 800 execs	in industry	Age	Birthplace	EDUCATION undergraduate	graduate
FOREST PRODUCTS & PACKAGING, Cont.						
Sonoco Products/Charles W Coker	264	6	63	Hartsville SC	Princeton, BA '55	Harvard, MBA '57
Stone Container/Roger W Stone	651	19	61	Chicago IL	U of Pennsylvania, BS '57	
Temple-Inland/Clifford J Grum	531	14	61	Davenport IA	Austin C, BA '56	U of Pennsylvania, MBA '58
Union Camp/W Craig McClelland	451	12	62	Orange NJ	Princeton, BA '56	Harvard, MBA '65
Westvaco/John A Luke Jr	560	16	47	New York NY	Lawrence U Wisc, BA '71	U of Penn-Wharton, MBA '79
Weyerhaeuser/John W Creighton Jr	228	4	63	Pittsburgh PA	Ohio State U, BS '54	JD '57
Willamette Inds/Steven R Rogel	626	18	53	Ritzville WA	U of Washington, BS '65	
HEALTH						
Abbott Laboratories/Duane L Burnham	215	24	54	Excelsior MN	U of Minnesota, BS '63	MBA '72
Allergan/William C Shepherd	546	43	57	San Francisco CA	U of Cal Berkeley, BS '63	Pepperdine U, MBA '76
ALZA/Ernest Mario	670	51	57	Clifton NJ	Rutgers, BS '61	U of Rhode Island, PhD '65
American Home Prod/John R Stafford	104	12	58	Harrisburg PA	Dickinson C, BA '59	George Washington U, LLB '62
AmeriSource Health/John F McNamara	14	4	61	Chicago IL		
Amgen/Gordon M Binder	6	1	60	St Louis MO	Purdue U, BSEE '57	Harvard, MBA '62
Baxter International/Vernon R Loucks Jr	167	20	61	Evanston IL	Yale, BA '57	Harvard, MBA '63
Becton Dickinson/Clateo Castellini	378	34	61	Italy	Bocconi U Italy, BA '58	
Bergen Brunswig/Robert E Martini	498	38	64	Hackensack NJ	Ohio State U, BS '54	

| TENURE (YRS) | | COMPENSATION | | | | | | | STOCK OWNED | | COMPANY DATA | | |
with firm	as CEO	salary	bonus ($thou)	% change*	other	stock gains	total	5-year total	%	market value ($mil)	sales	profits ($mil)	5-year return
38	26	634	1,000	26	230	314	2,178	7,671	1.25	31.7	2,706	165	12
39	17	790	0	8	—	—	790	5,089	1.72	26.9	7,351	445	−1
28	12	589	500	36	3	—	1,092	9,255	0.62	16.7	3,461	281	7
8	2	589	640	27	108	—	1,336	NA	0.04	1.5	4,212	451	7
17	4	783	200	40	61	—	1,044	3,986[4]	0.08	2.6	3,280	297	12
26	5	806	750	18	111	767	2,434	6,784	0.03	2.5	11,788	799	18
24	1	623	0	NA	127	115	864[9]	NA	0.05	1.8	3,874	515	22
		$605	**$446**	**10%**	**$227**	—	**$2,107**	**$8,410**	**0.19%**	**$11.6**	**$3,107**	**$118**	**17%**
14	6	818	1,000	14	755	—	2,574	20,620	0.05	16.4	10,012	1,689	14
30	4	605	160	−21	298	—	1,063	4,784	0.15	3.4	1,067	73	11
3	3	571	100	24	63	−1	732	1,643[5]	0.04	0.9	326	72	−1
26	9	1,185	1,185	7	377	2,238	4,985	23,491	0.05	15.2	13,376	1,680	18
15	7	415	250	11	54	15,104	15,822	17,491[4]	3.00	22.8	4,822	36	NA
14	8	613	900	20	129	19,991	21,634	25,755	0.07	9.1	1,940	538	22
30	16	751	800	12	1,607	—	3,158	16,110	0.19	22.4	5,048	649	10
18	2	544	600	51	141	298	1,583	NA	0.04	1.9	2,759	263	18
40	6	553	428	11	205	—	1,186	7,887	5.44	58.3	8,841	66	5

For footnotes 1–14 see page 17.

(Continued)

The 800 Highest-Paid CEOs *(Cont.)*

Company/chief executive	RANK among 800 execs	in industry	Age	Birthplace	EDUCATION undergraduate	graduate
HEALTH, *Cont.*						
Beverly Enterprises/David R Banks	514	40	59	Arcadia WI	U of Arkansas, BA '59	
Bindley Western Inds/William E Bindley[1]	518	41	55	Terre Haute IN	Purdue U, BS '61	
Boston Scientific/Peter M Nicholas[1]	540	42	55	Portsmouth NH	Duke U, BA '64	U of Penn-Wharton, MBA '68
Bristol-Myers Squibb/Charles A Heimbold Jr	231	26	62	Newark NJ	Villanova, BA '54	U of Pennsylvania, LLB '60
Cardinal Health/Robert D Walter[1]	429	36	50	Mansfield OH	Ohio U, BS '67	Harvard, MBA '70
Caremark Intl/C A Lance Piccolo	646	49	55	Somerville MA	Boston U, BS '62	
Chiron/Edward E Penhoet	68	9	55	Oakland CA	Stanford U, AB '63	U of Washington, PhD '68
Columbia/HCA/Richard L Scott[1]	484	37	43	Kansas City MO	U of Missouri, BBA '75	SMU, JD '78
Corning/Roger G Ackerman	389	35	57	Paterson NJ	Rutgers, BS '60	MS '62
FHP International/Westcott W Price III[1]	753	54	57	Glendale CA	U of Colorado, BS '61	USC, MBA '67
Forest Labs/Howard Solomon	11	3	68	New York NY	CUNY City, BA '49	Yale, JD '52
Foundation Health/Daniel D Crowley	280	30	48			
FoxMeyer Health/Abbey J Butler[15]	216	25	58	New York NY	American U, BS '58	
Genentech/Arthur D Levinson	685	52	46	Seattle WA	U of Washington, BS '72	Princeton, PhD '77
Guidant/Ronald W Dollens	583	44	49	Danville IN	Purdue U, BS '70	Indiana U, MBA '72
HBO & Co/Charles W McCall	41	5	52	Oskaloosa IA	U of Iowa, BBA	Roosevelt U, MBA
Health Systems Intl/Malik M Hasan[1,16]	7	2	57	India	King Edward Med C, MBBS '60	Royal C of Physicians, MRCP '63

| TENURE (YRS) | | COMPENSATION | | | | | | | STOCK OWNED | | COMPANY DATA | | |
with firm	as CEO	salary ($thou)	bonus ($thou)	% change*	other	stock gains	total ($thou)	5-year total	%	market value ($mil)	sales ($mil)	profits ($mil)	5-year return
24	7	539	173	1	414	—	1,126[8]	4,940	0.16	1.5	3,229	-8	0
29	29	599	247	8	267	—	1,113	4,671	26.71	46.6	4,670	16	0
17	17	621	430	42	20	—	1,071	3,093[4]	9.69	733.3	1,107	8	27[2]
33	2	1,056	1,304	24	47	—	2,407	9,774[5]	0.02	9.6	13,767	1,812	6
25	25	496	446	18	460	—	1,401	6,748	5.92	157.4	8,180	90	23
28	3	515	234	-14	59	—	808	3,316[4]	0.11	2.4	2,374	-116	18[2]
15	15	398	350	11	1,427	4,449	6,624	11,659	0.22	8.7	1,101	-513	8
9	9	858	0	-23	366	—	1,224[14]	4,005	1.38	316.4	17,695	1,064	26
34	—[10]	600	309	NA	112	521	1,542[9]	NA	0.11	8.3	5,313	-51	5
15	6	500	0	-5	10	—	510	4,701	0.91	11.1	4,021	23	2
19	19	551	60	6	24	16,416	17,050	79,263	1.25	25.4	437	108	4
7	7	753	750	-54	580	—	2,083	15,617	0.20	4.4	2,703	156	14
6	5	805	700	46	113	935	2,553	5,215[4]	9.39[12]	31.5	5,393	-11	4
16	1	425	250	NA	24	—	699[9]	NA	—[6]	0.3	857	146	16
24	8	320	161	9	494	—	975	2,135[5]	0.07	2.5	931	101	165[2]
5	5	521	669	5	35	7,952	9,176	17,248	0.28	13.3	496	-25	94
11	6	910	800	-26	181	18,793	20,685	26,385	8.95	136.7	2,732	90	28[2]

For footnotes 1–14 see page 17. [15]Office jointly held with Melvin J Estrin. [16]Office jointly held with Roger F Greaves.

(Continued)

The 800 Highest-Paid CEOs (Cont.)

Company/chief executive	RANK among 800 execs	in industry	Age	Birthplace	EDUCATION undergraduate	graduate
HEALTH, *Cont.*						
Healthsource/Norman C Payson[1]	75	10	48	New Brunswick NJ	MIT, BS '70	Dartmouth, MD '73
HealthSouth/Richard M Scrushy[1]	59	8	43	Florala AL	U of Alabama, BS '74	
Hillenbrand Inds/W August Hillenbrand	614	47	55	Batesville IN	St Joseph's IN, BS '65	
Humana/David A Jones[1]	180	21	64	Louisville KY	U of Louisville, BS '54	Yale, JD '60
IVAX/Phillip Frost[1]	735	53	59	Philadelphia PA	U of Pennsylvania, BA '57	Yeshiva U Einstein, MD '61
Johnson & Johnson/Ralph S Larsen	200	22	57	Brooklyn NY	Hofstra U, BBA '62	
Eli Lilly/Randall L Tobias	133	15	54	Lafayette IN	Indiana U, BS '64	
Mallinckrodt Group/C Ray Holman	166	19	53	Little Rock AR	U of Missouri, BS '64	
Manor Care/Stewart Bainum Jr	601	45	50	Takoma Park MD	Pacific Union C, BA '68	UCLA, MBA '70
McKesson/Alan Seelenfreund	43	6	59	New York NY	Cornell, BME '59	Stanford U, PhD '67
Medtronic/William W George	342	32	53	Muskegon MI	Georgia Tech, BSIE '64	Harvard, MBA '66
Merck/Raymond V Gilmartin	276	28	55	Washington DC	Union C, BSEE '63	Harvard, MBA '68
Mylan Labs/Milan Puskar[1]	258	27	61	Vintondale PA	Youngstown State U, BS '60	
Owens & Minor/G Gilmer Minor III	763	55	55	Richmond VA	VMI, BA '63	U of Virginia, MBA '66
Oxford Health Plans/Stephen F Wiggins[1]	205	23	39	Austin MN	Macalester C, BA '78	Harvard, MBA '84
PacifiCare Health/Alan R Hoops	154	18	48	Long Beach CA	UCLA, BS '69	U of Washington, MHA '73
Pall/Eric Krasnoff	613	46	43	Chicago IL	Columbia	
Pfizer/William C Steere Jr	46	7	59	Ann Arbor MI	Stanford U, BA '59	

| TENURE (YRS) | | COMPENSATION | | | | | | | STOCK OWNED | | COMPANY DATA | | |
| with firm | as CEO | salary | bonus | % change* | other | stock gains | total | 5-year total | % | market value ($mil) | sales | profits | 5-year return |
		($thou)			($thou)						($mil)		
11	11	483	0	25	10	5,863	6,356	8,714	6.81	161.4	1,167	56	55
12	12	1,738	5,000	110	650	—	7,388	29,283	0.21	11.6	1,557	79	24
30	7	658	0	3	225	—	883	7,507	6.44	177.5	1,625	90	10
35	35	936	477	−22	824	685	2,921	18,316	5.81	229.9	4,605	190	19
9	9	550	0	16	5	—	555	2,064	11.78	385.3	1,260	115	17
34	7	1,005	1,136	42	541	—	2,682	12,970	0.02	11.4	18,842	2,403	16
3	3	984	983	6	1,799	—	3,766	8,382[5]	0.03	8.6	6,764	2,291	15
20	3	618	470	9	2,079	—	3,166	5,604[4]	0.10	2.9	2,228	203	4
24	9	572	343	25	9	—	925	3,872	2.19	51.4	1,262	106	24
21	7	625	1,100	28	528	6,898	9,151	15,002	0.22	4.8	13,582	137	13
7	5	530	303	4	937	—	1,770[14]	6,779	0.09	11.2	2,090	400	33
2	2	1,000	1,100	NA	7	—	2,107	NA	—[6]	5.7	16,681	3,335	15
35	3	700	800	36	709	—	2,209	8,438[5]	2.00	46.5	409	118	19
33	12	375	0	−31	107	—	482	3,085	1.33	4.9	2,976	−11	17
12	12	450	360	37	52	1,781	2,643[8]	9,625	2.35	70.8	1,765	52	93[2]
19	3	578	350	10	478	1,966	3,373	7,484[4]	0.68	15.9	3,974	116	45
21	2	410	410	57	65	—	885	NA	0.06	1.8	902	129	10
37	5	1,030	2,060	5	2,461	3,373	8,924	18,480	0.03	13.0	10,021	1,573	23

For footnotes 1–14 see page 17.

(Continued)

The 800 Highest-Paid CEOs *(Cont.)*

	RANK among 800 execs	RANK in industry	Age	Birthplace	EDUCATION undergraduate	EDUCATION graduate
Company/chief executive						
HEALTH, *Cont.*						
Pharmacia & Upjohn/John L Zabriskie	279	29	56	Auburn NY	Dartmouth, BS '61	U of Rochester, PhD '65
Rhone-Poulenc Rorer/Michel de Rosen	616	48	45	France	Ecole Hautes Etudes, BA '72	Ecole Nationale d'Adm, MBA '76
St Jude Medical/Ronald A Matricaria	295	31	53	Derby CT	Mass C of Pharmacy, BS '66	
Schering-Plough/Richard J Kogan	82	11	54	New York NY	CUNY City, BA '63	NYU, MBA '68
Stryker/John W Brown	647	50	61	Paris TN	Auburn U, BS '57	
Tenet Healthcare/Jeffrey C Barbakow	360	33	52	Los Angeles CA	San Jose State U, BS '66	USC, MBA '68
United HealthCare/William W McGuire	151	17	48	Troy NY	U of Texas Austin, BA '70	U of Texas Galveston, MD '74
US Healthcare/Leonard Abramson[1]	131	14	63	Philadelphia PA	Penn State U, BA '54	Nova U, MPA '78
Vencor/W Bruce Lunsford[1]	129	13	48	Cincinnati OH	U of Kentucky, BA '69	Northern Kentucky U, JD '74
Warner-Lambert/Melvin R Goodes	135	16	61	Canada	Queens U, BA '57	U of Chicago, MBA '60
WellPoint Health/Leonard D Schaeffer	503	39	50	Chicago IL	Princeton, BA '69	
INSURANCE						
Aetna Life & Cas/Ronald E Compton	67	5	63	Chicago IL	Northwestern U, BA '54	
Aflac/Daniel P Amos	338	31	44	Pensacola FL	U of Georgia, BS '73	
Alleghany/John J Burns Jr	255	23	64	Cambridge MA	Boston C, BS '53	Harvard, MBA '55
Allmerica Financial/John F O'Brien	294	24	53	Brockton MA	Harvard, AB '65	MBA '68
Allstate/Jerry D Choate	303	26	57	La Habra CA	San Jose State U, BS '61	

| TENURE (YRS) | | COMPENSATION | | | | | | | STOCK OWNED | | COMPANY DATA | | |
with firm	as CEO	salary	bonus ($thou)	% change*	other	stock gains	total	5-year total ($thou)	%	market value ($mil)	sales ($mil)	profits	5-year return
2	2	904	1,173	36	7	—	2,083	NA	0.01	1.9	7,095	739	76[2]
3	1	436	276	4	171	—	882	NA	—[6]	0.5	5,142	357	11
3	3	523	549	29	956	—	2,029	3,781[5]	0.03	0.9	724	129	3
14	—[10]	803	691	NA	1,735	2,784	6,012[9]	NA	0.02	4.0	5,104	887	22
19	19	475	300	8	33	—	808	3,374	4.62	100.4	872	87	19
3	3	900	575	−15	227	—	1,702	NA	—[6]	0.4	4,671	376	−2
8	5	717	1,969	58	728	—	3,415[8]	25,846[4]	0.12	12.2	5,511	286	44
20	20	1,817	1,635	8	422	—	3,874[8]	26,654	10.20	843.5	3,518	381	27
13	11	500	1,338	75	5	2,071	3,913	11,875	2.99	70.0	2,324	8	25
31	5	943	778	2	348	1,679	3,749	18,562	0.08	11.7	7,040	740	10
10	10	636	305	3	231	—	1,172	5,728[4]	—[6]	0.2	3,107	180	1[2]
		$676	$529	10%	$261	—	$1,938	$7,377	0.32%	$7.3	$2,079	$198	16%
42	4	801	1,300	95	1,151	3,390	6,642	11,779	0.05	3.8	12,978	252	16
23	6	1,026	758	3	5	—	1,789	18,001	0.96	40.9	7,191	349	22
28	4	550	587	−4	1,109	—	2,246	7,365[4]	0.31	4.2	1,785	85	18
7	7	775	775	38	480	—	2,030	5,444[5]	—[6]	—[7]	3,239	146	NA
34	2	700	758	175	534	—	1,992	NA	—[6]	0.6	22,793	1,904	17[2]

For footnotes 1–14 see page 17.

(Continued)

The 800 Highest-Paid CEOs (Cont.)

| | RANK | | | | EDUCATION | |
Company/chief executive	among 800 execs	in industry	Age	Birthplace	undergraduate	graduate
INSURANCE, *Cont.*						
American Finl Group/Carl H Lindner	333	30	77	Dayton OH		
American General/Harold S Hook	100	7	64	Kansas City MO	U of Missouri, BS '53	MA '54
American Intl Group/Maurice R Greenberg	27	4	71	New York NY	U of Miami, BA '48	NY Law School, LLB '50
American Natl Ins/Robert L Moody	181	14	60	Galveston TX		
American Re/Paul H Inderbitzin	568	43	48	Rochester NY	St John Fisher C, BS '70	
Aon/Patrick G Ryan	331	29	59	Milwaukee WI	Northwestern U, BS '59	
WR Berkley/William R Berkley[1]	245	20	50	Newark NJ	NYU, BS '66	Harvard, MBA '68
Berkshire Hathaway/Warren E Buffett	789	52	65	Omaha NE	U of Nebraska Lincoln, BS '50	Columbia, MBA '51
Chubb/Dean R O'Hare	220	16	53	Jersey City NJ	NYU, BS '63	Pace U NY, MBA '68
Cigna/Wilson H Taylor	87	6	52	Hartford CT	Trinity College CT, BS '64	
Cincinnati Financial/Robert B Morgan	510	40	62	Yerkes KY	Eastern Kentucky U, BA '54	
Conseco/Stephen C Hilbert[1]	5	2	50	Terre Haute IN		
Equitable Cos/Joseph J Melone	157	11	64	Pittston PA	U of Pennsylvania, BS '53	PhD '61
Equitable of Iowa/Frederick S Hubbell	145	9	45	Des Moines IA	U of North Carolina, BA '73	U of Iowa, JD '76
First Colony/Bruce C Gottwald Jr	672	46	38	Richmond VA	VMI, BA '80	Col of William & Mary, MBA '84
Fremont General/James A McIntyre	175	13	63	Los Angeles CA	USC, BS '54	
General Re/Ronald E Ferguson	152	10	54	Chicago IL	Blackburn U, BA '63	U of Michigan, MS '65
Horace Mann/Paul J Kardos	625	44	59	Vandergrift PA	Grove City C, BS '62	

| TENURE (YRS) | | COMPENSATION | | | | | | | STOCK OWNED | | COMPANY DATA | | |
| with firm | as CEO | salary | bonus | % change* | other | stock gains | total | 5-year total | % | market value ($mil) | sales | profits | 5-year return |
		($thou)					($thou)				($mil)		
13	9	981	800	–6	49	—	1,830[8]	6,774	25.84	336.4	3,630	190	11
26	18	980	980	0	771	2,374	5,105	19,825	0.14	10.1	6,495	545	17
35	29	1,000	3,150	11	7	6,834	10,991	38,613	2.17	944.1	25,874	2,510	17
14	5	2,917	0	9	1	—	2,917	12,281	1.32	23.4	1,471	206	20
13	—[10]	437	550	NA	30	—	1,017	NA	0.02	0.4	1,797	–87	3[2]
32	14	887	743	23	217	—	1,847	6,558	12.42	691.7	3,466	403	20
29	29	1,023	996	105	275	—	2,293	7,158	12.48	108.3	1,022	61	11
31	26	100	0	0	—	—	100	500	43.22	16,770.0	4,488	725	33
33	8	803	1,227	46	484	—	2,515	11,759	0.06	4.4	6,089	697	8
32	8	872	1,575	42	3,107	146	5,699	12,986	0.09	7.3	18,955	211	22
30	5	576	399	9	—	165	1,140	6,623	0.60	20.8	1,656	227	19
17	17	250	7,416	–21	17,130	—	24,796	231,651	4.07	63.6	2,855	223	40
6	—[10]	600	2,000	NA	695	—	3,295[9]	NA	—[6]	0.2	7,274	350	32[2]
13	7	512	247	–13	2,435	406	3,600	8,950	1.76	18.5	765	85	48
4	4	386	324	17	16	—	725	1,923[5]	2.86	33.7	1,658	151	–9[2]
33	24	685	980	50	1,322	—	2,987	8,330	6.18	34.5	924	68	29
27	9	852	683	5	242	1,631	3,408	12,307	0.07	10.5	7,210	825	10
19	14	375	475	11	17	—	867[8]	3,897	2.26	14.6	741	74	15[2]

For footnotes 1–14 see page 17.

(Continued)

The 800 Highest-Paid CEOs (Cont.)

Company/chief executive	RANK among 800 execs	in industry	Age	Birthplace	EDUCATION undergraduate	graduate
INSURANCE, Cont.						
ITT Hartford Group/Donald R Frahm	165	12	64	St Louis MO	Washington U, BS '53	
Jefferson-Pilot/David A Stonecipher	358	34	55	Cleveland TN	Vanderbilt U, BBA '62	Georgia State U, MS '67
John Alden Financial/Glendon E Johnson	650	45	72	Cleveland UT	U of Utah, BS '48	Harvard, LLD '52
Leucadia National/Ian M Cumming	4	1	55	Canada	U of Kansas '62	Harvard, MBA '70
Liberty Financial Cos/Kenneth R Leibler	497	39	47	New York NY	Syracuse U, BA '71	
Life Partners Group/John Massey	732	49	56	San Antonio TX	SMU, BA '61	U of Texas Austin, JD '66
Life USA Holding/Robert W MacDonald[1]	527	41	53	Rochester NY	Western State U Col, BSL '74	
Lincoln National/Ian M Rolland	343	32	62	Fort Wayne IN	DePauw U, BA '55	U of Michigan, MA '56
Ohio Casualty/Lauren N Patch	762	50	45	Lexington KY	U of Kentucky, BS '73	
Old Republic Intl/A C Zucaro	683	47	57	France	CUNY Queens, BS '62	
Progressive/Peter B Lewis[1]	297	25	62	Cleveland OH	Princeton, AB '55	
Protective Life/Drayton Nabers Jr	359	35	55	Birmingham AL	Princeton, AB '62	Yale, LLB '65
Provident Cos/J Harold Chandler	218	15	47	Belton SC	Wofford C, BA '71	U of S Carolina, MBA '72
Providian/Irving W Bailey II	252	22	54	Cambridge MA	U of Colorado, BA '63	NYU, MBA '68
Prudential Reinsur/Joseph V Taranto	16	3	47	Brooklyn NY	CUNY Brooklyn, BS '71	
Reliance Group/Saul P Steinberg[1]	118	8	56	New York NY	U of Pennsylvania, BS '61	
ReliaStar Financial/John G Turner	244	19	56	Springfield MA	Amherst C, BA '61	
Safeco/Roger H Eigsti	447	38	54	Vancouver WA	Linfield C, BS '64	

| Tenure (yrs) | | Compensation | | | | | | | Stock Owned | | Company Data | | |
| with firm | as CEO | salary | bonus | % change* | other | stock gains | total | 5-year total | % | market value ($mil) | sales ($mil) | profits | 5-year return |
		($thou)					($thou)						
22	8	604	263	4	774	1,540	3,181	4,879[5]	0.02	1.3	12,150	559	NA
4	3	811	540	21	357	—	1,708	4,480[4]	0.07	2.6	1,569	274	27
11	11	667	0	-38	125	—	793	4,599[4]	0.34	1.6	1,671	7	6[2]
18	18	505	291	-45	251	27,996	29,042	45,448	17.07	246.8	1,504	79	30
6	1	655	491	NA	41	—	1,187	NA	—[6]	—[7]	1,027	74	17[2]
2	2	450	113	NA	3	—	566	NA	0.06	0.3	537	26	2[2]
9	9	500	500	100	100	—	1,100	3,615	9.71	15.9	273	19	5[2]
40	19	958	0	2	505	306	1,769	7,223	0.16	7.9	6,633	482	20
24	2	474	0	27	13	—	488	1,310[5]	0.58	7.2	1,462	100	16
20	6	494	200	-24	8	—	702	6,777	0.34	6.1	1,696	213	22
41	31	800	773	-18	441	—	2,014	14,006	12.15	374.9	3,012	251	18
17	4	499	459	14	746	—	1,704	5,125[4]	0.39	3.7	880	77	35
3	3	650	1,638	111	245	—	2,532	4,499[5]	0.23	3.1	2,555	116	12
15	8	745	519	8	389	603	2,255	10,561	0.16	6.9	3,388	345	16
2	2	815	300	NA	13,343	—	14,459	NA	0.87	9.5	949	1	NA
35	35	1,800	2,013	2	435	—	4,248	26,789	35.94	302.1	2,906	91	10
29	5	586	499	19	846	367	2,298	7,388	0.26	4.1	2,090	164	29
24	4	650	65	19	307	323	1,346	4,871	0.08	3.0	3,723	399	14

For footnotes 1–14 see page 17.

(Continued)

The 800 Highest-Paid CEOs *(Cont.)*

Company/chief executive	RANK among 800 execs	in industry	Age	Birthplace	EDUCATION undergraduate	graduate
INSURANCE, *Cont.*						
St Paul Cos/Douglas W Leatherdale	350	33	59	Canada	U of Manitoba, BA '57	
SunAmerica/Eli Broad[1]	233	18	62	New York NY	Michigan State U, BA '54	
TIG Holdings/Jon W Rotenstreich	556	42	52	Birmingham AL	U of Alabama, BS '64	
Torchmark/Ronald K Richey	328	28	69	Erie KS	Washburn U, BA '49	JD '51
Transamerica/Frank C Herringer	246	21	53	New York NY	Dartmouth, AB '64	MBA '65
Transatlantic Holding/Robert F Orlich	772	51	48	Hoboken NJ	St John's U NY, BBA '69	MBA '75
Unitrin/Richard C Vie	721	48	58	St Louis MO		
UNUM/James F Orr III	382	36	53	Minneapolis MN	Villanova, BS '65	Boston U, MBA '70
USF&G/Norman P Blake Jr	222	17	54	New York NY	Purdue U, BA '64	MA '66
USLife/Greer F Henderson	321	27	64	Jersey City NJ	St Peter's C, BS '54	
Western National/Michael J Poulos	393	37	65	Glens Falls NY	Colgate U, BA '53	NYU, MBA '63
METALS						
AK Steel Holding/Richard M Wardrop Jr	464	12	50	McKeesport PA	Penn State U, BS '68	
Alumax/Allen Born	449	11	62	Durango CO	U of Texas El Paso, BS '58	
Alcoa/Paul H O'Neill	29	1	60	St Louis MO	Cal St Fresno, BA '60	Indiana U, MPA '66
Asarco/Richard de J Osborne	234	5	62	Bronxville NY	Princeton, AB '56	
Bethlehem Steel/Curtis H Barnette	604	16	61	St Albans WV	West Virginia U, BA '56	Yale, JD '62
Commercial Metals/Stanley A Rabin	478	14	58	New York NY	Columbia, BS '59	U of Santa Clara, MBA '69
Cyprus Amax Mineral/Milton H Ward	164	4	63	Bessemer AL	U of Alabama, BS '55	U of New Mexico, MBA '74

| TENURE (YRS) | | COMPENSATION | | | | | | | STOCK OWNED | | COMPANY DATA | | |
with firm	as CEO	salary ($thou)	bonus ($thou)	% change*	other ($thou)	stock gains ($thou)	total ($thou)	5-year total	%	market value ($mil)	sales ($mil)	profits ($mil)	5-year return
24	6	738	630	6	377	—	1,745	7,574	0.11	4.8	5,410	521	14
39	39	600	1,528	18	271	—	2,399	21,584	17.72	442.1	1,122	214	47
3	3	600	400	4	54	—	1,054	2,624[5]	0.41	7.3	1,875	118	11[2]
32	11	1,167	500	−5	206	—	1,873	34,853	1.30	39.4	2,067	143	6
17	5	975	709	10	175	425	2,283	9,246	0.09	4.4	6,101	471	20
8	2	264	160	36	6	—	431	NA	—[6]	—[7]	1,165	132	14
13	4	475	100	19	—	16	592	2,157	—[6]	—[7]	1,447	151	7
10	9	691	249	50	616	—	1,556	11,042	0.19	8.7	4,123	281	16
5	5	806	1,500	22	168	—	2,474	12,152	0.05	0.9	3,459	209	12
21	—[10]	581	244	NA	970	89	1,883[9]	NA	0.48	4.7	1,740	105	14
3	3	750	750	0	29	—	1,529	3,708[5]	0.30	3.2	570	7	13[2]
		$625	$515	20%	$104	—	$1,543	$7,823	0.13%	$2.7	$3,198	$180	14%
4	1	443	436	NA	27	400	1,307	NA	0.17	1.8	2,257	269	31[2]
11	10	750	505	5	85	—	1,340	6,211[5]	0.15	2.3	2,926	237	NA
9	9	750	1,250	38	175	8,603	10,778	18,987	0.08	9.1	12,500	791	16
21	10	780	850	49	296	448	2,374	6,414	0.24	3.5	3,198	169	7
29	4	625	221	54	74	—	920	2,772[4]	0.09	1.3	4,868	180	−1
26	17	395	515	12	329	—	1,239	4,699	1.10	5.1	2,268	42	15
4	4	620	1,700	45	867	—	3,187	9,231[4]	0.36	9.3	3,207	124	10

For footnotes 1–14 see page 17.

(Continued)

The 800 Highest-Paid CEOs (Cont.)

Company/chief executive	RANK among 800 execs	in industry	Age	Birthplace	EDUCATION undergraduate	graduate
METALS, *Cont.*						
Engelhard/Orin R Smith	44	2	60	Newark NJ	Brown, BA '57	Seton Hall U, MBA '64
Freeport Copper/James R Moffett	313	8	57	Houma LA	U of Texas Austin, BS '61	Tulane U, MS '63
Homestake Mining/Jack E Thompson	769	19	46	Cuba	U of Arizona, BS '71	
Inland Steel Inds/Robert J Darnall	476	13	58	Normal IL	DePauw U, BA '60	U of Chicago, MBA '73
LTV/David H Hoag	253	6	56	Pittsburgh PA	Allegheny C, BA '60	
Maxxam/Charles E Hurwitz	506	15	56	Kilgore TX	U of Oklahoma, BA '62	
National Steel/V John Goodwin	667	18	52	Long Island NY	Clarkson U, BSEE '65	Monmouth C, MBA '77
Newmont Mining/Ronald C Cambre	630	17	57	New Orleans LA	Louisiana State U, BS '60	
Nucor/John D Correnti	388	10	49	Rochester NY	Clarkson U, BCE '69	
Phelps Dodge/Douglas C Yearley	142	3	60	Oak Park IL	Cornell, BS '58	
Reynolds Metals/Richard G Holder	271	7	64	Paris TN	Vanderbilt U, BA '53	
USX-US Steel/Thomas J Usher	337	9	53	Reading PA	U of Pittsburgh, BS '64	PhD '71
RETAILING						
Ames Dept Stores/Joseph R Ettore	654	37	57	Jersey City NJ	St Peter's C, BBA '61	
AutoZone/Joseph R Hyde III[1]	550	29	53	Memphis TN	U of North Carolina, BS '65	
Best Buy/Richard M Schulze[1]	433	21	55	St. Paul MN		
Caldor/Don R Clarke	641	36	50	Rexburg ID	Brigham Young U, BS '70	Washington State, MBA '71
Circuit City Stores/Richard L Sharp	315	12	49	Washington DC		

| TENURE (YRS) | | salary | bonus | % | COMPENSATION | | | | STOCK OWNED | | COMPANY DATA | | |
with firm	as CEO	($thou)		change*	other	stock gains	total	5-year total	%	market value ($mil)	sales ($mil)	profits	5-year return
19	12	735	925	25	1,481	5,967	9,108	29,752	0.59	19.6	2,840	138	28
26	12	1,819	0	−59	104	—	1,924	21,261[15]	0.44	23.7	1,834	254	25
15	—[10]	336	68	NA	38	—	442[9]	NA	—[6]	0.2	716	30	5
34	4	691	516	25	35	—	1,241	3,601[4]	0.13	1.6	4,781	147	4
36	5	588	340	2	1,321	—	2,249	9,476	0.08	1.2	4,283	185	52
18	16	609	450	7	97	—	1,156[8]	14,097	30.60	133.3	2,565	58	1
2	1	390	280	NA	73	—	743	NA	—[6]	—[7]	2,954	105	0[2]
3	3	513	333	1	9	—	855	1,854[5]	—[6]	0.3	636	113	16
16	—[10]	242	632	NA	468	201	1,543[9]	NA	0.05	2.7	3,462	275	25
36	7	640	643	15	280	2,070	3,633	17,937	0.17	8.5	4,185	747	20
43	4	700	975	72	101	341	2,117	5,034	0.13	4.6	7,213	389	3
30	1	675[16]	900[16]	NA	226	—	1,801	NA	0.04	1.2	6,456	303	12[2]
		$651	**$343**	**2%**	**$63**	**—**	**$1,283**	**$6,047**	**$0.51**	**7.8%**	**$4,448**	**$77**	**10%**
2	2	750	0	NA	37	—	787	NA	0.51	0.2	2,216	−2	4
31	24	602	451	−9	6	—	1,058	36,458	9.54	484.3	1,943	149	34[2]
30	30	728	0	−13	26	639	1,393	5,473	20.35	153.7	6,589	56	43
10	10	563	246	−2	8	—	816[8]	6,874[4]	0.78	0.5	2,764	1	−30[2]
13	10	652	975	39	286	—	1,913	20,276	0.96	31.4	6,686	181	29

For footnotes 1–14 see page 17. [15]Compensation paid by Freeport/McMoRan. [16]Salary and bonus is paid for services rendered to Marathon, Steel and Delhi.

(Continued)

The 800 Highest-Paid CEOs *(Cont.)*

| | RANK | | | | EDUCATION | |
| | among 800 execs | in industry | Age | Birthplace | undergraduate | graduate |
Company/chief executive						
RETAILING, *Cont.*						
CompUSA/James F Halpin	575	32	45	Chicago IL		
CUC International/Walter A Forbes	15	1	53	Rockford IL	Northwestern U, BS '61	Harvard, MBA '68
Dayton Hudson/Robert J Ulrich	159	4	53	Minneapolis MN	U of Minnesota, BA '67	
Dillard Dept Stores/William T Dillard Sr[1]	351	14	81	Mineral Spr AR	U of Arkansas, BBA '35	Columbia, MS '37
Eckerd/Francis A Newman	—	—	46	England		
Federated Dept Strs/Allen Questrom	299	11	56	Boston MA	Boston U, BA '64	
Fingerhut Cos/Theodore Deikel	368	16	60	Minneapolis MN		
Gap/Millard Drexler	—	—	51	New York NY	SUNY Buffalo, BS '66	Boston U, MBA '68
General Nutrition Cos/William E Watts	247	7	43	Buffalo NY	SUNY Buffalo, BA '75	
Hechinger/John W Hechinger Jr	661	38	46	Washington DC	Boston C, BS '72	
Home Depot/Bernard Marcus[1]	192	5	67	Newark NJ	Rutgers, BS '54	
Inacom/Bill L Fairfield[1]	487	24	49	Kearney NE	Bradley U, BSIE '69	Harvard, MBA '75
Intelligent Electron/Richard D Sanford[1]	445	22	52	New York NY	Hofstra U, BA '71	
Kmart/Floyd Hall	—	—	57	Duncan OK		
Kohl's/William S Kellogg	599	33	52	Milwaukee WI		
Limited/Leslie H Wexner[1]	285	10	58	Dayton OH	Ohio State U, BS '59	
Longs Drug Stores/Robert M Long	748	42	58	Oakland CA	Claremont McKenna C, BA '60	
Lowe's Cos/Leonard G Herring	610	34	68	Snow Hill NC	U of North Carolina, BS '48	
May Dept Stores/David C Farrell	93	3	62	Chicago IL	Antioch U, BA '56	
Melville/Stanley P Goldstein	554	30	61	Woonsocket RI	U of Pennsylvania, BS '55	

TENURE (YRS) with firm	TENURE (YRS) as CEO	salary ($thou)	bonus ($thou)	% change*	other ($thou)	stock gains ($thou)	total ($thou)	5-year total	STOCK OWNED %	market value ($mil)	sales ($mil)	profits	5-year return
3	2	550	440	124	—	—	990	NA	0.62	7.8	3,135	40	25[2]
20	20	733	725	9	28	13,115	14,600	32,601	0.18	10.3	1,415	163	35
29	2	982	750	65	179	1,349	3,259[8]	NA	0.07	4.8	23,516	311	6
57	57	885	660	−19	190	—	1,735	11,532	1.11	45.4	5,918	167	0
3	—[10]	NA	NA	—	—	—	—	NA	0.01	0.2	4,772	93	53[2]
6	6	1,250	750	67	—	—	2,000	10,540	—[6]	0.2	15,049	75	20[2]
7	7	577	519	102	547	—	1,643	20,231	3.13	18.3	2,110	51	3
13	1	NA	NA	—	—	—	—	NA	NA	—	4,395	354	19
12	5	599	200	0	25	1,453	2,277[8]	5,915	0.16	2.3	846	69	63[2]
24	6	483	172	−4	101	—	756[8]	3,212	2.70	4.0	2,253	−78	−14
18	18	600	2,000	0	167	—	2,767	12,957	3.12	688.7	15,470	732	22
17	9	374	729	134	113	—	1,216	3,307	1.65	2.9	2,200	12	2
14	14	850	0	−40	497	—	1,347[8]	7,920	11.24	22.4	3,475	−19	−17
1	1	NA	NA	—	—	—	—	NA	NA	—	34,654	−520	−22
30	17	814	111	−2	6	—	931[8]	3,605[4]	8.69	212.5	1,926	73	44[2]
33	33	1,150	768	−3	148	—	2,067	10,178	23.05	1,170.2	7,881	962	−4
35	19	100	291	10	133	—	524	2,201	10.75	94.9	2,644	46	6
40	18	625	96	−26	177	—	899	5,468	1.13	54.8	7,075	226	37
40	17	1,100	533	−7	3,541	222	5,396[8]	20,610	0.34	41.7	10,952	755	16
33	9	1,050	0	−32	4	—	1,054	8,825	0.17	7.0	9,689	−615	−4

For footnotes 1–14 see page 17.

(Continued)

The 800 Highest-Paid CEOs *(Cont.)*

| | RANK | | | | EDUCATION | |
| | among 800 execs | in industry | Age | Birthplace | undergraduate | graduate |
Company/chief executive						
RETAILING, *Cont.*						
Mercantile Stores/David L Nichols	502	27	53	Toledo OH	U of Toledo, BS '90	
Fred Meyer/Robert G Miller	707	41	52	Louisville MS		
MicroAge/Jeffrey D McKeever[1]	381	18	53	Marion IN	U of Arizona, BS '65	MBA '73
Nordstrom/Raymond A Johnson[15]	768	43	55	Seattle WA		
Office Depot/David I Fuente	322	13	50	Chicago IL	Purdue U, BS '67	MS '69
OfficeMax/Michael Feuer[1]	371	17	51			
Payless Cashways/David Stanley	692	40	60	Kansas City MO		Columbia, LLB '57
JC Penney/James E Oesterreicher	260	8	54	Saginaw MI	Michigan State U, BS '64	
Price/Costco/James D Sinegal[1]	785	44	60	Pittsburgh PA	San Diego State U, BA '59	
Revco DS/D Dwayne Hoven	411	20	54	Jackson AL	Auburn U, BS '64	
Rite Aid/Martin L Grass	501	26	42	Harrisburg PA	U of Pennsylvania, BA '76	Cornell, MBA '78
Sears, Roebuck/Arthur C Martinez	69	2	56	New York NY	Polytechnic Institute, BSME '60	Harvard, MBA '65
Service Merchandise/Raymond Zimmerman[1]	639	35	63	Memphis TN		
Spiegel/John J Shea	565	31	58	Newark NJ	La Salle, BS '59	U of Pittsburgh, MS '60
Staples/Thomas G Stemberg[1]	680	39	47	Newark NJ	Harvard, AB '71	MBA '73
Tandy/John V Roach	361	15	57	Stamford TX	Texas Christian U, BA '61	MBA '65
TJX Cos/Bernard Cammarata	394	19	56	Brooklyn NY		
Toys 'R' Us/Michael Goldstein	486	23	55	Brooklyn NY	CUNY Queens, BA '63	
Waban/Herbert J Zarkin	499	25	57	Haverhill MA		

with firm	as CEO	salary	bonus	% change*	other	stock gains	total	5-year total	%	market value ($mil)	sales ($mil)	profits	5-year return
32	4	725	394	12	59	—	1,179	3,631[4]	0.02	0.4	2,944	123	13
5	5	555	0	−25	67	—	623[8]	6,499[5]	0.69	5.2	3,429	30	12
20	9	463	37	−20	692	367	1,558[14]	4,162	3.06	4.5	3,047	−1	9
27	1	344	0	NA	12	87	444	NA	0.08	2.9	4,114	165	7
8	8	625	1,250	33	5	—	1,880[8]	33,679	0.25	8.0	5,313	132	26
8	8	624	1,000	95	—	—	1,624	3,770[4]	1.68	33.2	2,543	126	34[2]
16	14	650	0	−29	12	—	662	4,051	0.13	0.2	2,651	−132	−31[2]
32	1	395	413	20	1,286	102	2,197	NA	0.06	6.1	21,419	838	18
11	8	306	0	2	17	—	323	8,085	1.43	52.0	18,982	225	−3
9	3	600	878	65	—	—	1,478	3,052[5]	0.06	1.0	5,034	77	36[2]
18	1	927	165	NA	2	88	1,182[9]	NA	0.93	23.9	5,369	155	10
4	1	1,024	1,006	NA	4,559	—	6,589	NA	0.04	7.9	34,925	1,025	35
36	23	782	0	4	38	—	820	4,033	4.54	24.3	4,019	50	−2
16	11	600	0	−28	158	265	1,023	5,701	0.10	1.0	3,184	−10	6
10	10	423	281	8	—	—	704	5,062	0.70	21.1	3,068	74	44
29	15	735	183	−13	133	643	1,694	6,047	0.22	6.6	5,839	212	9
20	7	850	286	−1	388	—	1,525[8]	10,352	0.14	2.6	4,448	30	11
13	2	800	403	27	17	—	1,219[8]	NA	0.01	0.9	9,427	148	0
7	3	553	442	45	190	—	1,185[8]	3,163[5]	0.29	2.4	3,978	73	10

For footnotes 1–14 see page 17. [15]Office jointly held with John J Whitacre.

(Continued)

The 800 Highest-Paid CEOs *(Cont.)*

Company/chief executive	Rank among 800 execs	in industry	Age	Birthplace	Education undergraduate	graduate
RETAILING, *Cont.*						
Wal-Mart Stores/David D Glass	547	28	60	Mountainview MO	SW Missouri St U, BS '59	
Walgreen/Charles R Walgreen III	266	9	60	Chicago IL	U of Michigan, BS '58	
Woolworth/Roger N Farah	221	6	43	New York NY	U of Penn-Wharton, BS '74	
TRAVEL & TRANSPORT						
Airborne Freight/Robert S Cline	652	22	58	Urbana IL	Dartmouth, BA '59	
American President/Timothy J Rhein	729	28	55	San Francisco CA	U of Santa Clara, BS '62	
AMR/Robert L Crandall	163	8	60	Westerly RI	U of Rhode Island, BS '57	U of Pennsylvania, MBA '60
Burlington Santa Fe/Robert D Krebs	52	2	54	Sacramento CA	Stanford U, BA '64	Harvard, MBA '66
Caliber System/Daniel J Sullivan	716	27	50	Westbury CT	Amherst C, BA '69	
Circus Circus/Clyde T Turner	632	21	58	Las Vegas NV	U of Nevada Las Vegas, BS '60	
Conrail/David M LeVan	710	26	50	Gettysburg PA	Gettysburg C, BBA '68	
Consol Freightways/Donald E Moffitt	655	23	63	Terre Haute IN		
Continental Airlines/Gordon M Bethune	241	12	54	Austin TX	Abilene Christian U, BS '66	
CSX/John W Snow	102	5	56	Toledo OH	U of Toledo, BA '62	U of Virginia, PhD '65
Delta Air Lines/Ronald W Allen	545	20	54	Atlanta GA	Georgia Tech, BSIE '64	
Federal Express/Frederick W Smith[1]	462	18	51	Marks MS	Yale, BA '66	
Harrah's Entertain/Philip G Satre	170	9	47	Palo Alto CA	Stanford U, BA '71	U of Cal Davis, JD '75
HFS/Henry R Silverman[1]	418	17	56	New York NY	Williams C '61	U of Pennsylvania, JD '64

Tenure (yrs)		Compensation							Stock owned		Company data		
with firm	as CEO	salary	bonus	% change*	other	stock gains	total	5-year total	%	market value ($mil)	sales ($mil)	profits	5-year return
		($thou)					($thou)						
20	8	985	0	6	76	—	1,061[8]	4,658	0.11	58.3	93,627	2,740	4
44	25	827	493	17	841	—	2,160	8,649	0.47	36.9	10,682	331	16
1	1	1,500[3]	1,000	NA	—	—	2,500[8]	NA	0.15	3.6	8,224	−164	−11
		$533	**$320**	**4%**	**$89**	**—**	**$1,466**	**$8,142**	**0.14%**	**$5.2**	**$3,502**	**$163**	**18%**
31	12	487	0	−15	5	298	790	3,741	0.58	3.1	2,239	24	6
29	1	393	155	NA	23	—	572[9]	NA	—[6]	—[7]	2,896	30	18
23	11	663	395	76	2,131	—	3,188	18,590	0.08	5.7	16,910	196	9
30	9	525	265	11	1,351	6,021	8,163[14]	21,009	0.18	21.4	6,183	192	26
24	1	365	132	NA	100	—	597	NA	0.14	2.2	2,448	−27	−1
3	2	802	0	6	39	—	842[8]	NA	0.04	1.3	1,300	129	9
18	1	515	25	57	77	—	616	NA	0.06	3.6	3,686	264	28
41	5	650	31	−42	88	14	783	4,867	0.08	0.9	5,281	57	10
2	2	434[13]	1,500	NA	372	—	2,306[8]	NA	0.30	4.7	5,825	224	26[2]
19	7	896	1,688	37	2,407	—	4,990	21,376	0.30	29.5	10,504	618	23
33	9	475	561	118	28	—	1,063	3,964	0.06	2.6	12,250	510	3
25	25	700	516	9	99	—	1,315	4,420	8.51	357.9	10,005	280	14
16	2	477	134	−28	2,451	—	3,062	8,087[5]	0.33	11.3	1,550	79	45
6	6	1,000	434	5	7	—	1,441	5,035[4]	0.12	6.0	413	80	108[2]

For footnotes 1–14 see page 17.

(Continued)

The 800 Highest-Paid CEOs (Cont.)

| | RANK | | | | EDUCATION | |
| | among | in | | | | |
Company/chief executive	800 execs	industry	Age	Birthplace	undergraduate	graduate
TRAVEL & TRANSPORT, *Cont.*						
Hilton Hotels/Stephen F Bollenbach	745	30	53	Los Angeles CA	UCLA, BS '65	Cal St Los Angeles, MBA '68
Host Marriott/Terence C Golden	671	24	51	Horsham PA	U of Notre Dame, BSME '66	MIT, MSE '67
Illinois Central/E Hunter Harrison	407	15	51	Memphis TN	Memphis State U, BA '68	
ITT/Rand V Araskog	56	3	64	Fergus Falls MN	US Military Acad, BS '53	
Kansas City Southern/Landon H Rowland	85	4	59	Fuquay Springs NC	Dartmouth, BA '59	Harvard, LLB '62
Marriott Intl/J Willard Marriott Jr	400	14	64	Washington DC	U of Utah, BS '54	
Mirage/Stephen A Wynn	134	6	54	New Haven CT	U of Pennsylvania, BA '63	
Norfolk Southern/David R Goode	160	7	55	Vinton VA	Duke U, AB '62	Harvard, JD '65
Northwest Airlines/John H Dasburg	37	1	53	New York NY	U of Florida, BS '66	JD '73
Roadway Express/Michael W Wickham	786	32	49	Elmira NY	U of Delaware, BS '68	
Ryder System/M Anthony Burns	511	19	53	Las Vegas NV	Brigham Young U, BS '64	U of Cal Berkeley, MBA '65
Southern Pacific Rail/Jerry R Davis	408	16	57	Salina KS		MIT, MS '76
Southwest Airlines/Herbert D Kelleher	301	13	65	Camden NJ	Wesleyan C, BA '53	NYU, LLB '56
Trans World Airlines/Jeffrey H Erickson	708	25	51	New York NY	Rensselaer, BS '69	Polytechnic Institute, MS '73
UAL/Gerald Greenwald	225	11	60	Saint Louis MO	Princeton, BA '57	Wayne State U, MS '62
Union Pacific/Drew Lewis	193	10	64	Philadelphia PA	Haverford C, BS '53	Harvard, MBA '55
USAir Group/Stephen M Wolf	759	31	54	Oakland CA	San Francisco State U, BA '65	
Yellow/A Maurice Myers	737	29	56	California	Cal St Fullerton, BS '64	Cal St Long Beach, MBA '72

TENURE (YRS)		COMPENSATION							STOCK OWNED		COMPANY DATA		
with firm	as CEO	salary ($thou)	bonus	% change*	other	stock gains ($thou)	total	5-year total	%	market value ($mil)	sales ($mil)	profits	5-year return
—[10]	—[10]	540[3]	NA	—	—	—	540	NA	0.02	1.0	1,590	173	21
1	1	575[3]	152	NA	—	—	727	NA	—[6]	—[7]	484	−62	37
7	3	500	650	2	347	—	1,497	5,972[4]	0.51	8.9	644	130	31
29	17	2,000	2,331	7	3,326	—	7,657	34,593	0.41	29.0	6,346	147	NA
16	9	500	0	0	450	4,807	5,757	16,177	0.67	12.4	775	237	35
40	23	800	696	4	9	—	1,505	4,445[5]	7.54	467.5	8,961	247	29[2]
23	23	2,500	1,250	0	4	—	3,755	49,539	9.59	438.2	1,331	170	29
31	4	685	617	20	1,781	144	3,227	8,474[4]	0.03	2.8	4,668	713	17
7	6	404	480	4	197	8,694	9,776	11,660[5]	0.18	7.3	9,085	342	108[2]
28	—[10]	268	0	NA	47	—	315[9]	NA	0.05	0.1	2,289	−13	NA
22	13	725	320	−34	90	—	1,135	8,142	0.13	3.0	5,167	155	12
1	1	489[13]	0	NA	1,002	—	1,491	NA	—[6]	—[7]	3,151	−3	18[2]
29	15	395	172	0	40	1,391	1,999	5,604	0.87	39.7	2,873	183	26
2	2	370	250	NA	—	—	620	NA	0.01	—[7]	3,317	−228	NA
2	2	657	725	−65	1,068	—	2,450	NA	0.55	15.2	14,943	378	8
10	9	910	1,650	8	200	—	2,760	25,992	0.08	11.7	7,486	946	17
—[10]	—[10]	500[3]	NA	—	—	—	500	NA	0.51	6.1	7,474	119	−1
—[10]	—[10]	550[3]	NA	—	—	—	550	NA	—[6]	—[7]	3,057	−30	−14

For footnotes 1–14 see page 17.

The Forbes Four Hundred

As the nature of wealth is changing in America, so is the composition of The Forbes Four Hundred.

ANN MARSH

Edited by Peter Newcomb and Dolores A. Lataniotis

Reported by Ann Marsh, Josh McHugh and James Samuelson with assistance from Scott Bistayi and Saira Stewart

Photo editing by Lorna Bieber with assistance from Laurie DeChiara

Illustrations by Joyce Hesselberth

MEET THE CLASS OF 1996

Forget America's 50 families. Forget old money. Forget silver spoons. Great fortunes are being created almost monthly in the U.S. today by young entrepreneurs who hadn't a dime when we created this list in 1982.

There are 43 people in The Forbes Four Hundred Class of 1996. That means that nearly one in nine are newcomers this year.

Since 1990 alone 238 new people have made it into The Four Hundred, displacing an equal number of others. It's slippery up there, even in a roaring bull market.

Yet it's not easy to break the barrier to admission. With the Dow nudging 6,000, a mere centimillionaire hasn't a chance. The average net worth for the first time exceeds a billion dollars. This year's admission price was $415 million, a $75 million jump over last year.

Joe Liemandt cleared that hurdle with $85 million to spare. The youngest member of the Class of 1996, from Austin, Tex., dropped out of Stanford to start Trilogy Development Group, a software firm that helps companies streamline their sales processes.

Liemandt is all of 28. Poor Bill Gates. He didn't make The Four Hundred until he was 30—in 1986.

Another relative youngster, Kenneth Tuchman, 36, graduated from selling puka shells to providing telephone services. His TeleTech went public earlier this year, making Tuchman an instant billionaire.

The Forbes Four Hundred Class of 1996

Name	Worth ($mil)	Primary sources	Age
Anselmo, Mary	930	PanAmSat Corp.	55
Birck, Michael	660	Tellabs, Inc.	58
Chace, Malcolm G. III	440	Inheritance	61
Chowdry, Michael	600	Atlas Air	41
Connell, William	560	Scrap metal, presses	58
Davidson, Janice G.	475	Software	52
Davidson, Robert M.	475	Software	52
Fisher, John J.	435	Inheritance (The Gap)	35
Fisher, Robert J.	435	Inheritance (The Gap)	42
Fisher, William S.	435	Inheritance (The Gap)	39
Foss, Donald	550	Credit Acceptance Corp.	52
Friedman, Phyllis Koshland	490	Inheritance (Levi Strauss)	73
Giannulli, Mossimo	490	Clothes	32
Goergen, Robert B.	490	Candles	58
Goldman, Richard N.	1,200	Inheritance (Levi Strauss)	76
Goodnight, James	2,000	Software	53
Gosman, Abraham	480	Health care	67
Haas, Evelyn Danzig	1,100	Inheritance (Levi Strauss)	79
Harbert, Marguerite	870	Inheritance (construction)	73
Honickman, Harold	800	Beverage distribution	63
Hughes, Bradley Wayne	800	Public Storage Inc.	63
Krasny, Michael	620	Computer Discount Warehouse	43
Lenfest, Harold FitzGerald	425	Cable TV	66
Liemandt, Joseph	500	Trilogy Development Group	28
Lopker, Pamela M.	425	Software	42
Mays, L. Lowry	640	Radio	61
McCombs, Billy Joe (Red)	680	Autos, media, ranches	68
McNair, Robert C.	800	Energy	59
McVaney, C. Edward	550	Software	55
Morgridge, John P.	580	Data networking	63
Nash, Jack	475	Money management	66
Price, David G.	430	Real estate	64
Price, Michael	560	Money management	45
Sall, John	1,000	Software	48
Schwartz, Ted	1,100	APAC TeleServices Inc.	42
Scott, Walter Jr.	720	Construction, telecommunications	65
Sidhu, Sanjiv	415	Software	39
Silverman, Henry	600	Investments	56
Sykes, John H.	520	Computer support services	60
Troutt, Kenneth	1,400	Telecommunications	48
Tuchman, Kenneth D.	1,000	TeleTech	36
White, Dean	650	Billboards, hotels	73
Wold, Elaine Johnson	490	Inheritance (Johnson & Johnson)	68

Both these youthful Four Hundreders and many of the other relatively young ones represent a true sea change in society. In the not-so- distant past, wealth was almost always based on possession of physical assets— "the means of production," Marx called them. Control them and you got rich. Wealth was timber, oil, real estate, factories or printing presses. A bit over a decade ago a fourth of our members were engaged in heavy industry.

That was yesterday. Almost all today's new fortunes are based not on hard assets but on ideas and organizing principles. This year there are only 35 names on The Four Hundred list from heavy industry, down from 103 in 1985. Just as quantum physics overthrew our old assumptions about the physical world, so, too, in economics has innovation and adaptability become more precious than gold, more valuable than land. With quantum physics at the turn of the century, we came to realize that matter is energy. Now we are discovering that wealth is economic energy.

Which of course is why young entrepreneurs have been able to humble such mighty companies as IBM.

Look at the media business. The old press lords printed newspapers and magazines on paper. The new media barons—Disney, Warner, Murdoch, Redstone—deliver many of their products via bandwidth. Technology has helped the media business mightily. It helps explain why there are 62 names on The Four Hundred from media and entertainment, up from 58 a decade ago.

In this digital world where everything changes and nothing can be taken for granted, it's almost as hard to stay among The Forbes Four Hundred as it is to get on this list in the first place. Steve Jobs' comeback with his Pixar IPO late last year made him a billionaire in just a few days. Now he's worth just half that.

Peruse The Four Hundreds of past years. The membership is in constant flux.

When we started this list in 1982 there wasn't a single software magnate on it. Eight members of the Class of 1996 made their mark in computer software, swelling to 20 the number of software-rich on the list. Another 14 are involved with computer networking and hardware.

Software and PCs are part of the story. Just as the automobile revolution created ancillary fortunes in tires and glass and petroleum, so is the computer revolution spawning fortunes in related areas. Michael Krasny made a killing retailing computers at cut rates through catalog sales. His Computer Discount Warehouse stock is worth $620 million. John Sykes made his $520 million selling computer support systems. John Morgridge ($580 million) made his fortune in Cisco Systems by helping to tie computers together.

Yet old industries in turmoil also create entrepreneurial opportunities. Kenneth Troutt uses independent sales reps to sell long distance phone service. His Excel Communications stock is worth a scintillating $1.4 bil-

lion. Robert McNair of Cogen Technologies exploited electricity deregulation and became a serious competitor to utilities. His worth: $800 mil-
lion. Robert Goergen got on the list by selling candles—yes, candles *(see
p. 242–243)*. Mossimo Giannulli this year became the third fashion magnate to become a Four Hundred member.

Transportation? With just-in-time inventory systems creating demand
for air freight, Atlas Air's Michael Chowdry, 41, from a home base in Denver carries computer disk drives from Taiwan to the U.S. and fresh flow-
ers from Amsterdam to Singapore. Chowdry's worth: over $600 million.

Chowdry is an immigrant. He was born in Pakistan. He is one of 23
immigrants among The Four Hundred—all American citizens now.

What else do we know about the superrich? They defy stereotypes: 30
of them never went to college. We can't explain this, but 63 members having no college degree have a much higher average net worth than the
grads.

There are 45 unmarrieds among them, but they do tend to be family
people: Our Four Hundred have produced 1,150 children—2.88 on average. Nearly two-thirds are still with their first spouse; 89 are divorced at
least once.

This year's list has 60 women. That's a loss of 22% over ten years—
much of it old money.

But the truth is we can't really generalize about these folk: They come
in all sizes, colors and genders.

Writing in this issue seven years ago, cyberguru George Gilder pre-
dicted the 1990s would bring ". . . a global economy dominated more
and more by fortunes of thought rather than hoards of things."

Right on, George: Thought is the essential raw material of the Digital
Age, where steel and oil were those of the Industrial Age. No one can fore-
cast how many new fortunes and how much additional wealth will be created by ideas in the years ahead. But we will predict this: The tempo isn't
about to slow down.

JUDGMENT CALLS AND RULES OF THE CHASE

The two basic qualifications for membership in this year's Forbes Four
Hundred are: one, the candidate must be a U.S. citizen; and two, he or she
must have a net worth—assets minus liabilities—of at least $415 million,
up from a minimum of $340 million last year.

Estimating wealth for people with significant chunks of equity in public companies is pretty straightforward. For people whose wealth is tied
up in private companies, our fundamental operating principle is to ask
how prevailing public market prices would value the private assets. But
we aren't slaves to Wall Street valuations. We do use judgment. Other-

wise, using the earnings multiples Wall Street has placed on such companies as Netscape and Pixar would make George Lucas (who returns to our list this year) worth over $10 billion. Our best-informed estimate of Lucas' net worth: $2 billion.

Another judgment call: Jeffrey Katzenberg is not among The Forbes Four Hundred this year; he's a near-miss *(see p. 305)*. Katzenberg is one of the founding partners of DreamWorks SKG. Multibillionaire Paul Allen invested nearly $500 million for 18% of the studio; Allen's investment values Katzenberg's stake at $600 million. But we'd rather see DreamWorks produce something of value before we credit Katzenberg with that kind of money.

Other elements of our methodology:

- Blocks of publicly traded stock are priced at the market close of Aug. 23. The S&P 500 has climbed 2.4% since then, so in many cases our estimates are shy a few tens of millions. But not all. In late September apparel maker Mossimo Inc.'s stock plunged, making Mossimo Giannulli $150 million poorer.

- Privately held companies are usually valued on multiples of cash flow, earnings or sales. When these numbers are fuzzy, we rely on estimates from a broad network of experts and authorities who track particular industries professionally. We gratefully acknowledge these sources (except those who ask to remain anonymous) on page 307.

- Trusts and other intrafamily arrangements produce all sorts of complexities—their function, after all, is often to cloud issues of control and ownership. Using legal opinion but also common sense, we proceed on a case-by-case basis. Our primary concern: Who controls the wealth? For the most part, trusts are usually attributed to the person who created the wealth, provided he or she is still alive and in control. Lawyerly assertions that ownership is already in the hands of those who will ultimately receive the principal are difficult to take seriously, especially when some of these so-called owners are still children or not yet even born. But we are braced for the trusts-and-estates crowd's letters to the contrary.

With the computer revolution reaching into every nook and cranny of the economy, and the stock market eager to raise capital for the men and, increasingly, the women leading the revolution, we have added 43 new names to The Forbes Four Hundred this year, many of them from the computer world *(see list on p. 110)*. In the pages that follow, the biographies of the new members are highlighted.

The 400 Wealthiest Americans

OVER $7,000,000,000

William Henry Gates III

$18.5 billion
Microsoft. Bellevue, Wash. 40.
Married, 1 child.

Microsoft responds to explosive rise of Internet with new software, strategies. Slight snag as early version of new browser software to compete with Netscape stumbles—and Netscape is making antitrust noises. Brilliant student Gates quit Harvard to cofound Microsoft with Lakeside School classmate Paul Allen *(see p. 116)* 1975. Big break: selected to develop operating system for IBM's first PC 1980. Tight deadline: bought QDOS ("quick and dirty operating system") for $50,000; renamed MS-DOS. Handsome return: Microsoft gets royalty each time machine legally using MS-DOS is sold. Went public 1986. Early Internet skeptic quickly changed mind: Gates' May 1995 memo to staffers warned of "Internet Tidal Wave." New goal: dominate the Internet. Windows 95 shipped with Microsoft Network software; next Windows release to include built-in Web browser (Internet Explorer). Rivals protest: considered unfair advantage among on-line providers. Gates looking for content. Created high-profile on-line magazine, Slate; with NBC launched cable news channel and World Wide Web news service MSNBC July 1996. Recently bought Bettmann Archive, world's largest collection of historical photographs; plans to put digitized images on-line. Looking for Hollywood hookups; part-interest in DreamWorks Interactive. Also Teledesic: global wireless network with fellow Lakesider Craig McCaw *(see p. 154)*. Married Microsoft executive Melinda French New Year's Day 1994, daughter Jennifer Katharine born April 1996. Hard worker, brutally candid, but longtime employees rewarded well: Seattle property market inflated by "Microsoft millionaires." Wrote number one best-seller *The Road Ahead* (1995); every copy accompanied by CD-ROM, including computer-animated "virtual tour" of Gates' $30 million Bellevue waterfront home. World's richest man. Member since 1986.

Warren Edward Buffett

$15 billion
Stock market. Omaha. 66.
Separated, 3 children.

To silence the after-Buffett-what? nattering, Buffett indicated in March that Geico Corp. executive Louis Simpson, 60, could succeed him and longtime partner Charlie Munger (see p. 212) at helm of Berkshire Hathaway. Don't hold your breath. Buffett's been busy completing Geico buyout for $2.3 billion, warning public that Berkshire stock is overpriced and looking for ways to keep shareholders' money compounding—the latter increasingly difficult as the scale of his operation mounts. Credits the late Ben Graham with insight that launched most successful investment career in history; but in recent years, heavily influenced by partner Munger and by investment guru Phil Fisher (Forbes, Sept. 23). He has moved away from Graham's quantitative approach toward a more qualitative approach to investing—buying a stock as buying a piece of a business. Studied at Columbia Business School under Graham, started investment partnership age 25 with $100,000; after thirtyfold increase, dissolved 1969 at market peak; age 39. Picked up small, expiring textile firm Berkshire Hathaway 1965 and built it into an investment colossus. Biggest single investment: Coca-Cola. Of Gillette holding: "It's pleasant to go to bed every night knowing there are 2.5 billion males in the world who have to shave in the morning." Completes own tax returns. Proclaims computer illiteracy despite friendship with only American of greater net worth, Microsoft's Bill Gates. Buffett: separated from wife, Susan (see p. 161). Member since 1982.

Paul Gardner Allen

$7.5 billion
Microsoft. Mercer Island, Wash. 43.
Single.

Diversifying: investments in over two dozen new technology ventures. After Seattle's Lakeside School with childhood friend Bill Gates (see p. 115), dropped out of Washington State U.; worked for Honeywell in Boston. Teamed with Gates to write version of BASIC computer language; led to startup of Microsoft 1975. Left 1983 when diagnosed with Hodgkin's disease; in remission. Still major Microsoft shareholder with 9.5% equity. Once owned 25% America Online; sold at sizable profit after failing to get larger stake. Put up $300 million for 80% equity in market leader Ticketmaster 1993. Bought 18% stake in DreamWorks SKG for $500 million 1995; few projects delivered, yet Allen optimistic: "There are a lot of things coming down the pike." Takes credit for coining term "wired world" to describe electronically linked society. Investing $100 million in Interval Research over 10 years. Also substantial stakes in CNet and Starwave. Some misses: reportedly lost nearly $100 million on multimedia software company Asymetrix, $10 million on satellite venture SkyPix. Plays guitar in rock band the Threads. Jammed with buddy Dave Stewart at Las Vegas charity event November 1995. Avid Jimi Hendrix fan: paid $50,000 at auction for fragments of late musician's shattered Fender Stratocaster. With $60 million, founded Experience Music Project, interactive museum in tribute to Hendrix, Bing Crosby, Pearl Jam, other Northwest artists; slated to open 1999. "Voracious reader" science and tech magazines. Tried to give $21 million for creation of public park (Seattle Commons), but voters twice said no. Gives millions to AIDS research, libraries, museums. Funded search for extraterrestrial life: "It's a worthy thing." Bought 14-month option to purchase Seattle (football) Seahawks from California developer Ken Behring *(see p. 300)*; decision expected by July 1997. Recently under fire from Camp Nor'wester alum for forcing children's summer camp on his San Juan Islands property to relocate. Owns Boeing 757, 150-foot yacht and "significant . . . but not museum-size" impressionist art collection. Also owner of Portland (basketball) Trail Blazers. Avid scuba diver, lives with mother on a 6-acre waterfront estate that is equipped with 20-seat theater, skylit basketball gym, waterfall. Sister Jody Allen Patton oversees charitable foundations, real estate. Member since 1986.

John Werner Kluge

$7.2 billion
Metromedia Co. Charlottesville, Va. 82.
Thrice divorced, 3 children.

"I'm an operator, not an investor." Newest project: through new Metromedia International Group, bringing wireless cable TV, AM-FM radio, telephone and paging services to Russia, Eastern Europe, China. Born in Germany (*klug* is German for "clever"), immigrated to Detroit 1922 with mother, raised in tenement. Studied economics at Columbia, nearly lost scholarship after getting caught playing poker; $7,000 in winnings by graduation. Moonlighted as shoe salesman, secretarial work for son of president of China. Captain, Army intelligence WWII. Bought first Maryland radio station 1946 for $15,000. Bought FM stations when AM big, also independent TV stations. Formed Metromedia 1960. Amassed country's largest cellular network early 1980s. With right-hand man Stuart Subotnick *(see p. 261)* scoring big hits: realized $4.65 billion pretax liquidating Metromedia assets 1984. Bought Orion Pictures (rare moneyloser), restaurant chains. Sold cellular assets for $3.4 billion by 1992. Completed $2.5 billion long distance phone merger, called WorldCom, September 1993; sold WorldCom stake for $1.2 billion last year. Metromedia International stock faring poorly, but Kluge optimistic: "I'm forever raising the high bar and breaking my neck to clear it." Converted to Catholicism before third marriage to former model 1981. Divorced 1990. 10,000-acre Virginia estate boasts vintage carriage museum, working farm (profitable). Sold castle in Scotland to preservationists. Substantial art collection. Gave $110 million to Columbia for minority scholarships. Bootstraps every new acquisition: "The tighter you make things, the more people control costs." Member since 1982.

OVER $4,000,000,000

Lawrence J. Ellison

$6 billion
Oracle Corp. Atherton, Calif. 52.
Thrice divorced, 2 children.

Brash CEO pushing $500 network computers, stirring cyclical rumors he may buy friend Steve Jobs' *(see p. 250)* old Apple Computer. Investing with Michael Milken *(see p. 216)* in Education Technology partnership. Building $40 million authentic Japanese compound Woodside, Calif. Grew up Chicago's South Side; U. of Illinois dropout. "To quote Woody Allen, I had a real problem with authority." To Silicon Valley; worked at Amdahl: helped develop first IBM-compatible mainframe. To Ampex 1973. Began Oracle 1977 with $1,850 in small office in Santa Clara with Robert Miner (d. 1994; *see family*). Saw IBM study on new computer language for databases, beat IBM to market. Big success; went public. Pushed sales numbers too hard; Oracle stock collapsed 1990. Brought in high-powered outside management. Cut costs, refocused on quality; came out with industry-hailed Oracle 7. Now wants to provide interactive TV with monstrous database systems needed to archive video-on-demand. Majority owner NCube, computer hardware company. On arch-foe Bill Gates: "Microsoft is trying to create a proprietary network. We're going to provide a nonproprietary, video-enabled network." Gave up surfing, cycling for basketball after breaking ribs, elbow and neck. Heavy into sailboat racing. Now flying: owns $3 million Swiss military trainer, buying supersonic jet fighter. Jokes: "I must be desperately going through a midlife crisis. It's different from having your hair dyed black." Detective helped find natural mother. Member since 1986.

Philip Hampson Knight

$5.3 billion
Nike. Beaverton, Ore. 58.
Married, 2 children.

Explosive brand-name growth: Nike shares have more than quadrupled since January 1994. U. of Oregon track star, Stanford M.B.A.; wrote marketing paper on potential of manufacturing athletic shoes in Far East. Price Waterhouse CPA; moonlighted importing Japanese running shoes with former college track coach Bill Bowerman: "part genius, part madman, the best coach I ever had." Started making own shoes 1971. Bowerman, 85, designed famous "waffle sole" 1972: poured latex into wife's waffle iron. Paid grad student $35 for now ubiquitous "Swoosh" logo design. IPO 1980. Advertising blitz—then archrival Reebok introduced women's aerobic shoe. "We can't take our eye off the ball, because if we lose it, we'll have a bitch of a time getting it back." Got it back with "Just Do It" slogan, multimillion-dollar endorsements from Michael Jordan, Andre Agassi, Monica Seles, etc. Reebok (see Fireman) now fumbling in number two spot. Invaded apparel and accessories industry; passed on 1996 Olympic sponsorship, but high-profile TV blitz stole thunder from Olympic licensee Reebok. Largest customer: Footlocker. All of the footwear except the Cole Haan label is produced primarily in Asia; accused of operating sweatshops. Average cost for pair of Nikes: $63. Opened 6 Nike Town stores: part sports shrine, part retail. Avid runner, tennis player, fiercely competitive. Swoosh logo tattooed on left calf. Member since 1982.

Helen Robson Walton

Bentonville, Ark. 77.
Widowed, 4 children.

S. Robson Walton

Bentonville, Ark. 52.
Divorced, remarried; 5 children.

John T. Walton

Durango, Colo. 50.
Married, 1 child.

Jim C. Walton

Bentonville, Ark. 48.
Married, 4 children.

Alice Louise Walton

Rogers, Ark. 47
Divorced twice, no children.
$23.6 billion family fortune.
Wal-Mart Stores.

Widow and children of Wal-Mart founder Sam Walton (d. 1992). Young Sam started Ben Franklin five-and-dime store before opening first Wal-Mart, Rogers, Ark. 1962. Small-town discount store chain thrived in rural America. IPO 1970. Today largest U.S. retailer, with over 2, 200 stores and $95 billion in sales. Now biggest U.S. grocer after Kroger. Pressure to retain high growth rates took company into foreign territory: Canada, Latin America, Asia; also upper-middle-class American suburbs. Now balancing famed down-home image with high-end hopes of attracting affluent, value-minded customers. Sold photofinishing operations to Fuji Photo Film U.S. 1996. Wealth held in family partnership. Matriarch Helen: high school valedictorian, U. of Oklahoma graduate. S. Robson: Columbia Law grad, Wal-Mart chair and first company lawyer. "I probably wouldn't be effective if I tried to be [like Sam]." Ironman triathlete, Hawaii 1985. John T.: Vietnam veteran, former head of sailboat manufacturer Cosair Marine, Inc. Chairs global positioning systems manufacturer Satloc, Inc. Second Wal-Mart company pilot. VP of family investment partnership, Walton Enterprises. Jim C.: Walton Enterprises president, majority stockholder Community Publishers Inc. Alice L.: Trinity U. graduate, briefly a Wal-Mart buyer. Founded investment firm Llama Co. 1989. Former broker for E.F. Hutton: "This whole region gets left out by Wall Street and the money center banks." Members since 1989.

Samuel Irving Newhouse Jr.

$4.5 billion
Media. New York City. 68.
Divorced, remarried; 3 children.

Donald Edward Newhouse

$4.5 billion
Media. New York City. 66.
Married, 3 children.

Two sons of father Samuel Sr., ambitious journalist born to Eastern European immigrant parents. Ran *Bayonne (N.J.) Times* age 16, took over *Staten Island Advance* 1922. Tough distributor, cost-cutter; shunned unions. Built nation's largest private newspaper chain. Acquired magazine publisher Condé Nast 1959. Si Jr., brother Don took over on father's death 1979; beat IRS in huge estate tax case. Advance Publications now 29 newspapers (circulation: 3 million); 15 magazines (*Vanity Fair, New Yorker, Vogue* et al.); Random House (book publishing); cable TV (1.8 million subscribers); programming (Lifetime, The Learning Channel). Si: chairman, Advance Publications. At desk by 5 a.m. Shocked literary world when he moved *Vanity Fair*'s Tina Brown to editorship of *New Yorker;* new life into old book. Plans to launch first new title in almost 10 years: women's sports magazine to debut 1997. Record year for Random House: bestsellers by Oprah Winfrey *(see pp. 262 and 310)*, Michael Crichton, Colin Powell, the Pope. Don: Advance Publications president. Oversees newspapers, cable television operations. Brothers share fortune worth at least $9 billion. Members since 1982.

OVER $3,500,000,000

Barbara Cox Anthony

$4 billion
Newspapers, cable TV. Honolulu. 73.
Married, 2 children.

Anne Cox Chambers

$4 billion
Newspapers, cable TV. Atlanta. 76.
Twice divorced, 3 children.

Daughters of James Cox, poor farm boy, later teacher who bought *Dayton (Ohio) Daily News* 1898 for $26,000. Won 3 terms Ohio governorship; failed presidential bid 1920 (FDR his running mate) against Warren Harding. Left politics, bought *Atlanta Journal* 1939; *Atlanta Constitution* 1950. Merged. Now flagship paper Cox Enterprises. Died 1957. Brother James Jr. took over, moved into cable TV. James died 1974. Sisters have 98%. Control ceded to Barbara's husband, Garner Anthony, then in 1988 to Barbara's son by earlier marriage, James C. Kennedy, 48. Today privately owned Cox Enterprises: 18 dailies, 7 weeklies. Spun off cable systems as Cox Communications 1995: over 3 million cable subscribers; programming (The Discovery Channel, The Learning Channel, E! Entertainment). Sisters own Manheim Auctions, the world's largest car auction. Barbara: chairwoman Dayton papers; ranch in Australia; avoids press. Anne: Atlanta socialite; former ambassador to Belgium under Carter; Democratic Party giver. Chairwoman Atlanta papers. With families, sisters share fortune worth more than $8 billion. Members since 1982.

Ronald Owen Perelman

$4 billion
Investments. New York City. 53.
Twice divorced, remarried; 6 children.

More thumping from Perelman's investment machine MacAndrews &
Forbes: takes public Revlon, Consolidated Cigar; agrees to sell New World
Communications Group to Rupert Murdoch for $2.5 billion in July. Moves
ease debt load, but Marvel Comics stake down $500 million since last
year. Got start early: helped father in Philadelphia metal-fabricating business; then Wharton. First used debt in $1.9 million deal to buy minority
interest in jewelry distributor 1978; built into highly leveraged conglomerate with financing from Drexel Burnham. Concept: buy undervalued
assets with leverage, divest unwanted operations, use remaining cash
flows to bag bigger game. Bagged Revlon for $3 billion 1985, failed in $4.1
billion Gillette bid. Bought Marvel Comics, outdoor-equipment leader
Coleman Co., National Health Laboratories, First Gibraltar S&L, etc. Created New World Communications for television station, programming
assets 1994. After Murdoch invested $500 million, jolted television indus-
try when stations switched affiliation to Fox from CBS. Obsessive, frequent corporate restructurings for tax benefits. Cigar smoker, surrounds
himself with bodyguards. Now suing third wife Patricia Duff for divorce.
Member since 1987.

Gordon Earle Moore

$3.7 billion
Intel Corp. Woodside, Calif. 67.
Married, 2 children.

He of 1965 "Moore's Law": that power of microchips would double every
12 months (revised up to 18 months) with proportionate cost decreases.
Born San Francisco. UC Berkeley, Caltech Ph.D. 1954. He expected to join
academia, instead he became an "accidental entrepreneur." Briefly
researched weapons propulsion at Johns Hopkins before joining Shock-
ley Semiconductor as a research chemist. Cofounded Fairchild Semiconductor Corp. in 1957, developed first integrated circuit. "We had no
idea at all that [this] was going to be a $100 billion business." Cofounded
Intel 1968 with the late Robert Noyce. Developed world's first micropro-
cessor 1971. Today Intel rules the semiconductor industry with aggressive pricing, smart marketing, increasingly powerful chips and huge
capital investment. Says Harvard's business historian Alfred Chandler
about Intel: "That is where the great fortunes always come from, with
economies of scale. No one can compete because the barriers to entry
are there. That is what the Fords did, what Rockefeller did and what

Carnegie did." Moore and his wife recently gave $15 million to Berkeley. He still owns over 5% of Intel stock. Member since 1982.

Walter Hubert Annenberg

$3.7 billion
Publishing. Wynnewood, Pa. 88 .
Divorced, remarried; 1 daughter (1 son deceased).

America's greatest living philanthropist. Gave $365 million 1993 to 4 schools: Peddie School (he prepped there), USC, U. of Penn., Harvard; following year gave $500 million to spur public education reform. "Just to pile up money for my own sake—I can't view that as good citizenship." Son of Moses Annenberg (d. 1942), founder of what became Triangle Publications (*Philadelphia Inquirer, Daily Racing Form*). Walter took over debt-ridden company age 32, turned it around, expanded. Home run: took *TV Guide* national 1953, eventually largest circulation of any magazine in U.S. Later *Seventeen, Good Food.* Sold *Inquirer* to Knight-Ridder 1970. Nixon's ambassador to Great Britain 1969-74. Sold Triangle for top dollar to Rupert Murdoch *(see p. 125)* in 1988, the resulting debt burden nearly busting Murdoch. Major impressionist art collection worth near $1 billion. Appraiser: "Probably $200 million in van Goghs and another $100 million in Gauguins. You're halfway there before you start looking at the Monets and so on." Art will go to Metropolitan Museum of Art in New York City upon death. Still playing the market; big investments in banks paying handsomely: Walter's Wells Fargo stock up 40% in last year. "I like to sit, sit, sit with securities I believe in." Other Annenberg family heirs share estimated $800 million. Member since 1982.

Steven Anthony Ballmer

$3.7 billion
Microsoft. Bellevue, Wash. 40.
Married, 2 children.

Son of Swiss immigrant who worked 30 years at Ford Motor. Steven met Bill Gates at Harvard; studied economics, applied math; unlike Bill, he graduated. Worked at Procter & Gamble; assistant product manager. Left for Stanford business school, dropped out 1980 to join Gates at Microsoft; first nonprogrammer hired. Ran product development center: user education, marketing, testing of systems software. Conceived of innovative, brain-teaser recruitment questions like "How many gas stations are there in the U.S.?" Says, "They don't have to get the right answer. But I want to see how they go through the process." Enjoys spotlight: style called "engagingly direct, the decibel count unusually high." Blew out vocal cords at company meeting 1991; required surgery afterwards. Now executive VP worldwide sales and support. Runs 10 miles a day; shoots hoops. Currently owns 5.1% Microsoft. Member since 1990.

OVER $3,000,000,000

Kirk Kerkorian

$3.4 billion
Investments. Las Vegas. 79.
Twice divorced, 2 children.

Third time need not be a charm: just agreed to buy MGM for $1.3 billion from Crédit Lyonnais, having bought and sold the film studio twice before at huge profits. Son of Armenian immigrant fruit farmer. Junior high dropout, lightweight amateur boxer; trained U.S. fighter pilots, RAF, WWII. Flew surplus Air Force planes across Atlantic after war, built charter airline; sold for $104 million profit 1966. First takeover: $82 million for 40% MGM 1969. Added United Artists 1981; sold combined companies to Ted Turner for $1.5 billion 1986. Strapped for cash, Turner stripped out film broadcast rights, sold most assets back 5 months later for $480 million. Kirk resold all to Pathé for over $1.3 billion 1990. MGM sued for $750 million; Kerkorian countersued; won. Befriended Lee Iacocca, started buying Chrysler shares 1991; takeover threat 1994 blocked by management. Ended proxy fight; holds nearly 14% worth some $3 billion. Also 72% MGM Grand: hotels, casinos, luxury airline, billion-dollar Las Vegas theme park. Last time drew salary: $35,000 in 1966. Member since 1982.

Sumner Murray Redstone

$3.4 billion
Viacom Inc. Newton Centre, Mass. 73.
Married, 2 children.

Sacked longtime partner, Viacom chief Frank Biondi, in January. Took over as CEO, immediately struck $1.8 billion distribution deal with German media giant KirchGroup. Son of drive-in theater owner. Graduated Harvard Law 1947. Practiced law; joined father's theater business 1954. Built into National Amusements Inc.; today over 1,000 screens in U.S. and U.K. Survived 1979 Boston hotel fire by hanging from third-story window ledge; flames seared hand. Reaped big gains in 1980s as investor in Twentieth Century Fox, Columbia Pictures and MGM/UA. Acquired Viacom in $3.2 billion leveraged buyout 1987. Took public next day at profit: net worth nearly tripled. Battled with John Kluge *(see p. 117)* for Orion Pictures 1988. Luckily lost: Viacom took $18 million profit; Orion went bankrupt. Acquired Paramount Communications, Blockbuster 1994. Sold off Madison Square Garden, N.Y. (basketball) Knicks and (hockey) Rangers, cable TV systems to reduce still-huge debt. Age no deterrent: "If Dole thinks he can run America, I can run Viacom." But Viacom stock down 36% past year, cutting Redstone's net worth by $1.4 billion. Member since 1982.

Henry Ross Perot

$3.3 billion
Computer services. Dallas. 66.
Married; 4 daughters, 1 son.

Dallas demagogue's political stock down from 1992—not even fellow Reform Party member Richard Lamm supports him. But net worth up sharply: Perot Systems, 25% owned by Ross via grandchildren's trust, signed megadeal to handle Swiss Bank's data processing; doubled revenues over-night, now near $700 million. Son of East Texas horse trader. Eagle Scout. Annapolis; left Navy after 4 years for sales job with IBM, once filled annual sales quota in 19 days. Saw opportunity in data processing, but IBM wouldn't sell services, so founded Electronic Data Systems 1962. Billionaire in EDS stock by 1969; net worth plunged with stock 1970; recovered over the years: sold to General Motors 1984 for $1 billion cash, stock. Thorn in GM's side as gadfly director, bought out by company for $700 million 1986. Founded data processing company Perot Systems 1988 day after noncompete agreement with GM expired. During Iranian hostage crisis 1979 ran jailbreak rescue of 2 EDS employees, smuggling them 550 miles to Turkish border. Founded populist third party political group United We Stand America, ran on Independent ticket for President 1992, divided Republican voters, won 19% of vote. Running again 1996 on Reform Party ticket. Billions of dollars in tax-exempt bonds throwing off interest. Son Ross Jr., 37, overseeing family's huge real estate ventures, including Alliance airport, outside Fort Worth. Member since 1982.

Keith Rupert Murdoch

$3.2 billion
News Corp. Australia; London; NYC. 65.
Divorced, remarried; 4 children.

Father, Sir Keith, highly regarded editor *Melbourne Herald.* Rupert worked on London's Fleet Street after graduating Oxford 1952. Took over *Adelaide News* at 23; developed knack for tabloid headlines: "Queen Eats a Rat." Bought *Sydney Daily Mirror* 1960; expanded into TV, magazines, books. Purchased U.K. publications; to U.S. 1974. Bought Twentieth Century Fox 1985, 7 Metromedia television stations 1986; built Fox TV network. Paid Walter Annenberg (see p. 123) $3.2 billion for *TV Guide,* others, 1988. Climbed out of near-deadly debt hole 1990-91 by refinancing, selling equity. Repurchased *New York Post* out of bankruptcy 1993, squeezed unions for concessions. Also 1993: bought 63.3% Star TV, Hong Kong satellite network spanning Asia. In the U.S., grabbed broadcast rights to NFL football from CBS. Grooming son Lachlan, daughter Elizabeth, for top spots in worldwide media empire. Youngest son James started Rawkus Entertainment; acts include Motor Baby, Plastique and Whorgasm. Murdoch naturalized U.S. citizen 1985, owns roughly 30% of News Corp. Member since 1985.

Richard Marvin DeVos

$3.2 billion
Amway Corp. Ada, Mich. 70.
Married, 4 children.

Jay Van Andel

$3.2 billion
Amway Corp. Ada, Mich. 72.
Married, 4 children.

DeVos and Van Andel's global cosmetics machine also a national political player: bought cable coverage for GOP convention in August, spent millions on 1994 congressional campaigns. Several Amway distributors members of Congress. Partners were next-door neighbors, high school pals. Developed vitamin distribution system after WWII, started Amway in basements 1959. Bought distribution rights for biodegradable soap from broke Detroit chemist, sold enough in 2 years to open Grand Rapids plant. Now 2.5 million distributors selling nearly 7,000 Amway and brand-name products person-to-person in 64 countries. Company attracts salespeople with free-enterprise credo; distributors do recruiting, collect commissions on salespeople's take. Known to play hardball: lost $75,000 suit by Procter & Gamble for spreading damaging rumors. FTC investigation into pyramid scheme allegations 1979 went nowhere. Amway says sales up nearly 20% in last year, over $6 billion gross. Moved into People's Republic of China 1994 with public Amway Asia Pacific; also owns most of Amway Japan Ltd. Founders giving way to new guard: DeVos handed presidency to son Dick, 40, in 1992. Van Andel replaced as chairman by son Steve, 41. DeVos' Orlando (basketball) Magic lost superstar Shaquille O'Neal when LA Lakers offered more than $120 million. First appeared on list 1982.

Peter E. Haas Sr.

$3.1 billion
Inheritance. San Francisco. 77.
Divorced, remarried; 2 children.

Peter E. Haas Jr.

$1.2 billion
Inheritance. San Francisco. 48.
Married.

Frances Koshland Geballe

$1.2 billion
Inheritance. San Francisco. 75.
Married, 3 children.

Josephine B. Haas

$1.2 billion
Inheritance. San Francisco. 82.
Divorced, 2 children.

Robert Douglas Haas

$1.1 billion
Inheritance. San Francisco. 54.
Married, 1 child.

Daniel E. Koshland Jr.

$795 million
Inheritance. San Francisco. 76.
Married, 1 child.

Margaret E. Haas

$770 million
Inheritance. San Francisco. 41.
Divorced.

With families, heirs to Levi Strauss fortune. Fearing excess profits taxation, family executed LBO February 1996 on top of previously LBO'd company. Restructuring led by CEO Robert D. Haas, great-great-grandnephew of Levi Strauss. Family squabble ensued. Family of Rhoda Haas Goldman (d. 1996) cashed out. Remainder of shares owned by some 200 descendants placed in 15-year voting trust controlled by Haas families. Prescient move: another blockbuster year for Levi—over $700 million earnings on sales of $6.7 billion, due largely to sales of flagship 501 Blues. New Levi entity: LSAI Holding Corp. Founder Levi Strauss emigrated from Bavaria during California gold rush, started company 1850;

sold '49ers pants made of tent canvas; patented denim version, copper riveting technique 1873. Died bachelor 1902, left company to 4 nephews. Walter A. Haas Sr. (d. 1979) married Strauss' grandniece, ran company 1928–55. Son Peter Sr., Harvard M.B.A., joined to handle finance, operations; president 1970–81. Now chairs executive committee. Gives to Jewish causes, Smithsonian, United Way. Peter Sr.'s brother Walter Jr. (d. 1995) president 1958–70, took company public 1971. Retired 1981; honorary chair at death. His son Robert D., U.C. Berkeley, Peace Corps, Harvard M.B.A., took company private again 1985 in $1.7 billion LBO; nearly tripled revenues, paid debt early. Spending $850 million upgrading company's systems to provide quicker distribution, replenishment of merchandise. Capitalized on Levis' mystique abroad; now foreign sales half of total revenues. Josephine and ex-husband Peter Sr. share control of some Levi equity. Their son Peter Jr. is corporate foundation director; daughter Margaret Haas owns auto-racing team. Daniel E. Koshland Jr., retired editor of Science magazine and sister, Frances (Sissy) Geballe, children of Daniel Koshland Sr., brother-in-law to Walter A. Haas Sr. Today world's largest apparel firm; benefiting from casual-look trend. New incentive plan: every employee gets bonus equal to year's pay if company cash flow target is met by 2001. First appeared on list 1991.

Forrest Edward Mars Sr.

$3 billion
Candy. Miami. 92.
Widowed, 3 children.

Forrest Edward Mars Jr.

$3 billion
Candy. McLean, Va. 65.
Married, 4 daughters.

John Franklyn Mars

$3 billion
Candy. Arlington, Va. 60.
Married, 2 children.

Jacqueline Mars Vogel

$3 billion
Candy. Bedminster, N.J. 57.
Twice divorced, 3 children.

Father, 2 sons and daughter. Super-secretive candy giant Mars, Inc. continues push overseas; opens manufacturing plant Stupino, Russia in May. Company started 1911 by Forrest Sr.'s parents, Frank and Ethel; struck pay dirt 1923 after young Forrest suggested candy bar based on chocolate malted milk drink: Milky Way. Malt-flavored nougat became cornerstone of subsequent Mars bars, including Snickers, 3 Musketeers. Forrest Sr.: Built candy empire in Europe after falling out with father; returned to U.S. after father's death 1934. Developed M&Ms after seeing soldiers eating candy-coated chocolate drops in Spanish Civil War. Bought out family 1964, built one of world's largest candy companies, pet food makers (Whiskas, Kal Kan). Added snack and prepared foods, Uncle Ben's Rice et al. Retired 1973; runs Ethel M, fine-chocolate firm Las Vegas. Forrest Jr.: Established company's Dutch unit 1960s; now copresident. Advanced notion of candy as energy food, added granola bars, noncandy snacks. John: Set up Australian operations; now copresident. Jacqueline: victorious in recent divorce from Hank Vogel, who tried getting piece of Mars. Four share company worth over $12 billion.

Jay Arthur Pritzker

$3 billion
Finance, hotels. Chicago. 74.
Married, 4 children.

Robert Alan Pritzker

$3 billion
Finance, hotels. Chicago. 70.
Twice divorced, remarried; 5 children.

Brothers. Grandfather Nicholas emigrated from Russia to Chicago 1881; started law firm 1902; joined by 3 sons: firm still Pritzker & Pritzker. One son, Abram, diversified into real estate, light manufacturing late 1930s; died 1986. Lawyers minimized estate taxes so well IRS pressed for $53 million; settled. Sons increased holdings. Jay: Lawyer by education, financial wizard; used father's credit to finance early deals. Started Hyatt hotels 1957. Brother Donald (d. 1972) ran chain for years. Jay's son Thomas now in charge, expanding company. Donald's daughter Penny runs Hyatt's luxury retirement centers. Partnered with Donald Trump in NYC's Grand Hyatt. Family backed unsuccessful run on RJR Nabisco, lost to KKR. Robert: family engineer, runs 60-plus manufacturing, service companies through Marmon Group. Investments in Ticketmaster, Royal Caribbean Cruises, real estate, etc. With families, share fortune worth over $6 billion. Members since 1982.

OVER $2,500,000,000

William Redington Hewlett

$2.9 billion
Hewlett-Packard. Portola Valley, Calif. 83.
Widowed, remarried; 5 children, 5 stepchildren.

Longtime friend and partner David Packard died March 1996. Co-founders started HP in Palo Alto garage, now considered birthplace of Silicon Valley. Company name determined by coin toss. Hewlett: dyslexic, excelled in science/mathematics; focused on research. Designed first HP product, audio oscillator, as MIT grad school student. Sold 8 to Walt Disney for *Fantasia*. Lesser-known products: bowling alley foul-line indicator, automatic urinal flusher, weight-loss shock machine. Initial $538 capital investment; now $44 billion market cap. Left HP to serve WWII Army. Headed electronics section of War Dept. Special Staff; inspected Japanese industry after war. Returned to HP as VP. Rapid growth 1950s. IPO 1957. Father of pocket calculator: "I told the guys they ought to design a calculator to fit in my shirt pocket, so they came and measured my pocket." President 1964. Retired as CEO 1978, vice chair of board 1987. With Packard returned to company 1990 to fight bureaucracy; decentralized operations; increased sales by $6 billion in fiscal year 1995. Leading philanthropists: duo donated more than $300 million to Stanford University; gave $25 million for Stanford faculty fund research in honor of Frederick Terman, professor and mentor to both. "[Stanford] would not be the place it is without these two guys." But modest: No Stanford building bears either name. Member since 1982.

Edgar Miles Bronfman

$2.7 billion
The Seagram Co. Ltd. New York City. 67.
Married (4 marriages, 3 wives); 7 children.

With spirits market shrinking, Seagram expands into beer; ends industry-imposed moratorium on television liquor advertising. Father Sam refugee from czarist Russia to Canada 1889. Formed Distillers Corp., Montreal 1924. Acquired Joseph E. Seagram & Sons of Waterloo, Ont. Prospered along U.S. border during Prohibition; continued success after repeal. Holdings split among 4 children when Sam died 1971. Edgar M. (sole U.S. citizen among siblings) got U.S. branch, and brother, Charles R., Canadian post. Edgar established international distribution network for Seagram. Current chairman. Acquired Tropicana Products 1988, Dole worldwide juice business 1995. Son Edgar Jr., 41, current chief executive, steered investments toward entertainment: 80% MCA from Matsushita 1995 for $5.7 billion; 50% Interscope Records from Ted Field *(see p. 173)* 1996. Also 15% Time Warner. Plans to open new Universal theme parks in Florida and Osaka, Japan. Distribution agreement with DreamWorks SKG. Older brother Sam, 42, president Seagram Classics Wine Co. Younger brother Matthew, 37, cofounded Perfumes Isabell. Edgar M. president World Jewish Congress. Member since 1983.

Samuel Curtis Johnson

$2.6 billion
S.C. Johnson & Son. Racine, Wis. 68.
Married, 4 children.

Fourth-generation family business; still growing: $4 billion 1995 revenues, up $200 million from year before. Great-grandfather, parquet flooring salesman, founded famous floor-wax firm 1886. Sam, fourth generation, new products director 1955; encouraged non-Johnson's Wax items (Raid, Glade, Edge), now among company's most profitable lines. Expanded and contracted 1993: bought Drackett division of Bristol-Myers Squibb (Windex, Vanish, Drano) for $1.15 billion, sold parts of personal care products line (Cure, Agree). "They realized they were better at making household products than hair products." Very private about profitability, but took sideline company Johnson Worldwide Associates (outdoor recreation equipment) public 1987; family wanted liquidity. Also majority interest Johnson International (bank holding company, assets $1 billion). Sam's 4 children active in S.C. Johnson & Son: Curt, 41, VP global business development; Helen, 39, executive VP Johnson Worldwide Associates; Fisk, 38, home care business, consumer products North America; Winifred, 37, part-time public relations, also investor in Windmark music studio. Sam enjoys nature photography, flying planes, controls 60% of family company. Member since 1982.

Henry Lea Hillman

$2.6 billion
Industrialist, real estate. Pittsburgh. 77.
Married, 4 children.

Reserved son of fiery coal/steel/gas tycoon John Hartwell Hillman Jr., who followed lead of other Pittsburgh industrialists Carnegie and Mellon, built Pittsburgh Coke & Chemical, Texas Gas Transmission, etc. After Princeton, Henry joined business 1945, assumed control on father's death in 1959: "I'm not a table pounder, and he was." Bought out 5 siblings (now deceased). Sold smokestack assets, diversified into real estate, light industry. "When times change, you have to change." Holdings estimated $300 million 1969. Likes science, high tech; invested heavily in Silicon

Valley 1970s; now medical technology companies like Perrigo Co. Backed leveraged buyout shops like Kohlberg Kravis Roberts; later his own Exide Corp. Real estate holdings spanned nation, but sold 4.5 million square feet to Goldman, Sachs affiliate in $450 million deal 1994. Now said to be vying for Texas oil and gas reserves through Broughton Associates, joint venture of the Hillman Co. and smaller SK Resources. Wife, Elsie, a leading Republican. Henry owns 80% Hillman Co. empire; stepbrothers, Howard and Tatnall, own rest. Member since 1982.

OVER $2,000,000,000

George Soros

$2.5 billion
Money manager. London; NYC. 66.
Divorced, remarried; 5 children.

After lackluster 1994, early 1995, Soros and top fund manager Stanley Druckenmiller *(see p. 198)* swing heavily into U.S. securities. "They were buying up everything." Overall returns may be as much as 30% per annum. Hungarian-born, hid from Nazis in family attic. To London after war, London School of Economics; Wall Street analyst 1956, advised Americans on Europe after formation of European Common Market 1957: ". . . for a brief period I ruled as a one-eyed king among the blind." Spent 1963-66 revising never-published *The Burden of Consciousness*. Then Quantum Fund: Curaçao-based hedge fund 1969; brilliant long-term record. Currency speculator: the man who "broke" the British pound, forcing U.K. out of European exchange rate mechanism 1992; made $1 billion. Recovered from $600 million loss betting against yen early 1994. Considers Karl Popper a mentor. Substantially handed over fund investment to right-hand man Druckenmiller 1989; performance improved: "I became the coach, he became the competitor." Childhood belief he was God persisted into adulthood. In all seriousness: "It is a sort of disease when you consider yourself some kind of god, the creator of everything, but I feel comfortable about it now since I began to live it out." Claims to be giving away more than $300 million a year toward open society in Eastern Europe; also U.S. causes: drug policies, inner-city problems, people with fatal diseases. Advocates marijuana legalization for medical purposes. Member since 1986.

Abigail Johnson and family

$2.5 billion.
Fidelity Investments. Boston. 34.
Married, 1 daughter.

Edward Crosby Johnson III

$1.3 billion
Fidelity Investments. Boston. 66.
Married, 3 children.

Father and daughter. Humongous "pace car" of mutual fund industry with over $450 billion under management. Flagship Magellan Fund slipping a bit after departures of managers Peter Lynch and Jeffrey Vinik. Fidelity still worth at least $10 billion. Ned's father, Edward II, lawyer, acquired failing Fidelity Management Corp. 1946; built leading mutual fund manager: "The market is like a beautiful woman, always fascinating, always mystifying." Mr. Johnson excellent stock picker; son Ned, CEO 1972, master marketer. Created mutual fund for every investment strategy. Magellan Fund ($53 billion assets) biggest stock fund. When Charles Schwab & Co. started OneSource (offers no-loads from other fund families), countered with Funds-Network. Also real estate, publishing (suburban Boston newspaper chain, moneylosing *Worth* magazine). Ned cut own Fidelity shares by half 1995, to 12%, for estate planning, much turned over to employees. Principal heir apparent: daughter Abigail, 34, manages Fidelity's $1.2 billion Trend fund, retains 24.5% voting stock. Ned a member since 1985; Abigail since 1995.

Jon Meade Huntsman

$2.5 billion
Chemicals. Salt Lake City. 59.
Married, 9 children, 26 grandchildren.

Acquisition-minded Huntsman fuming over two failed takeover bids: Rexene rejected his $267 million bid in July; Sterling Chemicals, $670 million in April. Cyclical petrochemical margins squeezed, but Huntsman still strong performer. Two-time cancer survivor, Huntsman gave $100 million to cancer research last year. Wharton, USC M.B.A. Started 1965 joint venture in polystyrene egg containers after running in-laws' egg-processing plant. Founded plastic-products company with brother 1968. Company neared bankruptcy, then recovered; sold 1976. Founded Huntsman Chemical with big debt 1982. Sought acquisitions at bargain prices with aggressive leverage at cyclical lows in plastics markets. Bought Texaco's petrochemicals operation 1994 with Australian billionaire Kerry Packer for $1.06 billion; put in $80 million equity, got 80% stake. Recent purchase of Eastman Chemical's polypropylene business added 500 million pounds capacity. Staunch Republican: Nixon aide, Utah chairman Reagan, Bush campaigns. Devout Mormon, eventually intends to give fortune to charity. Member since 1989.

Robert Muse Bass

$2.3 billion
Oil, investments. Fort Worth. 48.
Married, 2 children.

Washington Mutual acquired Bass' largest single holding, American Savings, creating western banking power in July. Bass' continued investment worth $900 million-plus. Formed $1.75 billion investment partnership with Oak Hill Partners in August. Third son of oilman Perry Bass *(see p. 215)*, who expanded oil holdings inherited from tycoon uncle Sid Richardson (d. 1951). Perry stepped down 1968, leaving control to sons Sid, Lee, Edward *(see pp. 135 and 201)*. Eldest, Sid, diversified with help from Richard Rainwater *(see p. 163);* bought into Disney, Texaco, real estate, etc. Robert (Yale, Stanford Business School) felt overshadowed, split off 1983. Sold most of Disney, became major dealmaker: media (held stakes in *St. Petersburg Times,* Continental Broadcasting, Wometco); real estate (sold Plaza Hotel in NYC to Trump for profit); information (stake in Bell & Howell). American Savings, thrift bought from feds 1988, most profitable deal. Led consortium in $1.1 billion leveraged buyout of 8 related food companies (reportedly seeking buyer for troubled Specialty Foods Corp.). Sold Atlanta cable operators Wometco, Georgia Cable to US West for $1.2 billion 1994. Historical preservationist: bought Ulysses S. Grant's Georgetown home for reported $2 million. Gave $20 million gift to Yale in May after university rejected restrictive $20 million gift from younger brother Lee last year. Extremely private: "We seem to have gotten along very well without a lot of publicity." Member since 1983.

Philip Frederick Anschutz

$2.2 billion
Oil, railroads. Denver. 56.
Married, 3 children.

Finally unloaded his Southern Pacific railroad to Union Pacific September. Still laying fiber-optic network alongside rails to take on AT&T, MCI, others. Kansas native; B.S. from U. of Kansas 1961. Father Fred (d. 1993) oil rig operator, sold company for $10 million, unknowingly bought ranch on oil-rich land Utah, Wyoming. Struck it big at Anschutz Ranch East in Utah 1970s; one of 50 largest gas fields in U.S. Sold half of mineral rights to Mobil for $500 million 1982; retired debt. Amoco is operator, but family collects 17% royalties. Went into minerals, Denver real estate, stocks (nearly $100 million profit from ITT, Pennwalt). Bought Rio Grande Railroad for $500 million 1984, added Southern Pacific 1988. Two considered among worst-run railroads, but potential for improvement made IPO big hit: SP went public 1993 at $13.50; did secondary in 1994 at $21. Agreed to sell for $25 a share. With partner bought LA (hockey) Kings last year for $113 million; plans to build new team arena downtown LA. With partner bought downtown Denver Tabor Center for $123 million; building new Denver (basketball) Nuggets stadium. Railroad stock alone recently worth over $1 billion. Member since 1982.

Marvin Harold Davis

$2.2 billion
Oil, real estate. Beverly Hills. 71.
Married, 5 children.

A losing player in shareholder fight to kick T. Boone Pickens out of Mesa Inc. Teamed with Dennis Washington *(see p. 158)*, built up Mesa shares, but sold for loss when Richard Rainwater *(see p. 163)* cut white knight deal with Pickens. Davis got into oil after B.S. NYU 1947. Grabbed cheap Rocky Mountain oil leases, nicknamed Mr. Wildcatter. Sold bulk of massive oil operations to Hiram Walker 1981, some to Apache Oil. Still drilling in Argentina, China, south Russia; estimates $1 billion reserves from huge domestic strike last year. Also dealmaker: bought Twentieth Century Fox with fugitive Marc Rich 1981, broke company up, bought Rich's half for $116 million; sold pieces for big profits, including Fox to Rupert Murdoch for $575 million. Real estate operator: bought, sold Pebble Beach resort, Beverly Hills Hotel, Aspen Ski Co. Made money on runs for Northwest, United airlines 1989. Lost money on Spectradyne, pay-per-view provider. Called "tire kicker," walks away from many deals: passed on Lorimar Pictures, MGM/UA Communications, *Los Angeles Herald,* others. Son John movie producer; some winners *(The Firm, Courage Under Fire)*, one colossal bomb *(Waterworld)*. Member since 1982.

Lee Marshall Bass

$2.2 billion
Oil, investments. Fort Worth. 40.
Married.

Sid Richardson Bass

$1.9 billion
Oil, investments. Fort Worth. 53.
Divorced, remarried (to socialite Mercedes Kellogg); 2 children.

Two of four sons of Perry Richardson Bass *(see p. 215)*, who built on oil holdings inherited from oil tycoon uncle Sid Richardson (d. 1951). In 1968 gave reins to eldest son, Sid, newly minted Stanford M.B.A. With brother Lee and Stanford classmate Richard Rainwater *(see p. 163)*, started doing deals 1970. Marathon Oil ($160 million estimated profit), Texaco ($450 million); acquired big Disney stake (with father, shares recently $1.8 billion). Brothers Robert and Edward *(see pp. 134 and 201)* split off 1980s. With father, Perry have taken sizable positions in public companies (e.g., Beckman Instruments, Medical Care America, John Wiley & Sons). Lee graduated Yale, Wharton M.B.A. Red-faced Yale returned Lee's $20 million gift intended for politically incorrect Western Civilization curriculum development last year. Lee has more Disney shares than post-divorce Sid, whose ex, Anne *(see p. 305)*, now worth $400 million. Bass brothers investing together to renovate Fort Worth's historic downtown. Outside Las Vegas, Sid and Lee plan humongous residential community and casino-resort. Reported cost, shared with others: $3 billion to $4 billion. Members since 1982.

Leonard Alan Lauder

$2.1 billion
Estée Lauder Co. New York City. 63.
Married, 2 sons.

Ronald Steven Lauder

$2.1 billion
Estée Lauder Co. New York City. 52.
Married, 2 daughters.

Sons of cosmetics doyenne Estée Lauder. Family ended 50 years of private ownership November by taking cosmetics giant public. Generated centimillions to repay family members' debts to company. Ownership previously transferred from Estée (now in late 80s) to sons. IPO brilliantly constructed to outmaneuver IRS, doubling brothers' net worths. Estée born Josephine Esther Mentzer to Czech-Hungarian immigrants in Queens. Peddled skin creams for uncle, attached her name to several brands. Started company with 4 products 1946; pestered department store buyers until she landed orders. Discovered own strength after snub by wealthy beauty: "I could have helped her, but I didn't. I gave her nothing, and wherever she is, I'm sure her skin looks dreadful." Married Joseph Lauder (d. 1983) after summer resort romance. He: administrator, escort. She: social butterfly, product developer, promoter. Claims to "see" fragrances, consumer trends. Built one of world's largest cosmetics companies: Estée, Clinique, Aramis, Prescriptives, Origins. Leonard: CEO, outspent rivals on R&D, now credited with much of company's growth. Continuing overseas expansion: Russia, Eastern Europe, India, China. Overall sales nearing $3 billion. Wife, Evelyn, a senior executive. Son William running Origins, waiting in wings. Ronald: Republican, left company 1983 to become deputy assistant defense secretary (NATO), ambassador to Austria. Unsuccessful run for mayor NYC 1989, spent estimated $350 per vote; successfully sponsored term limit referendum 1993. Investing in TV, telecommunications ventures in Eastern, Central Europe. Renowned art collector, patron. Members since 1982.

Robert Edward (Ted) Turner

$2.1 billion
Turner Broadcasting System. Roswell, Ga. 57.
Twice divorced, remarried; 5 children.

After lengthy thumb-twiddling by FTC, Turner Broadcasting/Time Warner combo poised to become world's largest media conglomerate, Ted biggest Time Warner stockholder. Attended Brown U.; kicked out for girl in fraternity room, earned degree years later. Worked for father's ailing billboard business. Bought struggling Atlanta TV station 1970; turned into cable superstation TBS 1976. Launched first 24-hour all-news network CNN 1980. Unfazed by Rupert Murdoch's new all-news network challenge: "I'm looking forward to squishing Rupert like a bug." TBS empire now includes TNT, Castle Rock Entertainment, MGM film library, Turner Pictures and New Line Cinema. Also owns Atlanta (basketball) Hawks and 1995 World Series champs Atlanta Braves. Turner Foundation's $150 million endowment to be expanded to $500 million within next year: Green causes, please apply. Also pledged $75 million in stock 1995 to the Citadel, the McCallie School and Brown. Land rich, too: raises 12,000 bison on 6 ranches, including newly acquired 578,000-acre Vermejo Park Ranch, N.M. Married to Hollywood's Jane Fonda. Member since 1982.

Michel Fribourg and family

$2.1 billion
Continental Grain Co. New York City. 83.
Widowed, remarried; 5 children.

Fribourg upped his net worth by nearly $1 billion this year after spinning off his financial services company, ContiFinancial Corp. His ancestors: European grain traders early 1800s. Family founded Continental Grain, Chicago, 1921; immigrated during WWII. Michel intelligence agent U.S. Army. Left service to take over business one year after father's death 1944. For almost 30 years took lead in selling grain to Soviet Union. Diversified into other agribusinesses (poultry, animal feed, hogs, cattle). Formed partnership with Tosco Corp. in petroleum trading company (Continental-Tosco Inc.); since dissolved. Today more than $15 billion revenues, almost all from commodity marketing activities. Also stake in

Overseas Shipholding Group, big shipowner. Son Paul now president, COO; brought in smart outsider Michael Zimmerman, ex-Salomon Brothers, to help diversify. Michel now chairman emeritus, but "He's still here every day." Member since 1982.

George Lucas

$2 billion
Star Wars, special effects. San Rafael, Calif. 52.
Single, 1 child.

Raised on California walnut farm, earned allowance cutting grass. Indifferent high school student; USC film school. Nearly killed in 1962 car crash. Innovative filmmaking caught eye of director Francis Ford Coppola; sponsored Lucas with $777,777 (for luck) to turn student film into futuristic police state flick. Box office so-so, but second movie, *American Graffiti,* grossed $120 million. Realized early that control was key: when negotiating next film gave up large salary for ownership of merchandise, sequels. Smart move: *Star Wars* shattered box office records, made Lucas over $50 million. Next up: *Indiana Jones.* Took 77% of the profits for $100-million-plus gain. Abandoned moviemaking, poured money into digital studio Industrial Light & Magic. Produced special effects for other filmmakers (*E.T.: The Extra-Terrestrial, Forrest Gump, Jurassic Park*), advertisers; commercials now 25% of business. Lives on 4,700-acre Skywalker Ranch. "All studios are going to be exactly like us." First appeared on list 1982.

Charles de Ganahl Koch

$2 billion
Koch Industries, oil services. Wichita. 60.
Married, 2 children.

David Hamilton Koch

$2 billion
Koch Industries, oil services. NYC. 56.
Single.

Brothers. Two sons of Fred Koch (d. 1967), who developed thermal-cracking refining process to extract extra gas from crude 1928; U.S.S.R. early customer. Founding member (1958) John Birch Society—reportedly after seeing Russian friends liquidated. Four sons inherited $250 million (sales) oil marketer; renamed Koch Industries. Charles: "genius" joined Koch after management consulting gig. Three MIT degrees. Workaholic chairman. Bought refinery, then chemicals, pipelines, ranches. Now second-largest (revenues) family-owned U.S. business after Cargill; sales over $20 billion. David joined 1970, executive VP; 1980 Libertarian VP candidate. Broke with party 1983—it was "too radical." Helps fund market-oriented think tank Cato Institute. Bought Jackie Kennedy Onassis' Fifth Avenue apartment for $9.5 million. With Charles gives millions to support antitax measures, tuition vouchers for private schools. Survived USAir crash 1991 (34 killed): "I thought calmly, 'I have had a lot of interesting experiences in my life, and now I am about to have the experience of death.'" Pair drawn into bitter fight 1980 when brothers Fred and William (David's twin) waged palace coup for control of Koch Industries. Dissident brothers *(see p. 198)* took $1 billion 1983, still seeking more. David: "They wanted the cash and they got it. But we got the company." Members since 1982.

Lester Crown and family

$2 billion
Inheritance; industrialist. Wilmette, Ill. 71.
Married, 7 children.

Son of Henry Crown (d. 1990), renowned Chicago financier who created Material Service Corp., building supply firm, with 2 brothers and father 1919. Weathered fierce competition during Depression, gained dominant market share afterward. Career trademark: bold negotiations based on in-depth industry knowledge. Post-WWII acquired large stakes in real estate, stocks. Merged with General Dynamics 1959; sold stock after dispute with GD management. Waited for GD stock to drop, bought, booted management 1960s; turned company around. Family still holds nearly 7 million shares. Lester: Harvard M.B.A., Northwestern U. trustee. Conservative family man. Bought cousins out 1990; still believed to control most of family fortune, much in trusts. Member since 1982.

Donald Leroy Bren

$2 billion
Real estate. Newport Beach, Calif. 64.
Twice divorced; 4 children.

Bought outstanding shares in Irvine Co. June; now owns 100%. Speculation: Bren "unnerved" by stock dumping from outside investors. Days later pledged 21,000 acres for nature preserve; eco establishment (including Bruce Babbitt) attended ceremony. Eldest son of late Hollywood producer Milton Bren; stepson actress Claire Trevor. U. of Washington on ski scholarship; failed Olympic bid 1956. After Marines, built first house on $10,000 loan 1958 (later sold to actress Jane Wyman). Started new home-building company; sold 1970 to International Paper for $34 million; bought back 2 years later for reported $22 million. With Al Taubman, Max Fisher, Herb Allen *(see pp. 242, 250, and 188)* bought Irvine

Ranch, large tracts of land originally bought 1864 by James Irvine, 2 partners. Group paid $337 million 1977, Bren bought out most partners 1983 for $518 million. Minority owners Joan Irvine Smith, mother Athalie Clarke sued; eventually awarded $250 million. Irvine Co. now covers 90 square miles Orange County. Owns office, industrial, retail space; hotels; two 18-hole golf courses. Took public REIT with apartment properties 1993; Irvine retained 61%. Member since 1982.

Martha R. Ingram and family

$2 billion
Inheritance, distribution. Nashville. 61.
Widowed; 3 sons, 1 daughter.

Splitting distribution and shipping juggernaut created by late husband Bronson into 3 companies: $8.6 billion (sales) Ingram Micro, top computer distributor, going public; videocassette distributor, Ingram Entertainment, being run by son David, 33. Sons John, 35, and Orrin, 36, copresidents rest of Ingram Industries, Martha chairman. Bronson Ingram (d. 1995) inherited father's business 1963: oil refining, marketing, barges. With brother Fritz, brought in textbook supplier 1964, started distribution. Brothers built company into $1 billion powerhouse, split up firm after Fritz convicted of bribery 1978: Bronson took barges and books, Fritz served 16 months, held on to oil operations, sustained big losses. Bronson built his part into world's biggest book distributor, added videotapes; later added computers, software. Martha no stranger to business: board member at Baxter International, Weyerhaeuser, First American Corp. Was first woman on board of Nashville Chamber of Commerce 1975. Born Charleston, S.C. As Vassar student, met Princeton grad Bronson on blind date in New York City. Elected chairman Ingram Industries after Bronson's death. Member since 1995.

NEW TO THE FORBES FOUR HUNDRED

James Goodnight

$2 billion
Software. Cary, N.C. 53.
Married, 3 children.

John Sall

$1 billion
Software. Cary, N.C. 48.
Married, 4 children.

Partners. Jim: Son of hardware store owner, exposed to machine programming course N.C. State. Took to it immediately. "One night the light bulb went on, and I said, 'Oh, now I understand everything that's going on.'" Spent year with GE working on ground control system for Apollo space program. Programmed for university through college, teamed with faculty, developed SAS (Statistical Analysis System), software for data-warehousing, mining and analysis. By 1971 had program in place using punch-card computer. SAS Institute now largest private software company in U.S.: $600 million from 15,000 customers. Massive program: 6 million lines of code. Company has campus-like atmosphere: hundreds of acres, full-time doctors, day-care center. Cofounder John: no longer much involvement in SAS. Partners share company worth over $3 billion.

Ray Lee Hunt and family

$2 billion
Inheritance, oil, real estate. Dallas. 53.
Married, 5 children.

Runs fortune for "second family" of legendary Texas oilman H.L. Hunt. Bigamist H.L. legally married Ruth Ray and adopted her kids in 1957 after death of first wife in 1955 (wives long kept secret from each other). Ray's mom: Ruth Ray Hunt. Dallas. 79. Widowed; 4 children. Sister: Ruth Jane. Dallas. 51. Single. Professional Christian speaker-singer. Sister: Swanee. Vienna, Austria. 44. Divorced, remarried. U.S. ambassador; active Bosnia peace process. Supports social causes for mentally ill, poor. Family inherited Hunt Oil Co., etc. 1974, small part of H.L.'s empire. Split from first family, but on civil terms. Ray: turned company around, expanded, while first family, led by Bunker Hunt, sank into bankruptcy as result of silver debacle, oil bust. "Because of the way he spells his last name, Ray's had to earn his respect twice." Conservative money manager but aggressive on oil plays, especially in politically risky areas: hit big time with northern Yemen strike 1984; lucrative field bombed during recent Yemeni civil war but production now fully restored. Also 10% of less risky Beatrice North Sea oilfield. Dallas-Fort Worth real estate, oil refinery, etc. Active in politics, civic affairs. Member since 1982.

Laurence Alan Tisch

$2 billion
Loews Corp. Westchester County, N.Y. 73.
Married, 4 children.

Preston Robert Tisch

$2 billion
Loews Corp. NYC; Harrison, N.Y. 70.
Married, 3 children.

Close-knit brothers sold CBS to Westinghouse Electric Corp. 1995; concentrating on tobacco, insurance. Back in 1946 bought Lakewood, N.J. resort with father; expanded to 12-hotel chain by 1955. Gained control of Loews 1960. Loews' assets now include hotels, Lorillard (tobacco), CNA Financial (insurance), Bulova (watches), Diamond Offshore Drilling (oil), more. 1995 revenues: $18.7 billion. Larry: attended NYU, Harvard Law. Strategic planner. Took control of CBS 1986; accused of tarnishing Tiffany network. Son James S., 43, current Loews president, COO. Robert: U. of Michigan grad, left 20-month Postmaster General stint after negotiating union contract that eluded predecessors for 12 years. Owns 50% N.Y. (football) Giants. Son Jonathan M., 42, son-in-law of Saul Steinberg *(see p. 302)*, Loews Hotels president. Brothers Bob and Larry known for informal management style: first-name, free-flowing communications. Cochairmen and co-CEOs of Loews, together share fortune worth over $4 billion. Many charitable foundations with combined $400 million assets: each family member has one. Members since 1982.

OVER $1,500,000,000

Mary Alice (Dorrance) Malone

$1.9 billion
Campbell Soup. Coatesville, Pa. 46.
Married; 2 children, 2 stepchildren.

Bennett Dorrance

$1.8 billion
Campbell Soup. Paradise Valley, Ariz. 49.
Married, 2 children.

Son and daughter of John Dorrance Jr. Grandfather, Dr. John T. Dorrance, chemist who turned down professorships to work at uncle's Campbell Preserve Co.; invented process for making condensed soup. Bought uncle out 1914. Known for extravagant parties in Roaring Twenties. In Switzerland on vacation 1929, took broker's advice to sell stocks; made it through Crash unscathed. Health deteriorated thanks to heavy drinking, d. 1930. Son Jack (John T. Jr.) inherited $20,000-per-month allowance, drinking problem. Jack accomplished hunter, fisherman;

chairman 1962, but no day-to-day responsibilities. Kids John T. III, Bennett and Mary Alice moved to Switzerland with mother Mary Alice Bennett after 1963 divorce. After Jack's death in 1989, kids united to defeat the family members who wanted to sell Campbell stock; assured family control of company *(see Hamilton et al.)*. Eldest brother John T. III, 52, gave up U.S. citizenship for Irish 1994 to protest high U.S. taxes. Members since 1989.

David Geffen

$1.9 billion
Entertainment. Malibu, Calif. 53.
Single.

Has long claimed great wealth, now is Hollywood's richest guy. As child, learned negotiating skills watching mother run family's Brooklyn-based corset and brassiere business. Quit college, became CBS usher, then receptionist at television production company; fired for being too aggressive. Hustled his way into fabled William Morris mailroom after forging university stationery. Managed music acts, including Laura Nyro, who gave him 50% of her publishing company; sold to CBS; millionaire at age 26. Founded Asylum Records 1970, home to such acts as the Eagles, Linda Ronstadt, Joni Mitchell. Sold 1972 to Warner Communications for $7 million: "The biggest number I could think of." Retired briefly after being misdiagnosed with cancer; returned 1980. Started Geffen Records: Guns N' Roses, Peter Gabriel, Counting Crows. Also movies *(Interview with the Vampire, Beetlejuice, Risky Business)*, Broadway *(Cats, M. Butterfly)*. "The world is presenting itself to people who have cash." Has plenty of it: sold Geffen label to MCA 1990 for stock; netted $710 million when MCA sold to Matsushita. Frequent investor with Richard Rainwater. Formed new entertainment vehicle DreamWorks SKG 1995 with Steven Spielberg and Jeffrey Katzenberg *(see pp. 172 and 305)*; so far little to show for co-investor Paul Allen's near $500 million cash infusion. Past flings with Cher, Marlo Thomas, now active in AIDS causes. Member since 1988.

William Wrigley and family

$1.9 billion
Chewing gum. Chicago; Lake Geneva, Wis. 63.
Twice divorced, remarried; 3 children.

Chewing gum giant Wrigley expanded global empire: new plants in Europe, Asia; $25 million Russian affiliate in the works. Founded by William Wrigley Jr., salesman who came to Chicago 1891 to run father's soap business. Offered baking powder as incentive to buy soap; big hit. Threw in chewing gum as premium for baking powder purchase; bigger hit. Introduced Wrigley's Spearmint Gum 1893; by 1910 America's favorite. Aggressive advertiser: gum mailed to every American in phone book 1915. Succeeded by son Philip Wrigley; now run by grandson William. Today Wrigley's gum sold in over 120 countries; world's largest producer. Products include Doublemint, Juicy Fruit, Freedent. Winter-fresh star performer in U.S. market since 1994 debut. Former owner of Chicago (baseball) Cubs. Member since 1986.

John Richard Simplot and family

$1.9 billion
Potatoes, microchips. Boise, Idaho. 87.
Divorced, remarried; 4 children, 1 deceased.

Simplot's 32 million shares Micron Technology took huge hit last year. Simplot recently sold 7.6 million Micron shares to Canadian Imperial Bank of Commerce. Quit school, left home eighth grade. Sorted potatoes, raised hogs, saved up for first potato field. Became a millionaire by age 30. Company scientist developed freezing process 1950s. Simplot assured fortune when he convinced McDonald's to go with his frozen french fries. "Mr. Spud" now produces nearly 2 billion pounds annually, including 50% of McDonald's fries. Legal troubles: IRS fine 1977 for failing to report $1.3 million income, then caught manipulating Maine potato futures prices; banned from trading for 5 years 1978. Also owns cattle (fed with potato peels), large fertilizer business, meat processing plant, cheese factories, big stake Box Energy, more. "I love America. We've got the only system that works—it keeps everyone hustling." First appeared on list 1982.

Stanley Stub Hubbard

$1.8 billion
Broadcasting. St. Mary's Point, Minn. 63.
Married, 5 children.

Champion of satellite television finally got reward when United States Satellite Broadcasting went public February: his USSB stock alone worth over $1.3 billion. Son of Stanley Eugene Hubbard (d. 1992) who founded nation's first (unsuccessful) commercial airline; built one of first radio stations, WAMD ("Where All Minneapolis Dances"), 1923; added TV 1948. Stanley took charge after father's 1981 stroke. Hubbard Broadcasting now 8 TV stations, 2 radio stations; production co. Early interest in satellite

TV: leased or owned 3 transponders; also controls Conus Communications, satellite news gathering service with 100-plus member stations; developed satellite-borne program syndicator USTV. "The days of 3 people in New York planning the program fare for America are gone." Fortune held in trusts. First appeared on list 1984.

Gordon Peter Getty

$1.7 billion
Inheritance. San Francisco. 62.
Married, 4 sons.

Son of legendary oilman Jean Paul Getty. Joined Getty Oil, rebelled against corporate culture; showed more interest in music than oil. Attended San Francisco's Conservatory of Music 1960s. Became trustee Sarah C. Getty Trust (named for late grandmother), which held 40% of Getty Oil. Touched off Texaco-Pennzoil lawsuit by 1984 sale of Getty Oil to Texaco. Criticized as businessman, but sold business at height of oil prices, doubled family fortune to $3 billion, tripled income. Family suit against him settled 1988, with dissolution into separate trusts run by and for family members *(see other Gettys)*. Still active as composer, conductor; Russian National Orchestra performed his opera, *Plump Jack.* Also writes poetry; has interests in economics, genetics, anthropology. Oversees family trust currently valued at $1.4 billion. Member since 1982.

Theodore W. Waitt

$1.7 billion
Gateway 2000. North Sioux City, S.D. 33.
Married, 2 children.

After decade of direct marketing, Gateway begins selling $3,500-plus TV-PC combo in retail stores. Father Norm Sr. talked young Ted out of joining family cattle business. Ted, U. of Iowa dropout one semester short of degree, started computer mail-order business in Iowa farmhouse with $10,000 bank loan secured by grandmother's CD 1985. Brother Norman *(see p. 202)* joined with $5,000 investment 1986 to cofound Gateway 2000. Blind eye to Silicon Valley and retail market: direct-market PC seller and manufacturer based in South Dakota. First year revenue: $100,000. Staggering growth due to low costs, low prices. Sales now $3.7 billion. Ted: "Business is simple. It is not easy, but it is simple." IPO 1993. Expanded into Western Europe; foreign business now 13% of sales. Computers shipped in Holstein-spotted boxes inspired by family business. Once appeared in company ad as ponytailed janitor. Norm left 1991 amidst tensions with Ted; has since reduced 45% stake to 10%. Member since 1994.

Harry Brakmann Helmsley

Estimated over $1.7 billion
Real estate. New York City. 87.
Divorced, remarried.

Difficult times. Landmark buildings, including Empire State, creak under bad management; longtime Helmsley partners sue wife, Leona, for $40 million fraud; hospitalized for pneumonia 1995; reports (denied) of Alzheimer's disease: "Incapable of coherent conversation." Started in real estate firm mail room 1930s; collected rents. Brokered buildings; reinvested commissions for $1,000 down payment first building 1936. Bought unassuming buildings matching unpretentious manner. First wife Quaker; he converted 1940. Brilliant financial mind; pioneered real estate syndication with late Lawrence Wien. Moved up to prime NYC buildings 1950s; Empire State Building 1961 (since sold). "Money's the great motivator." Today Helmsley partnerships own 100 million sq. ft. commercial space, over 100,000 apartments, 5,000 hotel rooms. Mostly overseen by second wife, Leona, 76, onetime Chesterfield Girl described as having "a stevedore's mouth and the compassion of a cluster bomb." Did 18 months hard time for tax evasion through 1993, plus $8 million fines, restitution; finished sentence in $54-a-night hotel room. Fined $1.1 million for the alleged wrongful termination of an employee; performed only 1 of required 750 hours of community service for tax crimes—employees fulfilled commitment. Tax cheat may have been defrauded herself: personal pilot indicted on charges of stealing $884,000. Helmsley estate rumored to go to Quakers. Member since 1982.

Joan Beverly Kroc

$1.7 billion
Inheritance. Rancho Santa Fe, Calif. 68.
Divorced, widowed; 1 child.

Third wife of Ray Kroc (d. 1984), Chicago milk-shake-machine salesman who built McDonald's Corp. into world's largest fast-food service company. Joan first married at age 17. Worked as professional musician. Met Ray in St. Paul, Minn. 1956: she was performing in restaurant, he was lining up McDonald's franchises. Married 13 years later. Former big political donor; no longer: "I've decided I won't give another nickel to either party." Gives millions instead to children's causes. Donated $60 million to Ronald McDonald Houses 1993, followed by $50 million to Ronald McDonald Children's Charities in memory of her late husband 1995. Also more than $18 million to San Diego Hospice, $3.5 million to San Diego Zoo. "I'm in the prime of my golden years and loving it." Avid reader, animal lover.

Sold 144-foot yacht *Impromptu,* February 1996; bought 36-foot motor home instead. Travels U.S. with 4 granddaughters and Labrador retriever. Member since 1984.

Micky Arison and family

$1.7 billion
Carnival Cruise Lines. Bal Harbor, Fla. 47.
Married, 2 children.

Son of Carnival founder Ted Arison, who left earlier cruise line he founded (now Norwegian Cruise Line) after dispute with partners. Founded Carnival 1972 with 1 mortgaged ship. Micky spent high school summers on dad's ships. Ted worried about nepotism, but another Carnival executive secured Micky sales job. Still only 3 ships when named president 1979. By 1990 sales climbed to $1 billion. Carnival cruises known as floating Magic Kingdoms for adults: gambling, affordable ticket prices, pegged to middle-class wallets and tastes. Micky today commands 22 ships as Carnival CEO. Also hotels, resorts. Ted, now Israeli citizen, 72, retired, transferred majority voting control to son. Micky managing director of Arison family-owned Miami (basketball) Heat; separately owns Carnival Air Lines, formed to serve their Bahamas resort. Deal to merge into old Pan American Air shell collapsed in July. Member since 1995.

Stephen Davison Bechtel Jr.

$1.6 billion
Engineering, construction. San Francisco. 71.
Married, 5 children.

Riley P. Bechtel and family

$1.6 billion
Engineering, construction. San Francisco. 44.
Married, 3 children.

Father and son. One of largest U.S. construction firms. Patriarch Warren Bechtel, Stephen Jr.'s grandfather, headed west from Oklahoma working on railroads; supervised stone-quarrying operation, then bought own steam shovel, founded Bechtel Group. Company built Alaska pipeline, Hoover dam, San Francisco rapid transit (BART). Stephen Jr. took over global firm 1960, made big push into building nuclear facilities: in on 40% of nuclear power plants built in U.S. Continued international heavy construction. Company diversified into real estate, operates small power plants. Bechtel execs in Reagan's Cabinet: George Shultz, Forbes Chairman Caspar Weinberger. Several major projects in Arab countries 1970s. Windfall 1991: won post-Gulf war cleanup of Kuwait; profits jumped 34%. Remodeled U.S. Embassy in Moscow, helping manage $21 billion construction of Hong Kong airport; currently building 330-mile natural gas pipeline Thailand. 1995 revenues up 8%, to $8.5 billion. Riley current CEO. Members since 1982.

Peter M. Nicholas

$1.6 billion
Medical devices. Boston. 55.
Married, 3 children.

John E. Abele

$1.5 billion
Medical devices. Boston area. 59.
Married, 3 children.

Their Boston Scientific on acquisition spree: 9 companies in 18 months. Sales now over $1 billion; 8,500 products offered. Nicholas: Wharton grad, worked at Eli Lilly. Abele sold medical devices. Met at soccer game, cofounded BS in 1979. Abele: "He [Nicholas] is more interested in the deal and the structure. I'm more interested in the vision, if you will—what could happen, what might become." First product: catheters. Now developing devices used for less invasive procedures, reducing costs, trauma for patients. Abele helped establish Association for the Advancement of Medical Instrumentation 1965. Wife a descendant of American saint Elizabeth Ann Seton. Nicholas married to Ruth Virginia Lilly, great-great-granddaughter of pharmaceutical mogul Eli Lilly *(see family)*. Recently donated $20 million to the School of the Environment at Duke University. Members since 1994.

James R. Cargill

$1.5 billion
Cargill, Inc. Minneapolis. 72.
Married, 3 children.

Margaret Cargill

$1.5 billion
Cargill, Inc. La Jolla, Calif. 76.
Single.

Siblings, descendants of William W. Cargill, Long Island-born immigrant's son, moved West 1865, traded grain, quickly surpassed competition. Son-in-law John MacMillan Sr. took over after Cargill's death 1909. Company became world's largest grain trader: Cargill's world market share 25%. Also agricultural commodities, financial services, manufacturing, more. Privately held, but released earnings for first time: $902 million for 1995, up $231 million comparable year before. James: with Cargill since 1947, retired as senior vice president 1990, director 1963-95. Owns Dinnaken Properties, builds housing for University of Minnesota. Expert trout fisherman, owns three J.B. Hudson jewelry stores in Minneapolis. Sister Margaret: never married, reclusive. Whitney MacMillan *(see p. 174)* chairman 1977-95. Control via voting stock believed evenly split among 3 Cargill family branches. Members since 1982.

OVER $1,000,000,000

James LeVoy Sorenson

$1.4 billion
Medical devices. Salt Lake City. 75.
Married, 8 children, 44 grandchildren.

Devout Mormon: "That's what makes Utah so successful." Raised California. Quit medical school 1942 for missionary work; then Maritime Service. Doctor persuaded him to try pharmaceutical sales. Joined Upjohn, moved to Salt Lake City. On side, sold houses; bought, developed real estate; staked uranium claims, sold to penny-stock promoters. Tried medical devices; sold out 1960. Bought lingerie company. Customers include nuns: "There are people out there far beyond Utah who are interested in the elegance of modesty." Back to medical devices. Abbott Labs offer 1980. Bluffing: "Well, I'm building a $100 million company here." Abbott bit, his $100 million stock recently $1.1 billion: "I've never been public. That's why I'm as rich as I am." Helps kids, sons-in-law expand businesses he started. Current favorite: SorensonVision (formerly I.C. Imaging), face-to-face video communication over phone lines. Empire still growing: "Who the hell knows what they're worth these days with so much going on." Member since 1983.

David Rockefeller Sr. and family

$1.4 billion
Inheritance. New York City. 81.
Widowed, 6 children.

Grandson of John D. Rockefeller; youngest of 5 brothers *(see Rockefeller family, Laurance, Winthrop)*. Ph.D. economics. Became international statesman, banker, philanthropist. Founded the Council of the Americas; helped establish the Trilateral Commission, latest favorite target of conspiracy buffs. Led Chase into global expansion; aided the Thais in setting up National Institute for Development Administration; active in mobilizing business behind Nafta. Turned over Rockefeller Financial Services to son David 1992. Still has small piece of Rockefeller Center through Goldman Sachs group that bought it. While not the end of the saga, sale of this family landmark is perhaps the end of an age. Member since 1982.

Harry Wayne Huizenga

$1.4 billion
Entrepreneur, investments. Fort Lauderdale, Fla. 58.
Married, 4 children.

On buying binge: 19 companies in 12 months, including pending $3.4 billion acquisition of security-alarm giant ADT. Back in 1962 bought single used garbage truck; with partner built small trash-hauling operation into waste management behemoth WMX. Resigned 1984. Took over 19-store video-rental chain Blockbuster 1987; built into industry leader. Sold to Viacom for $8.4 billion 1994. Back to garbage: bought Republic Waste 1995 for $27 million; diversified into home security, preowned cars; now Republic Industries. Recently launched Extended Stay America: economy hotel chain offering rooms at $40/night. Occasional failure: had Blockbuster buy into Discovery Zone, chain of children's indoor play centers 1994; Discovery Zone filed for Chapter 11 March. Plans for massive "Wayne's World" Fort Lauderdale theme park collapsed. Owner Miami (football) Dolphins, Florida's (baseball) Marlins, (hockey) Panthers. May be worth well over $1.4 billion. Member since 1991.

NEW TO THE FORBES FOUR HUNDRED

Kenneth Troutt

$1.4 billion
Telecommunications. Dallas. 48.
Married, 2 children.

Raised in Illinois housing project, son of single mother. Capitalist genes: as preteen employed brothers, cousins for lawn-mowing outfit. High school quarterback; partial scholarship to Southern Illinois U. Sold insurance part time; company's top salesman senior year. Lost interest in law school: "Found out that I was good at sales." To Nebraska; started real estate and construction firm; dissolved when interest rates hit 20%. Moved to Dallas 1983 to broker oil; bailed out 1988 when oil prices dropped to $8 a barrel. Vision of perfect company: find product everybody uses; periodic payments after initial sale (like insurance); nonvolatile product (unlike oil). Turned on to telecommunications by accountant brother; started Excel Communications 1988. Avon-like multilevel marketing backbone of company: 500,000 independent sales reps sell long distance telephone service (MCI, WorldCom), recruit new reps. Took public in May at $15; Troutt retained 65%. Revenues first 6 months 1996 over $600 million, stock recently 19½. "We're well oiled."

Maurice Raymond Greenberg

$1.4 billion
American International Group. New York City. 71.
Married, 4 children.

"Hank" chairman of global insurance empire AIG. Resigned from Federal Reserve Bank of New York 1995. Raised on New York dairy farm. Army Ranger WWII: stormed Normandy beach. College, New York Law on G.I. bill. Learned insurance business with Continental Casualty Corp. Joined Cornelius Vander Starr's American International (now AIG) 1960. Starr founded company in Shanghai ("The Paris of the Orient") 1919, became first Westerner to sell insurance to the Chinese. Built into worldwide conglomerate. Rose quickly through AIG ranks, succeeded heirless Starr 1968. Continued aggressive expansion, acquisitions. Pilgrimages to site of Starr's original Shanghai office at least once a year. Nicknamed after Detroit Tigers hero "Hammering Hank" Greenberg. Eldest son, Jeffrey, 44, once heir apparent, left AIG abruptly 1995 after 17 years. Now at Marsh & McLennan; younger son Evan, 41, looking to pick up the slack. AIG now proxy for worldwide economic growth; Greenberg pushing hard internationally, returned to Chinese market 1992: "AIG was the first American insurance organization to enter the newly free countries of Eastern Europe. Change is in the wind, and AIG will be at the forefront of it." First appeared on list 1983.

Alfred Lerner

$1.4 billion
Banking, real estate.
Shaker Heights, Ohio. 63.
Married, 2 children.

Raised in 3 rooms behind father's Queens, N.Y. candy store; Columbia grad 1955; Marines. Earned $75 per week selling furniture. "I was just happy to be making a living." Saved, bought 59-unit Cleveland apartment building 1965. Founded Realty Refund Trust 1971. By 1979 could buy 11,000 Maryland, Pennsylvania apartment units with Andre Meyer (Lazard Frères) for $176 million. Director small Cleveland bank: "Whetted my appetite. I became a student of the banking business." Got control Equitable Bancorp 1981, promised turnaround. Invested $75 million Progressive Corp. (high-risk insurance) 1988; sold 1992, big profit split-adjusted. Merged Equitable with Maryland bank 1989; spun off MBNA 1991 as rescue tactic. Now has 29 million shares MBNA (largest U.S. issuer affinity credit cards), other assets. Recently took 13,000 apartments public via Town & Country REIT. Had interest in Cleveland (football) Browns; played key role in bringing Browns to Baltimore; longtime political and business ties in Baltimore. Now says trying to get new team in Cleveland. Gave $25 million to Columbia U., $10 million to Cleveland Hospital 1993. Wears same Countess Mara ties he wore in 1950s. "I'm no Joe Tycoon." First appeared on list 1988.

Donald Joyce Hall

$1.3 billion
Hallmark Cards. Mission Hills, Kans. 68.
Married, 3 children.

Barbara Hall Marshall

$650 million
Hallmark Cards. Kansas City, Mo. 72.
Widowed, 2 children.

Elizabeth Ann Reid

$650 million
Hallmark Cards. Denton, Tex. 74.
Divorced, 5 children.

Siblings, offspring of founder of greeting card juggernaut that keeps growing. Revenues up 13% in last year. Joyce Hall (d. 1982) preacher's son, started selling postcards 1906, age 15. Later sold holiday cards; buddy Norman Rockwell provided Christmas illustrations. Made card company into household name with advertising blitz 1920s. Beat WWII paper rationing by convincing government his greeting cards were essential to national morale. Insisted on approving card ideas personally. Don took over as CEO 1966, resigned 1986, now chairman. Tough boss ("The worst thing you can do in front of Don Hall is show emotion"), but rewards inventiveness in creative staff of more than 700. Over 11,000 new card designs, 8,000 redesigns a year in 20 languages. Bought Crayola crayonmaker 1984; added television miniseries producer RHI Entertainment 1994 for $365 million. "Good television is good business." Sisters not involved in running company, "just plain Midwest folk who happen to be the progeny of genius." Elizabeth: reclusive Texan. Barbara: design critic. "Looks like any midwestern lady who shops at Saks." These ordinary folk members since 1982.

Ralph Lauren

$1.3 billion
Apparel, home furnishings. New York City. 56.
Married, 3 children.

"I can feel the pulse of the world." Bronx-born son of Russian immigrant, became a billionaire marketing preppy, Waspy fashions. Never finished college, clerked at Brooks Brothers. Started Polo, Inc. 1967 with $50,000. Grows steadily richer by attaching name and image to wider range of goods, often via licensing: Fragrance, boyswear, house paint, etc. Opened flagship Madison Avenue boutique 1986. Bought womenswear license back from Biederman Industries in 1995. Launched Polo Jeans this year; 114 free-standing Polo Ralph Lauren stores. Also does big business in home furnishings. Total retail sales: $5 billion. Goldman, Sachs bought 28% for $135 million in 1994—a steal, apparently, but the capital infusion enabled Lauren to avoid going public. Member since 1986.

Samuel Jayson LeFrak

$1.3 billion
Real estate. New York City. 78.
Married, 4 children.

Joined immigrant father's construction firm after U. of Maryland, took over 1948. With postwar housing shortages, bought forests for lumber; later manufactured own bricks, concrete. Developed over 200,000 apartments, became one of largest U.S. apartment owner/managers (owns 61,000 units, manages another 32,000). "I'm like a farmer, but rather than reap 2 crops a year, I bring in 12 . . . each month when our rents are due." Developed in Brooklyn, Queens, N.Y. (5,000-unit LeFrak City); later Wall Street area (Battery Park City). Building 600-acre, $10 billion Jersey City, N.J. waterfront community, including 1.2-million-square-foot mall with Melvin Simon *(see p. 213)*. Bought 200 oilfields 1994 to build reserves of home heating oil, gas. Also interests in art, entertainment. LeFrak's Golden Rule: "He who has the gold makes the rules." Member since 1982.

Leslie Herbert Wexner

$1.3 billion
The Limited, Inc. New Albany, Ohio. 59.
Married, 2 children.

In move to bolster sagging stock price, the Limited spun off 17% of fast-growing retail division Intimate Brands (Victoria's Secret, Bath & Body Works) 1995. Plans to spin off casual apparel unit Abercrombie & Fitch. Wexner dropped out of Ohio State law school; worked in parents' clothing store. Disagreed on retail strategies; with $5,000 loan from aunt, opened own store specializing in women's sportswear 1963. First-year sales $160,000. Built into national chain; acquired Lane Bryant, Lerner New York, Cacique, Henri Bendel, Structure. Moved into men's apparel after women's market slumped late 1980s. Today more than 5,000 stores, over $7 billion in sales. Secret of success: "Narcissism. It's the key to the business." Decided to lead fuller life after brush with death in summer snowstorm atop Vail Mountain 1981. Married, for first time, 1993. Gives generously to Jewish causes, Columbus development and alma mater OSU. Member since 1982.

Craig O. McCaw

$1.3 billion
Telephony. Bellevue, Wash. 47.
Separated.

Estranged wife, Wendy, demanding half of billion-dollar fortune under Washington State community property laws; unlikely to collect, but already awarded 50% of Craig's AT&T stock options. Craig: graduate of Seattle's Lakeside School; Stanford history major. Father, John Elroy McCaw, early radio and cable TV baron, died 1969, leaving family heavily in debt. Mother one of first women to earn accounting degree at U. of Washington. Craig led brothers Bruce, John and Keith *(see pp. 191 and 173)* in building father's Twin City Cablevision into major cable TV systems operator. Sold cable assets to Jack Kent Cooke *(see p. 186)* for $755 million 1987. Reinvested (with help from Michael Milken, *see p. 216*) in cellular licenses; early partners in Arkansas license included Bill and Hillary Clinton. Became communications powerhouse McCaw Cellular. Sold to AT&T for $11.5 billion stock plus $5 billion debt 1994. Craig took control of Nextel Communications 1995 after family agreed to invest up to $1.3 billion to develop digital wireless network; replaced key senior management team. Also launching Teledesic, communications satellite venture with Bill Gates: constellation of hundreds of satellites, expected cost $9 billion. Avid yachtsman, pilot, largest individual AT&T shareholder. Member since 1986.

Dorrance Hill Hamilton

$1.3 billion
Inheritance. Wayne, Pa., Newport, R.I. 68.
Married, 3 children.

Hope Hill van Beuren

$1.1 billion
Inheritance. Middletown, R.I. 62.
Married, 3 children.

Charlotte Colket Weber

$1.1 billion
Inheritance. Ocala, Fla., New York City. 53.
Divorced, 4 children.

Tristram Colket

$470 million
Inheritance. Paoli, Pa. 58.
Married, 3 children.

Diana Strawbridge Wister

$610 million
Inheritance. Palm Beach, Fla. 57.
Divorced, remarried; 3 children.

George Strawbridge Jr.

$550 million
Inheritance. Cochranville, Pa. 58.
Married, 3 children.

Grandchildren of Campbell Soup pioneer Dr. John T. Dorrance, chemist who developed method of making condensed soup. Campbell Soup can's icon status captured, enhanced by pop artist Andy Warhol's paintings. These 6 are children of Dorrance's daughters, who split half of the U.S.' third-largest estate in 1930; other 50% went to John Jr. *(see Bennett Dorrance and Mary Alice Malone)*. Company now soup to nuts: owns Pepperidge Farm bakery, Swanson frozen dinners, bought salsa maker Pace for $1 billion 1995. Campbell's stock under Chief Executive David Johnson: "mm-mm good," up over 50% in last year. Almost sold family's 60% of Campbell after John Jr. (Jack) died 1989; move derailed by Jack's kids. Dorrance (Dodo): oldest of 9 cousins, only one born during John Sr.'s lifetime; led dissident (selling) faction. Hope (Happy): son Archbold on Campbell board, only family member active in company. Cousin Diana: splits time between horse farm "Runnymede," Coatesville, Pa., Vail ski chalet, home in Palm Beach. Her brother George Strawbridge Jr.: opposed sale; Widener University (Pa.) adjunct professor of Latin American History and Political Science. Cousin Charlotte: studied at Sorbonne; gave Chinese art worth $20 million to New York City's Metropolitan Museum of Art, rest of collection believed to be worth over $150 million. Her brother Tristram: after Trinity College, tried hand as entrepreneur, mixed results. His Altair Airlines, founded 1966, filed bankruptcy 1982. Members since 1982.

Amos Barr Hostetter Jr.

$1.3 billion
Cable TV. Boston. 59.
Married, 3 children.

Last February sold Continental Cablevision to U S West Media Group for total $10.8 billion—$5.5 billion debt, $5.3 billion cash and stock. Staying with company, will run U S West's cable operations after merger. Son of Short Hills, N.J. stockbroker. Harvard M.B.A. "Bud" did stint in utility finance; started company with friend H. Irving Grousbeck 1963; partners, dad put in $4,000. Acquired, built franchises. Grousbeck left 1981 to teach, held on to 10%. Dow Jones bought 24.5% same year, later sold part. Acquired McClatchys' *(see p. 284)* cable operations 1986, American Cable Systems 1988; bought out Dow Jones for $300 million 1989. Over 4 million subscribers. Getting into emerging markets: Singapore, Australia, Argentina. Investments in The Golf Network, E!, Home Shopping Network, TV Food Network. Member since 1986.

NEW TO THE FORBES FOUR HUNDRED

Richard N. Goldman

$1.2 billion
Inheritance. San Francisco. 76.
Widowed, 3 surviving children.

Evelyn Danzig Haas

$1.1 billion
Inheritance. San Francisco. 79.
Widowed, 3 children.

Phyllis Koshland Friedman

$490 million
Inheritance. San Francisco. 73.
Widowed, 2 children.

Heirs to Levi Strauss fortune, with families *(see Haas)*. Founder Levi Strauss emigrated from Bavaria during California gold rush, started company 1850, died bachelor 1902, left company to 4 nephews. Walter A. Haas Sr. (d. 1979) married Strauss' grandniece, ran company 1928-55. Son Peter Sr., Harvard M.B.A., joined to handle finance, operations; president 1970-81. Now chairs executive committee. Peter Sr.'s brother, Walter Jr. (d. 1995), president 1958-70, took company public 1971. Retired

1981; honorary chair at death. Widow, Evelyn D., executor of estate; fund created with husband supports arts, disadvantaged people. Their son, Robert D., U.C. Berkeley, Peace Corps, Africa (1964-66), Harvard M.B.A. 1968. Took company private again 1985 in $1.7 billion LBO. Greatly improved operations, capitalized on American West mystique abroad; now foreign sales half of $6.7 billion total revenues. Company LBO'd again 1996 by CEO Robert D. Haas, great-great-grandnephew of Levi Strauss. Prompted squabble with Rhoda Haas Goldman (d. 1996) family; they cashed out in 1996 LBO. Remainder of shares owned by some 200 descendants placed in 15-year voting trust controlled by Haas families. Richard: Rhoda's widower, an insurance executive, established Goldman Environmental Prize with Rhoda 1990. Phyllis, sister to Daniel Koshland Jr. and Frances Geballe *(see p. 127)*, children of Daniel Koshland Sr., brother-in-law to Walter A. Haas Sr. Today world's largest apparel firm.

Barbara Piasecka Johnson

$1.2 billion
Inheritance. Princeton, N.J. 59.
Widowed.

Third wife of Johnson & Johnson heir John Seward Johnson (d. 1983). Art history M.A. U. of Wroclaw, Poland; to U.S. 1968. Upstairs chambermaid; soon, scuba partner. Married 1971, 8 days after his divorce. He was 76, she, 34. Lovebirds built $15 million estate near Princeton. Ugly contest with his children over will. Offer to save Gdansk shipyards 1989 rejected: entailed $1/hour wages, 2,000 layoffs. Paid $15 million for 18th-century cabinet 1990: "This is to show you the quality—not the quantity—of my money." Converting Jasna Polana estate in Princeton into exclusive golf course/club. Will keep apartment on grounds. Still has large portion of husband's J&J stock. Member since 1986.

William Morse Davidson

$1.2 billion
Guardian Industries.
Bloomfield Hills, Mich. 73.
Thrice divorced, 2 children.

Dilettante lawyer, found talent saving failing businesses. Rescued Frank W. Kerr Co., drug wholesaling firm. Accomplished same with Rupp & Bowman in surgical supplies. Took over uncle's interest in Guardian Industries, then a failing windshield fabricator. Became president 1957; paid off creditors, acquired photo processing, broadened company focus

to architectural "float" glass. Took public 1968; private 1985 in $500 mil-
lion LBO. Built into world's fourth-largest glassmaker with 15% flat-glass
market, 8% auto market. Paid $40 million judgment in patent infringement
case 1991, $15 million for union-busting. Made 70% acquisition of auto
plastics company Automotive Moulding 1996; also controlling interest in
liquid display outfit Optical Imaging Systems. Endowed $30 million to U.
of Michigan business school. Also 70% Detroit (basketball) Pistons. Member since 1983.

Dennis Washington

$1.2 billion
Mining, railroads. Missoula, Mont. 62.
Married, 2 sons.

In May added Morrison Knudsen to private transportation, construction
empire for $263 million. Now more than $2.2 billion revenues on 40-some
ventures. Survived polio in childhood. Started as heavy crane operator;
with $30,000 loan built Montana's largest contractor. Went after big com-
panies with idle assets. Bought, reopened Anaconda copper mine for $18
million plus royalties 1985. Gave nonunion labor profit-sharing; soon low-
cost U.S. producer. Sold half 1989 for $125 million. Bought newly named
Montana Rail Link from Burlington Northern 1987. Got control Kasler
Holding, leading California road, bridge builder. Survived prostatitis 1991.
With Marvin Davis, lost out to Richard Rainwater *(see pp. 135 and 163)* in
bid for Mesa Inc. Owns big yachts, British Columbia island with golf
course, 68,000-acre Oregon ranch once owned by late Bhagwan Shree
Rajneesh. Member since 1989.

Kathryn McCurry Albertson

$1.2 billion
Albertson's, Inc. Boise, Idaho. 89.
Widowed, 1 child.

Aggressive expansion: 92 new stores in 18 months, to total 792 stores in
19 states; over 1,000 expected by the year 2000. Widow of Joseph
Albertson (d. 1993). He dropped out of college during Depression to
manage Kansas Safeway. Started first grocery store with $5,000 savings,
$7,500 loan 1939. Partnership with Leonard Skaggs *(see p. 177)* 1969;
developed grocery/drugstores under one roof. Partners split amicably
1977; each took 29 stores. Albertson's grew into nation's fifth-largest
retail food-drug chain: $12.6 billion sales 1995. Kay inherited half his
stock, other assets. Keeps low profile, sees old Boise friends regularly.
"She's never really gotten a sense of just how much money she's got."
Member since 1993.

Robert William Galvin

$1.2 billion
Motorola, Inc. Barrington Hills, Ill. 74.
Married, 4 children.

Father, Paul Galvin (d. 1959), founded Galvin Manufacturing with less than $600 capital 1928. Made car radios; sold first solid-state TV sets under $200. Developed walkie-talkies for WWII. Company renamed Motorola 1947. Robert groomed as successor from childhood; went with dad on business trips at age 7. Never graduated from college; learned on the job. Started in stockroom 1940; president 1956; CEO 1959. Greatest gift: anticipating change. Sold off TV division to Matsushita (Japan) 1974. Concentrated on semiconductor, wireless technology. Transformed fat company into limber giant 1980s. Important producer computer chips: PowerPC chip competes with Intel's Pentium. Unveiled StarTAC, world's smallest and lightest cellular phone, January 1996. Offered specially designed OlymPagers to all members Team U.S.A. at Atlanta Games. Motorola now proxy for worldwide telecommunications boom. Developing $3.4 billion Iridium project: global satellite system capable of transmitting instant cellular phone, fax and pager communications anywhere in the world by 1998. Spending big in China: $1.2 billion investment by 1998. Stepped down as chair 1990; son Christopher, 46, now president and COO. Sales now over $27 billion. Member since 1982.

Donald George Fisher

$1.2 billion
The Gap, Inc. San Francisco. 68.
Married, 3 children.

Doris Feigenbaum Fisher

$1.2 billion
The Gap, Inc. San Francisco. 65.
Married, 3 children.

Husband and wife. Cofounded first Gap (as in generation gap) store 1969; sold records, jeans. Denim biggest draw; stopped selling music after 3 months. Expanded with Banana Republic (1983), GapKids (1986), Baby-Gap (1989) and Old Navy Clothing Co. (1994). European-style clothing venture, Hemisphere (1987), discontinued (1989). Currently more than 1,700 stores in U.S., U.K., Canada, France, Germany, Japan; over $4 billion sales. Don: Berkeley swimming, water polo star; began career as real estate developer. Appointed by Reagan, Bush, Clinton to Advisory Committee of Trade Policy & Negotiations. Doris: Gap merchandising consultant. Sons Robert, William and John (see p. 255). First appeared on list 1986.

David A. Duffield

$1.2 billion
PeopleSoft Inc. Danville, Calif. 56.
Divorced, remarried; 5 children.

Cornell M.B.A., began as IBM engineer/marketing representative. Co-founded Information Associates 1968, developed payroll/personnel systems. Founded Integral Systems 1972. Clients: Rutgers, Penn, U. of Calif. Left mid-1980s, convinced that mainframe-based systems would be obsolete with new PCs. Founded PeopleSoft 1987; envisioned "Microsoft of application software" for accounting, logistics, personnel. IPO 1992; stock jumped over 60% first day. Recently joined forces with Price Waterhouse to provide financial services software. Created R&D partnership, PeopleSoft Manufacturing, with "sense of urgency, the startup mentality, needed to deliver a world-class application." No secretary; answers own phone: "It may be inefficient from time to time, but keeps me in tune." Member since 1995.

Fayez Shalaby Sarofim

$1.2 billion
Money management. Houston. 67.
Divorcing, 5 children.

Prenuptial agreement should keep fortune intact through second divorce. Buy-and-hold king still true to brand-name favorites: P&G, Coca-Cola, Philip Morris. Egyptian-born son of wealthy landowner. Harvard M.B.A.; naturalized 1961. Anderson Clayton 1951, advised pension funds. Launched own company 1958 with $100,000 from father. "The Sphinx" had early coup: landed Rice U.'s massive endowment. Early investor Teledyne, Intel. Very conservative, long-term strategist. Raging bull: thinks DJIA could hit 10,000 by 2000; $2 billion bond portfolio. Fund lost estimated $475 million on "Marlboro Friday" 1992, when Philip Morris cut cigarette prices. Thinks tobacco industry will survive recent defeats in court. Another reason won't sell positions: "You get haircut by taxes. I don't want to become a patriot." Son, Christopher, 32, Sarofim & Co. associate. Member since 1986.

Paul Mellon

$1.2 billion
Inheritance, finance. Upperville, Va. 89.
Widowed, remarried; 2 children by first wife.

Son of Andrew Mellon, inspired investor, financier, who hit peak of his career as U.S. Secretary of Treasury (1921-32), founded the National

Gallery *(see Mellon family)*. Paul lonely, vulnerable as a child, felt alienated as student (Choate, Yale, Cambridge). "My isolation in university allowed me to be completely unaware of unemployed farmers living at subsistence level only a few miles away as the Depression took its grip." Three years at Mellon Bank in Pittsburgh during his 20s; still uninterested in commerce. Felt grave responsibilities accompanied his great wealth; sessions with Carl Jung helped ease his way. "Wealth offers no immunity against pain and sorrow." In time settled down to life of gentleman farmer, art collector. Added to father's extensive holdings, creating an enviable collection (French impressionists, British art). Has given over $300 million in paintings alone to various institutes; helped buy land for Cape Hatteras National Seashore preserve; donated half of John Locke's library to Oxford. Staunch Anglophile: "Paul would be more comfortable in Georgian England than in 20th-century America." Member since 1982.

Susan Thompson Buffett

$1.2 billion
Marriage. San Francisco. 64.
Separated (from Warren Buffett), 3 children.

Daughter of Omaha educator; her parents knew Warren's. Met sage while rooming with his sister at Northwestern. Married 1952. Deeply involved in civil rights movement; couple's political shift to left rattled family. Heads Buffett Foundation: nuclear disarmament, population control. Once sought singing career, now spending time on foundation. Left Warren (who has steady live-in), moved to San Francisco 1977. Lives on West Coast, sees Warren regularly. Warren: "It works well this way. She sort of roams; she's a free spirit." Capital gains and estate taxes being what they are, he plans to leave his billions to her, then to their foundation. Member since 1991.

Samuel Zell

$1.2 billion
Real estate, investments. Chicago. 55.
Divorced, 3 children.

Another year at the ball for the Grave Dancer: After losing out in bid for NYC's Rockefeller Center, Zell-controlled Jacor Communications bought Citicasters from Carl Lindner for $770 million; Jacor now largest radio group in U.S. But battle brewing for real estate trust Chateau Properties; deal to merge Revco with Rite Aid nixed by FTC. Son of Polish immigrants, peddled *Playboy* in grade school for 200% profit. With U. of Michigan frat brother Robert Lurie (d. 1990) saw inflation, bought distressed Sunbelt, Midwest real estate 1970s, rehabbed for fraction of replacement cost, sold for big gains, picked up more. Applied same principle to companies, notably Itel. Now has 2 REITs public; 3 vulture funds with Merrill Lynch. Tried to buy 50% Italian motorcycle maker Ducati, favored bike of entourage "Zell's Angels." Deal collapsed, but "it's a lot easier buying motorcycles at $15,000 apiece than it is a $100 million building." Prefers denim to pinstripe. Holds treasure hunt on birthdays; has been known to play war games with paintball-pellet guns. Member since 1986.

Carl Henry Lindner Jr. and family

$1.1 billion
Insurance, investments, Chiquita bananas. Cincinnati. 77.
Married, 3 sons in business.

Despite giving $155,000 to Bob Dole-backed organizations, failed to get profit-protecting sanctions against Costa Rica and Colombia. High school dropout at 14; helped family dairy business during Depression. Opened ice cream store 1940 with brothers, $1,200. Built 220-store United Dairy Farmers chain. Began American Financial Corp. with small S&L 1959; added insurance 1971. Smart investor, tough greenmailer, teetotaler much tweaked by Gannett's Al Neuharth. AFC portfolio up sixtyfold 1961-80; took private 1981 for $340 million. Poor investments Mission Insurance, Chiquita Brands. Complex restructuring 1995: cutting debt; Moody's downgrades to junk status anyway. Been paring ostentatious salaries, bonuses. Strict Baptist, major contributor Jewish Welfare Fund. Member since 1982.

NEW TO THE FORBES FOUR HUNDRED

Ted Schwartz

$1.1 billion
Telemarketing. Chicago. 42.
Married, 2 children.

Founder APAC (all people are customers) TeleServices. Outsourcer handles 200 million phone calls a year. "If you call UPS to pick up your package, we take the order. If you need information regarding your Discover card, you're talking to us." College dropout, sold time for tiny Colorado radio station. Found more clients by working phones than by beating pavement. Founded Radio America in native Chicago, 1973. One day in 1985 friend asked what he did with his 200 phones after hours. Schwartz: "Nothing." Secured first contract with Xerox cold-calling for subscriptions to company's *Weekly Reader.* Sold radio sales business 1991; started persuading big corporations to let him handle their toll-free customer service. Today 40% of APAC sales comes from service calls. APAC went public October 1995, secondary offering March; still small: only $8 million earnings 1995. But Wall Street feverish: stock recently up sixfold since IPO. Schwartz and family own 29.5 million shares.

William Clay Ford

$1.1 billion
Ford Motor Co.
Grosse Pointe Shores, Mich. 71.
Married, 4 children.

With sister Josephine *(see p. 204)* last surviving grandchildren of Ford Motor Co. founder Henry Ford (d. 1947). Brother Henry Ford II (d. 1987) left Yale, Navy following father Edsel's death to join faltering company 1943; succeeded grandfather as president 1945. Engineered company turnaround, redevelopment of downtown Detroit. Reportedly settled arguments saying, "My name is on the building." Battled with Iacocca; fired him as president 1978. Retired as chairman 1980. William, Yale grad, began at Ford 1949. Vice president 1953. Retired as finance committee chair 1995. Son William Clay Jr., 38, Sloan (MIT) M.B.A., filled position. He and cousin Edsel II, 47, Ford Motor Credit chief operating officer, vying for fourth-generation leadership. William part-owner Detroit (football) Lions. Ford Foundation holds $7.5 billion assets. Ford family collectively owns 6% of company with 40% voting power, recently worth $2.2 billion. William Clay member since 1982.

Richard Rainwater

$1.1 billion
Investments. Fort Worth. 52.
Divorced, remarried; 3 children.

Rainwater used $80 million of his own cash to beat out Dennis Washington and Marvin Davis for Boone Pickens' troubled Mesa, Inc., July. Depleted reserves, big selloff small company stakes; all worth it: investment already at $180 million. Other big holdings up nearly 25%. "I like these stocks' being up." Son of middle-class wholesaler. Math, physics major U. of Texas; Stanford M.B.A. Met Sid Bass *(see p. 135)* at Stanford; after Goldman, Sachs stint, managed $50 million Bass family portfolio 1970. Lost money 2 years: "Mr. Bass Sr. commented to me that the tuition goes way up after college." Earned back tuition, then some: masterminded huge Disney investments 1984, still cornerstone of Bass family wealth. Left 1986 to run own investments: health care, oil, real estate.

Took Crescent REIT public 1994. Met, married banker Darla Moore 1991. Darla, dealmaster in her own right, has been running sizable assets since 1994. "This is the first year I've added a zero to my net worth." Says becoming a billionaire is "kind of nice." Member since 1986.

Michael Dell

$1.1 billion
Computers. Austin, Tex. 31.
Married, 2 daughters.

Dell Computer stock soared after enfant terrible brought in experienced management team: got inventories, chaotic growth under control; bolstered profits. Entered U. of Texas 1983, intended biology major; started computer resale business in dorm room. Dropped out 1984; grossed $80,000 a month. First to sell computers directly by phone. Sales boomed to $2 billion, spun out of control by 1993: lost $38 million in currency hedges, CFO deserted company. Introduction of notebook computers delayed; stock plunged as a result. New management has Dell back in saddle. Stock recovered. Sales $5.3 billion. Joined fellow Edifice-Complex high-tech moguls Larry Ellison, Bill Gates by erecting $19 million hilltop digs, biggest domicile in Austin. No chair in office, works standing up; "I think faster on my feet." First appeared on list 1991.

Reese McIntosh Rowling and family

$1.1 billion
Hotels, oil. Corpus Christi, Tex. 68.
Married, 4 children.

Reese's son Bob expanding hotel holdings: bought Omni chain February $500 million. Reese geologist for oil companies; started own Tana Oil & Gas 1972. Stayed virtually debt-free; in early 1980s bust "drilled a lot of wells while other companies were busy paying their bank loans." By 1989 one of largest independent U.S. explorers. Sold oil and gas production (kept pipeline) to Texaco for preferred stock 1989, avoiding big capital gains tax; later converted to common. Acquired Doubletree hotel in Dallas, 8 others since 1990. Added 20 more with Omni. Total debt on hotels, pipeline project: $450 million. "The Texaco stock's where we've made the money this year." Total return nearly 50% last 12 months. Family investments under TRT Holdings. Member since 1991.

Curtis LeRoy Carlson

$1.1 billion
Trading stamps, hotels, travel. Long Lake, Minn. 82.
Married, 2 children.

Son of Swedish immigrant grocer; started business life early: subcontracted paper routes to brothers for profit. U. of Minnesota 1937; Procter & Gamble soap salesman, $110 a month. Secured $50 loan, started Gold Bond Trading Stamps 1938. "The minute I was out on my own, I knew I'd found my own element." From 1960s on, built one-man travel, hotel, restaurant, marketing conglomerate. Today Radisson (hotels); Country Kitchen, TGI Friday's (restaurants); Carlson Wagonlit Travel (merged with France's Accor Group 1994). Son-in-law Edwin (Skip) Gage, former Carlson heir apparent, left 1992 to form competitor, Gage Marketing; took many managers with him. Then Hospitality Group CEO Juergen Bartels jumped ship 1995; now heads competitor Westin Hotel Co. Energetic daughter Marilyn 57, presumptive heir. Carlson Marketing experienced decline; now growing again. Curt, fully recovered from quadruple bypass, still at helm. Member since 1982.

Charles R. Schwab

$1.1 billion
Discount stockbroker. Atherton, Calif. 59.
Divorced, remarried; 5 children.

Discount broker giant Charles Schwab Corp. to expand by selling low-cost life insurance, mutual fund portfolios; draws ire from Fidelity Group. Stanford M.B.A., had eccentric early ventures: drive-through animal park, rock and classical music rodeo. Started San Francisco-based traditional brokerage 1971. Became pioneer discount broker 1974 to "offer an avenue [to] duck your financial affairs from some guy who has a very clear interest in converting your capital into his personal income." Brokers paid straight salaries, no commissions. Battled Wall Street brokerages with low prices, fast order executions through on-line system. Has offered 24-hour service since 1982. Sold to BankAmerica Corp. 1983; repurchased in $280 million leveraged buyout 1987. Published *How To Be Your Own Stockbroker* 1985. Introduced highly successful OneSource 1992: no transaction fee mutual fund service offering no-load funds. Chairs nonprofit agency for parents of children with learning disabilities; Charles and son also dyslexic. Modern art collector. Member since 1993.

Thomas F. Frist Jr.

$1.1 billion
Columbia/HCA. Nashville. 58.
Married, 2 sons, 1 daughter.

Legal problems slow Columbia/HCA's rapid growth: Michigan halts proposed acquisition of 369-bed nonprofit hospital 1996. Tom Jr. to Vanderbilt; Washington U. medical school. Air Force flight surgeon. Returned to Nashville 1968. Cofounded Hospital Corp. of America with father, family pal Jack Massey: showed hospitals can be run profitably. Public 1969. Acquisitive: by 1973, 51 hospitals. CEO 1987; now chairman. In 1988 led $5.1 billion leveraged buyout. Public again 1992; merger with Columbia Healthcare Corp. in February 1994. Cost-saving secret: big discounts on equipment, supplies through centralized buying; lower-paid nurse's aides, not registered nurses, read EKGs. Draws industry envy—and ridicule. Sneers Houston-based Northwest Medical CEO: "They're arrogant bullies." But big arrogant bullies: $2.3 billion cash flow. U.S. Senator Bill Frist his brother. Member since 1992.

Charles Cassius Gates Jr. and family

$1.1 billion
Manufacturing. Denver. 75.
Married, 2 children.

Liquidating: sold Gates Rubber Co. to Britain's Tomkins in July for $1.16 billion. Tomkins liked fit of Gates' businesses, connections in China, Japan, South America. Gates' father followed Gold Rush west, bought tire cover company 1911; senior Gates' brother invented V-belt 1917, became leading producer. Charles Jr. went to Stanford, studied engineering, inherited business with 4 sisters 1961. Diversified: bought Learjet Inc. 1967, turned around, sold 1987. Also hit home run with investment in Hamilton Oil: 1991 merger yielded over $100 million. Still owns oil, gas properties, plus 150,000-acres ranchland, 700 acres Colorado Springs. Active in Denver Museum of Natural History. Member since 1982.

Eli Broad

$1.1 billion
Home building, financial services.
Los Angeles. 63.
Married, 2 children.

This year sold 1,700 acres of Sacramento land to Morgan Stanley real estate fund for $43 million; 2,400 acres remain in portfolio. Founded Kaufman & Broad age 23 with Don Kaufman (d. 1983), built first houses with $25,000 loan from in-laws 1957. Left Michigan for California, added insurance business to hedge real estate cycles. Built thousands of homes for baby boomers; also overseas in France. Spun off home builder 1989 to concentrate on finance company: "After 25 years ... the thrill was gone." SunAmerica Inc. snapped up distressed financial companies like Anchor National Life (1986), Integrated Resources (1990). Vast art collection, founded LA Museum of Contemporary Art 1983. Member since 1989.

Jim Jannard

$1 billion
Sunglasses. Irvine, Calif. 47.
Divorced, 4 children.

Phenomenal wealth ride may be nearing end: in June Jannard dumped 4.5 million shares for over $200 million cash. Stake now less than 50%. Dropped out of USC, started Oakley (named after English Setter) in garage 1975; sold motorcycle handgrips from station wagon. Motocross goggles followed, then ski goggles. First sunglasses 1984. Tough, interchangeable lenses worn by Cal Ripken Jr., Andre Agassi, other top jocks for ultralow endorsement fees. Michael Jordan, Oakley board member, major shareholder. Secretive Jannard known as "mad scientist": fierce litigator, brings frequent patent infringement lawsuits. Will have his hands full as pal Phil Knight *(see p. 118)* pushes Nike into sports eyewear. Member since 1995.

NEW TO THE FORBES FOUR HUNDRED

Kenneth D. Tuchman

$1 billion
TeleTech. Denver area. 36, Married.

Son of LA home builder, youngest of 4 children. Early entrepreneur: worked at bicycle shop age 13; top salesman in 6 months; duplicated success at surf shop. Grew hair, became importer of puka shells "to meet women." Used two empty lots as clearinghouse to sell used cars; charged wealthy customers $55/week to "auto-sit" car until sold. Epiphany while working for dad: couldn't get answers about airconditioning systems, roofing, trusses, etc. "Some guy would show up a month later in response to our questions about the foundation and we were already rolling out sod." Started TeleTech 1982, age 22, to handle customer questions, complaints for big companies. First clients: ITT, Greenpeace, Herbal Life. First-year profits of $250,000 on $1 million revenues. Then 6 years of cash flow problems: shunned by traditional banks, turned to 24% interest rate loans. Borrowed against receivables, future earnings. "A dangerous thing ... almost bankrupted us." Survived. Explosive growth starting 1990; clients: UPS, CompuServe, AT&T.

Introduced to Sam Zell *(see p. 161)* 1994; he bought 17% stake. Went public August at $14.50; stock recently up to $29.25. Completed two years community college. "The university of life: You have to learn how to turn a nickel into a dollar."

Michael Rubens Bloomberg

$1 billion
Financial news. New York City. 54.
Divorced, 2 daughters.

Ever expanding: new monthly magazine, *Bloomberg Personal;* new publishing house, The Bloomberg Press. Overseas business now 45% of sales. Engineering and physics at Johns Hopkins. Harvard Business School. Salomon Brothers processing clerk 1966. By 1971 head of equity trading, sales; lost power struggle, left with some $20 million 1981. Developed computerized data service for Treasury bond traders; Merrill Lynch bought 30%. Business took off. Today over 65,000 Bloomberg terminals offer vast amounts sophisticated market, other data, including Letterman's Top Ten, *Forbes.* Added video, audio; NYC business news radio station. Also 24-hour satellite and cable all-news television. Doesn't have secretary, partly because "it impedes access to clients and customers." Wall Street still hungering for IPO. Bloomberg: "I don't need the capital." Apparently not. Gave $55 million to Johns Hopkins last fall. Member since 1992.

Laurance Spelman Rockefeller and family

$1 billion
Inheritance. New York City. 86.
Married, 3 daughters, 1 son.

Grandson of Standard Oil patriarch John D. Rockefeller *(see family).* With brother David *(see p. 149),* main investor of his generation. Bought John D. Sr.'s seat on the New York Stock Exchange. Generated hefty returns on sophisticated venture capital investments (seeded from huge 1934 trust): Eastern Air Lines (sold long before liquidation), McDonnell Douglas ($100 million gain), Apple Computer. Built remote, exclusive Rock Resorts in the Caribbean and Hawaii. Chaired Rockefeller Center Inc. 1953-66. Active environmentalist, gave thousands of acres, other real estate, money to national parks, reserves, etc. Donated $36 million to Memorial Sloan-Kettering, $21 million to Princeton, other gifts. Relaxes at Pocantico Hills, home of his grandfather. Introspective: interested in a number of religious and spiritual movements. Member since 1982.

Randolph Apperson Hearst

$1 billion
Inheritance. New York City. 80.
Twice divorced, remarried; 5 daughters.

Sole surviving son of media magnate William Randolph Hearst. Grandfather George Hearst (prospector, land baron, U.S. senator) took failing *San Francisco Examiner* from gambling debtor 1880. Only child, Harvard-expelled "Billie Buster" took over 1887 after writing to Dad. Built nation's largest newspaper chain. Country's most controversial media mogul: outsensationalized former employer Pulitzer *(see family)* in great NYC newspaper wars. Promoted Spanish-American War to increase circulation: "You furnish the pictures, and I'll furnish the war." Model for Orson Welles' *Citizen Kane*; built $30 million pleasure dome San Simeon, now owned by state of California. Died 1951; left control in foundation run by cronies. Heirs bought back 1974. Hearst Corp. 12 dailies, 5 weeklies, glossy consumer magazines (*Cosmopolitan, Esquire, Town & Country,* part *SmartMoney*). Also TV, radio stations, real estate, timberland. Interest in cable networks: ESPN, Arts & Entertainment, Lifetime. Investing in interactive media. Book division (William Morrow & Co., Avon) taken off block after failed attempt to unload 1994. *San Antonio Light* shut down 1993; *San Antonio Express* acquired next day. Stepped down as Hearst Corp. chairman March, ending 23-year reign; replaced by nephew George R. Hearst Jr. Five family branches *(see p. 237)*, each 20% beneficiary of trust estimated more than $5 billion. Member since 1982.

Fred A. Lennon

$1 billion
Pipe fittings, valves. Hunting Valley, Ohio. 90.
Widowed, 2 children.

Started at IBM in customer service, then salesman for Cleveland office machine company. Met Cullen Crawford, inventor of innovative highpressure pipe fitting, Swagelok. Became partners, started Crawford Fitting 1947; quickly bought Crawford out for $2,000. Expanded using controlfreak distribution system: vendors can sell only Crawford products, can be terminated with 60 days' notice. Now some 140 motivated distributors worldwide. Premium prices for superior products, often for specialized uses. Big contracts U.S. Navy, Du Pont, etc. Huge donor Republican Party. Company has no debt, big margins: "an absolute cash cow." Fanatically secretive: Crawford split into dozens of companies; work spread among small factories, many without signs on buildings, to conceal volume. Never talks to press. Unofficial company motto: "Secrecy is success. Success is secrecy." Wife died late last year; Lennon said to be extremely ill. Member since 1990.

Winthrop Paul Rockefeller

$1 billion
Inheritance. Morrilton, Ark. 48.
Divorced, remarried; 7 children.

Great-grandson of John D. Rockefeller, now making a bid for Lieutenant Governor of Arkansas. "I have two votes that I know of: mine and, I hope, my wife's." If elected he hopes to help his state recover from Whitewater and from former Governor Tucker's conviction. Father Winthrop (d. 1973, *see Rockefeller family*) revitalized GOP in Arkansas, was state's first Republican Governor (1967-71) since Reconstruction. After brief marriage to Win Paul's mother, Barbara (Bobo) Sears, moved South, picked up 927 acres (Winrock) atop Petit Jean Mountain; became famous among cattle buyers for his Santa Gertrudis stock. Like other Rockefellers, philanthropic as well as politically active. His foundation funds business development projects. Son Win (a "down-home Rockefeller") set up Law Enforcement Assistance Foundation to aid local sheriffs; has accompanied area police on patrol. Member since 1982.

Dirk Edward Ziff

$1 billion
Inheritance, investments. New York City. 32.
Single.

Robert David Ziff

$1 billion
Inheritance, investments. New York City. 30.
Single.

Daniel Morton Ziff

$1 billion
Inheritance, investments. New York City. 24.
Single.

Very eligible bachelors. Ziff Brothers Investments, founded with cash from 1994 sale of papa William Ziff Jr.'s publishing empire, reportedly posting 20% returns. Dirk: Columbia, Harvard M.B.A. Robert: Harvard, Cornell Law (first in class, passed New York bar last year), formerly vice president/ strategic planning Ziff Communications, now ZBI. Daniel: graduated

Columbia B.A. April, easing his way in. Dirk (got advice from Richard Rainwater) at ZBI helm, having snatched some of Wall Street's best traders. One of biggest, youngest contributors to Democrats: almost $500,000 1996. Played guitar on recent Carly Simon tour. Ziff fortune started by grandfather William Ziff, WWI aviator, noted lecturer, author, cofounded publisher Ziff-Davis 1927; died 1953. Son William Jr., then 24, now 66, took over: "I was saved from a life of abstraction by business." Bought out partner; expanded into upwardly mobile niches: *Car & Driver, Boating, Yachting,* etc., ultimately some 35 magazines, 6 TV stations. Sold off magazines while fighting cancer 1980 to Rupert Murdoch, CBS for total $713 million; stations for about $100 million 1983. Ziff kept, built up computer-related titles: *PC Magazine, PC Week, PC/Computing.* Cancer in remission, retired 1993, gave reins to Dirk and Robert (Daniel then in college). Three boys owned 90%, relatives rest. None interested in publishing. Auction of pieces of business announced June 1994; proceeds from Forstmann Little, Thomson Corp., AT&T, Softbank Corp., others total $2.1 billion. Other assets include REIT, Starwood Capital Group, mortgage hedge fund Ellington Mortgage Capital. All told, brothers may have $4 billion in assets. Members since 1994.

James Martin Moran

$1 billion
Toyotas. Hillsboro Beach, Fla. 78.
Widowed, remarried; 3 children.

Recently invested in used-car megastore AutoNation USA, along with H. Wayne Huizenga *(see p. 150)*; will compete with CarMax. Pumped gas age 14. Wangled own gas station, used-car dealership, then Hudson franchise. Then Ford. Own early-TV spokesman: "The Courtesy Man," local Chicago idol. Cancer diagnosis 1966, went to Florida. Remission. Acquired regional Toyota distributorship 1968. Built into world's largest independent: 200,000-plus cars sold annually. Tax-evasion conviction 1984; many lawsuits charged strong-arming of dealers: $150 million settlements. Japanese renewed franchise ahead of schedule 1993. Reportedly cleaned up act. Daughter Pat Moran president, CEO family business, JM Family Enterprises, Inc. Member since 1989.

Jack Crawford Taylor and family

$1 billion
Enterprise Rent-A-Car. St. Louis. 74.
Divorced, remarried; 2 children.

Biggest fleet of all rental car agencies. Left Washington U. to be Navy ace; flew fighters from aircraft carrier U.S.S. *Enterprise* in WWII. After war, sold cars, became regional Cadillac distributor. Took 50% pay cut to start own car-leasing business with boss. "If I failed, I figured that I could always do something else." Offered rentals as temporary replacements for stolen, wrecked cars. Business boomed in 1970s after courts made insurance companies pay for replacement rentals. Stayed out of crowded, competitive airport markets. Emphasizes training, motivation of employees. Son Andy, 48, now president and CEO, started working for Dad "as soon as I could drive." Tripled revenue in five years 1991–95. At 1996 fiscal year-end, July 31, total revenues: $3 billion. Member since 1990.

Steven Allen Spielberg

$1 billion
Movies. Palisades, Calif. 48.
Divorced, remarried; 5 children.

Hollywood's most commercially successful director. Son of GE engineer and concert pianist, ran kiddie movie house in Scottsdale, Ariz. living room. Mom: "We all worked for Steve." Sneaked onto Universal lot to watch filming age 16. With $400 borrowed from father, made first feature-length film, *Firelight*; grossed $500. Snubbed by top film schools, left Cal State Long Beach after 3 years, signed with Universal at $275 a week directing TV shows. Then *Jaws* 1975. Midas touch ever since: *Raiders of the Lost Ark, Close Encounters of the Third Kind, E.T.*, etc. Best deal in Hollywood: little upfront salary, huge slice of revenues, profits. Paid off with *Jurassic Park*, biggest-grossing film ever: thought to have pocketed over $300 million. Formed DreamWorks SKG with David Geffen and Jeffrey Katzenberg *(see pp. 143 and 305)* 1994; nothing yet delivered but extraordinary hype. First appeared on list 1987.

Carl Ray Pohlad and family

$1 billion
Banking, investments. Minneapolis. 81.
Married, 3 children.

Wants taxpayers to fund new baseball-only stadium; downplaying recent speculation that he'll move moneylosing and injury-prone baseball Twins from Minneapolis if they refuse. Grew up in West Des Moines, Iowa. Father was a railroad brakeman; mother, laundress. Carl to Gonzaga University on football scholarship; dropped out. Sold used cars; decorated fighter in WWII. Found his calling when brother-in-law, bank chief executive officer, died: Carl stepped in 1955; built banking fortune. Bought Pepsi bottler 1970s. Diversified into candy, snack foods. Sold bottling 1986, food 1990. Now he's back in bottling and distribution in Little Rock, New Orleans, Memphis; also medical and pension benefits processor DCA. Tried ill-fated hair care partnership: lawsuits, bankruptcy. Banks healthy, expanding into Texas, New Mexico, California. Member since 1984.

OVER $900,000,000

Frederick (Ted) Woodruff Field

$975 million
Inheritance, media. Beverly Hills. 44.
Divorced 4 times, 5 daughters.

Scion of Marshall Field, store clerk who built Marshall Field & Co. into world's largest department store. Grandson Marshall III sold 1941, started *Chicago Sun,* added *Times* 1947; later TV, cable. Marshall IV inherited; died 1965. Ted raised by mother in Chicago, Alaska. Clashed with half-brother Marshall V, liquidated company. Stint racing cars. To Hollywood to start Interscope movie company, record label. Sold 51% movie company to Poly-Gram 1992, the rest 1995, but still produces (*Jumanji, Mr. Holland's Opus*). Sold 50% record label to Time Warner for $125 million; bought back at discount after Time Warner attacked for Interscope's "gangsta" lyrics. Sold 50% months later to MCA for $200 million. Member since 1982.

Edward Lewis Gaylord

$975 million
Broadcasting, newspapers.
Oklahoma City. 77.
Married, 4 children.

Rumors persist that Gaylord may sell out to Westinghouse, other media giants; no deal yet. For years in shadow of father E.K., who bought into Daily Oklahoman 1903; became state power broker. Added TV, radio, more newspapers. E.L. took over at father's death 1974, age 101. Lover of country music, bought Grand Ole Opry, Opryland USA, Nashville (cable) Network 1983. Made over $100 million exchanging Telerate stock for Dow Jones shares, reportedly sold for additional $50 million gain 1993. Took Gaylord public 1991. Ed and family control 36 million shares. Member since 1982.

W. Duncan MacMillan

$975 million
Cargill, Inc. Wayzata, Minn. 66.
Married, 4 children.

John Hugh MacMillan III

$975 million
Cargill, Inc. Hillsboro Beach, Fla. 68.
Twice divorced, remarried; 9 children.

Marion MacMillan Pictet

$975 million
Cargill, Inc. Hamilton, Bermuda. 64.
Divorced, 1 surviving child.

Whitney MacMillan

$975 million
Cargill, Inc. Minneapolis. 67.
Married, 2 children.

Cargill MacMillan Jr.

$975 million
Cargill, Inc. Wayzata, Minn. 69.
Divorced, remarried, 4 children.

Pauline MacMillan Keinath

$975 million
Cargill, Inc. St. Louis. 64.
Married, 4 children.

Inheritance. Cargill, Inc., world's largest grain trader. Control split among 3 family branches, including James R. and Margaret Cargill *(see p. 148)*. Duncan MacMillan: with Cargill since 1953, director since 1966; vice chairman Waycrosse, Inc., family investment firm. Wrote 2-volume family history. John Hugh: not active in company. Barge company in bankruptcy. Sister Marion: owns, manages real estate holdings worldwide, many farming related. Whitney MacMillan: noted expert on East-West commercial relations; various U.S., international positions with company; CEO 1977 to August 1995. Brother Cargill: senior VP Cargill 1973-88. Retired, still active in company affairs. Philanthropic interests, public TV, banks. Sister Pauline: quiet lifestyle, works with handicapped children. Not active in company. Members since 1984.

Charles Feeney

$975 million
Duty Free Shoppers. London. 65.
Married, 5 children.

Feeney investment vehicle General Atlantic Partners reaped $173 million 1995 after Computer Associates bought software company Legent Corp. As Cornell student supplemented his GI Bill income by selling sandwiches to students who were studying at night. Opened duty-free shop with Cornell hotel administration classmate Robert Miller in Hong Kong 1960. Targeted Japanese tourists; rewarded tour guides with hefty commissions. DFS became the world's largest duty-free retailer. Retired from day-to-day operations 1970s to manage investments from huge cash flow. Also InterPacific: owns, manages South Pacific hotels, resorts. Duty Free Shoppers struggling with weak Japanese tourism, changing demographics. Described as reclusive, high-strung, fast talker. Member since 1988.

Bob John Magness

$960 million
TCI. Englewood, Colo. 72.
Widowed, remarried; 2 children.

Born Oklahoma; rancher, cottonseed seller. Patton's Third Army. Started cable system west Texas 1955. Strategy: create systems in small towns, rural areas, depreciate, sell; buy larger systems. Recognized managerial shortcomings in self; hired brilliant strategist, hard negotiator John Malone *(see p. 216)* as CEO. Magness chairman. Tele-Communications, Inc. now largest U.S. cable owner and operator, 14 million subscribers. Led 1987 bailout of Ted Turner *(see p. 137)*, came away with Turner stock, soon to be Time Warner stock. Spun off cable programmer Liberty Media 1991; reacquired 1994; spun off tracking stock 1995. Also stake in Discovery Communications, United Video Satellite Group *(see Flinn)*, Home Shopping Network, etc. Constant target of Justice Department, FTC; long-awaited IRS approval finally granted enabling TCI to buy Viacom cable systems; way also cleared for Time Warner/Turner Entertainment merger. Magness raises cattle, horses; collects Western art. Member since 1985.

Charles Bartlett Johnson

$960 million
Mutual funds. Hillsborough, Calif. 63.
Married, 6 children.

Rupert Harris Johnson Jr.

$765 million
Mutual funds. Hillsborough, Calif. 56.
Married.

Half-brothers. Their Franklin Resources (named after Ben Franklin for his common sense, frugality) recently bought Heine Securities for $610 million from value investor Michael Price *(see p. 225)*. Firm founded in 1947 as Franklin Distributors, Inc. by Rupert Johnson Sr. Son Charles took over fund management company with $2 million assets 1957. Went public as Franklin Resources 1970; now nation's fifth-largest mutual fund company with over $147 billion under management. Pioneered tax-free state bond funds. Acquired U.K.-based (Sir John) Templeton, Galbraith & Hansberger for $913 million 1992. Charles: Yale grad, now Franklin president. Rupert: executive vice president. Members since 1992.

Donald John Tyson

$950 million
Tyson Foods Inc. Springdale, Ark. 66.
Married, 3 children.

John Tyson founded Tyson Feed & Hatchery during Depression. Went public as Tyson Foods 1963. Son Don left U. of Arkansas senior year to join company 1952; took helm with half brother Randal (d. 1986) when father died in car-train wreck 1967. Company boosted by 1980s health-conscious craze as consumers turned from red meat to poultry. Growth by acquisition: built only 6 of 78 plants. Largest takeover 1989: Holly Farms at $1.5 billion. Corporate goal: "Provider of protein at the center of the plate." Expanded beyond poultry: acquired Arctic Alaska Fisheries 1992 for $243 million; also pork interests. But chicken still star performer. Today nation's leading supplier with 23% U.S. chicken market, over $5 billion sales; major accounts with likes of McDonald's, Kentucky Fried Chicken. Ships to 43 countries, including 70% of all U.S. chicken exported to Japan. Don stepped down as chairman April 1995; remains senior chairman. Member since 1986.

Carl Celian Icahn

$950 million
Finance. New York City. 60.
Divorced, 2 children.

Back in saddle: purchased 4.8% stake (with investor Bennett LeBow) in RJR Nabisco to force Nabisco spinoff; proxy suits follow. Severs LeBow ties, buys more RJR; stock price doesn't budge. Also investing in cheaply priced oil companies: 10% stakes in National Energy, Alexander and Pananco. Grew up middle class, NYC's Queens. Schoolteacher mother; father frustrated opera singer, cantor at local synagogue, read Schopenhauer to Carl. Princeton scholarship; medical school dropout. To Wall Street with $4,000 poker winnings. In 1962 crash had to sell convertible. Borrowed $400,000 for NYSE seat 1968; bought into firms that had to improve, spin off pieces or buy him out. In 1980s ACF, TWA, USX, Texaco.

Lately, debt restructurings, often pitted against fellow vulture investor Leon Black. TWA shaky after recent crash; Icahn trying to recoup his $200 million. Member since 1987.

Leonard Samuel (Sam) Skaggs Jr.

$950 million
American Stores Co.
Salt Lake City. 73.
Married, 4 children.

Skaggs recently threatened to unload his 18% American Stores stake, instigate management shakeup a year after stepping down as chairman. Wall Street unenthusiastic. Sam's grandfather, Baptist minister, founded Skaggs Cash Store in 1915 to help congregation. Run by 6 brothers, acquired Safeway supermarkets. Father bought Pay Less Drug Stores 1939 with Safeway shares. Sam took over in 1950, built second-largest U.S. grocery and drug chain. Other holdings: Acme Markets, Jewel Food Stores, Osco Drug, and Sav-on. Pioneered supermarket-drugstore combo with Joseph Albertson (see Kathryn Albertson) 1969. Partnership dissolved amicably in 1977. Merged with American Stores Co. in 1979. Remains as director, pest to company. Member since 1983.

Charles B. Wang

$940 million
Computer Associates. New York City. 52.
Married, 2 children.

Once little-known, now second-largest independent software publisher with $3.5 billion sales; trails only Microsoft. Born Shanghai, fled to U.S. with family 1952. Early years: "I know what it is to be hungry." Older brother to Yale, Cornell Law; Charles, Queens College grad. Became programmer: "I still love the technology better than the business." Worked at Columbia U., Standard Data Corp.; founded Computer Associates with staff of four 1976; today about 9,000 employees. Sold software for mainframe computers. Purchased CA's Swiss parent company 1980 for $2.8 million. Brother Anthony joined as president; IPO 1981. Ruthless growth strategy: more than 60 acquisitions in 20 years. Hit $1 billion sales 1989. Wrote book, *Techno Vision*, on keeping companies high-tech, lean, efficient. Brother resigned 1992. Entered client-server software market 1993; mainframe software still bulk of revenue. Employee perks: Montessori day-care center; breakfast provided in offices. Bans E-mail at work during prime hours. Stronghold: acquired competitor Legent Corp. for $1.8 billion 1995. Wang, chairman and chief executive, returned to China last fall for first time since fleeing 43 years before. Member since 1995.

NEW TO THE FORBES FOUR HUNDRED

Mary Anselmo and family

$930 million
PanAmSat Corp. Greenwich, Conn. 67.
Widowed, 3 children.

Late husband Reynold (Rene) Anselmo (d. 1995) was born in Boston, moved to Mexico to direct, produce shows for TV, theater after serving as marine in WWII. Befriended Emilio Azcárraga Milmo, heir to Televisa media empire. Azcárraga's father sent Anselmo back to U.S. 1963 to help run new Spanish-language TV network. Given equity; bought part of 5 Spanish-language stations in U.S. Concerns about FCC foreign ownership rules prompted partners to sell; personally netted $100 million. Moved into satellites: spent $65 million to build, insure, launch first privately owned international telecommunications satellite. Took company public last year, but didn't survive to see it: died 2 days before IPO, at age 69. PanAmSat now 4 satellites; stock left to wife, children and grandchildren.

Henry R. Kravis

$925 million
LBOs. New York City. 52.
Twice divorced, remarried; 2 children.

George R. Roberts

$925 million
LBOs. San Francisco area. 52.
Married, 3 children.

These cousins and partners pulled in massive gains this year in several deals, including a $3.7 billion return on their $350 million investment in Duracell, purchased by Gillette in mid-September. With mentor Jerome Kohlberg (see p. 197) left Bear, Stearns 1976 to form Kohlberg Kravis Roberts. Little firm quickly went after big fish: bought Houdaille Industries 1979 for $370 million; bought Wometco 1984, first $1 billion buyout. Others: Storer Communications, Safeway, Beatrice, Owens-Illinois, Walter Industries. Kohlberg left KKR 1987 after friendly "bootstrap" deals turned into mammoth, hostile takeovers. KKR's modus operandi: big deals, low risk, big fees—often 20% of profits, 1% investment banking fee, 1.5% management fee, etc. Sometimes risk just 1% of buyout equity. Bit off too much in 1988 LBO of RJR Nabisco, still history's biggest at $26.4 billion. RJR floundered, KKR slowly sold off until 1994, when traded last RJR stock in to buy Borden in hopes of milking Elsie the Cow. Greener pastures with American Reinsurance: bought 1992 for $300 million from Aetna, public 4 months later 3 times purchase price, Munich Re paying $4 billion for company, $1.7 billion profit for KKR. Other recent deal, K-III Communications, flat since IPO. Henry: now with third wife, Marie-Josée Drouin. Chairman of $53 million New York City Investment Fund for economic development. Keeps high social profile NYC, gives big to Metropolitan Museum. George: keeps low profile, stays away from NYC, runs West Coast office. Members since 1986.

Leonard Norman Stern

$925 million
Pet supplies, real estate. New York City. 58.
Divorced, remarried; 3 children.

Decides to give away once-venerable *Village Voice* for free in Manhattan 1996; decision cheers sales staff, demoralizes editorial. Funds son Emanuel's $45 million SoHo boutique hotel; first hotel in upscale art gallery neighborhood in 100 years. Father from Germany with 2,100 canaries 1926. Leonard took over floundering Hartz Mountain 1959, built pet supplies semi-monopoly; antitrust fines. Bought N.J. Meadowlands acreage from 1963: developed 33 million commercial square feet. Took Hartz public 1972, private 1979. Paid $55 million for *Village Voice* 1985. Gave alma mater NYU $30 million 1988, name now on business school. Sold Harmon Publishing for $104 million, says over $60 million profit. Bought Los Angeles weekly; then launched Orange County weekly. Sons Edward, Emanuel taking over day-to-day management. Member since 1982.

J. Paul Getty Jr.

$925 million
Inheritance. London. 64.
Divorced, widowed, remarried; 4 children by first wife, 1 by second.

Third son of oil baron Jean Paul Getty (d. 1976) *(see other Gettys)*. Ran Getty Oil Italian operations; got into Sixties counterculture, drugs. Divorced; married actress Talitha Pol 1966. Became addicts; she died, heroin overdose, 1971. Namesake son kidnapped 1973; ear cut off in ransom demand. Became virtual recluse. Recovered recent years; married companion, former model. Cricket enthusiast, collector rare books. Major philanthropist: $200 million in decade. Paid to prevent British national treasures from going to Getty Museum, Malibu, Calif. Partially controls $1.3 billion trust, other assets. First appeared on list in 1985.

Clemmie Dixon Spangler Jr.

$915 million
Investments. Chapel Hill, N.C. 64.
Married, 2 children.

Father left farm, started construction company; built motels, helped found bank that foundered. "Dick" Jr. after UNC and Harvard M.B.A. spent 2 years in U.S. Army. President C.D. Spangler Construction 1958. Developed Golden Eagle motel chain; sold off 1970s, 1980s. Sold bank started by father to NCNB 1982. Director of NCNB 1983-86 now NationsBank; wife, Meredith, a director. Together, largest single shareholders (over 8 million shares). NationsBank currently fifth-largest U.S. bank with $192 billion in assets. Recent acquisitions: CSF Holdings (Florida's largest S&L) for $516 million 1995; Florida-based Chase Federal Bank and parent TAC Bancshares for $280 million expected 1996. Spangler bought 2 million shares RJR before 1989 KKR buyout; also stake in Jefferson-Pilot. Not all business: Chairman N.C. State Board of Education 1982-86. Now president 154,000-student UNC: "best job in North Carolina." Repairs antique English grandfather clocks; backpacks summers in Rocky Mountains. Member since 1990.

Kit Goldsbury

$900 million
Salsa. San Antonio, Tex. 52.
Divorced, 2 children.

The salsa king. Sold Pace Picante Sauce to Campbell Soup 1995 for $1.1 billion. Political science major Trinity U. (San Antonio) 1966. Married daughter of David Pace, son of jellymaker from Louisiana who invented own hot and spicy salsa—"Syrup of the Southwest"—after WWII. Kit joined company 1966, started in production, then sales, oversaw 20% annual sales increases 1980s. Pace's appeal: low-cal alternative to high-fat condiments; surpassed ketchup sales in U.S. 1992. Kit bought father-in-law out 1982, then ex-wife in 1991 divorce. Spanish-speaking, private, said to be investing conservatively. Member since 1995.

David Sun

$900 million
Memory boards. Fountain Valley, Calif. 46.
Married, 2 children.

John Tu

$900 million
Memory boards. Fountain Valley, Calif. 56.
Married, 2 children.

Kingston Technology. In August partners agreed to sell 80% of memory-board maker to Japan's Softbank for $1.5 billion. Both immigrants, founded first memory company, Camintonn, 1982. Sold to AST for $6 million 1986. Lost most of profits in 1987 stock market crash. Started Kingston to make it back. Perfect timing: tapped boom in demand for memory upgrades; topped $1.2 billion sales 1995. Kingston's creed: buy memory chips in bulk, subcontract board assembly, make money on economies of scale, focus on customer service. Kingston relatively immune to chip sector volatility. Known for handshake deals ("trust everyone"), Sun and Tu will continue to run company after sale. Members since 1995.

Robert Henry Dedman Sr.

$900 million
Country clubs. Dallas. 70.
Married, 2 children.

Grew up Arkansas poor; to Texas during teens. Earned economics, engineering degrees, L.L.B. from U. of Texas while selling insurance and real estate and serving as commissioned Navy officer. Lawyer. Opened Brookhaven Country Club as sideline 1957. Profitable; others sold him clubs to get professional management. Added city clubs 1965. Now Club-Corp International: 83 country clubs, 79 city clubs, 40 public, 25 athletic and 9 resort properties worldwide. Also banking: Texas S&L Franklin Federal Bancorp. Son Bob Jr. president, heir apparent. Bob Sr. gives millions to health and education. Member since 1985.

OVER $800,000,000

Roberto Goizueta

$870 million
Coca-Cola. Atlanta. 64.
Married, 3 children.

No rest for archrival PepsiCo: Coke steals Pepsi's leading Venezuelan bottler in August. Son of rich Cuban sugar farmer; Yale grad. Answered newspaper ad for bilingual chemist at Coca-Cola 1954. Fled Castro 1961 with wife, kids, $20: "I wanted to see if I was worth anything or was just my father's son." Protégé of Coke patriarch Robert Woodruff (d. 1985). Chair and CEO 1981. Introduced Diet Coke 1982. Intense, hands-on CEO. As Coke's market cap went from $5 billion (1971) to $120 billion (1996), well compensated: last year $4.88 million salary and bonus; plus options, restricted stock, "performance and incentive units." Granted options on 1 million shares as "last equity award" after "remarkable" growth during tenure. Coke, world's leading soft-drink company; known to have world's most extensive distribution system. Trademark world's best-known brand. Company has 45% stake in Coca-Cola Enterprises, its largest bottler. Member since 1992.

Jackson Thomas Stephens

$870 million
Investment banking, media. Little Rock. 73.
Twice divorced, 2 children.

Raised on farm, son of Democratic power broker. Older brother Witt (d. 1991) sold belt buckles and bibles, then bonds in depressed 1933 municipals market. Jack joined 1946, cofounded Stephens, Inc. one of largest investment houses off Wall Street: underwrote Wal-Mart 1970, but no gratitude; Wal-Mart heir James Walton *(see p. 119)*, with Justice Department, foiled acquisition of tiny (circulation 13,000) *Northwest Arkansas Times* 1995. Suit on appeal. Also helped Tyson Foods' takeover Holly Farms 1989. Biggest asset believed Donrey Media, private newspaper and broadcast outfit bought in 1993 from pal Don Reynolds. Jack's son Warren, 39, CEO. Jack chairman of Augusta National, site of golf's Masters. Jack and late brother Witt's families share stake in Alltel worth near $500 million; also real estate, oil, gas. Late brother's heirs believed worth nearly $800 million. Member since 1983.

NEW TO THE FORBES FOUR HUNDRED

Marguerite Harbert

$870 million
Inheritance. Birmingham, Ala. 73.
Widowed, 3 children.

Wife of John Murdoch Harbert III (d. 1995); inherited control of sprawling family business, including diversified merchant banking operation now run by son Raymond, 37. John won $6,000 in crap game sailing home from WWII. Bought concrete mixer. Ran out of cash 3 times; finally carved niche in high-risk enterprises, e.g., water supply systems in Abu Dhabi. Bought Kentucky, Tennessee coal 1960s, early 1970s; sold for

Amoco stock during energy crisis. Diversified: real estate, power generation. Sold construction interests to brother Bill, now run under Bill Harbert International Construction by separate family branch. Raymond took over day-to-day 1990. Believed to hold 10 million Amoco shares.

Richard Mellon Scaife

$870 million
Inheritance. Pittsburgh. 63.
Divorced, remarried; 2 children.

Grandson of Richard Beatty Mellon *(see Mellon family)*. "Dicky" inherited over $200 million from Mellon mother 1965. Runs Scaife Newspapers; sold *Sacramento Union* 1989. Sued E.W. Scripps Co. *(see family)* over 1992 sale of Pittsburgh Press to Block family; claimed wasn't given chance to bid. Beat drinking problem. Won't use middle name (feels Mellon clan mistreated his parents). Reportedly gave $1 million to Nixon reelection campaign; big backer right-wing causes, think tanks. Long estranged from reclusive, liberal sister Cordelia Scaife May *(see p. 210)*. Reportedly lost "virtually nothing" in 1991 divorce. Member since 1982.

Marc Rich

$850 million
Commodities. Zug, Switzerland. 61.
Divorced, remarried; 3 children.

Pincus Green

$800 million
Commodities. Meggen, Switzerland. 61.
Married, 4 children.

Shadowy former trading partners, fled to Switzerland after U.S. charged them with tax evasion, fraud, racketeering 1983. Rich back in business after lying low for years: Marc Rich Investment Co., trading commodities again. Rich's Belgian family fled to U.S. 1941. Quit NYU to work in mail room of commodity trader Philipp Brothers. Rose, along with "Pinky" Green, to star trader status; pioneered spot-oil market 1968. Phibro balked at bonus earned, so Rich and Green left 1974, formed Rich & Co. AG, became Phibro's trading nemesis. Indicted after trading Iranian crude during hostage crisis early 1980s; also broke South Africa embargo 1980s. Left 1983. Paid $171 million in fines so U.S. arm Clarendon could do business 1984. Bought Twentieth Century Fox with Marvin Davis *(see p. 135)*, broke up company, sold out to Davis. Since 1990 at trading company: now called Glencore International; Pinky had heart bypass, cashed out. Profits down with exodus. Rich cashed out Glencore 1994. Tough times for Rich: ex-wife, Denise, still suing for half his assets; Interpol has "red notice" on him—priority arrest. Members since 1985.

Bernard Marcus

$840 million
Home Depot. Atlanta. 67.
Married, 3 children.

Arthur Blank

$440 million
Home Depot. Atlanta. 54.
Divorced, remarried; 3 children.

Marcus: humble beginnings; son of Russian immigrant cabinetmaker. B.S. Rutgers. Started in drug retailing; moved on and up. Blank: raised in NYC's Queens; studied accounting at Babson. Both fired from now-defunct Handy Dan Improvement Centers in 1978. Together opened do-it-yourself store Home Depot 1979. Went public 1981. Built chain; warehouse-size stores with broad range of merchandise, knowledgeable staff. Solid partnership: "The only thing we don't have is sex." Ross Perot almost a silent partner but was too loud. Opened first EXPO Design Center 1991, upscale interior design products; 4 more to date. Acquired 75% interest in Canadian retailer Aikenhead's 1994. Coproducing *House-Smart*, a series of daily 1-hour shows on Discovery Channel; subjects range from home repair to weekend projects. Home Depot integrating rural merchandise into some stores. Currently 474 stores in 35 states. Expanding aggressively: aiming for 900 stores by 1999. May expand overseas. Dominates home improvement industry with 12% market share, over $15 billion in sales. Marcus: CEO, avid golfer. Blank: president, likely to be Marcus' successor; frequent marathoner. Members since 1992.

Stuart Robert Levine

$830 million
Cabletron Systems. Stratham, N.H. 38.
Divorced, 1 son.

Craig Robert Benson

$800 million
Cabletron Systems. Rye, N.H. 42.
Married, 2 daughters.

Networking partners go on acquisition spree: Network Express ($110 million), Zeitnet ($137 million), Standard Microsystems. Cofounders started company in garage 1983 with cables connecting PCs/office networks. Quickly honed tough reputation with suppliers, distributors, own employees. First to install computer network in space: wired Russian Mir space station. Today major force in networking market: hubs, switches, asynchronous transfer mode. Levine: U. of Miami. In high school voted least likely to succeed. Benson: Syracuse M.B.A., Dole supporter. Together partners have sold over $600 million pretax Cabletron stock; still hold over 18 million shares. Members since 1991.

Harold Clark Simmons

$830 million
Investments. Dallas. 65.
Twice divorced, remarried; 4 daughters, 2 stepchildren.

Simmons-controlled Valhi Inc. agreed to sell Amalgamated Sugar to co-op Snake River Sugar for $250 million; proceeds speculated to pay down debt. Son of Texas teachers; saved $5,000, bought Dallas drugstore 1960. Built 100-store chain; sold for $50 million 1973. Built conglomerate with hostile takeovers. Most assets in public holding company Valhi: Medite (lumber), Tremont (titanium), NL Industries (chemicals), Sybra (Arby's restaurants), Dresser Industries (oilfield equipment), Keystone Consolidated (steel rods, wire products). Philanthropist: arthritis (longtime sufferer), cancer research; $41 million to U. of Texas Southwestern Medical Center 1988. Member since 1983.

Ollen Bruton Smith

$830 million
Speedway Motorsports. Charlotte, N.C. 69.
Divorced, 4 children.

Born, raised Oakboro, N.C. Interest in cars early on: "I wanted to be a racer, but my mother put a stop to that real fast." Instead, car dealer, race promoter. Built Charlotte Motor Speedway; held World 600 race 1960. Undercapitalized; bankrupt 1962. Regained majority control 1975. Added Atlanta Motor Speedway 1990. Company went public in February 1995;

first auto racetrack on NYSE. Also owns auto dealerships N.C., Tex. String of legal battles: divorce; discrimination suit; negligence, breach of fiduciary duty suit over failed S&L (Smith won). Reportedly bought Idi Amin's private jet. Member since 1995.

Jack Kent Cooke

$825 million
Real estate, investments. Middleburg, Va. 83.
Four divorces, 3 children.

Received green light for new state-funded 78,000-seat stadium for his Washington (football) Redskins; due to open May 1997. "This is the beginning of another series of winning streaks." Canadian-born, sold encyclopedias door-to-door. Bought radio station age 25; added newspapers, magazines; millionaire by 30. Naturalized by act of Congress 1960. Bought LA (basketball) Lakers, built Forum, sold both 1979. In 1980s bought, sold cable systems: $500 million profit. Now shopping *LA Daily News,* paying down debt on NYC's Chrysler building. "This [1996] is a banner year for me." Member since 1982.

Franklin Parsons Perdue

$825 million
Chickens. Salisbury, Md. 76.
Twice divorced, remarried; 4 children from first marriage.

Despite last winter's chicken recession, revenues up $400 million, to $2.1 billion, after acquiring Showell Farms. Grew up on father's egg farm, dreamed of big-league baseball career. Attended Salisbury State U.; dropped out, back to farm 1940. Chickens paid off: demand skyrocketed 1970s and 1980s. Added feed, processing: one of first integrated chicken companies. First to use brand name on commodity product: "It takes a tough man to make a tender chicken." Tough enough to meet NYC godfather Paul Castellano on quashing union organizers 1980. Perdue now fourth-largest in U.S. Son James runs company, replaced Dad as TV pitchman 1994. Member since 1986.

Joseph Dahr Jamail Jr.

$825 million
Lawsuits. Houston. 70.
Married, 3 sons.

Foul-mouthed pit bull of a trial lawyer: "You could gag a maggot off a meat wagon." Still scaring corporate America into big settlements. More than

$100 million in settlements forecast from multiple suits this year. His standard take: one-third. Started in D.A.'s office with U. of Texas law degree. Went on own, did well as personal injury lawyer. Struck Texas gold with Texaco-Pennzoil case 1987: estimated winnings $345 million (pretax). Low overhead, small staff: 5 associates, no partners (Kolius of firm Jamail & Kolius never a partner); some 90% of billings goes to bottom line. Brought antitrust case against American Airlines on behalf of Northwest and Continental; first case lost in 28 years. Representing American National Insurance against IBM. Son Randall owns Houston-based Justice Records. Member since 1989.

Dwight Darwin Opperman

$815 million
Legal publishing. Eagan, Minn. 73.
Married, 2 children.

Sold West Publishing to Thomson Corp. for $3.4 billion in February. Company started by John West after Civil War: sold law books from horseback. Became top U.S. legal publisher by turn of century. Opperman started with West Publishing 1951 as editorial counsel, rose to VP 1965, president 1968, CEO 1978. West compiled, copyrighted most complete index of citations, case histories; went on-line, charged Lexis, top competitor, for access. Beat heat from Ralph Nader et al. to turn index over to public domain. Lavished tropical trips on Supreme Court justices. West run by son Vance recently; one of top U.S. litigators, well connected politically: pals with Al Gore; ran Senator Dianne Feinstein's (D-Calif.) reelection campaign. Member since 1995.

Teresa F. Heinz

$800 million
Inheritance. Fox Chapel, Pa. 58.
Widowed, remarried; 3 children.

Daughter of Portuguese doctor. Born, raised Mozambique. U. of Witwatersrand and Geneva (Switzerland.) Interpreters School: speaks 5 languages. Married heir to ketchup company fortune and future U.S. Senator H. John Heinz III (R-Pa.), 1966. Husband died in plane crash 1991. Teresa married Senator John Forbes Kerry (D-Mass.) 1995; oversees $1 billion philanthropic foundation. Created Heinz Awards to honor "the kinds of things I saw in my [late] husband: zest, passion, excitement, joy." Remains registered Republican in Pennsylvania; avid environmentalist, arts benefactress. Heinz trusts, foundations sold 14.5 million Heinz shares to diversify 1995. Member since 1991.

Herbert Allen

$800 million
Investments. New York City. 88.
Widowed, remarried; 2 children.

Herbert Anthony Allen

$800 million
Investments. New York City. 56.
Twice divorced, 4 children.

Herbert Anthony, entertainment industry's eminent dealmaker: "Over a long weekend, I could teach my dog to be an investment banker." Herb Sr.'s brother Charlie Allen (d. 1994) was a legendary investor. Raised in Manhattan tenement, dropped out of high school to be Wall Street runner age 15. Trading bonds by age 19 with 2 phones and $1,000. Herbert joined 1928. Brothers made, and lost, first million within year. Herb's canny trades kept the firm solvent through the Depression. Since then stellar record investing in small, risky, cheap ventures. Charlie bought $1 million stake in Syntex 1958, reaped $290 million in sale to Roche 1994. Herbert invested $3 million in Benguet Mining, sold for $45 million. Herbert A. came aboard 1962, ignored elders' warnings about Hollywood and bought 6.7% Columbia for $2.4 million 1973; sold part to Coke for $40 million profit 1982, the rest to Sony for $70 million profit 1989. Now entertainment power broker: his annual Sun Valley weekend site of top-level deals, mandatory attendance for the likes of Edgar Bronfman, John Malone, Sumner Redstone, David Geffen, Barry Diller. Represented Diller in QVC's bid for Paramount, returned Diller's $1 million check when deal fizzled. Played major advisory role in sale of MCA to Seagram 1995. Coke stake nearing $500 million, director since 1982. Also invested in scores of high-tech and biotech companies. Charlie's heirs share balance of fortune believed well over $1.6 billion. Members since 1982.

NEW TO THE FORBES FOUR HUNDRED

Bradley Wayne Hughes and family

$800 million
Public Storage. Glendale, Calif. 63.
Married, 3 children.

As real estate syndicator early 1970s, noticed Texas roadside storage warehouse; checked it out, warehouse was full. With partner, bought California land next to busy freeway, built warehouse 1972. Put up sign "Private Storage Spaces;" only one customer: asked if storage available to public as well. Changed name to "Public Storage," business took off, broke even in 3 months. Had 20 mini-warehouses within 2 years. Raised $3 billion for expansion 1980s. Great economics: self-storage space generates 65% operating margin. Consolidating far-flung operations under main REIT Public Storage Inc.

Ronnie Chan and family

$800 million
Hang Lung Group. Hong Kong. 46.
Married, 2 children.

Family business in Hong Kong, but naturalized U.S. citizen. "I thought I would never go back." Took over late father's Hang Lung Group (Hang Lung Development, Amoy Properties, Grand Hotel Holdings) 1991. Refocused investments from West to Asia, especially Hong Kong. Traveled frequently in China; met local officials, leaders: "I became convinced that the open economic policy is pervasive and irreversible." Hang Lung now investing in Shanghai real estate; total market cap over $5 billion. Ronnie also founder, manager of private investment concern Morningside/Springfield Group: currently more than 60 investments in 16 countries (in Asia, Europe, U.S.). Does not believe in inherited wealth: "It's the best way to poison your family. I told my kids early on—you're not going to get a dime." Worth $800 million, perhaps far more. Member since 1995.

NEW TO THE FORBES FOUR HUNDRED

Robert C. McNair

$800 million
Energy. Houston. 59.
Married, 4 children.

Creative exploiter of electricity deregulation: "The utilities thought we'd go out and start 1-megawatt plants at the Holiday Inn. They had no idea we could go to industrial clients." Did so in a big way. His Cogen Technologies now owns 1,400 megawatts generating capacity nationwide; another 2,500 megawatts in works abroad: China, Pakistan. After B.S. psychology U. of South Carolina, turned first company, McNair Transport, into regional trucking power; early victim deregulation. Bankruptcy 1982. Determined to take advantage of deregulation next time around. Founded Cogen 1983 with $1 million capital, age 46. Bet correctly that gas prices would fall. Signed lucrative contracts with utilities, many with 20 years remaining. With 80% stake, McNair fielding buyout offers from energy behemoths. As much as Cogen's megawatts, potential buyers want its entrepreneurial spirit: "It's our corporate culture that's attractive to them."

E. Pierce Marshall and family

$800 million
Inheritance. Dallas, Tex. 57.
Married, 2 children.

Maybe it should be a TV comedy series: When J. Howard Marshall II died last year at age 90, he left behind his new bride: former stripper and Guess? jeans model Anna Nichole Smith, 28. She and stepson E. Pierce Marshall can't abide one another. They split old J. Howard II's ashes and held separate funerals. Now Smith is suing for a piece of the estate. So is E. Pierce's brother J. Howard Marshall III, who was disinherited by his father. The saga began with more promise. J. Howard II, Yale Law, became an Interior Department lawyer. Invested in Great Northern Oil Co. with Fred Koch; swapped for stake in Koch Industries, now second-largest privately owned company in U.S. E. Pierce Marshall, who, with his family, inherited 16% of Koch Industries upon his father's death, was moving aggressively to get power of attorney over the old man's affairs before he passed on. But Anna Nichole Smith looks determined, too. E. Pierce a member since 1995.

NEW TO THE FORBES FOUR HUNDRED

Harold Honickman

$800 million
Soft drink bottler. New York City, Philadelphia. 63.
Married, 2 children.

"I want 'stomach share,'" says this soft drink distributor whose territories stretch from Virginia to Rhode Island. His father talked Pepsi into giving young Harold bottling/distribution rights in southern New Jersey. Wealthy father-in-law built him bottling plant 1957. Harold took it from there. Acquired struggling Canada Dry bottling operations New York, suburban Philly; added private label bottlers. This is a tough business: Honickman indicted in 1981 for making an illegal payment to a union official, charges later dropped. Big in Manhattan since 1980s. Owns Pepsi-Cola Bottling of New York, Coors New York, Canada Dry of New York. Also Snapple's distributor in Baltimore, Rhode Island and suburban Philadelphia. To increase stomach share, puts Chocolate Moose, other goods on his trucks. The Honickman organization now $1 billion in revenue, one of the biggest independent soft drink bottlers in U.S. Wife Lynne photography buff.

Robert Earl Holding

$800 million
Refining, gas stations, real estate. Salt Lake City. 69.
Married, 3 children.

Currently beefing up second Utah ski resort, Snow Basin, for 2002 Olympics. Mormon parents lost everything in 1929 crash. Air Force; U. of Utah 1951. Managed isolated, moneylosing Wyoming motel/gas station 1952. Built up, bought out partners. Added pumps, advertised as world's largest gas station. Built chain. Borrowed to buy small refinery Casper, Wyo. 1968; mortgaged it 1976 to buy Sinclair Oil assets western U.S.: refinery, distribution, gas stations. Bought Sun Valley resort for $12 million 1977; now worth an estimated $115 million, constant improvements. Largest landowner Salt Lake City outside Mormon Church. Also 450,000 ranch acres Montana, Wyoming. Member since 1994.

Bruce R. McCaw

$800 million
McCaw Cellular. Bellevue, Wash. 49.
Married.

OVER $700,000,000

Keith W. McCaw

$775 million
McCaw Cellular. Seattle. 43.
Married, 2 children.

John Elroy McCaw Jr.

$750 million
McCaw Cellular. Seattle. 45.
Divorced, 3 children.

Brothers. Three of 4 sons of John Elroy McCaw, radio and cable TV pioneer (d. 1969). All attended Seattle's Lakeside School. Brother Craig *(see p. 154)* led family in building father's Twin City Cablevision into major cable TV systems operator. Sold cable assets for $755 million 1987, reinvested in cellular licenses. Became communications giant McCaw Cellular; sold to AT&T for $11.5 billion 1994. Family agreed to invest up to $1.1 billion in Nextel Communications. Bruce: never worked for Craig; aviation, race car enthusiast; recently married. Press-shy: "One of the reasons we spend less time in [Seattle] is because we got run out [by the press]." John: Lakeside classmate of Paul Allen *(see p. 116)*. Stake in Seattle (baseball) Mariners; majority owner Vancouver (basketball) Grizzlies, (hockey) Canucks. Flies helicopters. Keith: left McCaw 1991: "You can only work for your brother for so long." Just built mammoth house on Seattle's Lake Washington. Only brother without pilot's license. Member since 1987.

Henry Earl Singleton

$790 million
Teledyne, Beverly Hills. 79.
Married, 5 children.

Having thwarted raider Ronald LaBow's WHX Corp. takeover attempt early this year, Teledyne beat antitrust murmurs and merged with Allegheny Ludlum in August. Affluent Texas rancher's son and MIT grad, Singleton cofounded Teledyne with George Kozmetzky and Arthur Rock 1960. Expanded by acquiring undervalued businesses with steady cash flows. Early proponent of buying in stock to boost performance. "Buy very good value, and when the market is ready, that value will be recognized." Spun off insurers Argonaut Group 1986 and Unitrin 1990. Currently Argonaut chair. Proxies list him as a "rancher and investor." Divides time between 7 cattle ranches in New Mexico and California. Member since 1982.

George B. Kaiser

$780 million
Oil and gas, banking, real estate.
Tulsa. 54.
Married, 3 children.

Looking to merge his Bank of Oklahoma with an equal-sized bank. Snatched up 12 retirement centers over past 5 years because "the demographics are obvious." Father fled Nazi Germany 1938, settled in Tulsa 1940. George to Harvard for B.A., M.B.A.: says undergraduate experience was valuable, but B-school time could have been better spent. Took over Kaiser-Francis Oil; built into one of largest independent, private gas producers in U.S. Since diversified but "Oil and gas is still my first love." Recently shifted 50% of exploration efforts to Canada. Bought once distressed Bank of Oklahoma 1991, now worth $390 million. Merger would give liquidity, achieve critical mass. Member since 1992.

Frank Batten Sr. and family

$780 million
Media. Virginia Beach, Va. 69.
Married, 3 children.

Uncle Samuel Slover arrived Virginia 1900. Offered 50% of *Newport News* (now *Virginian-Pilot*) if he halted paper's losses within year; succeeded. Raised nephew Frank: Harvard M.B.A.; publisher 1954, age 27. Frank expanded Landmark Communications: now 7 dailies, 23 weeklies, more. First cable franchise 1964. Landmark also owns Weather Channel, Travel Channel. Frank owns 35% of Landmark. Sold Tele-Cable (over 740,000 subscribers) to TCI 1994 for over $1 billion then—but TCI stock in decline. Bright side: Landmark's broadcast properties (WTVF, Nashville; KLAS, Las Vegas) up sharply in value. Getting into on-line offerings. Son Frank Jr. now executive VP, involved in new ventures. Member since 1982.

John R. Menard Jr.

$775 million
Menard home improvement chain.
Eau Claire, Wis. 56.
Twice divorced, 3 children.

Menard thriving on upper-Midwest home turf despite onslaught by rival Home Depot: 17% growth, $2.7 billion sales 1995. Eldest of 8 children of teachers-turned-dairy-farmers. Built barns to pay for college. Opened home improvement store in Eau Claire 1972. Caught big do-it-yourself trend early: Menard's 115-store home improvement chain now third-largest in U.S. Little debt, specializes in low-priced imported hardware, good quality and inventory controls. Said to play both sides of political fence, big contributor both parties. "We'll do anything that's not immoral, illegal or unethical." Member since 1994.

Andrew Jerrold Perenchio

$750 million
Television, movies. Bel Air, Calif. 65.
Twice divorced, 3 children.

Swinging for the fences with pending Univision IPO, nation's leading Spanish-language broadcaster. Son of Fresno vintner. Attended UCLA; booked bands, catered frat parties. Joined MCA 1958; founded talent agency 1963; clients: Liz Taylor, Marlon Brando. Promoted Ali-Frazier fight. With Norman Lear 1974 created *All in the Family*, Embassy Pictures. Sold 1985 to Coca-Cola for $485 million. Bought Loews theaters for $160 million, sold 1986 for reported $300 million. Failed bid for Time 1989 with Charles Dolan, Robert Bass *(see pp. 236 and 134)*. Perenchio bought Univision from Hallmark 1992 with Mexican, Venezuelan billionaire partners who want to be in U.S. television but face complex foreign ownership rules. Perenchio paves their way. Member since 1985.

Robert Edward Rich Sr. and family

$750 million
Fake cream. Buffalo, N.Y.; Palm Beach. 83.
Married, 3 children.

Learned family dairy business, bought own milk company 1935; during WWII, milk administrator. "The cow is a very inefficient factory." Developed soybean-based whipping cream. Then Coffee Rich creamer 1960; cheap, nonspoiling; foundation of fortune. Added frozen products like breads, cookies, cakes, pies, pizza dough; 1995 revenues totaled $1.1 billion. Expanding internationally under son Robert Jr., 55. "We do more than fake cream." Now in China, India, Mexico, South Africa. Riches own AAA (baseball) Buffalo Bisons, AA (baseball) Wichita Wranglers; stake in Buffalo (hockey) Sabres. Member since 1983.

William Cook

$750 million
Medical supplies. Bloomington, Ind. 65.
Married, 1 son.

Ex-cabbie; Northwestern 1953; 5 years as medical supplies salesman. Quit to form own hypodermic syringe company. Hated big-city Chicago, bundled family into Corvair 1963, settled in bucolic Bloomington. Crafted then-new cardiovascular catheters after $1,500 investment in blowtorch, soldering iron, plastic tubing. Now leader in catheters, pacemakers, syringes; recently-developed cardiovascular shunt looks promising. Active in community, renovating properties downtown Bloomington. Strenuously denies Forbes' estimate of his net worth. Member since 1988.

Ernest J. Olde

$750 million
Discount stockbroker. Detroit, Cayman Islands. 58.
Divorced, remarried; 3 surviving children.

"High-end" discount brokerage founder with knack for getting his name in the papers. Successfully fought allegations of insider trading, workplace discrimination. Intensely private, but Olde Discount expanding its profile and earnings. Started career as broker with Kidder, Peabody. Left to pioneer discount brokerage. Introduced commissionless trading 1993. Started marketing with radio spots, mass mailings, now on national cable TV. Scaled back after 1987 crash, rebuilt. Now 200 offices nationwide, moving into high-visibility, free-standing former bank buildings. Most real estate owned by Olde Property subsidiary, founded 1992. Natty dresser; capricious leadership style. Member since 1995.

Leonard Abramson

$745 million
U.S. Healthcare. Blue Bell, Pa. 63.
Married, 3 daughters.

In July U.S. Healthcare agreed to be acquired by Aetna for $8.3 billion. New entity largest health care company in U.S., serving 1 in 12 Americans. Founder Leonard driven by father's small-business failures: "Not too many people started off with less than I did." Drove cab to support himself while attending Philadelphia College of Pharmacy & Science. Supersalesman Parke-Davis 1960; quit when denied promotion. Believed by early 1970s HMOs most promising health care alternative. Obtained $3 million federal loan to start not-for-profit HMO-PA 1975. By 1981 revenues up sixtyfold: smart marketing, low prices, efficient delivery, tough negotiation with doctors, other providers. Took public 1983. Thought Clinton's health plan "a perverse socialism" that would "open up legitimate enterprises to political influence." Member since 1992.

Roy Edward Disney

$740 million
Walt Disney Co. Los Angeles. 66.
Married, 4 children.

Nephew of Walt Disney, who started Walt Disney Productions 1923. Roy worked at studio for 24 years as film editor, writer, producer; quit 1977 after fight with management. Set up Shamrock Holdings as real estate, media investment vehicle. Teamed with Bass brothers *(see pp. 135 and 201)*, returned to Disney as vice chairman 1984; put new emphasis on animation, brought in Michael Eisner *(see p. 304)*. Sold Shamrock's radio holdings 1995 for $395 million. Now just 1 TV station. Refocusing Shamrock on food: investments in Fantastic Foods (veggie burgers sold at Disney theme parks), Cascadian Farms (organic food grower), Grand Union (grocery stores). Also stakes L.A. Gear, Koor Industries. Member since 1982.

William Michael Cafaro and family

$725 million
Shopping malls. Hubbard, Ohio. 83.
Widower, 3 children.

Recent focus: remodeling, repositioning existing properties, but suburban regional malls still main engine with over 34 million sq. ft. commercial, retail space. Immigrant's son, built first strip center late 1940s with brother John (d. 1987). Major contributors to postwar suburban sprawl: constantly built strip centers, later enclosed malls. Concentrated on middle market, Midwest; rarely sells property; little debt. Today among top developers in nation; strong ties to anchors such as J.C. Penney, Sears, Montgomery Ward. Eldest son, Anthony, president; daughter, Flora, VP; other son, J.J. (who had failed sports car company), also in family business. "If you make a friend today, you can always make a deal tomorrow." Member since 1989.

Richard T. Farmer

$720 million
Cintas Corp. Indian Hill, Ohio. 61.
Married, 3 children.

Rags-to-riches: grandfather started industrial rag cleaning business 1929. Richard joined company 1957. Persuaded father to switch focus to uniform rental. Cintas now second in uniform market after Aramark; annual revenues over $700 million. Company goal: $1 billion revenues by 1998. Currently more than 100 rental locations in 35 states, Canada; now eyeing Mexico, Europe. Richard controls 28% company shares; sister Joan, brother-in-law James also own sizable chunk. Richard chief executive 1968; stepped down 1995. Voracious reader. Second richest in Cincinnati after Carl Lindner (see p. 162). Member since 1991.

NEW TO THE FORBES FOUR HUNDRED

Walter Scott Jr.

$720 million
Construction, telecommunications.
Omaha, Neb. 65.
Widowed, remarried; 6 children.

Born Omaha; high school pal Warren Buffett (see p. 116). As teenager, worked for Peter Kiewit, where father was chief engineer. Back to Kiewit after civil engineering degree Colorado State 1953. Relocated 17 times in

10 years working way up corporate ladder. Took reins after Peter Kiewit Sr. died 1979. Diversified construction and mining concern into higher-margin businesses: telecom, cable TV, energy. Formed MFS Communications 1987 to get into local fiber-optic networks, spun off to public. WorldCom Inc. buying MFS. If sale goes through, Scott's MFS stake worth about $400 million. Kiewit owns 24% of partner Cal Energy, feeding development with big power plants in Indonesia, Philippines. MFS and Kiewit unit RCN now pushing into New York City phone, cable and Internet access market. Still Buffett's pal—and landlord: Sage of Omaha rents office in Kiewit Plaza building; with Scott, owns Omaha Royals minor league ball club.

Jerome Spiegel Kohlberg Jr.

$715 million
LBOs. Mount Kisco, N.Y. 71.
Married, 4 children.

Left Kohlberg Kravis Roberts 1987 when firm's LBOs began getting too big, too hostile. No longer getting a piece of KKR's new deals; gradually decreasing share closed out at 7%. New York-born lawyer, Harvard M.B.A. At Bear, Stearns, first 1965 "bootstrap" deal friendly; with investors, borrowed money, bought dental products maker for $9.5 million from aging chief who stayed on. Took company on buying spree, then public; turned $500,000 into $4 million. Blueprint: buy company cheap, cut costs, motivate executives with equity. Hired summer intern George Roberts *(see p. 178)*; Roberts moved to California, recommended replacement: cousin Henry Kravis. Trio formed KKR 1976. After leaving KKR, started own firm 1987 with son James. Member since 1986.

James H. Clark

$710 million
Netscape. Woodside, Calif. 52.
Married, 2 children.

Clark soared with the billionaires for a few months earlier this year, until his high-flying Netscape settled back down to $38 from its $87 high. No matter. This hyperenergetic entrepreneur is now looking for his third home run in Healtheon, an Internet-based health care information outfit he started in February. First home run was Silicon Graphics, producer of inexpensive, realistic 3-D computer graphics system (produced dinosaurs in *Jurassic Park*). Second home run: Netscape, commercial software to navigate World Wide Web. Stock jumped $30 above offering price on first day trading. "I grew up an absolute poor boy in Texas, so it doesn't bother me to spend money. In fact, if I have nothing left when I die, it'll be fine." His family now very wealthy—except for excluded father, who abandoned Clark when he was a child. Member since 1995.

Stanley Druckenmiller

$700 million
Soros Fund Management.
New York City, Palm Beach, Fla. 43.
Married, 3 children.

George Soros' *(see p. 132)* second-in-command. Profiting this year from big bets on the S&P, bonds. Normally reclusive, joined public debate last fall over national debt. Magna cum laude, Bowdoin College. Skipped graduate economics to become stock analyst, Pittsburgh National Bank. Quickly promoted. "I had a natural aptitude." At 28, left to start money manager Duquesne Capital Management 1981. To work for hero Soros 1988, who became mentor. Quick study: got day-to-day management of all funds 1989. Funds took off. "Soros has taught me that when you have tremendous conviction on a trade, you have to go for the jugular." Believed to get 30% of Soros' incentive fee. Member since 1995.

William Ingraham Koch

$700 million
Inheritance. Palm Beach, Fla. 56.
Married, 1 son.

Frederick Robinson Koch

$550 million
Inheritance. London, Monaco, NYC. 62.
Single.

Two of 4 sons of Fred Koch (d. 1967), founder of $23 billion (sales) oil giant Koch Industries. Family feud exploded 1981: Bill claimed mismanagement, stingy dividends by Koch Industries. Bill's twin, David, and older brother, Charles, *(see p. 60)* controlled firm, bought out Bill, Fred 1983 for over $1 billion. Bill's net share estimated $700 million. Massachusetts court ruled no capital gains tax applies; Bill got biggest Massachusetts tax refund ever 1993 ($47.5 million). Founded Oxbow Group mid-1980s: trading firm, high-tech and medical research, real estate, energy, etc. Revenues estimated $700 million. Bill: oenophile, art collector—Picasso, Cezanne, Miro. Engineering background helped him win sailing's America's Cup 1992. Sponsored first all-women team 1995. Now out of racing, calling field unsportsmanlike. Believes he and Fred undercompensated by Charles and David. Suing for additional Koch Industries payoff. Member since 1982. Fred: reclusive art collector, restorer. Attended Harvard, Yale Drama. Philanthropist: Morgan Library in NYC, Harvard Theater Collection; nearly $3 million building Swan Theatre at Stratford-upon-Avon. In London, lives in Jean Paul Getty's former mansion. Joins Bill in ongoing suits against brothers. Member since 1983.

Patrick Joseph McGovern

$700 million
Publishing. Nashua, N.H. 59.
Divorced, remarried; 4 children.

Built Tic-Tac-Toe machine tenth grade; won scholarship to MIT, studied biophysics, computer science. Worked briefly for first computer magazine (*Computers and Automation*); launched International Data Group 1964 as computer census service. Started flagship *Computerworld* magazine 1967. Has grown 20% to 30% annually by adding expositions, books, on-line services. Now over 280 titles read by 80 million-plus in 78 countries. Big push into Asia, Latin America, Eastern Europe helped fuel sales to $1.4 billion. Little debt, employees own 35%. Lives modestly; net worth could far exceed $700 million. Member since 1982.

John Orin Edson

$700 million
Leisure craft. Seattle. 64.
Divorced, remarried; 2 children.

Founded Bayliner Marine Corp., powerboat maker 1955, building boats in garage behind showroom. Sales, profits doubled every 3 years until 1986 (sales then over $400 million), when Brunswick bought Bayliner for $425 million. His secret: he simplified production in what had been custom boat industry, passed savings along to customer. Invested Bayliner proceeds conservatively: 60% in bonds, 40% in stocks. Made and launched 161-foot fiberglass yacht in July 1993. Edson and wife own several planes, helicopters. Bought land near Scottsdale, Ariz. airport. Takes yachting "business trips" to Caribbean, Costa Rica and Mexico. Member since 1986.

William A. Dart

$700 million
Styrofoam cups, investments.
Sarasota, Fla. 68.
Married, 3 children.

Ugly, epic Dart family dispute continues: W.A.'s eldest, estranged son Thomas suing for restoration of trust assets. So is grandson Thomas Dart

Jr., 19: "I want my family back, but I can't trust any of them." Small wonder. W.A.'s sons Kenneth and Robert expatriated to avoid U.S. taxes; Robert divorced wife through British courts to ensure stingy spousal settlement. W.A., son of steel tape measure manufacturer, experimented with plastics 1950s. Devised secret, lowest-cost method of making foam cups, built world's largest maker, Dart Container. Brought in sons Kenneth, Robert and Thomas. Kenneth invested profits brilliantly: Freddie Macs, Salomon Brothers; held up restructuring of Brazil's national debt. Kenneth and Robert secured citizenship Belize, Ireland. Brother Tom fears bulk of family lucre has been spirited overseas beyond his—or anyone's—reach: "Nobody's left." Member since 1991.

Ernest E. Stempel

$700 million
American International Group.
Hamilton, Bermuda. 80.
Widowed, 4 children.

Insurance kingpin. Referred by uncle, joined AIG predecessor as assistant manager 1938, then only 23 other employees. Officer on destroyer in WWII. Ascended AIG corporate ladder, attended law school at night. Sent to Bermuda by founder Cornelius Vander Starr 1953 to run subsidiary American International Reinsurance's general insurance operations. In 1963 took over Starr's life insurance division, made president. Serious international business traveler: says knows villages, cities of Southeast Asia better than U.S.; commutes weekly between Bermuda and NYC. Now in charge of AIG worldwide life insurance. Member since 1994.

George Lindemann

$700 million
Cable TV, cellular phones. Wellington, Fla. 60.
Married, 3 children.

"Every time everyone is talking about something, that's the time to sell." After Wharton joined father's cosmetics business 1958; developed new type contact lens, sold out to Cooper Labs 1971 for $60 million. Acquired New Jersey cable TV licenses, leveraged Vision Cable to 230,000 subscribers in 6 states; sold to Newhouse brothers (see p. 120) for $220 million 1982. Reinvested in cellular telephone licenses; sold Metro Mobile to Bell Atlantic for $300 million in Bell shares. Now building Southern Union natural gas company. Son George Jr. serious equestrian, convicted on charges that he commissioned killing a show horse for insurance money

1995. Lindemann Sr.'s Bell Atlantic stock recently worth over $460 million. Member since 1989.

OVER $600,000,000

Edward Perry Bass

$690 million
Oil, investments. Fort Worth. 51.
Single.

Second of 4 Bass brothers *(see pp. 134 and 135)*. Yale, Coast Guard, Yale architecture school; only non-M.B.A. Bass brother. Joined communal theater troupe in Santa Fe; owns properties worldwide, including hotel in Nepal. Oversees Sundance Square, part of Bass-financed 33-block development downtown Fort Worth (stores, restaurants, apartments, etc.) credited for Fort Worth revitalization. Spent reported $150 million on Biosphere 2, flawed experimental self-contained ecosystem in Arizona; sued over mismanagement, got top managers removed. Spent over $20 million establishing Institute of Biosphere Studies at Yale. Has 500,000-acre Australian ranch. Member since 1983.

NEW TO THE FORBES FOUR HUNDRED

Billy Joe (Red) McCombs

$680 million
Autos, media, ranches; San Antonio, Tex.; 69.
Married, 3 children.

Longtime Forbes Four Hundred wannabe, Red's Clear Channel Communications stock explodes with federal radio deregulation. Initial $175,000 investment now worth over $450 million. Auto mechanic's son, set goal age 9 to be rich. Washed dishes, delivered newspapers age 11. Quit law school U. of Texas after a year and a half, began selling new Fords on commission 1950. Entered used car market; became partner in dealership 1958. Taught sales seminars for Ford Motor Co. Made first million by 1960. Teamed with Lowry Mays *(see p. 208)* to start Clear Channel Communications 1972. Red focused on car dealerships, ranching. Sold interest in Denver (basketball) Nuggets 1985 for $20 million profit; also 85% stake in San Antonio (basketball) Spurs 1993. Consolidated extensive ranch holdings in early 1990s. "Success is the journey, not the destination."

Norman W. Waitt

$680 million
Gateway 2000. North Sioux City, S.D. 42.
Married.

With brother Ted *(see p. 145)* started computer mail order business in Iowa farmhouse 1985 with $10,000 bank loan secured by grandmother's CD. Norman, Morningside College grad, joined with $5,000 investment 1986; incorporated as Gateway 2000. Bypassed Silicon Valley and retail market; became direct-market PC seller and manufacturer based in South Dakota. First year revenue: $100,000. Staggering growth due to low costs, low prices. Norm designed accounting system and handled finances. Computers shipped in Holstein-spotted boxes inspired by family business; same motif in Norm's office. Left company 1991 amidst tensions with Ted. Created foundation with wife, Andrea. Reduced stake to 10% from 45% in 5 years. New venture: music production company Antipreneur. "As an entrepreneur at Gateway, I made a lot of money and had a little fun. With Antipreneur, I hope to make a little money and have a lot of fun." Keeping to word: one year, one album. Member since 1994.

Steven Ferencz Udvar-Hazy

$675 million
International Lease Finance Corp.
Beverly Hills. 50.
Married, 4 children.

Born Budapest. Family fled to Sweden, then NYC; LA 1962. Steven, UCLA grad, had own aircraft brokering, consulting business. With Leslie and Louis Gonda *(see p. 226)*, pooled $150,000, plus $1.7 million bank loan, to found ILFC in 1973. Deregulated airlines eager for cheap, low-risk, short-term leases. Public 1983; now one of world's largest aircraft lessors. Merged with AIG 1990. Known as demanding businessman, shrewd negotiator. Keen sense of industry: $4.7 billion Boeing jet order in mid-1980s, including generation not in use; today those flying are industry standard. Recently ordered 18 Boeing aircraft, valued at $2.7 billion. ILFC president. Certified pilot; flies company jet around world scouting business. Member since 1993.

Samuel Heyman

$675 million
GAF Corp. New York City. 57.
Married, 4 children.

Yale (tennis champ), Harvard Law; under Bobby Kennedy at Justice, chief assistant U.S. Attorney Connecticut. When father died 1968, drawn into family real estate: "It became so fascinating I decided to stay." Shopping malls 1968-83. Bought GAF shares 1981; successful proxy fight against "selfish management." With Michael Milken's *(see p. 216)* help, went after Union Carbide, Borg-Warner; made over $450 million. Took International Specialty Products public 1991. Founded Heyman Center on Corporate Governance at Cardozo Law School, NYC, 1987. Extensive art collection. Much debt. Member since 1991.

Patrick G. Ryan

$670 million
Insurance. Winnetka, Ill. 59.
Married, 3 children.

Son of Milwaukee Ford dealer. Northwestern on football scholarship. Sold Penn Mutual insurance before founding Pat Ryan & Associates 1964. Specialized in providing policies with "altar boy" image at car dealerships. Renamed Ryan Insurance Group, Inc. 1971; merged with Aon Corp. (formerly Combined International Corp.) 1982. Acquired majority of corporate training company Pecos River Learning Centers 1994. Disposed of two life insurance subsidiaries 1996 to focus on insurance brokerage. Current chair and CEO. Part-owner Chicago (football) Bears. Founded Pathways Center for Children with wife, Shirley, a not-for-profit center for children with neurological, sensory-motor, learning disorders. Slowed down since quadruple bypass surgery 1994. Member since 1985.

Alan Gerry

$665 million
Cable TV. Liberty, N.Y.; Naples, Fla. 67.
Married, 3 children.

Sold Cablevision Industries to Time Warner last year for $2.8 billion; Gerry's take: $795 million in Time Warner stock and cash. Age 17, U.S. Marines, then electronics school; studied television 1949. Put up TV antenna towers with $1,500 1956 in Catskills town of Liberty. "Just trying to get a good picture on the 3 networks." Acquired cable franchises, built systems, steady growth to 2,000 subscribers 1970; then up to 52,000 by 1980. Acquisition push through 1980s jacked CVI, subsidiaries to 1.3 million subscribers in 18 states; Philadelphia, LA, etc. Says not worried about underperforming Time Warner stock, eagerly awaiting Time Warner/Turner merger. Now running own investment company: venture capital, currency trading, etc. Member since 1993.

John Charles Haas

$665 million
Rohm & Haas Co. Villanova, Pa. 78.
Married, 5 children.

Father Otto Haas (d. 1960) and Otto Röhm formed German company to manufacture leather products 1907. Fifty-fifty partnership: Haas came to U.S. to set up American branch 1909; Röhm developed German side. Company added pesticides 1929, Plexiglas 1932. U.S. government seized German assets WWI, WWII; sold in public offering 1948. Haas family kept their stake. Company split into two independent firms: Rohm & Haas (Philadelphia) and Röhm GmbH (Germany). John's brother Fritz Otto Haas (d. 1994) took over when father retired 1959. John: chairman 1974-78. Expanded into paint and paper coatings, adhesives, chemicals. Created RohMax July 1996: joint venture with Röhm GmbH of Germany; reunited petroleum additives divisions. Sales expected to exceed $4 billion 1996. Member since 1986.

Josephine Ford

$660 million
Inheritance. Grosse Pointe Farms, Mich. 73.
Married, 4 children.

With brother William Clay (see p. 163), last surviving grandchildren of Ford Motor Co. founder Henry Ford (d. 1947). Brother Henry Ford II (d. 1987) left Yale, Navy following father Edsel's death to join faltering company 1943; succeeded grandfather as president 1945; retired as chairman 1980. Engineered company turnaround, redevelopment of downtown Detroit. Josephine (Dodie) married to Walter B. Ford of unrelated old Detroit banking family. Ford family has donated more than $10 million to Detroit Institute of Arts. Ford Foundation holds $7.5 billion assets. Ford family collectively owns 6% company with 40% voting power, recently worth $2.2 billion. First appeared on list 1983.

NEW TO THE FORBES FOUR HUNDRED

Michael Birck and family

$660 million
Tellabs, Inc. Hinsdale, Ill. 58.
Married, 3 children.

Born in Missoula, Mont.; raised on chicken, corn farm in Indiana. Father was rural mail carrier, mother English teacher. Turned on to science, math by high school teacher; only student in class of 11 to go to college.

After electrical engineering degree at Purdue (1960), joined vaunted Bell Laboratories. Bureaucracy nearly suffocated him: "I really wanted to design something." Left in 1966 after NYU master's in engineering; started Tellabs in 1975 with 2 partners, plywood workbench, $25 used soldering machine, old oscilloscope. Public 1980; sales, profits skyrocketed in 1990s on strength of Titan digital cross-connect system: helps regional Bells manage phone traffic. Affable, down-to-earth, but stock up 2,100% since 1993.

John William Berry Sr.

$650 million
Yellow Pages. Dayton, Ohio. 74.
Twice divorced, remarried; 5 sons.

Son of Loren M. Berry, horseradish salesman, then train schedule ad space boy. Arrived Dayton 1910 with ambition, $200. Convinced Dayton Home Telephone Co. to sell ads on yellow paper he could buy cheap. "Mr. Yellow Pages" died 1980 at 91, his product by then a part of the language. John Sr. bought out siblings, expanded. Sold L.M. Berry & Co., then second-largest Yellow Pages agent, for BellSouth stock 1986; retired 1987. Son John Jr.: 48, CEO Berry Investments (hunting supplies, security devices). With family, believed to still hold some 14 million shares BellSouth. Member since 1983.

Leon Hess

$650 million
Amerada Hess Corp. Deal, N.J. 81.
Married, 3 children.

Son of Lithuanian immigrant who started small fuel-delivery firm; went broke 1933. Leon, 19, reorganized business: rebuilt trucks with heaters to deliver fuel oil in liquid form; bought resid for pennies, sold for near-full price per BTU of coal. Expanded into refining, exploration. Hess went public 1962 through merger. Acquired Amerada Corp. 1969. Company produces oil in U.S., U.K., North Sea, Middle East, Gabon. Also sells gasoline in over 500 Hess stations (primarily in New York, New Jersey, Florida). Over $7 billion in sales last fiscal year. Stepped down as chairman and CEO 1995; still on board. Son John, 41, now CEO. Leon owner of New York (football) Jets. Member since 1982.

Robert Allen Naify

$650 million
Movie theaters. San Francisco. 74.
Married, 6 children.

Marshall Naify

$445 million
Movie theaters. San Francisco. 76.
Divorced, 3 children.

Brothers. Two sons of Lebanese immigrant who opened Atlantic City movie theater 1912. Founded California Theaters 1920s; later purchased 50% United Artists Theater Circuit. Early pioneer cable television 1950s. Young Robert and Marshall started in movie business as ushers, projectionists in father's theaters; gained control after UCT-UATC merger 1963. Brothers eventually sold out to Tele-Communications, Inc. 1986 for stock, convertible notes, cash. Brothers low-key, but older brother Marshall making noise investing in Canadian gold stocks. First appeared on list 1987.

Oakleigh Blakeman Thorne III

$650 million
CCH. Millbrook, N.Y. 64.
Divorced, remarried; 4 children.

CCH (formerly Commerce Clearing House) agreed to $1.9 billion buyout by Dutch media powerhouse Wolters Kluwer in January. Deal strengthens position in U.S. tax and legal publishing market. Great-grandfather Oakleigh Thorne bought company 1892, 21 years before income tax enacted. Company became largest publisher of tax guides for lawyers, accountants and government. Biggest subscriber: IRS. Oakleigh III less committed to company; spent more time on 900-acre "Thorndale" estate. CCH's net income dropped from $53 million 1987 to $31 million 1991. Enter founder's great-great-grandson, Oakleigh IV. Joined company after Columbia M.B.A., engineered company makeover: trimmed payroll, reorganized management, pushed for dramatic shift toward electronic publishing. Rewarded for turnaround with CEO title April 1995. Nearly doubled fortune selling family's controlling CCH stake: "We found the offer very compelling." Resigned in August. Thorne family no longer associated with company. First appeared on list 1982.

NEW TO THE FORBES FOUR HUNDRED

Dean White

$650 million
Billboards, hotels. Crown Point, Ind. 73.
Married, 4 children.

The new Clinton/Gore restrictions on tobacco companies' advertising may take a piece out of White's wealth. Cigarette companies big spenders on billboards, and Whiteco Outdoor now nation's fourth-largest billboard company. Father started sign company 1935; Dean sold ads at 13. U. of Nebraska dropout. U.S. Merchant Academy 1945; returned to take over business. Surpassed father's challenge to net $1 million: landed billboard contract with Holiday Inn founder Kemmons Wilson; capitalized on interstate highway growth. Has diversified into go-cart/batting-cage entertainment centers. Hints he may take Whiteco public while the taking is good: "When [Whiteco is] valued at 14 times cash flow, I'm heads up on that." Or may not: "I can't spend the money I got."

Mark Hume McCormack

$650 million
Sports management. Cleveland, NYC. 65.
Divorced, remarried; 2 sons, 1 daughter.

Lost $1 billion bid for broadcast rights to 2002 soccer World Cup. But no matter. Still explosive growth for worldwide sports business juggernaut International Management Group. Son of Chicago farm journal publisher. Childhood injury ruled out contact sports, chose golf. As top golfer at William & Mary, competed against, befriended Arnold Palmer. Yale Law, Army stint followed by job in Cleveland law firm. On side, booked exhibitions for pro golfers. Palmer, others asked McCormack to review endorsement contracts. Started IMG late 1950s, Palmer first client; then signed Jack Nicklaus, Gary Player. Gradually built business to global proportions. Five IMG divisions: client management (sports, entertainment, literary); event management (owns several golf and tennis events); corporate marketing; television and film production (covers badminton in Asia, soccer in Europe, golf everywhere); financial management. Member since 1995.

Edward J. DeBartolo Jr.

$650 million
Shopping centers. Youngstown, Ohio. 50.
Married, 3 daughters.

Ed Jr. dislikes debt, unlike dad Ed Sr. (d. 1994): stock swap with Melvin Simon *(see p. 213)* wipes out $1.5 billion loan 1996; now holds 22 million shares in nation's largest REIT. Ed Sr. wrote contracting bids for non-English-speaking stepfather at age 13. Studied civil engineering Notre Dame; Army engineering WWII. Took over family business 1944, built first shopping center 1948. Saw suburban malls as "the new downtown." Took risks, built vast shopping center empire; net worth over $1 billion before early 1990s real estate crash, debt crunch. President Ed Jr.'s biggest single personal asset: San Francisco (football) 49ers; little sister Marie active in running private real estate. Member since 1995.

James Evans Stowers Jr.

$650 million
Mutual funds. Kansas City, Mo. 72.
Married, 4 children.

"The eternal bull." Founder, Twentieth Century Mutual Funds. WWII Army fighter pilot. After graduating U. of Missouri 1948, did short stints medical school, life insurance sales, local mutual fund firm. Founded Twentieth Century Mutual Funds 1958 with $100,000 and 24 shareholders. Believes earnings momentum predicts stock prices: "Money follows earnings." First tracked dozens by hand with calculator; developed computer model 1973, now tracks 15,500. Last year acquired $11 billion Benham Group. Assets now over $50 billion. Lunch: homemade peanut butter sandwiches in employee cafeteria. Son, James Stowers III, now president. With wife, both cancer survivors, big givers to medical research. Member since 1993.

NEW TO THE FORBES FOUR HUNDRED

L. Lowry Mays

$640 million
Radio. San Antonio, Tex. 61. Married, 3 children.

Texas A&M, Harvard M.B.A. Ran small investment banking concern. "I had no intention of getting into the broadcast business." Teamed with local car dealer B.J. "Red" McCombs (see p. 201) to buy struggling San Antonio radio station WOAI-AM for $175,000 in 1972. Quit banking to run fledgling media properties 1974. Bought distressed stations in mid-size markets. Stepped up promotion: heavy use of billboards, on-air contests, giveaways. Clear Channel Communications public 1984 at $10 a share; secondary offering 1991 at $14.25. With FCC ownership rules easing, shares now trade in the 80s. Mays still owns 20%. Cash flow compounded annually by 50% over past 5 years. Clear Channel now 18 TV stations, 140 radio stations nationwide. Three kids in business; Mark, 33, current chief operating officer, being groomed to take over.

Sidney Kimmel

$630 million
Jones Apparel Group. Philadelphia. 67.
Single.

Son of Philly cab driver. Dropped out of college, worked in knitting mill. Rose to president women's sportswear company Villager Inc. 1968. Founded Jones Apparel Division of W.R. Grace & Co.; bought unit 1970 with former Grace accountant Gerard Rubin. Moderately priced career sportswear: "Armani for the working woman." Dangerously overexpanded by 1987, sold weak divisions, held on to moneymakers: Jones New York, Evan-Picone, Saville. Bought out Rubin 1989; took public 1991. Cinematic sideline: Jones Film, started 1983: *Blame it On Rio*, *9 1/2 Weeks*. Recently donated $10 million to Thomas Jefferson U. for cancer research. Member since 1992.

Morton L. Mandel

$630 million
Premier Industrial Corp.
Shaker Heights, Ohio. 75.
Married, 3 children.

Joseph C. Mandel

$615 million
Premier Industrial Corp.
Lyndhurst, Ohio. 82.
Married, 2 children.

Jack N. Mandel

$600 million
Premier Industrial Corp.
Shaker Heights, Ohio. 84.
Married.

Brothers. Morton: dropped out of Western Reserve U. at 19, pooled $900 with Joe and Jack, bought auto-parts business from uncle 1940. Public 1960; bought Newark Electronics 1968 to expand beyond auto parts: provides hard-to-find, rare electronic parts to mostly low-volume customers. Heavy emphasis on customer service: employees answer telephone by third ring. Jack and Joe chaired finance, executive committees. Active in Cleveland redevelopment efforts. Merged Premier Industrial with England's Farnell Electronics Plc. in $2.8 billion deal 1996; now Premier Farnell Plc. Brothers received cash, stock. Morton still active, Premier Farnell deputy chairman. First appeared on list 1983.

John Thomas Lupton

$630 million
Coca-Cola bottling. Lookout Mountain, Tenn. 70.
Married, 4 children.

Elizabeth Lupton Davenport

$630 million
Coca-Cola bottling. Lookout Mountain, Tenn. 63.
Divorced, remarried; 3 children.

Siblings. Grandfather John T. (d. 1933) landed rights to distribute Coke 1899. Used part of patent medicine fortune to finance early bottling plants. Father, Thomas Carter, bought, sold Coke franchises at frenzied pace. John: started 1954 as chief bottle washer; ran family's Great Western Coca-Cola Bottling Co. after father's death 1977; board member until 1983. became largest U.S. Coca-Cola bottler. Sold to Coke 1986 for $1.4 billion. Major pillar Chattanooga society. Joined moneylosing golf club maker ProGroup as CEO 1995; company in black after 4 months. Member since 1982. Elizabeth: lives quietly, but shares in fortune worth over $1.2 billion. Member since 1986.

Cordelia Scaife May

$630 million
Inheritance. Ligonier, Pa. 68.
Divorced, widowed.

Great-granddaughter of Judge Thomas Mellon *(see Mellon family)*. Married briefly 1950. Wed Pittsburgh D.A. Robert Duggan, longtime friend, 1973. Duggan shot to death during corruption investigation 1974. Brother, Richard Mellon Scaife *(see p. 183)*, convinced Duggan was guilty, had turned against him. She never forgave him. Funds, supports environmental, educational causes. Carried on family tradition of funding emerging companies: $10 million for alternative energy into venture capital firm Roldiva (named after her favorite horse). Member since 1982.

Michael Ilitch

$625 million
Pizza. Detroit area. 67.
Married, 7 children.

Pizza problems: after Little Caesar's entry into delivery business, competitor Pizza Hut takes big slice of Caesar's take-out market. Also stung by Kmart store closings: lost scores of Caesar's in-store outlets. Son of Macedonian immigrants, opened first pizza parlor with wife, Garden City, Mich. 1959. Added second 1961; started franchising 1962. Saw chain possible: by 1967, 50 Little Caesar's. Started high-voltage ad campaigns: "Pizza! Pizza! Two great pizzas! One low price" 1976. Ilitch opened Czech, Slovak stores 1993. Sales now top $2 billion. Owns Detroit (hockey) Red Wings;

bought (baseball) Tigers from rival Domino's Pizza owner Tom Monaghan *(see p. 229)*; pledged $175 million for new stadium. Invested in blighted downtown Detroit properties. Member since 1991.

David Howard Murdock

$625 million
Real estate, finance. Bel Air, Calif. 73.
Divorced, widowed, remarried; 2 sons.

In 4 years lost nearly $200 million on 2 Hawaiian luxury hotels. A "tactical error." High school dropout. To Phoenix after World War II. Made fortune building houses; lost nearly all when housing market collapsed 1964. Put last million into Los Angeles real estate, small companies. Now Pacific Holding. Merged Iowa Beef Processors into Occidental Petroleum, made $100 million. Now chief executive, 23% owner Dole Food. Also lots of real estate, Arabian horses. "As long as we want to achieve, we're alive. If we're satisfied, we're already half dead." Member since 1982.

Betsey Cushing Roosevelt Whitney

$625 million
Inheritance. Manhasset, N.Y. 88.
Divorced, widowed; 2 children.

One of the 3 famous "Cushing sisters," she married James Roosevelt, FDR's eldest son; became White House hostess. Divorced 1940. Remarried 1942, to John Hay (Jock) Whitney, heir to vast oil, tobacco fortune. Jock invested in startups, media (*International Herald Tribune,* TV, radio stations). Died 1982. Betsey inherited almost all, including large art collection appraised over $200 million. Media holdings greatly reduced several years ago, but not so family trusts. She still comes in to the family office every day. "She keeps us all hopping." Member since 1982.

Richard Edwin Marriott

$620 million
Hotels. Potomac, Md. 57.
Married, 4 children.

John Willard Marriott Jr.

$565 million
Hotels. Washington, D.C. area. 64.
Married, 4 children.

Sons of John Willard Marriott Sr. (d. 1985). Willard Sr. started Washington, D.C. 9-stool root beer stand, Hot Shoppe, with wife, Alice, 1927; expanded into airline catering, restaurants. Opened Marriott Twin Bridges Motor Hotel 1957. Deeply religious Mormon, often worked 18-hour days in early years. Willard Jr. (Bill): U. of Utah grad, started as teen cook at father's Hot Shoppes. Marriott Corp. CEO 1972, succeeding father. Richard: U. of Utah, Harvard M.B.A., also began at Hot Shoppes; Marriott's vice chairman 1986. Hotel count surged from 75 (1980) to 539 (1989). Company split in two 1993: Host Marriott Corp. owns, manages real estate; Marriott International manages hotels, provides food/facilities management. Expansion drives second split 1996: new Host Marriott Services Corp. operates concessions at airports, toll roads, sports/entertainment venues. Bill runs Marriott International; brother Dick heads Host Marriott, also chairs First Media Corp., broadcasting firm privately owned by Marriott family. Brothers active Mormons, philanthropists. First appeared on list 1986.

Nelson Peltz

$620 million
LBOs. Bedford, N.Y.; Palm Beach, Fla. 54.
Divorced, remarried; 8 children.

With wife, Claudia, and investor partner Peter May, sued factoring firm Rampell 1996; claimed they were illegally lured into deal that promised 30% return. Peltz's Palm Beach estate, Montsorrel, on block for $75 million, twice as much as next-highest property. Wharton dropout. Built up family food distributor, sold 1978. With May, met Michael Milken 1979. Gained control Triangle Industries 1983; National Can 1985; American Can 1986. Sold Triangle 1988 to France's Péchiney S.A. for $834 million profit. Not as successful after: put $100 million 1989 into U.K.'s Montleigh Group (real estate), lost all when firm collapsed. With May, paid $80 million for 25% Victor Posner's DWG 1993, now Triarc Cos. Also partner Hollywood Inc. (Florida real estate). Member since 1989.

Charles Thomas Munger

$620 million
Berkshire Hathaway. Los Angeles. 72.
Married, 8 children.

Curmudgeonly partner of Warren Buffett for past 30 years; his tough-guy approach makes possible Buffett's Mr. Nice Guy. Helped push Buffett toward more qualitative, less quantitative analysis. Buffett: "He expanded my horizons." U. of Michigan 1941-42, Cal Tech 1943 while in Air Force. Postwar, Harvard Law School, J.D. 1948, magna cum laude. Lawyer in L.A. 1948-65; met Buffett 1959; co-invested mid-1960s. Berkshire Hathaway officer 1976; director, vice chairman since 1978. Enjoys golf, bridge, fishing. Says life's goal to stay below radar screen of The Forbes Four Hundred. "I've been associated with Warren for so long, I thought I'd just be a footnote." No way. Member since 1993.

NEW TO THE FORBES FOUR HUNDRED

Michael Krasny

$620 million
Mail-order computer sales. Buffalo Grove, Ill. 43.
Married, 1 child.

Graduated (barely) U. of Illinois 1975. Went to work for father's Toyota dealership. Hated selling cars, liked computerizing agency's sales and finance data. Became freelance computer programmer; lousy living. Needed cash, sold his IBM PC through ad in *Chicago Tribune*. First caller bought, second asked him to assemble, install computer system. Made a few hundred dollars. Calls kept coming, developed sales pitch. CDW Computer Centers went into business 1985 with first national ad in *PC World*. CDW's catalog now carries around 20,000 items, sales over $600 million. Learned from Toyota lot days: CDW salespeople have authority to haggle with customers. Krasny: "We negotiate everything." Took CDW public 1993. Krasny's 43% stake recently worth $620 million.

Melvin Simon

$620 million
Shopping centers. Indianapolis; Manalapan, Fla. 70.
Divorced, remarried; 5 children.

Herbert Simon

$425 million
Shopping centers. Indianapolis. 62.
Divorced, remarried; 5 children.

The "Marx Brothers" of malls tell each other to shut up during negotiations. Must've been a lot of cackling as they merged with DeBartolo *(see p. 207)*, creating a $3.7 billion company and the nation's largest shopping center REIT, the Simon DeBartolo Group. They can now further leverage their holdings on favorable terms and keep expanding beyond current holdings of 111 regional shopping centers, 66 strip shopping centers. Sons of New York tailor, Mel moved to Indianapolis, became leasing agent. Sent for Herb; made fortunes covering Midwest with unpretentious shopping malls. "Meshuggener Mel" known for colorful clothing, exuberant manner. Pair own Indiana (basketball) Pacers; 22.5% Minneapolis' Mall of America. Put 53% of their 69 million sq. ft. shopping mall empire in 1993 IPO of Simon Property Group. "We are just a couple of naive guys from the Bronx, right?" Mel a member since 1982; Herb first appeared on list 1986.

Jennifer Johnson Duke

$610 million
Inheritance. Jacksonville, Fla. 55.
Twice married, 2 children.

James Loring Johnson

$610 million
Inheritance. Pottersville, N.J. 51.
Married, 6 children.

Children of John Seward Johnson (d. 1983), with sisters, Elaine (see Wold), Diana, brother J. Seward Jr., heir to Johnson & Johnson fortune. Most of estate went to third wife and former chambermaid, Barbara Piasecka Johnson (see p. 157). She battled the kids in court, settled 1986. Jennifer: photographer; husband, Joseph, designs furniture. James: gentleman farmer, painter. Sister Diana Johnson Firestone: breeds and races horses; shares recently worth $380 million. Brother J. Seward Johnson Jr: accomplished sculptor, director of Harbor Branch Oceanographic Institute; shares recently worth $230 million. Oldest sister Mary Lea Johnson Richards (d. 1990) produced Broadway hits (22 Tonys), films (The Shining) with husband Martin. Half of estate to Martin, half to children, grandchildren; those shares recently worth $200 million. Siblings first appeared on list 1992.

Stewart Bainum Sr.

$610 million
Manor Care, Inc. Silver Spring, Md. 77.
Married, 4 children.

College dropout; plumbing contractor. Became builder during 1950s D.C. real estate boom. With brother developed nursing homes. Founded Quality Inns motel chain 1966 (renamed Choice Hotels 1990). Merged companies 1980. Choice operates Comfort, Clarion, Econo Lodge Inns. Manor Care now 200 nursing homes and assisted living facilities (most for affluent elderly). Also owns 82% Vitalink Pharmacy. Son Stewart Jr., 50, ex-state senator, lost race for U.S. House 1986; succeeded father as chairman 1987. First appeared on list 1985.

Perry Richardson Bass

$610 million
Oil, investments. Fort Worth. 81.
Married, 4 sons.

Nephew of oil tycoon Sid Richardson (d. 1951). Sid started with $40 from Perry's mother; left part of fortune to Perry, who built new oil empire. Perry ceded control to his son Sid 1968; Sid joined forces with Richard Rainwater (see p. 163), younger brother Lee in deals. With Bass partnership Airlie Group, Perry has large positions in nearly a dozen companies: RJR Nabisco, Beckman Instruments, John Wiley & Sons, others. Also cotrustee for Bass family entity controlling 5.9% Walt Disney Co., recently worth $1.8 billion. Member since 1982.

William Barron Hilton

$600 million
Hilton Hotels Corp. Holmby Hills, Calif. 68.
Married, 8 children.

Hilton Hotels goes gambling; just acquired Bally Entertainment Corp. in a $3 billion deal. Son of hotel magnate Conrad Hilton (d. 1979). Father wanted Barron to start at bottom of ladder. Barron left ladder, became WWII Navy photographer. Orange juice distributor at 19. Joined family business 1951 in operations. Founded LA (football) Chargers 1960. Moved team to San Diego following year, sold 1966. A founder of the American Football League. Bought 2 Las Vegas hotels 1970; gaming division now accounts for 46% operating profit. Toyed with selling company 1989, 1995; bids too low. Recently lured Stephen Bollenbach from Walt Disney Co. to become first nonfamily president in Hilton's 77-year history: stock has since skyrocketed. Barron balloon enthusiast. First appeared on list 1982.

NEW TO THE FORBES FOUR HUNDRED

Michael Chowdry

$600 million
Atlas Air. Denver. 41.
Married, 2 children.

Orphaned as a teenager. When his father died, young Chowdry was shipped off to England from Pakistan in 1968: his mother feared his uncle would kill him for his inheritance. Chowdry made his way to the U.S. to study aviation. Flew crop dusters in North Dakota before dropping out of U. of Minnesota-Crookston. Started buying, selling prop planes, then bigger jets for carriers 1980s. Increased world trade coincided with narrow-body trend. Result: shortage of cargo space. Bought used 747s, converted for cargo-only transport. First order: Nike sneakers, computer disk drives from Taiwan to U.S. for China Air. Took Atlas Air public August 1995 at $16; stock surged to $65. Projected 1996 sales: $320 million. "Unless people start beaming things from Hong Kong to New York, we'll be here."

John C. Malone

$600 million
Cable TV. Parker, Colo. 55.
Married, 2 children.

"Doctor" Malone has Johns Hopkins Ph.D. philosophy; undergraduate Yale. Stint at AT&T Bell Laboratories. Joined cable magnate John Magness *(see p. 175)* at Tele-Communications, Inc. 1973. TCI now largest U.S. cable systems owner and operator, 14 million subscribers; has stakes in Discovery Communications, United Video Satellite Group *(see Flinn)*, Home Shopping Network. U.S. Vice President Al Gore calls TCI the "ringleader of the cable Cosa Nostra," Malone, "Darth Vader." Gore and friends at FTC, appear to have vendetta against Malone, denying TCI important satellite broadcast licenses, crimping cash flow. Malone creative financier: keeps spinning off pieces of TCI, trying to get stock value up, so far to little avail. Planned merger with Bell Atlantic 1994 aborted; stock off 50% since. Wall Street down on cable in general and TCI in particular, but Malone keeps buying cable systems; latest purchase Viacom's systems 1996 after long awaited IRS ruling. Is there an exit strategy? Keeps yacht at his marina in Maine. Member since 1993.

Michael Robert Milken and family

$600 million
Investments. Los Angeles. 50.
Married, 3 children.

OVER $500,000,000

Lowell Jay Milken and family

$500 million
Investments. Los Angeles. 47.
Married, 4 children.

Did Michael Milken violate the terms of his disbarment from the securities business? His probation was recently extended to Oct. 25 while the

Securities and Exchange Commission ponders the question. So a cloud remains over him. Spends much time these days raising money, promoting cancer research; his own prostate cancer currently in remission. Helped bring Ted Turner and Time Warner's Jerry Levin together for recently consummated merger. Will get $50 million fee. By-product: cover story in Time Warner's Fortune, a sheet that frequently beat up on him in the past. Book due out soon. Has invested in real estate, Educational Technologies L.L.C. with Larry Ellison *(see p. 118)*. Educated Berkeley, Wharton M.B.A. Joined Drexel Burnham Lambert 1969; built into powerhouse for high-yield "junk" bond financing; fueled 1980s LBO boom. Salary and bonus exceeded $550 million in 1986 alone. Became thorn in the side of Wall Street, business establishments. Pleaded guilty to 6 felony counts security laws violations. Case mishandled by super-lawyer Arthur Liman. Milken went to prison in 1991; released after serving 22 months of a 10-year sentence. Paid $900 million settlement to government, creditors, litigators. When probation ends says he plans "to build a company with my own ideas rather than pass them all off to others." Believes nation's educational shortcomings offer giant opportunities for business. Brother/partner Lowell in many ways is his alter ego.

Charles C. Butt and family

$600 million
Supermarkets. San Antonio. 58.
Single.

Grandmother started small grocery 1905 with $60 to support sick husband, 3 kids in Kerrville, Tex. Son Howard (d. 1991) renamed it H.E. Butt Grocery 1944; chairman to 1984. Today H-E-B Foods. Grandson Charles began bagging groceries age 8: "About all I could do was carry groceries—I did a lot of that." Wharton 1959, H-E-B president 1971. Family built one of largest private U.S. supermarket chains (projected 1996 sales, $5.7 billion). Reclusive—"Poor man's Howard Hughes"—but releases net worth information. Has 100% voting control. Member since 1988.

Anne Catherine Getty Earhart

$600 million
Inheritance. Laguna Beach, Calif. 44.
Married, 2 children.

Claire Eugenia Getty Perry

$600 million
Inheritance. San Francisco Bay area. 42.
Married, 4 sons.

Caroline Marie Getty

$600 million
Inheritance. San Francisco. 39.
Single.

Daughters of George Getty (d. 1973), son of renowned oilman Jean Paul Getty (d. 1976); collectively dubbed "Georgettes" by family. Anne began squabble over half-uncle Gordon's *(see p. 145)* control of Sarah C. Getty Trust, then backbone of Getty family fortune; also disliked handling of Getty Oil. Husband John former Peace Corps volunteer; now general partner San Diego Padres baseball team. Claire also married to Peace Corps man. Amid initial Getty-Pennzoil deal, petitioned California judge for temporary restraining order that gave investment banker Bruce Wasserstein chance to bring in Texaco, resulting in Getty Oil sale, vast increase in family wealth, rise of Pennzoil lawyer Joe Jamail. Caroline active in preserving wildlife, environment. All very private. Members since 1989.

Helen Kinney Copley

$600 million
Publishing. La Jolla, Calif. 73.
Divorced, widowed; 1 son.

In July bought *Peoria Journal-Star* for $174 million. Daughter of Iowa railroad man. Saw ad, became secretary to James S. Copley, adopted son of newspaper magnate Colonel Ira Copley. Secretary became confidante, wife. "I'll never know what he saw in me. I was so pathetically shy." Dutiful wife, gracious hostess until James' death 1973; then shocked Copley crony-lieutenants who expected to take over operations: took over herself as publisher, chairman. Sold unprofitable papers, slashed payroll. Flagship *San Diego Union,* 9 other dailies; James' 2 children from first marriage beneficiaries of trust. Member since 1982.

Marvin J. Herb

$600 million
Bottling. Chicago. 59.
Married, 2 children.

Born upstate New York; University of Toledo M.B.A. Bronx plant manager for PepsiCo; president Pepsi-Cola Bottling of Indianapolis 1972. To Borden; became president consumer products division. Saw opportunity: bought Coca-Cola's bottlers for Indianapolis (competing against old Pepsi organization), Chicago 1981. Later added plants Milwaukee; Rochester, N.Y.; Pittson, Pa. Now Coke's third-largest bottler, estimated 90 million cases sold in 5 states. Intensely private; shuns publicity. Also frugal: flies coach for business. Notoriously tough manager, aggressive labor negotiator. Member since 1991.

Leonard Litwin

$600 million
Real estate. New York City. 80.
Married, 2 daughters.

Began in landscaping with father on New York's Long Island; still retains tree nurseries there. Branched into apartments with pioneering highrises on Manhattan's Upper East Side. Newest building—the Brittany—went up 1994. Also had Queens apartment buildings, Manhattan office space (since sold). Shuns publicity: "He operates like an old-fashioned real estate man." Today 26 Manhattan rental properties, at least 5,000 prime units. "Everybody who has a job in New York can't spend $5,000 on a co-op." Old-fashioned enough to keep rents very competitive. First appeared on list 1984.

Sydell L. Miller and family

$600 million
Matrix Essentials. Cleveland. 58.
Widowed, 2 children.

Married hairdresser Arnold Miller (d. 1992); couple founded Ardell Inc. eyelash products 1971. "We didn't understand distribution." Prospered anyway until 1984 sale for $3 million. Started hair care Matrix Essentials 1980; built extensive customer relations base with beauty salons nationwide. Successful Système Biolage product line prefaced development of skin and beauty care products. Sales hit $250 million by 1994. Sold to Bristol-Myers Squibb 1994 for 7.4 million shares of stock. Unit reportedly experiencing clash in management style since merger. Miller recently retired as chair. Member since 1995.

NEW TO THE FORBES FOUR HUNDRED

Henry R. Silverman

$600 million
Investments. New York City area. 56.
Married, 3 children.

This son of well-to-do New York family has ridden red-hot HFS stock to riches. Law degree University of Pennsylvania. 1964. Served in Vietnam

War as a lieutenant in Navy. To Wall Street as investment banker; became partner with Drexel Burnham in leveraged buyouts 1983. Hooked up with Blackstone Group 1990, borrowed heavily, bought Ramada, Howard Johnson franchises, bundled them into HFS, took public 1992 with $300 million market cap; now $9 billion. Added Park Inn International, Super 8 chains to portfolio. Invested in gambling startups 1993. Now consummating $800 million deal to buy Avis rent-a-car. Shrewd financial engineer, good businessman, workaholic—but what will happen to high-flying HFS stock when earnings growth inevitably slows?

Robert Addison Day Jr.

$590 million
Money management. New York City. 52.
Married, 3 children.

Trust Company of the West back on track after 1995 departure of high-profile fund managers. Grandson of Superior Oil founder William M. Keck and of Addison Day, onetime president of Los Angeles Gas Co. He succeeded his uncle Howard B. Keck (see p. 303) as head of W.M. Keck foundation ($1 billion assets) in January. At Claremont McKenna College he was a classmate of Henry Kravis (see p. 178). White Weld salesman. Started own money management firm. Launched TCW with $1.5 million from investors 1972. Found profitable niches: growth stocks, Latin securities, junk bonds, etc. Today manages diversified $52 billion. "There are only two kinds of players in this game: winners and losers. My grandfather always said 5% of the geologists discovered 95% of the oil." Member since 1993.

Peter Benjamin Lewis

$590 million
Progressive Corp. Beachwood, Ohio. 62.
Divorced, 3 children.

Surely the most colorful chief executive in the tepid insurance industry, Lewis said to advocate in-office romance and therapy of all stripes: Freudian, couples, group, individual, whatever. "They're all great." His fortune was built insuring high-risk drivers, an untapped corner of the market. Since taking over the business in 1965 (inherited from his father who cofounded it in 1937), Lewis increased revenues from $6 million to $3 billion. Provides immediate claims service, 24-hour policy hotline. Now creeping into standard market. A Democrat who favors reducing the size of government. Progressive has a sizable modern art collection;

Lewis' ex-wife Toby is the company curator. Gave $10 million to New York City's Guggenheim Museum in 1995. Likes to throw parties and claims his single-guy sex life keeps him healthy at the helm of the company. Penned unpublished book, *Progressive History*. Member since 1993.

Roger Milliken

$580 million
Textiles, investments. Spartanburg, S.C. 80.
Married, 5 children.

Milliken quickly built new factory after last year's fire that wiped out his company's largest manufacturing facility. Poor worldwide cotton crop 1995, but revenues, net profits rise. The company was cofounded in 1865 by Seth Milliken and William Deering (who left to join what became International Harvester) as dry goods jobber. Financed fledgling Southern mills, became owner of many in the Depression. Grandson Roger longtime head of Milliken & Co., largest private U.S. textile firm. Dependent on automotive fabric sales: Roger hard-nosed on General Motors' price demands. Stresses research and development, latest technology. Also controls Mercantile Stores Co. Secret about business; virulently anti-Nafta. Siblings Gerrish, Anne Franchetti, also share in company worth estimated at $1.2 billion. Member since 1982.

NEW TO THE FORBES FOUR HUNDRED

John P. Morgridge

$580 million
Data networking. San Jose, Calif. 63.

Born Elmhurst, Ill. Bachelor's U. of Wisconsin-Madison 1955; Stanford M.B.A. ('57), concentration marketing and transportation. Worked 20 years for Honeywell Information Systems; left 1980 for Stratus Computer; VP sales and marketing 1980-86. Spent 2 years as president, chief operating officer of laptop computer maker GRID Systems. Took helm at Cisco Systems 1988. Main product: router, device used to connect groups of computers—allows different networks to access same database. Sales exploded from less than $30 million 1989 to $4 billion 1996. Stock up more than 9,000% since IPO in 1990. Low key, has reputation for frugality: rented old Subaru from Rent-A-Wreck while on vacation. Ceded CEO spot to John Chambers 1995; stepped into chairman's role.

Edmund Wattis Littlefield

$580 million
Utah International. Burlingame, Calif. 82.
Married, 3 children.

Grandson of Edmund O. Wattis, founder Utah Construction; company took on huge projects, including Hoover Dam, San Francisco-Oakland Bay Bridge. Edmund, waterboy for UI workers, Stanford M.B.A. General manager Utah International 1958; construction business sold to Fluor Corp. 1969; became major coal/copper miner. Director General Electric 1964-84. While UI chairman, merged with GE; then-largest merger: $2.2 billion. Edmund and Wattis family received GE shares recently worth $3.6 billion. First appeared on list 1987.

John Edward Anderson

$575 million
Beverage distribution. Bel Air, Calif. 79.
Married, 4 surviving children.

Peddled popcorn outside father's Minnesota barber shop; Western Union messenger. UCLA: hockey team, taught ice skating. Harvard M.B.A. 1942; night school for law degree. Cofounder LA law firm Kindel & Anderson 1953. Some clients beverage distributors. Saw business, liked it. Formed Ace Beverage Co. 1956; learned business from distributor clients, distributed then-minor beer brand, Budweiser. Grew with Bud; added banks, insurance, real estate. "You need enough cash cows to feed your pigs." Member since 1988.

Kenneth Feld

$575 million
The Greatest Show on Earth.
Potomac, Md. 48.
Married, 3 children.

Circus, entertainment sales way up; now at least $600 million. Taking ice shows worldwide, producing *Big* on Broadway. Son of Irvin Feld, record store and pharmacy owner turned promoter. Bought Ringling Bros. and Barnum & Bailey Circus 1967 for $8 million. Rejuvenated, sold to Mattel 1971 for $50 million; repurchased 1982 for $23 million. Groomed son for business; died 1984. After Boston U., Kenneth built on father's base: cut salaries, costs to the bone. "The tightest man in show business." Believed aiming for $1 billion sales 1999. Also owns Siegfried & Roy magic show; 200-acre Florida elephant farm, clown college. Continually updates Circus; recent addition: Airiana, the Human Arrow. Member since 1993.

Leon Levy

$575 million
Money manager. New York City. 71.
Divorced, remarried; 1 child.

He and partner Jack Nash *(see p. 249)* shun publicity, play cards close to vest, look for investments others haven't yet identified. Favorite quote: "Money is not made in the light"—i.e., you don't make money following conventional wisdom. Earned returns averaging 30% since 1982. Typical of Levy, never studied economics or finance, instead music, psychology at CCNY. Joined Oppenheimer & Co. 1951, met future partner Nash. Ran research, made killing on bankrupt railroad bonds 1950s when others thought rails hopeless. Bought Oppenheimer; later sold and formed Odyssey Partners. Levy sociable, Nash uptight and secretive. "I think gossip is half the fun of life. Jack doesn't." Member since 1994.

Richard Alexander Manoogian

$570 million
Masco Corp. Grosse Pointe Farms, Mich. 60.
Married, 3 children.

Son of Alexander Manoogian (d. 1996), founded Masco Corp. 1929. Alex perfected the single-handle Delta faucet 1954; led to family fortune. Richard, Yale grad, took over 1968. Guided company through expansion, diversification. Acquired well over 100 companies; targeted low-tech industry, high-margin firms. Made unfortunate decision to enter home furnishings 1986: bought leading furniture makers Henredon, Drexel Heritage, etc. for $1.7 billion. Drag on profits: home furnishings accounted for 42% of sales but only 14% operating profits 1994. Sold division August 1996 for $1 billion. New strategy: "We want to get back that shareholder following we lost because of the distraction of home furnishings." Respected collector of 19th-century American art. Late father Alex renowned leader in Armenian community, well-known philanthropist: pledged tens of millions of dollars to charity, education. Member since 1986.

James Lee Clayton

$570 million
Mobile homes. Knoxville, Tenn. 62.
Twice divorced, 4 children.

Son of sharecropper: "I [recently] picked a little cotton just for fun and confirmed that I never want to do that again." Played guitar, had radio program. "There's a lot of money to be made in entertainment, but it was always going in the wrong direction." At 22 had own used-car lot. Bankrupt at 27. Got U. of Tennessee law degree while working nights at radio station. In 1966 started mobile-home business. Took Clayton Homes public 1983. Knew market; smart on credit. Today largest U.S. retailer mobile homes thanks to high demand for low-income homes in Southeast for chicken-processing plant workers, families. Sales now over $900 million. Also banks: under Smoky Mountain Bancorp. Gives to Tennessee cultural, educational institutions, but "still a used-car salesman at heart." Member since 1992.

Lawrence Flinn Jr.

$570 million
United Video Satellite Group.
Greenwich, Conn. 60.
Married, 3 children.

Yale, Columbia M.B.A.; got start with investment bank Morgan Stanley. Entered cable television 1965; became CEO/chairman 1976 of United Video Satellite Group, distributor of programming via satellite to cable TV systems, radio networks, paging industries, etc. UVSG's Prevue Network Channel reaches 42 million U.S. homes. Public 1993. Merged with telecommunications giant TCI *(see Malone, Magness)* 1995. Still chair and chief executive. With *TV Guide* parent News Corp., planned to create print and video hybrid, TV Guide Channel; collapsed. Recently parceled away privately held United Video Cablevision, cable operator providing service in 11 states. Member since 1995.

William B. Turner

$560 million
Coca-Cola. Columbus, Ga. 73.
6 children.

Sarah Turner Butler

$560 million
Coca-Cola. Columbus, Ga. 76.
Married, 3 children.

Elizabeth Turner Corn

$560 million
Coca-Cola. Columbus, Ga. 70.
Married, 5 children.

Siblings. Grandfather W.C. Bradley founded eponymous company 1885; currently in real estate, timberland, sports apparel, barbecue grills. Real wealth from spectacular long-term investment: Coca-Cola. W.C. helped fellow Columbus native Ernest Woodruff and others buy Coca-Cola Co. for $25 million 1919. Watched Woodruff build soft-drink empire, held on for the ride; was director, owned what is now 1.3%. Shares passed through trusts to grandchildren. William stepped down as Coke board director April 1996. Three sons active W.C. Bradley Co. Members since 1993.

NEW TO THE FORBES FOUR HUNDRED

Michael Price

$560 million
Money manager. Far Hills, N.J. 45.
Divorced, 3 sons.

Less-than-motivated student University of Oklahoma. Hired after graduation 1975 as $200-a-week research assistant by money manager Max Heine, founder Short Hills, N.J.-based Heine Securities; Price's father was a Heine client. Heine, then 62, took young Price under his wing, slowly handed over the reins of the company. "We ran it together. It was more him in the 1970s, more me in the 1980s." Heine killed in car accident 1988. Price bought company for a song from Heine's estate. By then funds had grown from $5 million under management to $2.5 billion. Company running $17 billion when bought out in June by Franklin Resources for up to $800 million (hinges on growth targets). Price is to stay on for at least 5 years. Price also ran brokerage firm Clearwater Securities, offshore Orion Fund. Divorce in 1994 lopped estimated $50 million off net worth.

NEW TO THE FORBES FOUR HUNDRED

William Connell

$560 million
Scrap metal, presses. Swampscott, Mass. 58.
Married, 6 children.

"Industrial America is alive and well." Founder and 100% owner (with family) $1.2 billion (sales) Connell Limited Partnership. Boston-Irish born and bred: Boston College, Army, Harvard M.B.A. Intended to become professor, but fell for business instead. Rose to treasurer, VP of New York-based Ogden Corp. When Ogden decided to sell off heavy industrial holdings 1987, Connell put together investor group, bought Ogden scrap metal yards Luria Brothers (Cleveland), Wabash Alloys (Wabash, Ind.), Danly Machine and Danly Die Set (Chicago), Mayville Metals (Mayville, Wis.), Yuba Division (Tulsa, Okla.). Market leaders each. Bought out other investors 1990. Well-connected with Boston Irish old guard; former member of the Vault. Importing scrap for minimills; strong dollar, low interest rates strengthened margins. Connell: "We can produce steel more cheaply in this country than anywhere in the world."

NEW TO THE FORBES FOUR HUNDRED

Donald A. Foss

$550 million
Car loans. Farmington Hills, Mich. 52.
Married, 2 children.

Graduated from Detroit's Cooley High 1964; used-car salesman from 1967. Saw opportunity where most lenders shied away: making loans for used-car purchases to people with spotty employment and credit records. Founded Auto Finance Corporation 1972, later changed name to Credit Acceptance Corp. Public 1992. Company provides funding, receivables management, other services to automobile dealers. Since 1989 buying loans from dealers in 48 continental states. Foss still owns over 51% of the stock.

Leslie L. Gonda

$550 million
International Lease Finance Corp.
Beverly Hills. 77.
Married, 3 children.

Louis L. Gonda

$535 million
International Lease Finance Corp.
Beverly Hills. 48.
Married, 5 children.

Father and son. Leslie and wife Susan survived Holocaust concentration and work camps; fled Hungary 1947. Began buying commercial real estate; moved to California 1963 in time to prosper from construction boom. With son Louis and friend Steven Udvar-Hazy (see p. 202), pooled

$150,000, $1.7 million bank loan to found International Lease Finance 1973. Deregulated airliners eager for cheap, low-risk, short-term leases. Public 1983; now one of world's largest aircraft lessors. Merged with AIG 1990. Leslie ILFC chair; Louis executive VP. Leslie and wife established foundation 1988; sponsors medical research at UCLA, Mayo Clinic, City of Hope. Also U.S. Holocaust Museum, humanitarian projects in U.S. and abroad. Members since 1993.

George Phydias Mitchell

$550 million
Oil & gas, real estate. Houston. 77.
Married, 10 children.

Son of Greek immigrant, graduated top of class in petroleum engineering Texas A&M; tennis team captain. WWII Army engineer. Discovered huge natural gas field northern Texas 1953: soon supplying 10% of gas used in Chicago. Mitchell Energy bought the Woodlands early 1960s: created 25,000-acre ultimate planned community north of Houston: "Give us 40 years and we'll transplant the entire social, economic and ethnic/minority mix into the Woodlands." Transforming Houston region into center of biotech R&D: "Biotech takes a long time, but if you get a hit, it's a real hit." Mitchell lately cutting work force, selling underproducing oilfields, much property outside Woodlands. Still avid tennis player. Member since 1982.

Alfred A. Checchi

$550 million
Leveraged buyouts. Los Angeles. 48.
Married, 3 children.

Gary L. Wilson

$510 million
Leveraged buyouts. Los Angeles. 56.
Married, 2 sons.

Partners. Took Northwest Airlines private 1989, public again 1994; stock took off. Now feuding with partner Dutch airline KLM over business strategy; will be eligible to sell stock in 1997 for first time since taking public. Wilson: Duke, Wharton M.B.A.; as CFO at Marriott, hired Checchi 1975. Checchi: Amherst, Harvard M.B.A.; left Marriott 1982 to work for Bass family. Introduced Wilson to Michael Eisner *(see p. 304).* Wilson became Disney CFO 1985, just in time for cheap stock options. Joined

Northwest board 1987, resigned 1988, began buying stock with pal Checchi. Brought in KLM, other investors. Beat out Marvin Davis *(see p. 135)*, KKR in LBO bid. Checchi and Wilson piled on debt, squeezed unions, needed emergency Minnesota state bond issue to stay afloat. Good results since going public. Each has seen original $20 million NWA investment multiply more than 20 times. Members since 1995.

John Arrillaga

$550 million
Real estate. Palo Alto, Calif. 59.
Recently widowed, 1 son, 1 daughter.

Richard Taylor Peery

$550 million
Real estate. Palo Alto, Calif. 56.
Married, 3 sons, 1 daughter.

These partners hooked up 1967 and with Bank of America financing bought cheap farmland in Silicon Valley, built top-shelf office space for high-tech crowd. Sold much at top of 1980s market; then built more. They insist on conservative, ultra low debt operation. Thousands of acres are yet to be developed. John: visionary architect, master salesman; son of immigrant Basque produce wholesaler; won Stanford basketball scholarship, third team all-America; worked as landscaper during college, personally assisted landscapers working on his $50 million, 200-acre private Shangri-La (man-made lakes, 70,000 new trees, etc.). Active again after early 1990s dormant years. Dick: Mormon, son of Bank of America executive; Stanford M.B.A.; managed his father's Bay Area real estate. Tough businessman, writes leases, minds books; outdoorsman. Members since 1986.

Bruce Kovner

$550 million
Money manager. New York City. 51.
Married, 3 children.

Returned $1.25 billion of $2 billion under management 1995 after flat returns. Smaller is beautiful: funds back up by 16% end 1995, 8% so far 1996. At Harvard: writer's block on dissertation. Drifted 6 years; drove cab, studied harpsichord at Julliard. Age 31 taught self to trade commodities on $3,000 MasterCard line. Made quick $40,000, didn't hedge; lost $23,000 in hours. Joined Commodities Corp., learned from veteran

Michael Marcus: "He taught me that you could make a million dollars." And keep it. Started own firm, Caxton, 1983. Phenomenal returns: 87% 1985, 98% 1987. Closed to new investors 1992. Member since 1992.

NEW TO THE FORBES FOUR HUNDRED

C. Edward McVaney

$550 million
Software. Englewood, Colo. 55.
Married, 3 children.

"Nebraska farmboy," born Omaha, dyslexic. B.S. mechanical engineering U. of Nebraska 1964; M.B.A. Rutgers 1966; CPA. Worked for Peat, Marwick; then to Grant Thornton & Co. Left with 2 co-workers—Jack Thompson, Dan Gregory—to write business accounting software. Founded J. (Jack) D. (Dan) Edwards & Co. on St. Patrick's Day 1977. Sold programs to small companies; shifted early 1980s from developing custom program for each customer to one-size-fits-all package. Linked up with IBM early, still partners. Over last 10 years expanded software to encompass all manufacturing uses; over half clients now outside U.S. Historical focus on companies with sales up to a couple billion dollars, but beginning to compete for bigger fish against Oracle, Baan and SAP. Claims sales growth averaging 53% annually since 1977. Still private. This year sales expected to top $400 million.

Thomas Stephen Monaghan

$550 million
Domino's Pizza. Ann Arbor, Mich. 59.
Married, 4 daughters (one is spokeswoman).

Fatherless at 4, raised with brother in Catholic orphanage. Expelled from seminary; joined Marines. With brother, $500 loan, bought pizzeria Ypsilanti, Mich. 1960. Traded VW for brother's share 1961. Started "30-minute delivery" system; built giant Domino's chain. Got arrogant, took eye off business: bought $40 million of Frank Lloyd Wright artifacts, $3 million home; company experienced $200 million technical default 1992. Closed 100 stores 1993, sales dipped to $2.2 billion. Put himself back on track by selling Detroit (baseball) Tigers to rival Michael Ilitch *(see p. 210)* 1992, other toys, including Frank Lloyd Wright designs, at "fire sale" prices. Recovered: 1995 revenues $2.6 billion; expanding overseas. Little brother Jim joined lunatic fringe group Michigan Militia 1996. Member since 1984.

Claude B. (Doc) Pennington

$550 million
Oil, gas. Baton Rouge, La. 96.
Married, only son killed in oil rig accident.

Labored summers in Louisiana oilfields. Joined father as optometrist 1925; hated profession, closed clinic day after father's death. Returned to oilfields. On leased land made first known oil discovery east of Atchafalaya River. Began deep offshore drilling 1970s. Local banks' favorite depositor: rumored to have over $100 million cash. Unloading $1 million a year to charities. Gave LSU $125 million for nutrition center: ardent believer in healthfulness of peanut oil, vitamins E, C. "Someday I'm going to be an old man. I'd like for science to prolong my health." Old as the century, still comes to the office every day. Member since 1984.

Donald J. Schneider

$550 million
Trucking. Green Bay, Wis. 60.
Married, 5 children.

Father, Al, started one-truck business Green Bay 1938. Employed son Don part time during college, full time after Wharton. Schneider National now over $1.7 billion in revenues. Very efficient operator, prospered during deregulation, pioneered intermodal rail/road combinations. Excellent logistics: satellite antennas on every truck by 1988. Championed merit pay over union scale. For competitive reasons refuses to file required data with ICC. Recently sold long distance provider Schneider Communications and its 80% ownership in Link USA to Rochester-based Frontier Corp. for $127 million. "A lot of opportunity goes to those willing to take the risk." Member since 1994.

Walter Herbert Shorenstein

$540 million
Real estate. San Francisco. 81.
Widowed, 1 son, 2 daughters (1 deceased).

The dean of downtown San Francisco: 12 Fogtown office properties, others across country. Prize trophy: Bank of America building at 555 California. Son of Long Island haberdasher. Army Air Force WWII. Postwar, visited San Francisco, never left. Worked as real estate broker, bought out employer 1960, renamed Shorenstein Co. 1985. Became preeminent SF building owner, "on sidelines" 1986-93. Then back in game with vengeance: bought 8 new buildings (Boston, Denver, Minneapolis, Phoenix, etc.). Prefers class A space, low debt, institutional partners. Total: over 25 million square feet. Major Democrat fundraiser, adviser to LBJ, Carter; now Al Gore pal; Son, Douglas, 41, company president. Member since 1982.

Steven M. Rales

$540 million
Danaher Corp. Washington, D.C. 44.
Married.

Mitchell P. Rales

$540 million
Danaher Corp. Washington, D.C. 39.
Married.

Brothers. Left father's real estate firm 1979; "raiders in short pants" in 1980s junk-finance frenzy. Loaded up on leverage; bought hand tool, tire-making, other businesses. Acquired 30% near-bankrupt REIT 1983; renamed Danaher Corp. after favorite Montana stream where brothers once caught trout. Applied real estate lessons: "Tax losses can be good for cash flow." Lost bid for Ohio-based Scott & Fetzer Co. to Warren Buffett 1985. Brothers have confounded skeptics: Danaher stock up twenty-fold over past decade. Acquired electric power product maker Joslyn Corp. for $245 million 1995; completed $200 million tender offer for Acme-Cleveland Corp. July 1996. Sales now over $1.4 billion. Publicity shy. Intense. Family-oriented. Members since 1995.

Ann Walton Kroenke

$540 million
Inheritance. Columbia, Mo. 46.
Married, 2 children.

Nancy Walton Laurie

$540 million
Inheritance. Columbia, Mo. 44.
Married, 1 child.

Daughters and apparent heirs of James L. (Bud) Walton (d. 1995); cousins of Sam Walton's children *(see p. 119)*. Bud operated small five-and-dime store in Missouri. Pooled assets with older brother Sam Walton (d. 1992) when Sam's merchandising concept took off. First Wal-Mart, Rogers, Ark., 1962. Bud, low profile, handled real estate. Today Wal-Mart largest U.S. retailer, with over 2,200 stores and $95 billion in sales. Ann: U. of Missouri, Columbia dropout. Husband, E. Stanley Kroenke, Wal-Mart director; real estate developer. Owns shopping centers, many anchored with Wal-Mart stores. Minority owner St. Louis (football) Rams. Sister, Nancy: U. of Arkansas, Fayetteville dropout, owns 350-acre Crown Center Farms with husband, Bill; breed Appaloosa and quarter horses. Donated $10 million to U. of Missouri, Columbia for new basketball arena. Members since 1995.

Harry V. Quadracci

$540 million
Printing. Racine, Wis. 60.
Married, 4 children.

After Columbia law degree 1960, joined Milwaukee printing firm. Advocated tough management line; out after company caved in to union wage demands. "This onetime unemployed, lapsed lawyer" (company bio) raised $250,000 toward $900,000 high-tech press 1969; took bank loan, mortgaged house for the rest. Counted on high press productivity: investors repaid in 24 months. Quad/Graphics revenues now more than $1 billion, prints most of *Newsweek,* a third of *Time.* Harry famous for inspirational leadership. Also high jinks: walked high-wire across factory floor. Eight family members currently work for company, including Dad (board chairman), 2 brothers, wife, 2 kids. Together they own 60% of private company worth estimated $900 million. Member since 1995.

Caroline Rose Hunt and family

$540 million
Inheritance, oil, real estate. Dallas. 73.
Twice divorced, 5 children.

Second daughter legendary oilman H.L. Hunt *(see also Ray Hunt).* After failed try by brothers (William, Lamar, Nelson) to corner silver market 1980, she and older sister separated their holdings 1983. Caroline's trust invested in luxury hotels, thrifts. Rosewood Hotel & Resorts manages Lanesborough Hotel, London, 3 in West Indies, others; owns The Mansion on Turtle Creek, Dallas. Her healthy Southwest Savings took over 4 insolvent thrifts 1988. Sold most domestic oil properties for about $275 million 1990. Now rebuilding U.S. oil and gas reserves. Retains lucrative North Sea oil interests. Caroline said to live frugally, taking no part in management of trust. Member since 1982.

John Hammond Krehbiel Jr.

$540 million
Molex Inc. Lake Forest, Ill. 59.
Married, 3 children.

Frederick A. Krehbiel

$425 million
Molex Inc. Hinsdale, Ill. 55.
Married, 2 sons.

Brothers. Grandfather Fred invented "molex," inexpensive plastic molding material originally used in flowerpots, toys, etc. Father, John Sr. (d. 1993), joined company 1940. Switched from commercial to electrical products: connectors, terminals, cables. Took Molex public 1972. Brothers now run business. John Jr.: Molex president since 1975. Fred: established Molex's International Division 1967, with factories in Japan, Singapore, Ireland. "What we have learned globally has vastly increased our ability to compete locally." Now chairman/CEO. Company topped $1 billion in sales in fiscal 1996. Ambitious growth strategy: to double sales by 2000. Second in the worldwide electronics connector industry behind giant AMP Inc. Forty-six plants in 21 countries, including India, Poland, Mexico. Pete, son of John Jr., fourth-generation Krehbiel to join Molex; elected to board 1993 after grandfather's death. Members since 1994.

Paul Barry Fireman and family

$535 million
Reebok. Newton, Mass. 52.
Married, 3 children.

Lagging behind archrival Nike, stock down. Dissident shareholders put heat on Fireman. He suggests they shut up or sell out; later sets 2-year deadline to end sales slump or step down: offer expires 1998. Amidst takeover rumors, Reebok offers to buy back as much as 33% outstanding common, giving Fireman family more control. Family had camping, sporting goods business. Paul, Boston U. dropout, saw British Reebok shoe label at trade show 1979; bought U.S. rights, then company 1984. IPO 1985. Introduced women's aerobic shoes 1982. Great timing, Reebok premier athletic shoe company 1986. Then Nike recovered. Fireman settled government price-fixing charges for $9 million 1995. Opened Reebok Sports Club/NY, bought golf club same year. Official licensee 1996 Summer Olympics, but Nike's unofficial campaign scored more points. Bought Rockport brand 1986; recently agreed to make footware under Ralph Lauren label. Human rights activist. Member since 1986.

Robert Boisseau Pamplin Jr.and family

$525 million
Textiles. Lake Oswego, Ore. 55.
Married, 2 daughters.

Sharp spike in cotton prices depressed profits last year; recovering this year. Ordained minister. Beat cancer. Eight degrees, including 2 doctorates. Runs R.B. Pamplin Corp., one of country's biggest denim producers. Father, Robert Sr.: penniless, rose to chief executive of Georgia-Pacific. On retirement bought sand and gravel company, built today's company. Later addition: Mt. Vernon Mills, now 95% of sales. Consumes 5% of cotton used in the U.S. Gives 10% pretax profit to charity. Started small Christian entertainment companies: musical artists and videos (superhero "Bible Man"). Member since 1992.

Gary Campbell Comer

$525 million
Lands' End. Chicago. 67.
Married, 2 children.

Profits drop as Lands' End wrestles with costs of international expansion, hike in paper, postal prices. Gary skipped college, became award-winning ad copywriter Young & Rubicam 1952-62. Started Lands' End 1963, Chicago-based mail-order supplier of sailing gear. Began selling luggage, clothing, dropped boat hardware by 1977. Went public 1986. People-first philosophy: "Take care of your people, take care of your customers, and the rest will take care of itself." First U.K. catalog 1991. Expanded with mailings to France, Germany, Netherlands, Japan by 1994; plans for continued overseas expansion. Today 22.4-million-member mailing list, $1.3 billion sales. Avid sailer. First appeared on list 1987.

NEW TO THE FORBES FOUR HUNDRED

John H. Sykes

$520 million
Computer support services. Tampa, Fla. 60.
Divorced, remarried; 2 daughters, 1 son.

An outsourcer, his Sykes Enterprises handles hardware, software product support for Apple, Hewlett-Packard, Novell, IBM, Digital Equipment, others. Also develops software, information systems for NationsBank, Monsanto, etc. Decentralized organization; using telephones and computers, 1,800 of Sykes' 2,800 employees work in out-ofthe-way spots like Ponca City, Okla.; Overland Park, Kans.; Sterling, Colo.; Klamath Falls, Ore.; Bismarck, N.D. "People like to live and work where they grew up." Early 1960s, Sykes at McDonnell Aircraft at Cape Canaveral; worked on Mercury and Gemini space programs, left company before Apollo program. Worked for technical support company to Wall Street firms before starting own company 1977: offered contract engineering expertise, engineers for civil projects, then focused on technical graphics (manuals, etc.), then into software support. Took Sykes public April, still owns 70%.

Guilford Glazer

$520 million
Real estate. Beverly Hills. 75.
Divorced, remarried; 2 children.

July birthday present to himself: retirement—more time for golf and grandchildren. Expanded father's welding shop Knoxville, Tenn.; began building with apartment house for widowed mother 1950. Built Oak Ridge, Tenn. shopping center 1954; sold 1989 for $45 million. Moved to LA 1960 for the climate. Has office buildings Atlanta, Boston, Pittsburgh; Holiday Inns; industrial buildings. Says there is no debt on many properties: "Pay your debt, then you don't have somebody else controlling you." Active in U.S.-Israel relations; built Israeli community center with buddy Armand Hammer. Member since 1986.

Richard Alan Smith and family

$520 million
Harcourt General. Chestnut Hill, Mass. 71.
Married, 3 children.

Nancy Smith Lurie Marks and family

$520 million
Harcourt General. Chestnut Hill, Mass. 69.
Married, 3 children.

Brother and sister. Father, Philip, founded General Cinema, drive-in theater chain 1922. Richard, Harvard grad, assumed control 1961. Largest movie theater operator by 1973. Also Pepsi bottling plants: largest independent soft drink bottler by 1981. Bought 37% department store retailer Carter Hawley Hale 1984. Entered high-end retailing 1987, exchanging CHH for 60% Neiman Marcus Group. Acquired textbook publisher Harcourt Brace Jovanovich 1991. Divested struggling Contempo-Casuals from NMG 1995. Nancy's son, Jeff Lurie, owns Philadelphia (football) Eagles. With families, Richard and Nancy share fortune worth more than $1 billion. Richard a member since 1982; Nancy since 1994.

Charles Francis Dolan

$510 million
Cable TV. Oyster Bay, N.Y. 70.
Married, 6 children.

Bought Madison Square Garden 1995 with ITT for $1 billion; brought back boxing. Cablevision Systems stock taking it on the chin since: down almost 40% in last year. Grew up in Cleveland, convinced city paper to run his Boy Scout column for $2 a week age 15. To NYC 1952, made industrial films. Breakthrough 1960: wired news service into NYC hotels. Scored Manhattan cable franchise 1961; covered Knicks, Rangers games. Financed high-cost growth through limited partnerships. Created Home Box Office 1970, sold to Time Inc. 1973. Built Cablevision Systems, took public 1986. With ITT, now controls distribution of all NYC-area pro baseball, basketball, hockey via MSG and SportsChannel New York. Member since 1986.

Richard J. Egan and family

$500 million
Data storage. Hopkinton, Mass. 60.
Married, 5 children.

EMC Corp. founder and family still "diversifying," i.e., selling lots of stock. Marine in Korean War. Northeastern U., B.S. electrical engineering. At MIT, helped develop computer system to guide *Apollo* back from moon. Worked for Intel. Cofounded EMC 1979 with college roommate. Sold solid-state memory boards. After mid-1980s IPO had problems, then breakthrough: EMC engineers adapted data storage scheme devised at Berkeley using groups of cheap disk drives simultaneously to store and back up data. Beat IBM (selling big stand-alone disks) to market by 4 years. Overtook Big Blue 1995, selling more storage; revenues grew more than tenfold since 1990. Member since 1994.

Sheldon Adelson

$500 million
Trade shows, gambling.
Boston; Las Vegas. 63.
Married, 5 children.

Sold computer trade show Comdex 1995 for $900 million to Softbank. Adelson not satisfied. On the site of his Sands casino/hotel in Las Vegas, planning $1.3 billion gambling fantasia patterned after Venice. And the current structure? As we go to press, he's set to blow it to smithereens for Chevy Chase film. To work in corporate finance, real estate. Tried venture capital, lost big in 1969 market slide. Formed Interface Group, started trade shows 1971. First Comdex—Computer Dealers Expo—in 1979. Added more shows; into Japan 1985. Bought Sands for $135 million in 1989. Comdex Fall in Las Vegas became must-attend event for computer industry. Member since 1995.

William Randolph Hearst III

$500 million
Inheritance. San Francisco. 47.
Married, 3 children.

Austin Hearst

$500 million
Inheritance. New York City. 44.
Married, 1 child.

George Randolph Hearst Jr.

$500 million
Inheritance. Los Angeles. 69.
Widowed, divorced, remarried; 4 children.

Phoebe Hearst Cooke

$500 million
Inheritance. San Francisco. 69.
Divorced, remarried; 1 daughter.

Millicent V. Boudjakdji

$500 million
Inheritance. Los Angeles. 56.
Married, 3 children.

David Whitmire Hearst Jr.

$500 million
Inheritance. Los Angeles. 51.
Single.

Grandchildren of William Randolph Hearst, media magnate who built nation's largest newspaper chain, model for Orson Welles' *Citizen Kane* (d. 1951). William Randolph Hearst III: stepped down as publisher of San Francisco *Examiner* December 1994. Computer buff interested in new media. Austin Hearst: VP Hearst Entertainment & Syndication. George Jr.: ran *Herald-Examiner* 1962-77; supervises real estate. His sister Phoebe: major role with current husband in family's 1974 trust buyback. Four children of John Hearst Sr. (d. 1958) share estimated $1 billion. With uncle Randolph Apperson Hearst *(see p. 169),* family fortune exceeds $5 billion. First appeared on list 1982.

William Gordon Bennett

$500 million
Gambling. Las Vegas. 71.
Married, 2 children.

William Norman Pennington

$480 million
Gambling. Reno. 73.
Widowed, remarried; 2 children.

Ex-partners. Cofounded Circus Circus Enterprises after recognizing unserved gambling market: vacationing families, middle class. Opened Circus Circus 1968, Vegas casino with clean image, entertainment. Hit jackpot. Bennett: former furniture store owner, known as aggressive cost-cutter who won't give gamblers credit. Stepped down as CEO 1994, officially to spend time with wife, hobbies of boating, sailing. Reportedly forced to step down as chair amid takeover rumors. Bought Sahara Hotel for $193 million months later. Pennington: WWII bomber pilot, president Circus Circus from 1979, retired 1988; enjoys boating, horseback riding. Members since 1985.

Amar Gopal Bose

$500 million
Loudspeakers. Wayland, Mass. 66.
Married, 2 children.

Born Philadelphia to Indian immigrant. MIT Ph.D. electrical engineering 1956. Holds patents in acoustics, electronics, communication theory.

Started Bose Corp. 1964. First, R&D contracts with military, NASA. Consumer loudspeakers best in field 1968. Introduced world's first factory-installed customized car stereo system 1982: Cadillac, then Mercedes, Nissan, etc. Also corporate jets, home theater systems. One of country's biggest suppliers nontrademarked speakers. Sales thought to exceed $700 million. Reinvests profits in R&D, growth. Still MIT professor (electrical engineering, computer science). Member since 1994.

Grover Connell

$500 million
Equipment leasing, rice. Westfield, N.J. 78.
Married, 3 children.

After WWII Navy service, took over family's $10 million (sales) rice and sugar company 1950. Built Connell Co. into country's largest independent broker/trader in rice, sugar; U.S. export share over 20%, much to Japan. Added heavy equipment leasing (railroad, aircraft, power plants) 1973; now some $1.4 billion in assets. Also prime N.J. real estate. Known for lunches featuring lectures by congressmen. Hosted party for politicos with Zaire dictator Mobutu. Member since 1982.

Wallace Henry Coulter

$500 million
Blood cell analysis. Miami. 83.
Single.

Brother and business partner Joseph Coulter died 1995 age 71. Wallace studied electrical engineering at Georgia Tech, dropped out 1932. Held down series of technical and service jobs, tinkered in basement, developed "Coulter principle" 1949: automated electronic method of counting microscopic particles. In 1953 invented Coulter Counter, blood cell counter, with government funding. Started Coulter Electronics with Joseph 1958; never went public. Now private Coulter Corp. Big success: near 95% automated blood counters worldwide are Coulter or clones. Snapped up 104-acre Amerifirst campus in Miami from Resolution Trust Corp. 1992. Wallace's heirs share estimated $475 million. Member since 1988.

Lawrence Fisher

$500 million
Real estate. New York City. 86.
Married, 1 child.

Zachary Fisher

$500 million
Real estate. New York City. 85.
Married, 1 child.

Brothers. Third-generation New York real estate family. Larry: "We've been in business over 100 years." As teens, bought Philadelphia bank building 1926; built Queens apartments 1930s-40s. Moved into Manhattan office market 1960s. Now over 6 million sq. ft. in 5 A-list buildings NYC, including Westvaco Building, Park Ave. Plaza, Burlington House. Politically connected Zach greased delivery of $4.5 million HUD grant 1981 for pet project *Intrepid* Sea-Air-Space Museum; aircraft carrier racked up $3 million in debt; bankruptcy 1985. In 1980s moved excess cash into stocks: made $60 million from runs on Disney, CBS; execs had Quotrons on desks. Bidders for troubled New York Post 1993; dropped out. Also Zachary and Elizabeth Fisher Armed Services Foundation scholarships to family members of servicemen killed in 1983 Beirut bomb blast; $25,000 to family of each person killed in explosion U.S.S. *Iowa*. Larry: active in NYC Police, Fire Department charities; avid baseball fan. With families, brothers share real estate fortune estimated to be at least $1 billion. Members since 1982.

NEW TO THE FORBES FOUR HUNDRED

Joseph Liemandt

$500 million
Software. Austin. 28. Single.

Youngest self-made member of The Forbes Four Hundred; probably only one who rents his primary residence. Started Trilogy Development Group 1989 with four Stanford pals, dropped out 1990 halfway through senior year. "My market window's closing!" Goal: beat IBM, Hewlett-Packard to the punch with "sales configuration" software. Eliminates errors, wasted time from manufacturers' sales and ordering processes. Couldn't get venture capital backing, relied heavily on credit card debt to keep going. After three years of trial-and-error programming, success: $3.5 million contract from H-P, 1993. Orders from Boeing, IBM, Silicon Graphics followed. Sales believed over $120 million. Father Gregory (d. 1993) friends with Jack Welch at GE. When informed of Joe's plan to drop out of Stanford, dad replied: "You're a moron."

Lynne Pasculano and family

$500 million
Auto parts. NYC; Greenwich, Conn. 55.
Married, 2 children.

Daughter of Harry Lebensfeld (d. 1994); Brooklyn native; high school dropout: started at father's furniture company. Founded UIS 1945 with purchase of small desk manufacturing company, Shelbyville, Ind. Growth strategy: buy small firms with growth potential. Acquired over 20 companies to form mini-conglomerate. Manufactures original and replacement auto parts. Sales now over $870 million; 80% auto/truck parts. Also owns New England Confectionery Co., maker Necco wafers. Lean operation: 14 employees in N.J. headquarters. Lynne's husband, Richard Pasculano, executive vice president. Lynne a longtime volunteer NY Public Library. UIS in trust for Lynne and her children. Member since 1994.

Frank Pritt

$500 million
Attachmate Corp. Seattle. 54.
Married, 3 children.

After joining The Forbes Four Hundred last year, Pritt made some bad moves with his Attachmate software company—namely turning it over to a misguided new management team. A botched attempt to reposition Attachmate as "The Intranet Company" confused many of its basic customers. Attachmate's CEO, other executives let go; Pritt back at helm. But Pritt's been through tough times before. He started his career working for IBM (sales), Harris Corp. (product manager). Witnessed dawn of personal computer, foresaw market for connecting PCs to mainframes. Harris uninterested so Pritt quit 1984; started Attachmate in living room with $150,000 in retirement money. Hours after resignation, he stumbled across ad for "his" product from computer firm DCA. "I thought I was the only one who thought of this thing. It was sort of gruesome." Went ahead anyway. Bought out DCA 1994. Pritt owns 70 of $400 million sales company. Member since 1995.

John R. Stanley

$500 million
Gas. Houston. 57.
Married, 4 children, 1 son disowned.

Stanley's debt-laden TransTexas scored big discovery 1995 southern Texas. Increased reserves by 56%. Son of Mass. schoolteacher; pumped gas, leased Gulf station while student. By mid-1970s 230 Gasland outlets; bought refinery Good Hope, La., began oil drilling. Hit gas big-time in Laredo field. Invested in ammonia; prices plunged; bankrupt 1975. Held off creditors; saved by 1979 oil shock; paid off, borrowed $750 million to expand refinery. Bankrupt 1983. Sued creditors; bought time. Out of

Chapter 11 in 1993; kept gas, borrowed $500 million to revamp refinery. Borrowed $800 million more in 1995 to refinance, explore new fields. Analyst: "You take John out of the picture and [the company's] probably worth a lot more." Member since 1994.

A. Alfred Taubman

$500 million
Real estate. Bloomfield Hills, Mich. 71.
Divorced, remarried; 3 children.

Immigrant father built homes; "Al" teased as child for dyslexia, stuttering; college dropout. Got $5,000 loan 1950; developed retail stores, then strip malls, shopping centers. For Max Fisher *(see p. 250)* built 200 gas stations. Large regional malls 1960s. Perfectionist, tight control over selling environment; major U.S. shopping mall developer. Made $150 million in Irvine Ranch buyout *(see Bren)*; Sotheby's shareholder, chairman. Floated REIT 1992 to repay $600 million loan. Has given more than $40 million to hospitals, colleges. Son Robert now Taubman Centers chief executive officer. Member since 1982.

Albert Lee Ueltschi

$500 million
FlightSafety International. Irving, Tex. 79.
Widowed, 4 children.

Raised on Kentucky dairy farm. Opened hamburger shop age 16 to pay for flying lessons. Bought open-cockpit biplane with $3,500 loan. Joined Pan American Airlines 1941; personal pilot to Pan Am founder Juan Trippe. Saw lack of properly trained pilots for commercial aircraft: started FlightSafety 1951; mortgaged house 1954 to purchase own simulator. Used off-duty hours for business; quit Pan Am 1968. Expanded to training in marine operations 1976. Joint venture with Babcock & Wilcox for power plant personnel training 1984; sold interest 1994 to focus on core business. Today 40 training centers, more than 160 simulators. Sales over $325 million. First appeared on list 1983.

NEW TO THE FORBES FOUR HUNDRED

Robert B. Goergen

$490 million
Candles. Greenwich, Conn. 58.
Married, 2 children.

Wharton M.B.A.; worked at Procter & Gamble, McCann-Erickson and McKinsey & Co. Ran Donaldson, Lufkin & Jenrette's Sprout venture capital funds. Left DLJ 1978. With 3 partners bought Brooklyn candlemaker from founder's children for $100,000. Company was doing $3 million selling candles to churches and religious goods stores. Partners innovated with citronella candles in colorful ceramic pots; wide variety of scents and shapes. Acquired 6 competitors in 12 years. Sales up 500% to $331 million last 6 years. Took Blyth Industries public 1994. Accessorizing candles: horse-shaped candleholders for $28.95, high-margin replacement candles at $11.25 the half-dozen. "We are in the razor business, except our razor blades burn."

Hugh Rodney Sharp III & family

$490 million
Inheritance (Du Pont). Wilmington, Del. 61.
Married, 5 children.

Member of vast, blue blood du Pont clan. A grandson of Isabella du Pont Sharp (see du Pont family); a sister of Pierre Samuel II; known as H. Rodney. Father Hugh Jr. (d. 1990) active in Du Pont 1938-82, flew combat missions during WWII; with brother Bayard, donated $11 million parcel of beach and wilderness for use as a Florida state park. Hugh Jr. left his inheritance to his three children; Hugh III, H. Donan Sharp and William M.W. Sharp. Hugh III still a director at Du Pont; retired as manager of computer systems for company 1991. Member since 1992.

Phillip Frost

$490 million
Medicine. Miami Beach. 60.
Married.

The founder of Ivax (maker of generic drugs) is now trying to revive Pan Am; plans to go public by folding into investment vehicle Frost Hanna Merger Group. "I'm looking at it as a minor diversification." But possibly losing focus: Ivax quarterly earnings 74% below expectations this summer. U. of Pennsylvania, Albert Einstein College of Medicine. Dermatologist, invented disposable biopsy device, took over struggling Key Pharmaceuticals 1971, fixed up company, sold to Schering-Plough 1986. Founded Ivax 1987, now one of the largest generic drug firms. Began with small companies, rights to salable drugs to generate immediate revenues, fund growth, acquisitions. Motivation: "ego . . . the chase and success." Active civic affairs, philanthropy. Member since 1991.

Philip Evans Kamins

$490 million
Plastics, chemicals. Beverly Hills. 60.
Married, 4 children.

Born Chicago. Parents divorced when Philip was 12; worked to support family. At 16 got job with H. Muehlstein & Co., plastics scrap dealer. Took night classes in finance, Northwestern; never graduated. To LA as salesman for Muehlstein 1957; on his own 1963, formed Kamco Plastics with wife, brother; now PMC, Inc. Acquired specialty chemicals, plastics firms. "Bottom fisher." Gave equity to managers to enhance performance, switched to cash 1986. Refused financing offer from Mike Milken. PMC now 17-business conglomerate with sales over $730 million. Member since 1993.

NEW TO THE FORBES FOUR HUNDRED

Elaine Johnson Wold

$490 million
Inheritance. Boca Raton, Fla. 68.
Married, 2 children.

Daughter of John Seward Johnson (d. 1983); with siblings *(see Duke, Johnson)* she is heir to Johnson & Johnson fortune. Most of estate went to John Seward's third wife and former chambermaid, Barbara Piasecka Johnson *(see p. 157)*. Her bitter court battle with 6 grown children, who had own trusts, settled 1986. Very low profile; Elaine married to retired physician.

Alexis Felix du Pont Jr.

$490 million
Inheritance. Wilmington, Del. 90.
Divorced, remarried, widowed; 4 children.

Alice Francis du Pont Mills

$490 million
Inheritance. Middleburg, Va. 83.
Widowed, 3 children.

Siblings. Children of A. Felix du Pont, distant cousin of Pierre Samuel II *(see du Pont family)*, who sided with Pierre in family split 1915, was rewarded with stake in Christiana Securities (family holding company). Their brother Richard, noted pilot, killed in WWII glider crash. His widow,

Helena Allaire Crozer du Pont, horse breeder, one of first women admitted to Jockey Club (1983). She and children worth estimated $490 million. Member since 1982.

NEW TO THE FORBES FOUR HUNDRED

Mossimo Giannulli

$490 million
Clothing. Los Angeles. 32.
Divorced, 1 child.

Son of Los Angeles landscape architect; Generation X fashion aesthetic flourished while riding funky old-model bicycles, skateboards. USC dropout 1987. Borrowed $100,000 from dad; made T shirts, neon volleyball shorts. Marketed to surf shops; grossed $1 million first year. Hired designer 1991, broadened line: woven sweaters, knit shirts, fleece sweatshirts. Now upscale casual clothing line. Mossimo Inc. went public in February at $18, climbed to $36. Now launching line of women's apparel and men's tailored suits. "Clothing is pretty basic. We're not talking rocket science here."

Frank Lyon Jr. and family

$490 million
Bottling. Boca Raton, Fla. 55.
Married, 2 stepdaughters.

Father Frank Sr., now 86, genteel southerner, door-to-door suit salesman, youngest district manager General Foods. RCA distributor 1942; sweetheart deal with fellow Arkansan Wal-Mart 1970s. Acquired Coca-Cola bottler 1969, became biggest in Arkansas. Also acquired bank; turned operations over to Harvard M.B.A.-armed Frank Jr. 1967. Jr. sold bottler to Coke 1989 for huge capital gain: same year battled cancer, now in remission. Acquired more banks, sold to Mercantile Bancorporation for stock. Also farming, real estate, Wingmead (13,000-acre duck hunting retreat and farm). Member since 1993.

Joseph Reeves Hyde III

$480 million
Auto parts. Memphis. 53.
Twice divorced, remarried; 3 children.

Grandfather started Malone & Hyde food wholesaler 1907. Hyde III (known as "Pitt Hyde") attended UNC, became president when father fell ill 1968. In 1972: youngest chairman of NYSE-listed companies. Expanded business:

sporting goods, drugstores, supermarkets. Biggest hit: auto parts division. AutoZone spun off 1987. Service is key: sales force trained to ask customers if they need help within 30 seconds. With KKR, did leveraged buyout of Malone & Hyde 1984; sold to Fleming Cos. for $600 million 1988. Hyde now chairman and CEO of AutoZone. Currently 1,423 stores in 27 states, sales over $2.2 billion. Chairs executive committee National Civil Rights Museum in Memphis. Funds UNC scholarships. Member since 1992.

NEW TO THE FORBES FOUR HUNDRED

Abraham Gosman

$480 million
Health care. Palm Beach. 67.
Married, 2 sons.

Son of Russian immigrants, propelled to riches by accident. Rejected by Harvard. After University of New Hampshire (economics), borrowed $800 from mother to start first business: selling fake alligator skin to shoemakers. College roommate invested in nursing home. Abe joined 1957 with $10,000. Home run. Medicare began coverage. By 1968 partners had 1,172 beds. In late 1970s, government declared alcoholism disease. Rushed to build alcohol treatment and drug rehabilitation centers, became Mediplex. Started Meditrust REIT with Mediplex properties 1985. Assets today: $2 billion. Sold Mediplex, operator of rehab centers, to Avon Products for $245 million 1986, bought back for $48 million 1989, sold again 1994 for $315 million to Sun Healthcare. Also physician practice management company PhyMatrix. "Abe sees markets in the health care arena before anyone else." Two sons run health care real estate company CareMatrix. Yacht: *Octopussy*. Favorite companion: his spaniel, Chancellor (Chancy).

Irénée du Pont Jr.

$480 million
Inheritance. Montchanin, Del. 76.
Married, 5 children.

Irene Sophie du Pont May

$480 million
Inheritance. Wilmington, Del. 95.
Widowed, 4 children.

Constance Simons du Pont Darden

$480 million.
Inheritance. Norfolk, Va. 92.
Widowed, 3 children.

Octavia Mary du Pont Bredin

$480 million
Inheritance. Greenville, Del. 83.
Married, 6 children.

Brother and sisters. Children of Irénée du Pont Sr. (d. 1963), who was president of Du Pont Co. 1919-26 *(see du Pont family)*. Irénée Jr. retired as senior VP 1978 after 32 years with Du Pont, continued to serve as director until 1990; on Wilmington Trust board until 1992. Oversaw merger (1977) of Du Pont with family holding company (Christiana Securities), ending family's 173-year reign of company. With the family of the late Lucille du Pont Flint, these 4 siblings and families share fortune estimated at $2.4 billion, much in trusts.

Patrizio Vinciarelli

$475 million
Vicor Corp. Boston. 49.
Divorced.

University of Rome, Ph.D. physics 1970. Taught physics at Princeton University. Left Princeton, founded Vicor Corp., maker of power supplies for electronic equipment, 1981. Inspired by incident in 1970s: His stereo system's power component blew up in smoke: vowed to make better gear. Borrowed $500,000 from friends, family. No business experience: "I just knew that I could do this. I may have been naive, but I wasn't scared." Went public 1990. Expanded to Germany, Taiwan. Loves classical music; listens to Mozart at work. Also likes to cook; best dish: Roman artichokes. President/chairman since 1981. Member since 1995.

Norman Hascoe and family

$475 million
Semiconductor materials, investments.
Greenwich, Conn. 67.
Married, 3 children.

Engineering degree. Started on own 1957 with $8,000. Accumulated over 100 patents advanced semiconductor materials. Sold part of business

1969, later bought back. Sold large portion 1983, got cash, 1,345 million AlliedSignal shares; total over $100 million. Separately, sold other assets, also stock, after rise. Portfolio now managed by sons Lloyd, Andrew; some in hedge funds, but mostly liquid. Lloyd handles securities. "We are completely diversified." Andrew handles real estate, buying shopping centers. Member since 1993.

NEW TO THE FORBES FOUR HUNDRED

Robert Davidson

$475 million
Educational software. Torrance, Calif. 52.
Married, 3 children.

Janice G. Davidson

$475 million
Educational software. Torrance, Calif. 52.
Married, 3 children.

This wife-and-husband team sold their 14-year-old educational software company Davidson & Associates to CUC International in July for $1 billion. "We worried about wiping out the kids' savings. Now we've made them rich. I don't know which is worse." As a neophyte programmer, Janice was stood up by software publisher at lunch in 1982. Her husband, Robert, a construction executive, persuaded her to publish herself. The pair raided $6,000 from their 3 kids' college fund to get going. Jan's program Speed Reader was a quick hit: 5,400 copies first year, netted $270,000. More programs; by 1986 sales were $4 million. Built distribution, bought competitors. "We wanted to avoid being the consolidatee." But CUC's offer was too good to pass up.

William Russell Kelly

$475 million
Kelly Services. Fort Lauderdale. 90.
Married, 1 son.

Born Vancouver Island, B.C., family had castle in France until father lost oil millions. Died 1928, left 7 children, no estate. Russell: left U. of Pittsburgh to support siblings. Stint as car salesman; WWII Army civilian headquarters auditor. Started Russell Kelly Office Service with $10,000 savings 1946; among pioneers of modern temp help industry. IPO 1962. Then 153 offices, today nearly 1,400 globally. Acquired Top Interim, Luxembourg-based temp help company in financial services, launched

Kelly Scientific Resources for scientific professionals 1996. Son Terence E. Adderley, president, CEO. Russell remains chair. Member since 1985.

Anne Windfohr Marion

$475 million
Inheritance. Fort Worth. 57.
Thrice divorced, remarried; 1 daughter.

Arts patron: financed Santa Fe museum dedicated to works of Georgia O'Keeffe last year. Her cattle ranching great-grandfather Burk Burnett amassed 448,000 West Texas acres: valuable oil underneath. Her mother, "Big Anne," controlled until death; player in oil, weddings; married 4 times, lastly to Charles Tandy, founder Tandy Corp. Oil, land to "Little Anne." Daughter keeps up traditions: collects oil royalties, art, husbands. Married to former Sotheby's chairman John Marion. "Underestimated as a businesswoman." Fearless horsewoman, good shot. Member since 1988.

NEW TO THE FORBES FOUR HUNDRED

Jack Nash

$475 million
Money manager. New York City. 66.
Married, 2 children.

Cofounder, with Leon Levy (see p. 223), of Odyssey Partners. Keeps low profile. Partner Levy: "He's so reliable, he's not colorful." Fled Berlin with family 1941; City College of N.Y. Trainee at Oppenheimer & Co. 1951, where met Levy. Meteoric rise: within 3 years managing partner. Formed Odyssey Partners with Levy through proceeds of Oppenheimer sale 1982: $40 million of their own money plus $75 million from investors. Credited with ability to tell good deals from dogs. Says one Odyssey insider: "This firm has stayed out of trouble remarkably well in large measure due to Jack's instincts." But not infallible: while at Oppenheimer, financed John DeLorean's car company. Son Joshua now an Odyssey managing partner.

Jesse Mack Robinson and family

$475 million
Banking, insurance. Atlanta. 73.
Married, 2 daughters.

College dropout, used-car salesman; built chain of auto loan companies. Mack financed Yves St. Laurent 1960; sold 80% in 1966 for $1 million. "One doesn't always keep the right things." Bought, opened 22 banks, branches in 72 towns. Led merger of First National Bank of Atlanta with Wachovia Bank (N.C.) 1985; retains sizable Wachovia stake. Also lumber mills, insurance, etc. Heart attack 1986 spurred slow sale of businesses, but acquired others, e.g., retailer Leath Furniture; expanding Midwest, Florida. Avid golfer, breeds racehorses. Wants daughters, sons-in-law to succeed him. Member since 1986.

Joyce Raley Teel

$475 million
Supermarkets, drugstores.
West Sacramento. 65.
Married, 5 children.

Father, Tom, Safeway store manager, opened first Raley's grocery store, Placerville, Calif. 1935. Tried combination drug and grocery "superstore" 1958. Introduced precut, prepackaged meat. Joyce worked at Raley's as teenager; Sacramento City College 1951. Married Jim Teel also from Raley's; raised five children. Talked Dad into letting her return 1986; cochairman (with husband) after father died 1991. Company expanded dramatically under Joyce, yet recently growing slower. 1995 revenues: near $1.9 billion. Member since 1994.

Steven Paul Jobs

$470 million
Software, computers. Palo Alto, Calif. 41.
Married, 3 children.

Ever the showman, linked Silicon Valley with Hollywood: bought movie animation software maker Pixar from George Lucas *(see p. 138)* for $10 million 1986, took public last year after huge box-office debut of *Toy Story*, Pixar-animated Disney flick. Stake soared over $1 billion before investors cooled; great technology, but Disney gets lion's share of profits until at least 1999. College dropout, started Apple Computer 1976 in garage with pal Steve Wozniak. Success of consumer-oriented Apple II followed by hit Macintosh. Brought in PepsiCo's John Sculley as CEO; Sculley ousted Jobs. Started Next Software, to make high-end PCs, got financing from Ross Perot. Next's computers bombed; hoping for better results with Internet software. First appeared on list 1982.

Max Martin Fisher

$470 million
Oil. Franklin, Mich. 88.
Widowed, remarried; 5 children.

Grew up middle class in Ohio, son of Russian immigrant peddler who built small oil reclamation plant. Graduated Ohio State 1930, joined father's business; plant burned down 2 years later. Gas brokers agreed to finance refinery: "I guess I must have hoodwinked them." Rebuilt business barrel by barrel, offered top price for oil during 1930s to lock in suppliers. Made killing World War II. Sold for Marathon Oil stock 1959; shares sold to U.S. Steel for more than $150 million 1982. Reinvested in real estate, Sotheby's. Big supporter Israel: after Six Day War 1967 raised over $100 million in a month. Also supports Detroit Renaissance, Republican Party, Dole campaign. Member since 1982.

George Joseph

$460 million
Mercury General Corp. Los Angeles. 75.
Married, 5 children.

Born W. Va. Army Air Force WWII. Numbers nut: completed mathematics and physics degrees in 2 years, 9 months; Harvard 1949. Started as an acturial trainee at Occidental Life making $225 a month. Saw sales guys make more. Started property and casualty agency. In 1962 founded Mercury General Corp. for area other LA insurers shied away from: auto. Focused on personal, not commercial, vehicles; aggressively investigated suspicious claims. Grew; took public second time 1985; now California's seventh-largest auto insurer. Expanded Atlanta and Illinois. Goal by May 1997: $80 million monthly run rate. Active in industry. What drives him: "A desire to see my ideas put into effect." First appeared on list 1993.

Lewis Robert Wasserman

$460 million
MCA. Beverly Hills. 83.
Married, 1 daughter.

Hollywood's eminence grise. Born Cleveland; to Chicago 1936 to join Music Corp. of America. President 1946 at 33; hobnobbed with Alfred Hitchcock, Ronald Reagan, Jimmy Stewart. Brought dark business suits, ties to Tinseltown. Acquired Universal Studios for television production 1962; turned down Secretary of Commerce offer from LBJ 1965. Distributed Spielberg *(see p. 172)* hits *Jaws, E.T., Jurassic Park*. Bought Geffen Records for $545 million 1990; sold MCA months later to Matsushita for $6.1 billion. Lew took high-yielding preferred stock, retained much control, reportedly bickered with new owners. Seagram *(see Bronfman)* bought 80% of MCA 1995; Lew still honorary chairman. First appeared on list 1982.

Viola Sommer

$460 million
Inheritance. New York City. 75.
Widowed, 3 children.

Sommer Trust bought Las Vegas' Aladdin Hotel December 1994. In 1940s and 1950s husband Sigmund Sommer built small apartment buildings Brooklyn, single-family homes N.J. By the mid-1970s building shopping malls, huge luxury apartment buildings. Branched into racehorses, owned top Thoroughbred moneywinner 1971-72. Sigmund died of heart attack at the racetrack in 1979. Lawsuits over estate begun in 1987, heirs claimed breaches of fiduciary duty by coexecutor and his law firm. Settled 1994; defendants paid Sommer estate $3.5 million; the estate paid $1.25 million fees to court-appointed guardian for the grandchildren. Lawyer recalls, "She's a fun lady to litigate with." Viola in Racing Hall of Fame. Member since 1990.

Thomas H. Lee

$450 million
LBOs. Boston. 52.
Divorced, remarried; 2 children.

The Snapple King last year finalized divorce, paid Barbara Lee estimated $200 million, though confidentiality clause prevents confirmation. Lee: "Maybe I'm coming off [The Forbes Four Hundred]." Maybe not. Deals humming, 4 investment funds way up. Harvard B.A. 1965. Securities analyst for L.F. Rothschild; later headed high-tech lending at Bank of Boston. Started buyout firm Thomas H. Lee Co. with $100,000 savings and inheritance 1974: "I knew I wanted to own companies, but I didn't quite know how to do it." Found out: by 1980 controlled 12; invested own money alongside funds. Specialty: small-growth companies. Some flops, more home runs: Snapple, $900 million profit in sale to Quaker. Sold big General Nutrition stake this year, also Ghirardelli Chocolate. Still flush post divorce: gave $22 million to Harvard in September. Unassuming: "Excuse me while I eat a jelly bean." Member since 1993.

Clayton Lee Mathile

$450 million
Pet food. Dayton, Ohio. 55.
Married, 5 children.

Former Campbell Soup buyer hired 1970 by Paul Iams, animal-nutritionist-turned-pet-food-maker. Mathile succeeded Iams 1975; bought him out 1982. Brought in upgraded management, board. Increased sales from $16 million to over $400 million 1994. Convinced breeders that his premium product would produce healthier animals. Pioneered fast-growing yuppie puppy food market pitching ultra-premium product the "pros" use; got premium prices, margins. Expanding internationally, and just introduced a premium cat food. Member since 1991.

Robert Einar Petersen

$450 million
Publishing. Beverly Hills. 70.
Married.

Sold 32-title Petersen Publishing to group headed by Claeys Bahrenburg, ex-head at Hearst magazines, for around $450 million in August. Auto mechanic's son; short-order cook, gas pumper, car fancier. Started *Hot Rod* magazine 1948 with partner, $400; hawked for 25 cents a copy at races. Bought out partner in 1950. Familiar titles: *Guns & Ammo, Motor Trend, Skin Diver.* Biggest circulation: *Teen,* "for nice, clean-cut girls." Bagged polar bear with revolver in 1965. Also has Petersen Automobile Museum, air chartering business, real estate. This may be his last year on The Forbes Four Hundred, at least for a while—the taxman cometh. Member since 1982.

Thomas John Flatley

$450 million
Real estate. Milton, Mass. 64.
Married, 5 children.

Massive Boston-area holdings said to be "sizzling": hotel values up 15% or more in last year. Also up: Flatley's 5,000-plus apartments, over 6.5 million sq. ft. office, retail, industrial space. Born Ireland, came to America 1950, age 18, with $32 in pocket. Night school; started electrical installation company, then discovered real estate. Started with apartments, expanded into wide variety of properties. Retained frugality, Irish accent. The anti-Trump: hates the spotlight, keeps debt low. Saw net worth drop in real estate bust, but rode out storm with no new debt, holdings intact. First appeared on list 1988.

John D. Hollingsworth

$450 million
Textile machinery, real estate.
Greenville, S.C. 78.
Divorced, 1 daughter.

Still said to be running company from the same trailer on factory grounds he's lived in since 1964. Overseas operations troubled as shakeout con-

solidates textile machinery industry: one of the few big players left in
yarnmaking machinery game. Father serviced cotton mill and yarnmaking machines during Depression. John took over 1942, age 24. Navy
machinist WWII while wife, Ella Mae, ran company. Refined carding
machines; upped productivity from 10 pounds of yarn an hour to 40.
Guaranteed repair service within 48 hours. Bought prime Greenville real
estate. Family, tax problems 1960s; bought thousands of obsolete carding
machines, arranged in neat rows covering entire large field. Member
since 1989.

Donald Trump

$450 million
Casinos, real estate. New York City. 50.
Divorced, remarried; 4 children.

Trump, polite but unhappy, phoning from his plane: "You're putting me
on at $450 million? I've got that much in stock market assets alone.
There's 100% of Trump Tower, 100% of the new Nike store—they're paying $10 million a year in rent!" Add it all up, said Trump, and his net
worth is "in the $2 billion range, probably over $2 billion." Who knows?
Maybe it is. Just as financial leverage can knock fortunes down very fast
(Trump's estimated net worth fell to minus $900 million in 1990), so it
can rapidly restore fortunes when values rise again—and New York's
real estate market has lately regained much of its old vigor. Ditto
Atlantic City, where Trump's Castle, Taj Mahal, other properties have
30% of the gaming market. So yes, Donald, we have lowballed the current value of your holdings, but, given your love of leverage, it seems
the smart thing to do.

NEW TO THE FORBES FOUR HUNDRED

Malcolm G. (Kim) Chace III

$440 million
Berkshire Hathaway. Providence, R.I. 61.
Married, 3 children.

Longtime minority owner in Warren Buffett's *(see p. 116)* famed investment vehicle. Ancestor Oliver Chace founded textile mill Berkshire in
1806 in Providence, R.I. Father Malcolm Chace, Berkshire president,
oversaw merger with Hathaway 1955. Had 14 plants and $112 million
sales. Malcolm III spent "absolutely terrible" summer working in dye

mill as teenager. "I think they call it 'character building.'" Failed to move south; mills were losing money. In 1962 young Buffett started buying shares. Family ambivalent but takeover completed 1965. Chaces kept most of their stock, later reconciled to change: "We sort of sat there and smiled and watched him [Buffett] do his thing." Father stayed on as chairman, son inherited seat. Last mill closed in the mid-1970s. Chace currently owns 13,435 Berkshire Hathaway shares recently worth $32,000 each. Also chairman of newly formed Bank of Rhode Island. "I do consider myself lucky."

NEW TO THE FORBES FOUR HUNDRED

Robert J. Fisher

$435 million
The Gap, Inc. San Francisco. 42.
Married, 3 children.

William S. Fisher

$435 million
The Gap, Inc. San Francisco. 39.
Married, 3 children.

John J. Fisher

$435 million
The Gap, Inc. San Francisco. 35.
Married, 4 children.

Sons of Gap, Inc. founders Donald and Doris Fisher *(see p. 159)*. Robert began his career in Bloomingdale's merchandising training program. Started at The Gap as store manager 1980; chief financial officer 1991; chief operating officer 1995. Founded Gap Environmental Organization: "We believe that business profitability and environmental responsibility are not mutually exclusive." William established store operations in Canada 1989. Now president, international division: heads strategic planning, merchandising for Gap stores in Canada, United Kingdom, France, Japan, Germany. John not involved in company; part owner San Francisco (baseball) Giants with father. All three brothers Princeton graduates, Stanford M.B.A.s.

Jerral Wayne Jones

$435 million
Oil and gas, sports. Dallas. 54.
Married, 3 children.

Irascible Cowboys owner looking to topple NFL licensing dominance. Football league suing for $300 million. Jones' countersuit: $750 million. Born LA; to North Little Rock, Ark. early 1940s. U. of Arkansas football, M.B.A.; joined father's insurance business 1965. Dad taught flamboyance. Bought, developed gas properties as Arkoma with gas engineer Mike McCoy. Bought undeveloped wells from Arkla 1982, sold back for big profits 1989. Bought Dallas (football) Cowboys, fired legendary coach Tom Landry; first season disastrous: 1–15. Turned around; Texas Stadium (Jones owns lease) revenues by far league's highest. Says making money is "like trying to quench a thirst . . . I've never gone to sleep yet without wanting something more to drink." Paid $105 million in players' bonuses; $13 million to Deion Sanders alone. Member since 1994.

NEW TO THE FORBES FOUR HUNDRED

David G. Price

$430 million
Real estate. Santa Monica, Calif. 64.
Married, 5 children.

Immigrant Welsh father; raised LA. UCLA law school. Through sister, met LA real estate mogul Joseph Drown, became personal attorney. Bought 2 golf courses, country club 1969; 5 years before his American Golf turned profit. Now manages 240 properties. Prefers privacy—"If it's a public company, you have to answer to too many people"—but took National Golf Properties public anyway 1993. American Golf still private. Critics cite AG-NGP cozy relationship; speculation that Price props up NGP's earnings through AG's cash flow. Born-again Christian but likes B-52s, potent rum drink introduced to him by friend Bill Gates (see p. 115). Also enjoys airplane racing, basketball. Ambivalent about Forbes Four Hundred: "I don't know whether to celebrate or commiserate."

Jane B. Engelhard

$430 million
Inheritance. Far Hills, N.J. 78.
Twice widowed, 5 daughters.

Father was Brazilian diplomat. Family fled war-ravaged Europe for Buenos Aires with "nothing but our passports and our personal belongings." Second husband, "Platinum King" Charles Engelhard Jr. (d. 1971), inherited small Engelhard Minerals & Chemicals, built what is now Engelhard Corp.; prototype for James Bond character Goldfinger. Globe-hopped with Jane in private airplane: left $300 million estate. Jane retired socialite. Collects rare books, documents; e.g., original proclamation of Louisiana Purchase signed by Jefferson. Fortune "not as dependent on Dow Jones as some." Resigned from her $80 million foundation 1996; daughters will continue its operation. Member since 1982.

Virginia McKnight Binger

$430 million
3M. Wayzata, Minn. 80.
Married, 3 children (1 deceased).

Only child of William McKnight (d. 1978), S. Dakota farm boy who climbed from bookkeeper to key exec in fledgling sandpaper company; now industrial giant 3M Corp. ($13.5 billion sales 1995). Virginia honorary chair $1.3 billion McKnight Foundation; this year pledged $33.5 million over next 5 years to Minnesota arts organizations. Started own foundation, VMB fund, for Minn. poor. Husband, James, former Honeywell CEO, runs Broadway's Jujamcyn theater chain (now showing *Grease!*, *Smokey Joe's Cafe*, etc.). Once raised Thoroughbreds at top Fla. horse-breeding farm; won Preakness 1980. Sold major parcel in 1994; still trying to sell the rest. "A result of our getting out of the horse business," says James. First appeared on list in 1982.

Howard Phipps Jr.

$430 million
Inheritance. Old Westbury, N.Y. 62.
Married, 3 children.

Anne Phipps Sidamon-Eristoff

$430 million
Inheritance. New York City. 64.
Married, 3 children.

Brother and sister. Grandchildren of Pittsburgh steel magnate Henry Phipps, children of Howard Phipps (d. 1981). Family-founded Bessemer Trust Co. now more than $12 billion; other groups (Bessemer Securities, Bessemer Group) prospering as well. Family's share believed over $4.3 billion. Howard Jr.: "not a lot of laughs," lives quietly, represents sister on Bessemer Trust board. Anne: married to prominent lawyer; active on boards of American Museum of Natural History, Museum of Modern Art.

Phipps family known for outstanding racehorses. Four other family branches split wealth not controlled by Howard, Anne. First appeared on list 1982.

Robert Freeman Weis

$425 million
Weis Markets. Sunbury, Pa. 77.
Married, 3 children.

Weis Markets in midst of self-financed expansion program: 9 new super-stores 1995, 9 more by year-end. This is the most ambitious expansion program in Weis Markets' history. Father and uncle opened neighbor-hood grocery store 1912. Became Weis Markets 1955. Robert, Yale grad, cousin Sigfried (d. 1995) became cochairmen. Expanded to 151-super-market empire in 6 states. Added own manufacturing; also construction division, truck fleet. Best-seller: over 2,000 private-label items: "We have people who understand what quality is." Strict cost controls, no debt; over $1.6 billion in sales 1995. Bought 80% interest in pet supplier Super-petz 1994. Member since 1982.

Fitz Eugene Dixon Jr.

$425 million
Inheritance. Lafayette Hill, Pa. 73.
Married, 1 son, 1 daughter.

Great-grandfathers were P.A.B. Widener (streetcar magnate, d. 1915 with reported $100 million estate) and William Elkins (d. 1903 leaving reported $30 million fortune). Fitz: Harvard dropout, taught 16 years at Episcopal Academy: "Happiest days of my life." Big giver medicine, education. Investments mostly blue chips, bonds, some real estate, including Grind-stone Neck, Me. (resort where he was born). Philadelphia power broker. Owns 10% (baseball) Phillies. Grandfather George died on *Titanic;* Fitz wears emerald ring given to grandmother as she stepped into lifeboat. Member since 1982.

Timothy E. Gill

$425 million
Quark, Inc. Denver. 42.
Single.

Farhad Fred Ebrahimi

$425 million
Quark, Inc. Denver. 57.
Married, 2 children.

Gill: "I figured if I started my own business, I'd be the last person fired." U. of Colorado B.S. in applied math, computer science. After sacked from company started by high school buddies, borrowed $2,000 from parents, started Quark, Inc. ("A nice, cool, scientific word") in bedroom 1981. Met Ebrahimi through mutual attorney, brought in as 50% partner to handle finances 1986 for $100,000. Quark XPress out 1987, quickly became top desktop software for page layouts. Company reports sales over $200 million, extremely profitable. Gill heads design team, Ebrahimi deals with business end. Gill lives with companion of 10 years: "I'm as married as a gay person can be." Members since 1993.

Ralph L. Engelstad

$425 million
Gambling. Las Vegas. 66.
Married, 1 daughter.

Grandson of potato farmer, grew up Thief River Falls, Minn. B.S., U. of North Dakota 1954. Made money in construction. To Las Vegas, built Imperial Palace 1974: nonunion casino. Largest private casino/hotel on Strip: 2,700 rooms, no debt. Held parties on Hitler's birthday in casino "war room" 1986, 1988; fined $1.5 million by Nevada Gaming Commission 1989 for damaging state's image. Lying low since, refuses most interviews. Third-largest antique automobile collection in U.S.: 43 Duesenbergs, Hitler's parade car, Father Divine's Throne Car given to him by his congregation. Member since 1994.

NEW TO THE FORBES FOUR HUNDRED

Harold FitzGerald Lenfest

$425 million
Cable TV. Huntingdon Valley, Pa. 66.
Married, 3 children.

Son of traveling entrepreneur; mother died when he was 13. Raised on farm of religious Pennsylvania Dutch woman; developed rebellious personality. Columbia law degree; took post as in-house counsel to Walter Annenberg 1965. Editorial director, Seventeen magazine 1970. Bought two cable systems from Annenberg for $2.3 million 1974. Lenfest Communications struggled early 1980s; John Malone (see p. 216) bankrolled further growth. Slowly bought up small cable systems in Pennsylvania, N.J., now 12th largest cable operator in U.S., over 1 million subscribers. Also owns Jaguar dealerships, real estate. Legal troubles: he and wife, Marguerite, sued in 1995 for alleged insider trading violations; case pending. Lenfest Communications paid $5 million fine 1994 to settle Justice Department's allegations that it cheated motion picture industry of programming royalties. Otherwise low profile: avid yachtsman, flies coach.

NEW TO THE FORBES FOUR HUNDRED

Pamela M. Lopker

$425 million
Software. Carpinteria, Calif. 42.
Married, 2 children.

Richest self-made woman on The Forbes Four Hundred. Graduated U.C. Santa Barbara, 1977. Started QAD in 1979, wrote program that kept track of shoemakers' sales orders; later expanded program to take care of accounting and inventory. Moved from cobblers into factories, upgraded software to handle materials planning, forecasting, cash management for Philips Electronics, Unilever, Ford. Bought partners out 1981. Private QAD now replacing old-fashioned, monolithic applications with "object-oriented programming"—independent, interchangeable modules of programming that can be assembled to create complex, flexible programs. Gearing up to be compatible with Microsoft's NT 4.0 operating system. QAD known for nontechie approach: learn customer's industry inside and out, so "we look like we come from that industry."

Raymond J. Noorda

$425 million
Computer software. Provo, Utah. 72.
Married, 3 children.

Served U.S. Navy WWII. U. of Utah grad; GE computer engineer. Then chief executive power-supply-systems maker, sold 1981. Joined Novell as CEO 1983; $3.8 million revenue then, $1.8 billion 1993. Expanded with joint ventures, acquisitions. Two merger talks with Bill Gates failed; subsequently cooperated with government antitrust efforts against Microsoft. Ray: "Microsoft would like to consume the business; if they can't do that they'll inhume it or subsume it." Acquired WordPerfect Corp. in $855 million merger 1994. Noorda retired 1994, allegedly for health reasons. Same year Novell reached a settlement with the Justice Department to resolve allegations it overcharged the government for equipment. Novell recently unloaded WordPerfect and QuattroPro in sale to Corel Corp.; took 20% Corel stake, $11 million cash. Noorda's investment vehicle, the Canopy

Group, has stakes in more than 12 high-tech ventures. Litigation continues: Caldera, Inc., owned mainly by Noorda, recently filed antitrust suit against Microsoft. Member since 1992.

Edmund Newton Ansin

$420 million
TV stations. Miami Beach. 60.
Divorced, 3 children.

Son of Massachusetts shoe manufacturer who bought Florida property 1940, FCC license for $3.4 million 1962. After Andover, Harvard, Wharton, Edmund took over WSVN-TV 1971. NBC affiliate, no debt; prospered. Dropped by NBC 1987. Big mistake. Revamped as tabloid news station: crime, sex, flashy graphics. Soon revenues higher than competing NBC, CBS stations. Bought Boston's WHDH-TV for $215 million 1993. Son Andrew, 32, in real estate division; James, 30, TV marketing, sales. With TV stations again trading at record multiples, Ed's 2 stations worth over $400 million. First appeared on list 1984.

Stuart Subotnick

$420 million
Metromedia. New York City. 54.
Married, 2 children.

Right-hand man to legendary dealmaker John Kluge *(see p. 117)*: "We both came from very modest backgrounds. We know what a dollar is all about." Subotnick now aiming to build a radio station empire without his mentor/boss. Grew up city projects, Bensonhurst, N.Y. While working for IRS 1967, answered blind ad for tax position at Metromedia. Urged full review of competing candidates: "If you still think I'm the right person for the job, give it to me then." Hired, promoted to CFO 13 years later. Has since propelled Metromedia through biggest deals. Gets 5% equity in most. Also owns horses, real estate. Co-owner with boss of NY-NJ soccer franchises. Sits on the Thelonious Monk Institute of Jazz board. Member since 1995.

Ernest Gallo

$420 million
Wine. Modesto, Calif. 87.
Widower, 2 children.

Surviving brother of famous wine-making duo. Italian immigrant father bought 230 Modesto wine acres during Prohibition, sold grapes. Ernest and Julio sweated in vineyards as teens, raised younger brother Joseph Jr. after taskmaster father killed wife, self 1933. Brothers took over operations, built on inexpensive wines: Thunderbird, Night Train. Stepped up to varietal wines 1970s, 1980s. Also wine coolers. Julio died in car crash 1993. Ernest still runs the show, but being sued by Kendall-Jackson Winery over trademark infringement; case pending. Member since 1982.

NEW TO THE FORBES FOUR HUNDRED

Sanjiv Sidhu

$415 million
Manufacturing software. Dallas. 39.
Married, 2 children.

Another young software mogul joining The Forbes Four Hundred, Sidhu is the founder and 67% owner of i2 Technologies; it makes software that figures out the most cost-effective production schedules for manufacturers, others. Son of a research chemist, he was born in Hyderabad, India. Grew up among other scientists' families; attended school, college near home, then to Oklahoma State for master's in chemical engineering. Took job in Texas Instruments' artificial intelligence lab, saw how AI techniques could be used to organize factory work. Left TI to start own company 1988, first named Intellection, later i2. Early clients: Caterpillar, Black & Decker and Timken Steel. Said no thanks to venture capitalists: "It took less effort to sell $3 million of software than to negotiate $3 million in venture capital."

Oprah Gail Winfrey

$415 million
Talk. Chicago. 42.
Single.

Oprah Winfrey Show in eleventh straight season America's number one daytime program. Just cut new distribution deal with Disney/ABC for feature films, TV movies. Born rural Mississippi, moved to Milwaukee, then Nashville. Miss Black Tennessee age 19. Left Tennessee State U. 1973, became Nashville TV newscaster. News anchor Baltimore ABC station 1976; emotional ad-lib delivery got her pulled off air after 9 months; switched to morning talk show. To Chicago, boosted city's third-rated talk show to number one in Phil Donahue's hometown. Television 1986 with nationally syndicated *Oprah Winfrey Show*. Negotiated best deal in syndication: believed to get over 60% of show's revenues. Oprah now owns vertically integrated entertainment machine; owns, produces show from Chicago's city-block Harpo studios facility. Member since 1995.

GREAT FAMILY FORTUNES

Some of the largest fortunes in America are so divided among heirs or family members that no one individual qualifies for The Forbes Four Hundred. Many are echoes from fortunes past.

Alfond

$875 million
Dexter Shoe. Maine

Harold Alfond, 82, son of shoemaker; started in shoe factory at 25 cents per hour. "In 1934 we didn't know what college was, we went to work." Bought, sold Norrwock Shoe Co. Founded Dexter Shoe 1956 with $10,000. Joined 1958 by nephew Peter Lunder (now president). Currently 7.5 million pairs shoes produced annually in Maine, Puerto Rico; 77 owned retail outlets. Key to success: "Make a product that's good value, good quality, and you get the customers." Customers include J.C. Penney, Nordstrom, May, etc. Dexter acquired by Berkshire Hathaway 1993; atypically, Buffett paid with BH stock, since much appreciated. Harold Alfond also part-owner of Boston (baseball) Red Sox. Pledged $2.5 million in challenge grants to University of New England for health sciences facility 1995. Three sons, all in the business.

Andersen

$700 million
Windows. Bayport, Minn.

"All together, boys." Hans Jacob Andersen's legendary first words in English, became company motto. He arrived Portland, Me. 1870 from

Denmark. Founded Andersen Lumber Co. with sons 1903. Revolutionized window industry 1905 with standardized window frame featuring interchangeable parts. Penny-pinching Hans signed company's first profit-sharing check hours before death; plan grew, recently 25% of employees' salaries. Hans' son Fred came up with advertising gem: "Only the rich can afford poor windows." Tough year in window industry, but Andersen still top player in U.S. market.

Asplundh

$560 million
Tree trimming. Willow Grove, Pa.

Many fortunes trace to tree-cutting. Brothers Griffith, Carl, Lester owe their fortune to *trimming* trees. Sons of Swedish immigrant after college formed Asplundh Tree Expert 1928, courted electric and phone companies: growth industries even during Depression. Rapid expansion. Other businesses for utility customers: maintaining telephone poles, streetlights and pipelines. Founders' sons took over 1960s. Now nearly 20,000 employees in 50 states, 8 foreign countries; $935 million sales, no long-term debt. Tough field training for family members: 8 years as trimmer, foreman, etc. "No one is above failure." Third generation poised to take over, benefit from outsourcing trend. Utilities, others who need to deal with trees increasingly farm out work. Fortune shared by 132 family members.

Bacardi

$2 billion
Liquor. Puerto Rico, Miami et al.

Wine merchant Don Facundo Bacardi (b. 1816) immigrated to Cuba 1830. Distilled "civilized rum," founded Bacardi 1862, built into world's most popular liquor brand. Castro stole operations after revolution, but family kept trademark. Expanded internationally: Bacardi now two-thirds of world rum market. Family credited with invention of daiquiri. Company mixed rum with vermouth 1993 by buying major stake in Martini & Rossi for $1.4 billion. Profits now estimated at $225 million. Integrated corporate structure: Bacardi Corp. of Puerto Rico sells to Bacardi Corp. of Miami; royalties go to Bacardi & Co. Ltd. Bahamas. Company now run by Don Facundo's great-grandson Manuel Jorge Cutillas, but fortune divided among some 500 family members, some of whom are squabbling.

Bancroft

$1 billion
Dow Jones & Co. California et al.

Heirs of Clarence Barron (d. 1928), Barron's magazine. Bought *Wall Street Journal,* Dow ticker from Charles Dow, others 1902. Began Barron's 1921 at suggestion of son-in-law Hugh Bancroft (d. 1933), husband of Clarence's adopted daughter Jane. Fortune split among their children: Jane Bancroft Cook, Jessie Cox (d. 1982), Hugh Bancroft Jr. (d. 1953). Hugh's 4 children share his third. Bettina Klink, LA; Hugh, Newport Beach, Calif., designs and builds antique car kits; Chris runs real estate company, ice-cream shops in Denton, Tex.; Kathryn Kavadas, Newton, Mass., active in fine arts, philanthropy. Jane Bancroft Cook, 84, thrice widowed, once divorced, 3 daughters; quiet but big donor education, hospitals. "Zealous guardian of the journalistic independence of the *Journal.*" Jane Cox MacElree, 67, child of Jessie Cox, active in Philadelphia charities, votes 8.8 million shares Dow Jones held in trust.

Barbey

$715 million
Textiles, apparel. California et al.

Heirs of John Barbey, cofounder Reading Glove & Mitten Manufacturing Co. 1899. Bought out 5 partners 1911; name changed to Schuylkill Silk Mills. First product: silk gloves. Began selling brand-name lingerie as Vanity Fair 1917. First to use live underwear models. Son J.E. designed lingerie: "He just loved beautiful things." Moved beyond white and pink: introduced leopard and mermaid prints. Died 1956; left stock in trust, handpicked outside management. Company became VF Corp. 1970. Other brands: Lee, Wrangler, Jantzen.

Belfer

$1.2 billion
Heirs of oilman Arthur B. Belfer. NYC

Sold original Belco Petroleum 1983, now back with Belco Oil & Gas, founded 1992, public in March. Family's 80% stake adds $550 million to family net worth. Arthur Belfer to U.S. from Poland WWII. Made sleeping bags for U.S. Army. 1952 discovered oil and gas. Took Belco Petroleum public 1959. Created large resource base in Peru, also domestic natural gas. After oil venture in Israel flopped, added U.S. coal mining 1969. Friendly takeover by InterNorth (now Enron) 1983. Motto: "If the price is right, we sell." Peru operations nationalized same year; Belco Petroleum's output chopped in half. Arthur died 1993. Son Robert, 60, Harvard Law grad, Enron director. Now chairman and president Belco Oil & Gas. Brother Laurence, COO. Arthur's heirs also include 2 daughters; 9 grandchildren, 14 great-grandchildren.

Blaustein

$1.3 billion
Amoco. Baltimore
Heirs of Louis Blaustein (1869-1937)

Lithuanian-born immigrant delivered kerosene door-to-door, invented predecessor of RR tank car. Only son, Jacob (d. 1970), invented metered gasoline pumps, antiknock gas, drive-in stations. Founded Amoco 1910; merged with Standard Oil of Indiana 1954. Part-time diplomat: convinced U.N. conferees to accept human rights provisions 1945. His son Jacob inherited 50%; daughters Fanny Thalheimer (d. 1957), Ruth Rosenberg (d. 1992), 25% each. Family still owns 16.6 million Amoco shares. Family's private American Trading & Production Corp. in manufacturing (office supplies, security systems), real estate, oil and gas.

Breed

$470 million
Airbags. South Padre Island, Tex.

Allen Breed: 69, thrice divorced, remarried. Son of Chicago doctor; engineering degree Northwestern 1959. Became expert on triggers; started Florida-based Breed Corp. on military contracts 1961. Applied trigger technology to air bags; first air bag crash-sensor produced 1968. Met fourth wife and business partner, Johnnie Cordell Breed, at Pritikin Longevity Center after heart attack 1984. Married 1987. Johnnie, 52, former owner of big travel company; brought cash, organization and key $45 million loan guarantee to help expand Breed's company. Boosted by 1991 Congress decree that all new cars for sale in U.S. must include air bags. Public 1992; renamed Breed Technologies. Now dominates North American air bag sensor market with 62% market share, sales over $400 million.

Brittingham

$525 million
Ceramic tile. Mexico, Dallas.

Brothers Jack and Robert filled ceramic tile niche in post-WWII building boom. Headquartered in Dallas, but made tiles cheap in Mexico. Built Dal-Tile to one of largest U.S. ceramic tilemakers. Jack, a.k.a. Juan, commuted Dallas-Mexico; former chairman Robert ran Dal-Tile U.S. Sold 1990 to AEA Investors for $640 million. Robert fined $4 million 1993 for dumping lead sludge; court mandated community service, 5 years' probation. Avid hunter. Son Bobby in Dallas real estate, etc., as Rosebriar Holdings Corp. Sold land to AMC Theaters for largest U.S. cinema—some 20 screens—at family's Stemmons Crossroads development in Dallas.

Brown

$1.3 billion
Brown-Forman Corp. Louisville, Kentucky

Young pharmaceuticals salesman George Garvin Brown created first sealed bottles (barrels then customary) for whiskey 1870. Started company with half-brother and $5,000. Family adapted well to times. Prohibition: government license to bottle whiskey for medicinal purposes. WWII: converted whiskey plant to manufacture industrial alcohol. Acquired Jack Daniel Distillery 1965, makers of classic Tennessee mash whiskey. Started wine division 1991. Other brands include Southern Comfort; Fetzer, Korbel, Bolla wines. Also Lenox china, Dansk tableware, Hartmann luggage. Fourth generation Owsley Brown II now CEO. Five other family members active in company management.

Busch

$1.6 billion
Anheuser-Busch. St. Louis.

Bavarian immigrant Adolphus Busch married Lilly Anheuser 1861; joined father-in-law's brewery 1864. Grandson August Jr. (d. 1989) president 1946, steered company into modern marketing era with inspired brand advertising: made Budweiser "King of Beers." Also bought St. Louis (baseball) Cardinals. August III, 59, unseated father 1975 to take company helm. Fierce competitor: "The goal is dominance. I have to win." Established Eagle Snacks 1979; since sold to PepsiCo. Increased domestic beer market share from 23% to 45%. Expanding internationally; Bud now in U.K. pubs, 70 countries. Divesting: sold Cardinals to loyal fan group; spun off baking subsidiary Campbell Taggart. Now back to brewing, and theme parks. Fifth-generation August IV, 32, VP brand management.

Campbell

$1 billion
Land, investment portfolio. Hawaii

Patriarch James Campbell (d. 1900) left Ireland as 13-year-old stowaway on NYC-bound ship 1839. Kept going: 1850 sailed for Hawaii; survived shipwreck. Profits from sugar-growing business paid for land on Oahu, Maui, Hawaii; turned 41,000 arid Oahu acres into fertile sugar plantation by drilling artesian well. Called "Kimo-Ona Milliona." Estate now 72,000 acres on 3 islands: much conservation, agro land; some commercial development—30,000 Oahu acres becoming city of Kapolei. Also, 9 million square feet stateside (shopping malls; office, industrial). Kimo-Ona's last surviving daughter died 1987. Massive historic trust dissolves 2007, proceeds to more than 100 beneficiaries.

Carter

$500 million
Direct selling. Dallas area.

Sisters-in-law Mary Crowley (d. 1986), Mary Kay (cosmetics) both founded direct-selling companies. Crowley started Home Interiors & Gifts on savings, $6,000 loan 1957: home decorations (gilt wall sconces, butterfly plaques, etc.). Today over 500 products, 50,000 "displayers" organize parties to sell in homes. Sales by distributors $850 million. Son Donald Carter's financial acumen helped build on mother's legacy. Donald, 63, owns 30% (rest family, key employees with 23%), also piece of Dallas (basketball) Mavericks. Donald rejected proposed $1 billion LBO (7.5 times cash flow) 1994: "They don't necessarily think bigger is better."

Carver

$430 million
Bandag, Inc. Muscatine, Iowa

Widow and three children of Roy James Carver (d. 1981). Roy learned about tire retreading process at wine-tasting party in Germany 1957. Acquired rights. Nearly drained family pump business to perfect Bandag method. Built predominant company in field. Bandag's retreading materials franchised to 1,300 dealers. Recently entered litigation at threat of losing 26 franchises. Widow, Lucille, 79, remains treasurer. Youngest son, Martin, 48, now president. Oldest son, Roy Jr., 53, owns original Carver Pump business. John, 51, raises horses. Family controls 75% Bandag stock.

Cayre

$1.1 billion
Media. New York City

Three sons of Jack Cayre, Syrian immigrant who ran whiskey and cigarette concession on Miami-Bahamas tourist boat 1940s. Eldest two sons came to New York, started Caytronics 1969 to license unwanted Latin and disco music from major labels. Sold music contract to RCA worth $100 million 1979. With music business proceeds started Good-Times Home Video: distributor of cheap movies, public domain cartoons. Now ubiquitous titles at Wal-Mart, Toys "R" Us. Disney sued, lost over Cayre's *Aladdin* and *Snow White* knockoffs. Video business slowed, started PC game division GT Interactive 1993: *Doom*, huge hit. IPO 1995. Estimated 1996 sales $375 million. Private GoodTimes Entertainment Group also sells music, books, toys. Estimated 1996 sales $600 million. Also merchandising, real estate. Brothers Stanley, 60, Joseph, 55, and Kenneth, 53, grew up poor. No college degrees. Share in fortune estimated over $1.2 billion.

Chandler

$2.1 billion
Times Mirror Co. Los Angeles

Heirs of Henry Chandler, clerk who married daughter of *Los Angeles Times* owner Harrison Gray Otis 1894. Built media empire, died 1944. Son Norman pushed news over ads during WWII newsprint shortage, won readers. Conservative: "We only gave management's side in [covering] labor disputes." Liberal guilt: Henry's grandson Otis took over 1960, moved paper leftward. Also raced cars, hunted big game, still surfs at age 68. Company diversified into book publishing, broadcast, cable. Sold 4 TV stations 1993; cable to Cox Communications 1995. Publishing *Hartford Courant, Baltimore Sun,* etc. Tightening belts: new CEO, scrapped NYC edition Newsday 1995, cut LA staff. Scores of heirs share family trust. Politically conservative family members now trying to assert themselves as flagship paper luffs.

Clapp

$1.4 billion
Lumber. Seattle

Norton brothers Matthew G. and James started lumber company Laird Norton late 1800s with cousin William Laird. Helped Frederick Weyerhaeuser start Weyerhaeuser Co. Eben Clapp, a physician, married daughters of both Matthew and James. Eben's son Norton main heir, d. 1995 at 89. Largest Weyerhaeuser shareholder. Married widow of one of sons. Laird Norton's Lanoga Corp. in lumber, building supplies Pacific Northwest, Midwest, Alaska. Also Washington State real estate. Much tied up in Laird Norton Trust. More than 100 heirs share fortune.

Clark

$630 million
Sewing machines. Cooperstown, N.Y.

Edward Clark (1811-82) helped Isaac Singer sell sewing machines in the 1850s. Clark got 40% of Singer Manufacturing and passed it on to his son

Alfred (d. 1896). Alfred's sons Edward, F. Ambrose (racehorse owner), Stephen and Robert (art collectors) put their dinky hometown, Cooperstown, on the map claiming that baseball was invented there. The story caught on, and Baseball's Hall of Fame opened there in 1939. Museums followed, as did a hotel, a golf course and a hospital. Family's fifth generation includes Anne Labouisse Peretz, 57, co-owner of *New Republic* magazine, and Jane Forbes Clark, 41, who chairs the Clark Foundation and Clark Estates, Inc. in NYC.

Close

$500 million
Textiles. Fort Mill, S.C.

Colonel Leroy Springs founded Lancaster Cotton Mill 1895, took over Fort Mill Mfg. Co. Son Elliot White Springs (d. 1959), ace pilot WWI, writer 1920s, returned to family textile business at father's request 1931, wrote racy ad copy: "A buck well spent on a Springmaid sheet." Big profits WWII. Son-in-law Hugh W. Close (d. 1983) took over, pushed into fashion areas. Springs Industries now major manufacturer home furnishings. Elliot's granddaughter Crandall Close Bowles, 48, executive VP. Family interests in real estate, insurance, railroad held through investment firm Springs Co. Family controls nearly 66% voting stock.

Collier

$1.4 billion
Real estate. Naples, Fla.; Phoenix

Descendants of Barron Gift Collier (d. 1939), pioneered streetcar advertising, used $5 million annual income to purchase southwest Florida land starting 1911. By 1930 over 1 million acres; renamed Collier County. Heirs disagreed on investment strategy, split empire with coin toss 1980. One branch: Collier Enterprises, led by Miles Collier, 49. Other: Barron Collier Co., 3 principal heirs. Combined holdings: 144,000 acres farmland, 20,000 citrus, 100,000 ranchland; 10,000 other in Naples area. Families have additional acreage Phoenix, elsewhere. Private Capital Management now over $1 billion.

Coors

$600 million
Beer. Golden, Colo.

Descendants of German immigrant Adolph Coors, stowaway on Baltimore-bound sailing ship; founded small beer company 1873. Company survived

Prohibition making malted milk, ceramics, near-beer. Now near 10% of domestic beer market. Founder's great-grandsons run businesses. Peter, 49, fourth-generation Coors, worked summer vacations at brewery; now at helm. Joseph Jr., 54, and Jeffrey, 51, head ACX Technologies: industrial ceramics, aluminum, consumer packaging. "If the 3 of us were over there, we'd be all over each other." Some 70 family members own 55% Coors through trust.

Cowles

$575 million
Media. Minneapolis, NYC.

Descendants of Gardner Cowles Sr. (d. 1946), who invested $110,000 into sickly *Des Moines Register* 1903, added evening *Tribune,* controlled monopoly. Son John (d. 1983) pulled off own monopoly in Minneapolis 1935. Gardner Jr. sold *Family Circle,* etc., to *New York Times* for 23% of NYT stock 1971. Third generation squandered profits; 1984 sold Cowles Broadcasting to Oveta Culp Hobby, flagship *Register* to Gannett for $200 million 1985. John (Jay) III, 42, chairs Cowles Media: "We still have plenty to do." Roughly 70 heirs share 59% Cowles Media, also *New York Times,* Affiliated Publications stock.

Cullen

$550 million
Oil. Houston

Heirs of Hugh Roy Cullen (d. 1957), grade school dropout, legendary wild-catter who hit big drilling deeper in played-out fields. Used "creekology," reading bends of creeks, rivers for oil. Hit famed Tom O'Connor *(see family)* field early 1930s. "Father of U. of Houston": family has given $100 million. Quintana Petroleum runs wells for family, Exxon. Quintana executive committee includes 1 daughter, 2 grandsons, granddaughter's husband. Grandson Enrico di Portanova, born to daughter (now deceased) and Italian playboy, long ago renounced U.S. citizenship; sued for more income, lost 1984.

Damon

$750 million
Banking, real estate. Hawaii, California

Heirs of Samuel Mills Damon, early partner First Hawaiian Bank, wrote will 1914. Carefully managed estate includes: First Hawaiian shares, 4,000 acres walnut groves near Sacramento, Calif., commercial real estate San

Francisco area, 235 acres commercial/industrial warehouse real estate near Honolulu, over 117,000 acres total on Big Island, much of it not worth much. Also part of Moanalua Valley on Oahu: park and wilderness reserve. Trust value said to increase about 12% annually. Historic trust due to dissolve at death of Damon's septuagenarian grandchildren; 20 to 30 heirs will benefit.

Davis

$2.3 billion
Winn-Dixie stores, Jacksonville, Fla.

Descendants of founder William Milton Davis. Purchased Rockmore Grocery in Lemon City, Fla. 1925 with $10,000. Named Winn-Dixie 1955: "To win Dixie was our ambition." Four sons built company to largest grocery chain in the Sunbelt. Now 1,178 stores in 14 states. Sales now $13 billion. Artemis Darius (A.D.) retired as vice chairman 1982; died 1995. His son Robert, 64, chairman 1983-88: "I'm just stepping down to give myself a little more elbowroom." Now heads DDI, family holding company. Robert's cousin A. Dano, current Winn-Dixie chairman.

Dayton

$1 billion
Retailing. Minneapolis

Heirs to George Draper Dayton who founded Dayton's department store 1902. Son George Nelson Dayton ran company 1938-50. Brothers joined by 1950, knew value of work: "The only thing worse than a bum is a rich bum." Since 1946, 5% of pretax profits to charity. Added low-margin discount stores 1962; created book retailer B. Dalton (sold 1986). Merged with J.L. Hudson Co. 1969. No family member active in company since 1983. Today over 1,000 stores in 37 states, $23 billion sales. Operates Dayton's, Hudson's, Marshall Field's, Target, Mervyn's. Founder's grandson Bruce Dayton, art collector; most of collection promised to Minneapolis museum.

Demoulas

$675 million
Supermarkets. Boston area.

Demoulas family executives found to have violated rules governing company's profit-sharing fund; paid $15,000 to Department of Labor 1996 to resolve accounting issues. Greek-American patriarch Arthur Demoulas, wife opened small grocery 1917. Sons, George and Telemachus, took over

1954. Today over 56 Demoulas/Market Basket stores Massachusetts, New Hampshire; estimated revenues $1.6 billion. Also real estate. Agreement that if one brother died, survivor would care for other's family. George died heart attack 1971; Telemachus removed George's widow from board 1978; transferred all but 8% of stock to himself. George's heirs (4 children) alarmed by 1989 tax notice, sued 1990. Verdict 1994: Telemachus liable for fraud, breach of trust. Will appeal.

de Young

$1.4 billion
Publishing. San Francisco

Descendants of Michael H. de Young, cofounder of *San Francisco Chronicle* 1865 (other cofounder Charles de Young shot mayoral candidate in feud 1879; victim's son then shot Charles to death). Paper entertained public with local scandals, Wild West shoot-outs, mudslinging. De Youngs long feuded with rival Hearsts *(see pp. 237 and 169)*; now jointly publish Sunday edition to save costs under joint operating agreement with Hearst-owned *San Francisco Examiner.* Granddaughter Nan Tucker McEvoy inherited largest share of *Chronicle* after mother died 1988, but cousins forced her off board 1995.

Dillon

$650 million
Finance. Far Hills, N.J.

Patriarch Clarence Dillon (d. 1979), Harvard 1905, joined William A. Read & Co. 1914, worked way to top of company (renamed Dillon, Read) by 1919. Firm became Wall Street power; locked horns with J.P. Morgan. Wrote personal check for $146 million to buy Dodge Brothers Auto Co. Son C. Douglas became statesman: Eisenhower's ambassador to France; Treasury Secretary for JFK, LBJ; former chair Metropolitan Museum, NYC. Dillon, Read sold to Bechtel *(see p. 147)* 1981. Family also owns large pieces choice N.J. land; 2 world class Bordeaux vineyards, including Haut-Brion.

Donnelley

$1.4 billion
R.R. Donnelley & Sons. Chicago

Heirs of Richard R. Donnelley, Canadian saddlemaker's apprentice. Started own print shop, Chicago 1864. Destroyed by Great Fire of 1871; rebuilt by family into R.R. Donnelley & Sons. Went public 1956. Son

Reuben (d. 1929) formed publishing company; produced Yellow Pages; sold to Dun & Bradstreet 1961 for $80 million. Grandson Gaylord (d. 1992) took over main family business 1964. Company known for "The Good Book" and "The Big Book," i.e., the Bible and the Sears catalog. Sears dropped catalog, but Donnelley still prints more Bibles than anyone else. Also *Time, New Yorker, TV Guide,* Forbes Inc.'s *American Heritage.* Operations in 26 countries; revenues $6.5 billion 1995. Largest commercial printer in U.S.

du Pont

$10.5 billion
Inheritance. Delaware

Descendants of Pierre Samuel du Pont de Nemours (1739-1817), French Physiocrat who fled Revolutionary Terror for America 1800. Son Eleuthère Irénée, chemist's apprentice, founded gunpowder factory on Brandywine Creek 1802. Company and family prospered, dominated Powder Trust late 1800s. After interfamilial battle for control, Pierre S. du Pont II emerged as leader. WWI munitions contracts produced massive growth (also sobriquet "Merchants of Death"). Founded Christiana Securities as family holding company for DuPont; later, under antitrust pressure from the Justice Department, merged into DuPont 1977. Rescued nascent General Motors 1920s, took about one-third. Bought out cousins in further struggles. Childless, divided bulk of fortune among 6 siblings before his death in 1958. His branch of the family built Wilmington Trust Co., dissident branches, Delaware Trust Co. Numerous descendants of P.S. II still control over 15% of DuPont. Family member: "The thing about the du Ponts is that some are very, very rich, and others are just plain old rich."

Durst

$650 million
Real estate. New York City area

Descendants of Joseph Durst (d. 1974), Austrian immigrant 1902, who began Durst Organization 1915 to oversee handful of NYC buildings. Sons Seymour (d. 1995), Royal (d. 1993), Edwin (d. 1990), David and daughter Alma. Seymour bought midtown office property 1940s; pioneered Third Avenue development. Heeded Dad's advice: "Never buy farther than you can walk." Eventually 5 million square feet midtown office space. August 1996 groundbreaking for Durst's 48-story Times Square skyscraper marks first Manhattan tower construction in 8 years; Condé Nast to occupy 40% of building's 1.6 million square feet. Quirky passion: set up the National Debt Clock near Times Square; former columnist for homeless paper

Street News. Next generation now manages: Seymour's son Douglas; David's sons Jonathan, Joshua.

France

$550 million
Auto racing. Daytona Beach, Fla.

Heirs of auto mechanic, amateur stock car racer William France (d. 1992). Car broke down 1934 in Daytona Beach en route to Miami; decided to stay. Raced Ford on Daytona's hard sand beach on weekends. Better at promoting races than winning them; founded sanctioning body Nascar 1947; strict rules as to which car models would be allowed to race under Nascar banner. Built $3 million Daytona International Speedway track 1959; financed in part by borrowing money from Dallas' wealthy Murchison family. Bread-and-butter income from race sanctioning: crown jewel Winston Cup series. Other Nascar income: merchandising, memberships, television. Son Bill Jr. succeeded father as Nascar president 1972. Bill Jr.'s brother James president of public company International Speedway Corp.; family owns 61%. Bill Jr.'s son Brian head of Nascar marketing. Big question: What happens to revenues after Clinton ban on sports sponsorships by tobacco companies?

Goldman

$600 million
Inheritance. New York City area

Widow Lillian, 4 children of Sol Goldman, NYC real estate mogul (d. 1987). First moved into big leagues with Chrysler Building purchase 1960. Known for squeezing "every nickel out of every building." Lillian filed for divorce 1983; "reconciliation" won 33% of Sol's $760 million estate of 550 parcels. Later sued to void deal, claiming conspiracy; lost 1987. Trust was created on Sol's death. Ugly intrafamily battle with children. Lillian sued again; won 1991. Family's energy now focused on IRS, trying to knock down big estate tax bill. Most properties are listed in name of children, Amy, Diane, Jane and Allan.

Gore

$950 million
Gore-Tex. Newark, Del.

Wilbert L. Gore (d. 1986) worked on Teflon 1957 as Du Pont employee. Du Pont not interested in selling finished Teflon goods; Wilbert and wife, Vieve, started own business 1958 in basement. First insulated cable, then

Gore-Tex, durable membrane later used in space suits. Son Bob took over business 1986. Gore-Tex best known for outerwear, but also used in medicine (surgical patches; artificial blood vessels), telecommunications (cables) and industry (filters). Fat margins on unique material. Fiscal 1996 sales over $1 billion. "Associates" (employees) get stock. Motto: "To make money and have fun."

Gorman

$480 million
L.L. Bean Inc. Freeport, Me.

Descendants of Leon Leonwood Bean (1872-1967), sportsman, founder L.L. Bean. Tired of soggy, cold feet: attached rubber soles to leather boots, became famous "Bean boot." After 90 of first 100 pairs returned defective, introduced Bean money-back guarantee: still in effect. One of first junk mailers: first ever direct-mail campaign to Maine's first hunting licensees 1919; sales exceeded $1 million 1942. "That wasn't bad for a boy who never got through the eighth grade." Sales now over $1 billion; still private. Grandson Leon Gorman, 61, increasing advertising, expanding women's line; guards quality, service. Low-profile family now selling to preppy Japanese.

Gottwald

$875 million
Ethyl Corp. Richmond, Va. et al.

Floyd Gottwald (d. 1982) made fortune in paper, acquired Ethyl Corp. 1962, expanded Ethyl into plastics, metals. Sons, Floyd Jr., Bruce, diversified into chemicals for computer chips, insurance, pharmaceuticals, etc.; spun off plastics, aluminum, energy, specialty chemicals. Now focusing on petroleum additives: added Amoco's lubricant additives 1992; purchased Texaco's worldwide lubricant additives business February 1996 for $136 million. Grandsons now in business.

Graham

$775 million
Washington Post. Washington, D.C.

Financier Eugene Meyer bought *Washington Post* in bankruptcy auction 1933. Daughter Katharine married young hotshot lawyer Phil Graham 1940. Katharine worked in circulation while Phil fought in Pacific WWII. Phil made publisher, editor-in-chief *Post* 1947, received voting control of paper 1948. Close friend of JFK's. Rebuilt *Post* to profitability. Committed suicide 1963. Widowed Kay took over, pushed paper to new heights: Pentagon Papers 1971, Watergate 1972-74. Published Unabomber manifesto 1995. Son Donald, 51, publisher 1979, CEO 1991, chairman 1993. Holdings include *Newsweek,* 6 television stations, cable. Kay, 79, Washington grande dame, still chairs *Post* executive committee.

Gund

$2.1 billion
Sanka, banking. Cleveland

Six children of George Gund Jr. (d. 1966). Harvard Business School grad sold family brewery during Prohibition. Bought decaffeinated coffee firm, later Sanka, 1919. Sold to Kellogg 1927 for stock. Moved into real estate, banking. Cleveland Trust president 1941. Son Gordon: "We didn't know the extent of our wealth until our father's death." George III, Gordon own Cleveland (basketball) Cavaliers. Paid $14 million in 1994 for rights to name city's arena Gund Arena. George, SF financier, has majority San Jose (hockey) Sharks. Gordon, blind from retinitis pigmentosa, is a venture capitalist. Graham, Boston architect. Agnes, president NYC Museum of Modern Art.

Haebler

$860 million
International Flavors and Fragrances.
Milwaukee et al.

Descendants of American-born William T. Haebler (d. 1956); founded IFF 1929 with Dutch émigré A.L. van Ameringen. Leading maker of flavors, fragrances for perfumes, soaps, household products, food and beverages. Company does not disclose clients, but perfumes reportedly include Calvin Klein's Eternity, Liz Taylor's Black Pearls, Yves St. Laurent's Champagne. IFF generates over two-thirds of sales and profits from operations outside the U.S.; over $1.4 billion revenues 1995. William's 3 daughters, main heirs. Polly: Milwaukee; married to William Van Dyke, Smith Barney executive. Ellen: Darien, Conn.; married to Phillip Skove. Ann: died 1988; left shares to 2 sons.

Haworth

$750 million
Office furniture. Holland, Mich.

Founded 1948 by Gerrard Haworth, 84, as maker of wood and glass office partitions. Growth took off 1975 when one-upped office furniture rival

Herman Miller's movable panel concept: installing electrical wiring inside panels. Copycats beat back by litigation: Miller agreed to pay $44 million in damages for patent infringement. Since 1988, 16 acquisitions for $300 million. Lean production and sales operations: computerization of manufacturing process, ruthless undercutters of competitors' bids. Now broadening presence in Europe, Asia. Gerrard's son, Richard, owns more than 50%; Richard's four sisters split rest.

Hillenbrand

$1.3 billion
Hillenbrand Industries. Batesville, Ind. et al.

Descendants of John Hillenbrand, son of German immigrant who rescued Batesville Casket Company from bankruptcy 1906. First to mass-market airtight, watertight caskets 1940. Created Hill-Rom, manufacturer of hospital beds, 1928. Batesville Casket and Hill-Rom combined under parent Hillenbrand Industries 1969. Public 1971. Founded Forethought Group 1985: offers life insurance for prearranged funerals. Also manufactures high security locks. Still world's largest casket maker. Daniel A., 73, chairman. W August (Gus), 56, President/CEO. Three other Hillenbrands on the board. Family owns 60% of company.

Hixon

$1.2 billion
Electronics. Pasadena

Joseph Hixon secured family fortune with major investment in AMP stock. Company world leader in manufacturing of electrical connectors vital for computers, telecommunications systems; 57% revenues from global operations in 45 countries outside U.S. Current Hixon generation merged family holding company into AMP 1981. Joseph's son Frederick (d. 1978) moved to San Antonio, invested in ranches, oil; venture capital. Another son, Alexander, 81, AMP director to 1987; Joseph III, 57, director since 1988, chair of Hixon Properties, San Antonio. Some 70 family members believed to own AMP shares.

Hoiles

$1.2 billion
Newspapers. Colorado Springs et al.

"The kind of newspaper a man takes has a lot to do with what kind of man he becomes." Descendants of Raymond C. Hoiles (d. 1970) who started as a printer's assistant for $2 a week, worked his way up to buy the *Bucyrus (Ohio) Telegram* in 1927, then the *Santa Ana Register* in 1935. Used his papers as pulpit to air libertarian philosophy against public schooling, police forces, public highways, etc. Survived 2 bomb attacks. Three children. Son Clarence ran company after Raymond's death; Clarence's death spurred bitter dissent in family ranks. But wounds have healed. "Everyone works together now." Daughter Mary Jane Hoiles Hardie died April. Last of Raymond's children, Harry Howard, lives in Colorado Springs, celebrated 80th birthday; said to be in poor health. Family company owns 6 TV stations, *Orange County Register,* other papers, magazines. Family majority on board giving way to outside managers.

Horvitz

$1 billion
Media, real estate, construction.
Cleveland, Fort Lauderdale

Heirs of self-made media, real estate mogul Samuel A. Horvitz (d. 1956): hawked newspapers at age 8 to support family; started building roads 1916; acquired 5,000 Florida acres in bankruptcy sale, 2 Ohio newspapers. Built both up, left in trust for three sons, who split operations: papers to Harry, construction to Leonard, real estate to William. Sons expanded: added 3 newspapers, cable TV. But battles among brothers raged; fistfights, lawsuits after mother's death 1977. Exasperated probate judge liquidated trust 1987, split 3 ways. Fighting long over, Leonard says. Harry died of cancer 1992, age 71. Leonard now 73, William 70.

Houghton

$500 million
Corning Inc. Corning, N.Y.

Descendants of Corning Glass Works founder Amory Houghton. Entered glass works 1851. Bought Brooklyn Flint Glass Co. 1864; moved upstate to Corning, N.Y. 1868. Produced first glass bulbs for Thomas Edison 1879. Family company later pioneered: Pyrex 1915; silicone late 1930s; fiberglass 1939; TV picture tube 1947; optical fibers late 1960s. Subsidiary Dow Corning Corp., silicone producer, filed for bankruptcy 1995 after breast implant litigation. Corning to spin off its healthcare services division 1996. James (Jamie) Houghton, 60, retired as chair and CEO 1996 ending five generations of family management. Brother Amory (Amo) Jr., 70, left company 1986 to serve in Congress (R.–N.Y.). Family stake held directly or through Market Street Trust Co.

Huber

$525 million
J.M. Huber Corp. Rumson, N.J.

Descendants of Joseph Maria Huber (d. 1932), German immigrant inkmaker who founded J.M. Huber Corp. 1883. Company expanded dramatically under grandson Michael's 42-year reign, 1951-93: oil and gas, industrial chemicals, clay, carbon black, contract electronic manufacturing (AVEX Electronics). Sold three divisions 1995. Still revenues rise: $1.5 billion 1995. Company is maker of ingredients from tires to toothpaste. Global player: plants in Europe, Pacific Rim, India. Peter Francis now chairman.

Hughes

$1 billion
Inheritance. California et al.

Some 250 heirs (including attorneys) of reclusive tycoon Howard Hughes recently agreed to sell Hughes Corp. to Rouse Co. to alleviate cash crunch. Smaller Rouse also acquired 22,000-acre Las Vegas, Los Angeles land holdings. Howard: inherited father's patented oil well drill bit at age 18. Daredevil who set flight records, created Hughes Aircraft, owned TWA, discovered Jane Russell. Turned eccentric and secretive. Died 1976 leaving no will, no immediate family. Most went to Howard Hughes Medical Institute. Cousin William Lummis, attorney who had not seen Hughes in 40 years, took over the rest, estimated at $168 million. Search for heirs amid outrageous claims. Built Summa Corp. to Las Vegas real estate powerhouse: sprawling Summerlin is one of largest planned communities in United States.

Idema

$1.1 billion
Steelcase. Grand Rapids, Mich.

Descendants of Henry Idema (d. 1951). Steelworker Peter Wege (d. 1947) invented fireproof metal office furniture, started firm 1912. Big hit: first metal wastebasket. Idema saw potential, became major investor. Did well 1920s, patented suspension cabinet 1934. Became top office furniture maker in U.S. Henry's son Walter (d. 1979) set up company's financial controls; daughter Mary married Robert Pew, now chairman, 73. Founder's son, Peter Wege, vice chairman. Idema heirs control estimated 70% of company. Earnings up 60% since last year to $124 million.

Jenkins

$1.3 billion
Publix Super Markets. Lakeland, Fla.

Descendants of George Washington Jenkins (d. 1996), who hitched from Georgia in 1925 to seek fortune in Florida real estate. Found janitorial work in Piggly Wiggly grocery instead; became manager 8 weeks later. Snubbed by new owner, opened store next door 1930 named Publix, after movie chain. "Do what you do better than everyone else. We win on execution." Offered a few Florida firsts: shopping music, air-conditioning, automatic doors, self-serve meats. By 1950, 21 stores. Today more than 520 stores in 4 states, over $9.4 billion sales. Now 9th largest U.S. supermarket chain. George's son, Howard, 45, current CEO.

Jordan

$950 million
Retailing, publishing
Washington, D.C., New Hampshire

With $1.25 as capital, Eben D. Jordan (d. 1895) left Danville, Me. 1836 at age 14 to seek fortune in Boston. Farmhand, errand boy; at 29, founded Jordan Marsh department stores 1851 with partner Ben Marsh. Eventually sold to Allied Stores. Greatest investment: funding Charles H. Taylor's *(see family)* effort to revive *Boston Globe*. Recently terminated family trust owned large block of parent Affiliated Publications, acquired by *New York Times* 1993. Also early investors with significant stake in McCaw *(see p. 191)* Cellular. Charlotte Kidder Ramsay, Eben's great-great-granddaughter died Sept. 1995 of an aneurysm two days prior to her mother Dorothy Robinson Kidder's death from cancer; both were well-known Washington philanthropists.

Kleberg

$800 million
King Ranch. Texas

Descendants of Richard King (1824-85), Rio Grande steamboat captain, bought Spanish land grants south Texas 1850s. Over 700,000 acres willed to daughter and husband Robert Kleberg. Big oilfields developed with Exxon have dwindled to a trickle, but King Ranch now 825,000 acres; also 12,000 acres Florida sugarcane. Cattle ranches overseas sold, except 50,000 acres in Brazil. Oil and gas exploration in Texas; acquired 15,000 acres of Florida orange groves from Coca-Cola; sold power generation plant in Guatemala 1994. Bought out heir Belton Kleberg Johnson. Stephen Kleberg runs agricultural operations.

Kohler

$770 million
Toilets, etc. Kohler, Wis.

John M. Kohler bought iron foundry 1873. Enameled a hog scalder/cattle watering trough, put legs on it, sold to local farmer as bathtub for 1 cow, 14 chickens. Expanded to toilets, other bathroom fixtures. Son Walter pioneered color-coordinated fixtures 1920s; governor of Wisconsin 1929-31. Walter Jr. governor 1951-57. John's grandson Herbert Jr., 56, dabbled in theater before joining family company, took over 1972. Marketing whiz, design-oriented: "I felt we could change the whole function of the bathroom and make it stimulating, possibly even social." Bathrooms not yet replacing living rooms as gathering-place, but business has been stimulating, with latest revenues over $1.7 billion. Rare stock in circulation at $120,000 a share.

Landegger

$700 million
Paper and pulp. NYC; Rye Brook, N.Y.

Karl Landegger bought broken-down Austrian paper mill 1920s, turned around. Fled Hitler to U.S. 1938 with $40,000. Bought Parsons & Whittemore, small pulp trader, built into world's largest trader of paper and pulp. Also bought Black-Cawson, maker papermaking equipment. Died 1976. Sons Carl and George now run things. Carl: 66, married, 6 children; archeologist: discovered pre-Columbian cities. George: 58, married, 5 children. Pulp, paper prices down from last year's cyclic highs, but looking forward to big demand from abroad, especially developing countries. George: "A billion and a half people are becoming consumers!"

Lilly

$1.5 billion
Eli Lilly & Co. Indianapolis et al.

Colonel Eli Lilly, Civil War veteran, started making "Lilly Pills" 1876. Son Josiah took over 1898; introduced first commercial insulin 1920s. Leader in barbiturates 1930s; antibiotics 1940s; Salk polio vaccine 1950s. Many legal problems 1970s, 1980s: DES, Darvon, Oraflex. Added medical devices, diagnostics. Introduced antidepressant "wonder drug" Prozac

1988; produced over $2 billion in revenues 1995. New drugs: Zyprexa (schizophrenia), Gemzar (pancreatic cancer), Humalog (diabetes mellitus). Family no longer in management. Charitable: Lilly Endowment, set up 1937, now $5.2 billion trust for educational, religious, and community development.

Louis

$1.3 billion
Johnson Wax. Winnetka, Ill.

Wife, 3 children of John Jeffry Louis, whose mother was a Johnson of Johnson Wax (see first cousin Samuel Johnson). Late Louis worked in dad's advertising agency; then Johnson Wax international marketing 4 years. Venture capitalist; equity in about 27 companies 1960-80; "4 or 5 succeeded." Biggest: Combined Communications—billboards, television and radio stations, newspapers; chairman until Combined merged into Gannett 1981. Big Republican contributor; ambassador to Britain for Reagan 1981-83. Died February at age 69. Thirty percent ownership of S.C. Johnson & Son remains family holding benefiting some 15 descendants.

Lykes

$1.1 billion
Banking, real estate. Tampa; New Orleans

Howell Tyson Lykes (d. 1907) inherited 500 acres Florida land, gave up medicine for ranching 1870s. Made fortune with 7 sons raising and shipping cattle to Cuba. Lost substantial Cuba holdings to Castro. Luckily, Lykes Bros. had diversified in 1940s into insurance, banking, real estate, citrus groves, natural gas, steel. Merged steel, other parts with LTV Corp. 1978; bought steamship line back 1983, got most of money out before LTV crash 1986. Got 8% of Barnett Banks in exchange for 37% First Florida Banks 1992. Holdings distributed among some 250 family members; Thompson Lykes Rankin, 55, heads family business empire.

Martin

$700 million
Inheritance. Tampa, Fla.

Heirs of banking mogul Alpheus Lee Ellis, who died in November 1995 at age 90. Alpheus's first bank job was as a spittoon-cleaner for $8 a week in 1920 Alabama bank where his father worked. Stayed in the business:

moved to Florida, bought control of Sarasota State Bank 1943. Ellis and wife eventually snapped up 81 bank branches in Florida, then merged their Ellis Banking Corp. with NCNB in 1984 for 4 million shares and guarantee of lifelong job. After several mergers and acquisitions, NCNB became today's NationsBank Corp. Ellis worked until the end: "I don't do anything but work. I used to play golf, but I made a hole in one once, so I quit." NationsBank stock faring better than par, up over 40% in last year, believed spread among Ellis' daughter, Carol Martin, and his granddaughters.

McClatchy

$625 million
McClatchy Newspapers. Sacramento, Calif.

Descendants of Irish immigrant James McClatchy, cofounder of *Sacramento Bee* 1857. Granddaughter Eleanor (d. 1980) took over 1936; supported liberal causes. Shunned publicity: "I am content to have people think I live in a cave and wear horns." Nephew Charles (d. 1989) took over 1978. Company went public 1988. Acquired the News & Observer Publishing Co. for $373 million 1995: publisher of the *(Raleigh) News & Observer,* as well as 7 other North Carolina publications. Announced sale of 5 community newspapers in 1996: "We believe we need to focus our newspaper strategy on mid-sized growth markets." McClatchy currently owns 13 dailies, including *Fresno Bee,* in California; 15 nondaily publications. Revenues $540 million in l995. Family still active in company.

McGraw

$850 million
McGraw-Hill Cos. New York City et al.

Pending Times Mirror Higher Education Group acquisition, McGraw-Hill to become world's largest educational publisher. Heirs of James H. McGraw, schoolteacher who sold magazine subscriptions 1800s. Took stake in ailing railroad publication in lieu of back pay 1888; revived it. Acquired other trade publications. Founded McGraw-Hill with partner John Hill 1909: 20 magazines, book business by late 1920s. Today: *Business Week,* 38 trade magazines, 4 TV stations, hundreds of CD-ROM titles, book publishing, on-line database services, etc.; 1995 sales over $2.9 billion. Grandson Harold W. McGraw Jr., 78, CEO 1975-88; blocked American Express takeover bid 1979. Great-grandson Harold III (Terry), 48, now president, COO. Family has 20% interest.

Mead

$860 million
Consolidated Papers. Wisconsin Rapids, Wis.

Illinois furniture salesman George W. Mead (d. 1961) took over father-in-law's dam construction and paper mill business 1902. Built first electrically powered paper machine; reinvested profits. Company expanded, modernized under son Stanton 1950-66 (d. 1988). Grandson George II, 69, (B.S. Yale) president 1966; chairman since 1971. Frugal, conservative; flies coach unless frequent-flier points bump him up to first class. Consolidated still has first account; also Forbes. Now North America's largest producer of coated printing paper. Sales over $1.5 billion last fiscal year. Family stake owned by about 80 scattered heirs.

Meijer

$1 billion
Retailing. Grand Rapids, Mich.

Recurring annual flat sales and brutal discount competition downgrades Meijer family's net worth by $200 million this year. Hendrik Meijer emigrated from Holland 1907. Opened barbershop 1914, added storefront. During Depression started grocery to pay the rent. Food store grew faster than barbershop. Son Frederik shirked college for family business. Pioneered "one-stop shopping" concept with combination grocery, discount stores 1960s. Concept caught on; became Meijer Inc., now over 100 hypermarkets. Attempt to move into "warehouse clubs" failed. Stores run by Fred, 76, and sons: Hendrik, 44; Douglas, 42; Mark, 38. Fred: "I am more poor than you think."

Mellon

$5.8 billion
Finance. Pittsburgh area

Andrew Mellon's grandfather arrived in the U.S. in 1818. His son Judge Thomas Mellon studied law, attended Western U. (now U. of Pittsburgh), began investing in coal, real estate. Successful enough to start own bank (T. Mellon & Sons—predecessor of today's Mellon Bank). Resigned common pleas judgeship 1869: "I was making too great a pecuniary sacrifice." Sons Andrew and Richard B. developed holdings into one of 3 largest pre-World War I American fortunes (Rockefeller and Vanderbilt were other 2). Andrew created financial institutions; early venture capital projects included Gulf Oil, Alcoa. Named U.S. Treasury Secretary, served 1921-32. Exonerated of income tax fraud charges after his death in 1937. Richard King, son of Richard B., managed family business for 3 decades: merged existing banks, centralized control in Pittsburgh. Revitalized Pittsburgh, instrumental in over $160 million going to Carnegie-Mellon U.

Mennen

$1.1 billion
Mennen Co. Morristown, N.J.

Gerhard Mennen arrived in NYC 1871 at age 15. Worked for apothecary; bought Newark drugstore on installment plan for $1,600. Founded Mennen 1878. Known for marketing innovations: first talcum powder in shaker can, shaving cream in tube, stick deodorant. Grew to big toiletries name: Speed Stick, Skin Bracer. Also paper party goods: Paper Art, C.A. Reed. Grandson G. Mennen Williams became governor Michigan (d. 1988). Fierce competition from multibillion-dollar marketing giants convinced family to sell company to Colgate-Palmolive for $670 million 1992. Family got 80% in Colgate stock, cash.

Miner

$600 million
Oracle Corp. San Francisco

Family of late Oracle cofounder Robert Miner (d. 1994). Attended George Washington University Law, also School of Engineering. Honed programming skills at Applied Data Research Corp., National Institutes of Health, IBM's Federal Systems Division. Later designed minicomputer operating system for Phillips. With Lawrence Ellison *(see p. 118)* founded Oracle Corp. 1977. Responsible for product design, development, marketing. Retired after lung cancer diagnosis 1994. Ellison: "He did a magnificent job and got us to where we are today. I just hope I can do as good a job as he did." Widow, Mary, and 3 children, Nicola, Justine and Luke, fiercely guard privacy. Family foundation gives to cancer research.

Murphy

$600 million
Murphy Oil. El Dorado, Ark.

Charles Sr. ("Mr. Charlie") built timber and farming operation, drilled for Louisiana oil 1907. Son Charles Jr., 76, started oil production company at 16 with $5,000 from grandfather. Schooling: private and personal. Authors, professors, Shakespearean actor tutored him; studied Latin,

Greek, French, Spanish. "I don't care about business schools. They don't teach people to think. You get that from the classics." At 21, took over Murphy Oil after father suffered stroke. Built successful oil and gas company, but now needs revitalization. Nephew Claiborne P. Deming, 41, now running company, selling some assets. Charles Jr.'s son, R. Madison Murphy, 38, is chairman. Extended Murphy clan owns 25% Murphy Oil stake.

Nordstrom

$1.3 billion
Retailing. Seattle

John W. Nordstrom emigrated from Sweden to U.S. 1888 with $5; learned English as mine worker, lumberjack; made $13,000 in 1896 Klondike gold rush. Opened Seattle shoe store 1901; retired 1928. His 3 sons built into largest independent U.S. shoe chain by 1963. Family company diversified into specialty retailing, adding women's fashions; menswear 1968. Public 1971. Today 83 upscale department stores in 18 states; $4.1 billion sales. Incredible service: caters to the needs of every customer. Entered direct sales with first catalog 1994. Realigning women's merchandise: making room for cutting-edge designers. Six fourth-generation family members act as copresidents. Unwieldy, but so far seems to work.

Norris

$1.1 billion
Lennox International. Texas area

D.W. Norris, owner of Marshalltown, Iowa Times-Republican, helped father-in-law get job by buying coal-furnace patent from machinist-inventor Davis Lennox for $40,000. Pioneered sheet-metal furnaces; huge success when U.S. moved to central heating. Son John Norris developed oil and gas furnaces 1930s. Later, refrigeration, air conditioners. John Jr. took over 1980. Also own Heatcraft, Armstrong Air Conditioning. Revenues now estimated over $1.5 billion. Ownership shared by more than 175 family members.

O'Connor

$440 million
Inheritance. Victoria, Tex.

Descendants of Thomas O'Connor, Irish immigrant who arrived in Texas early 1830s, built up 500,000-acre ranching empire southern Texas (d. 1887). Two sons expanded holdings. In mid-1930s discovered "Tom O'Connor" oilfield: one of largest, most productive in Texas; Exxon has big interest. Cullen family *(see p. 271)* runs wells for family. O'Connors also owned big stake in Victoria Bankshares (place to stash royalty money), recently sold to Norwest. Steeped in ranching tradition, wealth preservation. "We're just caretakers for the next generation."

O'Neill

$590 million
Real estate. Southern California.

Irish-born Richard O'Neill (b. 1825) came to U.S. with family as a child, headed west for California gold rush, found success as rancher: borrowed to buy half of $457,000 Santa Margarita ranch, worked off debt over 24 years. Grandchildren inherited 52,000 acres 1943. Developed 10,000-acre Mission Viejo with Donald Bren *(see p. 139)*, sold to Philip Morris 1972. Great-grandson Anthony Moiso now developing 5,000-acre Rancho Santa Margarita in Orange County.

Pigott

$775 million
Paccar Inc. Bellevue, Wash.

Descendants of William Pigott Sr., who founded Seattle Car Manufacturing Co. 1905; made railway cars for logging industry. Built tanks WWII. Entered truck manufacturing with 1945 purchase of Kenworth; added Peterbilt. Now a leading U.S. heavy-duty truckmaker with 21% market share; $4.8 billion in revenues. Also sells auto parts, winches, oilfield equipment. Exports to over 30 countries; now looking to expand in China. Family currently believed to own approximately 40%; very private. Grandson Charles, 67, chairman and CEO. Plans to resign December 1996. Son Mark, 42, current vice chairman, will fill both positions.

Pitcairn

$1.3 billion
Glass. Bryn Athyn, Pa.

Devout Scottish immigrant John Pitcairn (d. 1916) founded glassmaking plant on Allegheny River 1883, built into PPG Industries. Family out of active role in company by 1935; retained 14% equity interest. Descendants admit they "inherited neither the great financial wealth of our fathers nor the capabilities and energy required to be creators and builders." Sold PPG stake 1985, formed Pitcairn Trust Co. to manage their money, some wealthy outsiders' too. Firm receives favorable reviews from investors. Family devoted to Swedenborgian faith: designers and main supporters of Bryn Athyn cathedral.

Primm

$530 million
Primadonna Resorts. Las Vegas

Ernest Primm bought 400 acres of land and an old gas station from a "crusty Old West character known as Whiskey Pete" for $15,000 in 1952. Turned into 12-room motel and casino 1977; named after original proprietor. Son Gary took over after father's death 1981; expanded Whiskey Pete's to current 777 rooms. Opened Primadonna Resort & Casino 1990. Latest addition: 1,239-room Buffalo Bill's Hotel & Casino 1994: boasts one of the world's tallest roller coasters running through the casino. "Everybody driving the I-15 is our customer." Joint venture with MGM slated to open December 1996: New York-New York, a resort fashioned after the famous NYC skyline. Gary, CEO/chairman. Five siblings—not in casino business—plus Gary own more than 70% of Primadonna Resorts.

Pulitzer

$1 billion
Pulitzer Publishing Co. St. Louis et al.

Pulitzer purchased 16 daily, 30 nondaily publications from Scripps League Newspapers July 1996 for $214 million. Descendants of Joseph Pulitzer (d. 1911), Hungarian immigrant, settled in St. Louis after Civil War. Bought bankrupt Dispatch 1878 for $2,500; stressed muckraking, yellow journalism. Built national chain. Founded first journalism grad school 1903: Columbia. Later established Pulitzer Prize. Company went public amid family dissension 1986. Grandson Joseph Jr. (d. 1993) led company 38 years; brother Michael, 66, current chairman/chief executive. Pulitzer also operates 2 radio stations, 9 television stations. Became part-owner of St. Louis (baseball) Cardinals 1996.

Reed

$1.4 billion
Timber, paper. Seattle et al.

Descendants of Sol G. Simpson, cofounder Simpson Timber in 1890. "Sleepy lumber company" until 1950s, diversified into papermaking. Known for bargain hunting, buying timber properties at fire-sale prices, replanting. Now over 760,000 acres West Coast timberland, including 200,000 acres second-growth California redwood. Simpson's great-grandson William Reed, 56, heading company since 1971. Bought out last few nonfamily shareholders 1987 after legal battle. Environmental pressure to limit timber harvests on public lands adds value to Reed holdings. Ownership split among fewer than 50 relatives.

Richardson

$800 million
Inheritance. Greensboro, N.C.; Connecticut

Descendants of teacher-turned-pharmacist Lunsford Richardson, who bought drugstore 1890s. In 1905, with $8,000 savings, founded Vicks Family Remedies (picked name from ad for Vick's Seeds). Main product: Vicks VapoRub. Aromatic ointment caught on during flu epidemic 1918-19. Family added other over-the-counter products. Richardson-Merrell sold to Dow Chemical 1981 for $80 million stock. Richardson-Vicks later merged into P&G for another $400 million. Holdings in Lexington Global Asset Managers, Chartwell RE Corp., Vanguard Cellular. Over 200 heirs share fortune.

Robinson

$450 million
Real estate. Kauai, Hawaii

Scottish ancestors arrived Niihau, Hawaiian island, 1863. Bought it from King Kamehameha V for $10,000 in gold. Later added 50,000-plus acres on Kauai's undeveloped west side. Passionate preservationists: some 3 dozen family members oppose development. Family farms sugarcane; also cattle. Preserves last pure Hawaiian community (pop. 200) on Niihau. Patriarch Warren Robinson: "I'm still a cowboy." But cash flow, inheritance taxes a problem. Developing ecotourism venture on family island, rain forest: wild boar, ram safaris, resort-cottage complex, but developing slowly. Robinson waterfall, helicopter used in *Jurassic Park.*

Rockefeller (John D.)

$6.5 billion
Standard Oil. New York City et al.

Descendants of John D. Rockefeller, America's first billionaire and founder of Standard Oil. Thrifty accounting clerk who set up merchant grain business 1858; with $4,000 capital, made first investment in oil refining. Seven years later: Standard Oil. Furor led by muckrakers forced breakup 1911. Only son, John Jr., married Abby Aldrich, daughter of Senator Nelson Aldrich. Father and son donated over $1 billion to charity. John D. Jr. had 6 children: daughter Abby, 5 sons (the Brothers): J.D.III, Nelson, Winthrop (all deceased), Laurance and David *(see both)*. Nelson: ("Rocky," d. 1979), 4-term liberal GOP N.Y. governor, Vice President under Ford. John D. IV: son of John D. III, (d. 1978), Democratic W.Va. senator (also governor 1977-84). David Jr.: apparent leader of his generation (a.k.a. the Cousins). Standard Oil was the source of another fortune for the family. John Sr.'s brother, William (d. 1922), left his heirs a substantial inheritance, believed to be now worth at least $500 million, perhaps considerably more.

Rollins

$780 million
Inheritance. Atlanta; Wilmington, Del.

Heirs and brother of O. Wayne Rollins: farm boy who worked 72-hour week for $10 in textile mill during Depression. Younger brother John came into business, a onetime used car dealer who became Delaware's lieutenant governor mid-1960s. Brothers built separate interests. John W.: owns Brandywine, Dover Downs raceways in Delaware; other real estate, stock. O. Wayne: pest control (Orkin Exterminating), media (Rollins Communications), oil and gas, security systems, real estate, etc. O. Wayne died 1991. Sons: R. Randall, 64, chairman and CEO Rollins, Inc.; Gary W., 52, president Rollins, Inc. Plan to take raceway Dover Downs public this fall; cash proceeds to pay debt, expand gambling and track seating.

Sammons

$550 million
Cable TV, insurance. Dallas

Orphan Charles A. Sammons born Oklahoma 1898, raised by aunt. Started as grain and hay merchant; founded Postal Indemnity Co. in Waco, then Reserve Life Insurance in Dallas. Moved into cable TV after WWII: "Cable is like *Alice in Wonderland*. You have to run just to keep up." Died 1988 after arranging estate: 60% to foundations, 10% in ESOP, 30% for family. Descendants still own Midland National Life. Sold cable 1995: 60% to Marcus Cable for $1 billion, 40% to TCI-led consortium for $800 million. Fortune split among only child, Maryanne Sammons Cree, and 11 or so of her descendants.

Schwan

$1.5 billion
Frozen pizza, food delivery. Marshall, Minn.

Marvin Schwan (d. 1993) put self through college, joined milk bottling business started by father, a German immigrant who arrived Minnesota 1921. Took business on road to beat local price cap. Isolated families in rural Minnesota eager to buy more than milk from Schwan trucks: frozen foods, groceries, etc. Ran with convenience-stores-on-wheels concept, expanded routes to include suburbs, some urban areas. Built Schwan Sales Enterprises to 2,500 trucks in 48 states. Delivered frozen pizzas to school cafeterias, hospitals, etc. Now has as much as 90% institutional pizza market. Sales estimated over $2 billion. Marvin's heirs said to be up in arms over disposition of estate.

Scripps (E.W.)

$2.6 billion
Publishing. Cincinnati

Descendants of E.W. Scripps (d. 1926), who founded Cleveland Press age 24, 1878; founded UPI. Built nation's once-largest newspaper chain, Scripps Howard. Long history of family feuds: bitter estrangement from half-brother James *(see J.E. Scripps family)*. Other children broke away at E.W.'s death. Son James G. started Scripps League Chain 1931; today considered "low-key operation." Original Scripps company IPO 1988; now 15 dailies in 11 states. Diversified: Scripps Howard Broadcasting (TV, radio, cable) merged into parent 1994; also cable TV programmer Cinetel Productions. Selling cable systems to Comcast Corp. for $1.6 billion Comcast stock. Wealth in family trust that terminates after death of the last of E.W.'s 4 grandchildren.

Scripps (J.E.)

$1 billion
Newspapers. Detroit et al.

English immigrant James Edmund Scripps arrived in Illinois 1844. Half-brother of E.W. Scripps *(see above)*. Started *Detroit News* 1873, kept stories short, simple for minimally educated factory workers; kept paper cheap. Circulation rocketed to 5 times nearest competitor's. Formula worked in Cleveland, Cincinnati, other cities. Bitter split with E.W.; J.E. merged with other papers, built Evening News Association. Great-grandson Peter Bruce Clark sold to Gannett for $717 million 1986. George Booth, Scripps executive who married into family, started Booth Newspapers, sold to Newhouse for $300 million 1976. Fortune spread among more than 200 relatives.

Searle

$1.2 billion
Inheritance, drugs. Chicago

Gideon Daniel Searle bought small Indiana drugstore 1888. Got into drug-making business as G.D. Searle. Grandson John president 1936: introduced motion sickness remedy Dramamine; also first oral contraceptive.

John's son Daniel CEO 1966-77: made bad acquisitions, probe by FDA blackened Searle's image. Former defense secretary Donald Rumsfeld turned company around. Sold out to Monsanto 1985. Fortune now diversified, monitored by G.D.'s great-grandchildren William and Suzanne.

Smith (Byron)

$2.8 billion
Illinois Tool Works. Chicago et al.

Scions of Solomon A. Smith, early president Merchants' Savings, Loan & Trust Co. Son Byron founded Northern Trust 1889; family still has large holdings. Financed 2 Swedish toolmakers to form Illinois Tool Works 1912; later took control. Expanded into fasteners, screws, washers. Great-grandson Harold (d. 1990) diversified into packaging systems, engineering components, medical and computer supplies. Over past 5 years, expanded aggressively, averaging 20 acquisitions per year. Currently 360 operations in 34 countries. Family holds 25%. Harold Smith Jr., 62, (Princeton, Northwestern M.B.A.) now heads Illinois Tool Works executive committee. Also chairman of Illinois GOP; led state's 1994 election sweep.

Smith (Charles E.)

$600 million
Real estate. Washington, D.C.

Russian immigrant Charles E. Smith, now 95, started building business in Brooklyn, lost shirt in Depression. To Washington, D.C.; lost big in first venture there, considered career change: bartender; wife talked him out of it. Back into building apartments, luck finally improved. Son Robert joined 1950. Pair amassed land, including railroad yard in Arlington, Va.; yard now Crystal City, vast commercial property holding; also Skyline City, more office space in Virginia. Total land up to 16 million square feet. Navy relocation could be big problem for Crystal City. Charles' son Robert, 68, and son-in-law Robert Kogod run company. Took public Charles E. Smith REIT in 1994, more than 11,000 apartments.

Smith

$1 billion
Broadcasting. Baltimore

This low-profile media fortune got its start in 1965 when engineer Julian Smith quit his job at Martin Marietta and mortgaged everything he owned to buy a broadcasting license. Julian's second son, David, was bitten by the entrepreneurial bug, too: he dropped out of electronics school in 1979 to start Comark, a television transmitter company, with $20,000 seed money. Sold Comark in 1986 for $5 million. "My father was too much of a visionary to care about profits," David says. "What I wanted was purely to make money." Joined the ailing Julian in 1981, engineered buyout of outside investors in 1986. With debts under control, Dave began acquisition march with WPGH in Pittsburgh in 1991 for $55 million cash, now worth over $300 million. Sinclair Broadcast Group now owns 28 television stations, 34 radio stations in 15 states. Now moving into broadcast modems: plans to deliver Internet content over the air.

Stryker

$580 million
Stryker Corp. Kalamazoo, Mich.

Grandchildren of Homer Stryker, orthopedic surgeon, invented mobile hospital bed. Received Army contract during WWII; turned to civilian market afterward with professional managers' help. Son Lee (d. 1976) ran company. Invented new products like cast cutter that spares patient's skin. Chairman John Brown (non-family member) took over 1977; public 1979. Develops surgical instruments, bone implants, replacement joints, hospital beds. Acquired Dimso, French producer of spinal implants 1992. Bought majority stake in Japanese distributor Matsumoto Medical Instrument. Family stake in trust controlled by Lee's children, Ronda, Patricia, Jon.

Stuart

$825 million
Carnation Co. Seattle

Grandfather Elbridge Amos Stuart founded Carnation Co. 1899 in Kent, Wash. Paid $25,000 for German evaporated milk process, supplied prospectors en route to Yukon. Overtook leader Pet with unsweetened canned milk (Pet's was heavily sugared). Famous tag line: "From contented cows." Built major food company. Much later: Coffee-mate, Instant Breakfast, Friskies, etc. Sold to Nestlé 1985 for $3 billion. Grandson Dwight: 72. Divorced 4 times; 5 children. President 1973-83; had idea to sell family's one-third share. Brother Elbridge: 79. Married to noted paleontologist Marion Butler Stuart; 3 children. Carnation vice president to 1961; lives on Idaho ranch.

Sulzberger

$600 million
Publishing. New York City

Tennessee newsman Adolph Ochs (d. 1935) bought *New York Times* 1896 for $75,000; alternative to era's "yellow journalism." Built one of world's most respected newspapers. In 1950s, 1960s: labor costly, readers fled to suburbs. Grandson Arthur Ochs (Punch) Sulzberger revamped 1970s: new design, special sections recaptured elite readers. Also diversified: 21 newspapers, 10 magazines, 6 TV, 2 radio stations. Acquired *Boston Globe* for $1.1 billion 1993. This year marks 100 years of control of the *Times* by the Sulzberger and Ochs families. Punch, 70, publisher 29 years, now chair, CEO; his son Arthur Jr., 45, now publisher, most likely candidate to take reins when father resigns. "Gray Lady" on-line June 1994. Family also owns *Chattanooga Times.*

Swig

$575 million
Real estate. San Francisco

Descendants of Ben Swig, who worked real estate deals in Boston while partner Jack Weiler operated in NYC. Ben moved to San Francisco 1946. Together, families built, bought hotels, residential and commercial properties. Swig, Weiler & Arnow currently more than 5 million square feet, largely New York City office space. Ben died 1980; his family bought Weilers ("non-growth-oriented") from hotel operations 1982. Ben's son Richard, 71, chairman; other son, Mel, died 1993. Brother-in-law Richard Dinner, 75, recently retired. Democrats, philanthropists. Ben's philosophy: "Give it away while you're alive, because there are no pockets in shrouds."

Taylor

$700 million
Publishing. Boston

General Charles H. Taylor (d. 1921) revived fading *Boston Globe* 1872 with funding from Eben Jordan *(see family)*; families established co-ownership of *Globe.* Expanded readership to working class; aligned with Democratic Party early 1900s. *Globe's* management since dominated by 4 successive generations of Taylors. William O., 64, great-grandson of general, ran company under Affiliated Publications; acquired by *New York Times* for $1.1 billion 1993; now *Globe* publisher. Early investor in McCaw Cellular, acquired by AT&T 1994.

Temple

$825 million
Timber, containers. Diboll, Tex.

Descendants of Thomas Louis Latane Temple Sr., cofounder Southern Pine Lumber Co. 1894 with 7,000 acres East Texas timber. At his death

(1934): 200,000 debt-ridden acres. Grandson Arthur Jr. took over 1951; by 1973 half-million acre forest earning $9.6 million a year. Merged with publisher Time Inc. 1973. Arthur Jr. Time chairman 1978-83. Temple-Inland, corrugated container producer, spun off 1984. Arthur, 76, retired. Son Arthur (Buddy) III, 54, die-hard Democrat, once had political aspirations; now heads family investment company. Temple Foundation holds $300 million assets; grants $15 million each year.

Upjohn

$3.2 billion
Upjohn Co. Kalamazoo, Mich. et al.

Descendants of William Erastus Upjohn, inventor of first dissolvable pill. Founded Upjohn Pill & Granule Co. with brothers 1885; bought them out. Company went public 1958. Developed Phenolax, premier flavored laxative (mint), 1908; Rogaine, baldness treatment, 1988; injectable contraceptive Depro-Provera 1993. Patent expirations: Halcion (sleeping pill); Xanax (antianxiety); Ansaide (anti-inflammatory); Micronase (diabetes). Swedish drugmaker Pharmacia AB and Upjohn merged through a tax-free stock swap November 1995; new entity, Pharmacia & Upjohn, Inc., one of world's 10 largest pharmaceutical companies. Family spread out, but many in Kalamazoo area.

Ward

$575 million
Russell Stover Candies. Kansas City, Mo.

Louis Larrick Ward (died in February): Stanford, Navy WWII, bought small paper box company 1950. One customer: Russell Stover. Bought control for $7.5 million, took public 1960. "There are only so many ways you can put chocolate, butter, cream, eggs, milk, fruit and nuts together. The real competition is in the packaging." Brought automatic packaging, economies of scale to boxed chocolate; spread fixed costs over huge volume. Took private 1981. Now dominant in market. Acquired Whitman's Candies 1993. After Louis' stroke 1993, sons Scott and Tom took over company, expanded.

Watson

$575 million
Real estate. Southern California area

Progenitor Juan José Dominguez, Spanish soldier, was awarded 76,000-acre land grant 1784 by King Carlos III of Spain for service in what is now

Los Angeles and Mexico. Juan bequeathed Rancho San Pedro to nephew Cristóbal, whose granddaughter Marie Dolores married Scottish gunslinger James Watson 1855: "a deadlier shot never fingered a revolver." Their great-granddaughter Susana married William Huston, now chairman Watson Land Co., owned by some 90 family members. Massive southern California real estate holdings: offices, warehouses, business parks; also oil interests.

Weyerhaeuser

$1.3 billion
Timber, paper. St. Paul, Tacoma et al.

German immigrant Frederick Weyerhaeuser (d. 1914) worked in Illinois sawmill, bought it out of bankruptcy 1857 with brother-in-law. Cut massive swath through forests of north central U.S. to Pacific. Bought 900,000 acres timberland at $6 per acre from railroad pioneer James Hill 1900. Merged several companies to form Weyerhaeuser Co., with separate directorates eliminated by Frederick's grandson John Philip Jr. 1947. Pioneered tree-farming techniques 1940s, won praise of environmentalists: "The best of the s.o.b.s." Pacific Northwest business juggernaut. Frederick's great-grandson George, 70, retired as CEO 1991. Fortune spread among more than 260 heirs.

Whittier

$800 million
Oil. Southern California.

Descendants of Mericos H. (Max) Whittier, cofounder Belridge Oil 1911. Bought option on Bakersfield property when oil discovered seeping from ground. President of Belridge until death 1925. Son Leland president 1965-79; secretive: driver's license didn't have home address (San Marino, Calif.). Two families sold out to Texaco, Mobil 1930s; Whittier, Buck, Green families sold to Shell for $3.6 billion 1979; at time biggest takeover ever. Whittier family netted $475 million. Assets include small oil company M.H. Whittier. Philanthropists; low-profile.

Wirtz

$650 million
Real estate, sports. Chicago

Arthur Wirtz, Chicago cop's son, began buying real estate 1922; owned or managed 80 lakefront properties within 5 years, then cleaned up in wake of Depression, snapping up cheap real estate with grain speculator James

Norris. Next on agenda: sports. Brought figure skater Sonja Henie to U.S. 1936; bought several sports arenas, including Madison Square Garden; sold some after 1957 antitrust suit; died 1983. Son William, 67, runs family liquor distributorships, real estate, banking. Family still cutting imposing figure in sports: owns hockey's Blackhawks, piece of NBA champion Bulls; 50% of Bulls' new stomping ground, United Center.

Died or Left Behind

This year 53 people fell off The Forbes Four Hundred, few because their fortunes fell.

DIED

Coulter, Joseph R.

Medical equipment. Miami area
Died last November age 71. Older brother Wallace *(see p. 239)* still on list.

Ellis, Alpheus Lee

Banking. Tarpon Springs, Fla.
Died last October age 89. Fortune split between heirs *(see Martin family)*.

Flint, Lucile du Pont

Inheritance (Du Pont Co.). Greenville, Del.
Died in April age 80 *(see Bredin, et al.)*.

Goldman, Rhoda Haas

Inheritance (Levi Strauss). San Francisco
Died in February age 71 of heart attack *(see Richard Goldman)*.

Hardie, Mary Jane Hoiles

Publishing. Marysville, Calif.
Died this spring age 74 *(see Hoiles family)*.

Packard, David

Hewlett-Packard. Los Altos Hills, Calif.
Died in March age 83 after complications from pneumonia. Most of estate left to foundation *(see William Redington Hewlett)*.

Reinhart, Dewayne B.

Wholesale foods. La Crosse, Wis.
Died in April age 75. Fortune left to 4 children, 10 grandchildren.

Rinker, Marshall Edison Sr.

Concrete. Palm Beach, Fla.
"Doc" died in April age 90, leaving estimated $370 million fortune.

Sakioka, Katsumasa

Real estate. Costa Mesa, Calif.
Roy died October 1995 age 97. Real estate fortune left to 6 children.

Terra, Daniel James

Lawter International. Northbrook, Ill.
Died in June age 85.

LEFT BEHIND

Ackerman, Peter

Junk bonds. Washington, D.C. 49
The former Drexel executive and Michael Milken protégé falls short.

Ashton, Alan C.

WordPerfect. Orem, Utah. 54
Sold his company for Novell stock, which lately has been languishing.

Bass, Anne Hendricks

Divorce. NYC, Fort Worth. 55
Ex-wife of Sid Bass, pillar of society didn't keep pace.

Behring, Kenneth Eugene

Real estate. Blackhawk, Calif. 68
Recent efforts in Seattle, including football's Seahawks, subpar.

Bloch, Henry Wollman

H&R Block. Shawnee Mission, Kans. 74
Tax specialist's stock down, struggling to unload CompuServe unit.

Boyd, William Samuel

Casinos. Las Vegas. 64
Boyd Gaming Corp. stock down.

Brennan, Bernard F.

Montgomery Ward. Chicago. 58
Though sales hit $7 billion, retailer's earnings dropped precipitously.

Brown, Jack Eugene

Oil. Midland, Tex. 71
With partner Cyril Wagner Jr. short of this year's minimum.

Carver, Lucille

Bandag, Inc. Muscatine, Iowa. 79
Her shares of Bandag down since last year *(see Carver family)*.

Cook, Jane Bancroft

Inheritance (Dow Jones). Mass.; Fla. 84
Gave up control over family's Dow Jones shares *(see Bancroft family)*.

Cook, Scott D.

Intuit. Menlo Park, Calif. 43
Intuit stock down from last year.

Cumming, Ian

Banking, insurance. Salt Lake City. 55
His Leucadia stock didn't keep pace.

du Pont, Willis Harrington

Inheritance (Du Pont Co.). Palm Beach. 60
Son of Lammot du Pont. Fortune estimated at $390 million.

Eisner, Michael D.

Walt Disney Co. Los Angeles. 54
Eisner should have exercised some of those Disney options.

Fritz, Lynn C.

Shipping agent. San Francisco. 53
Shares in his Fritz Companies stock down sharply since last year.

Harbert, Raymond

Inheritance. Birmingham, Ala. 37
Wealth now correctly attributed to mother Marguerite Harbert.

Hill, Margaret Hunt

Inheritance, oil. Dallas. 80
Failed attempts to boost oil reserves, new details reveal dwindling trust.

Hoiles, Harry Howard

Publishing. Colorado Springs. 80
Still worth over $400 million (see Hoiles family).

Jacobs, Jeremy Maurice

Sports concessions. East Aurora, N.Y. 56
Business flat, but net worth still estimated at over $400 million.

Jacobs, Richard E.

Shopping centers. Lakewood, Ohio; NYC. 71
His playoff-bound baseball Indians boost net worth over $400 million.

Keck, Howard Brighton

Inheritance (oil). Los Angeles. 83
The Superior Oil scion falls off the list this year, but is still worth $415 million.

Lauder, Estée

Cosmetics. New York City. Ageless.
Shares in Estée Lauder Co. now held by sons Leonard, Ronald (see both).

Marshall, James Howard III

Inheritance (oil). Pasadena, Calif. 60
Wealth now attributed to younger brother E. Pierce.

McEvoy, Nan Tucker

Publishing. San Francisco. 77
Still worth over $370 million (see de Young family).

McGlothlin, James

Coal. Bristol, Tenn. 55
Coal business hurting but, with family, still worth over $400 million.

Milstein, Monroe Gary

Burlington Coat Factory. Burlington, N.J. 69
Stock is down, but family's holdings still worth over $300 million.

Pearson, Edith du Pont

Inheritance. Montchanin, Del. 84
Daughter of Lammot du Pont. Still worth over $390 million.

Posner, Victor

Financier. Miami Beach. 78
Bankruptcies, convictions, penalties, family squabbling. No surprises here.

Roberts, Ralph J.

Comcast Corp. Coatesville, Pa. 76
His Comcast shares down sharply.

Saul, Bernard Francis II

Banking, real estate. Chevy Chase, Md. 64
Short of this year's minimum.

Scharbauer, Clarence Jr.

Inheritance (oil, land). Midland, Tex. 71
Still collects plenty of oil royalties, but not enough to stay on list.

Simmons, Richard Paul

Allegheny Ludlum. Sewickley, Pa. 65
His shares of the big steelmaker down since last year.

Smith, Athalie Irvine

Inheritance, lawsuits. Va.; Calif. 63
Heiress of Orange County's Irvine Ranch failed to keep pace.

Smith, Frederick Wallace

Federal Express. Memphis. 52
Still king of overnight delivery, but FedEx up only slightly.

Solheim, Karsten

Ping golf clubs. Phoenix. 85
Failure to pursue red-hot titanium woods leaves him short of the green.

Solomon, Russell

Tower Records. Sacramento, Calif. 71
Best music chain in nation, but margins being squeezed.

Solow, Sheldon Henry

Real estate. New York City. 68.
New life for Manhattan real estate, but not enough to stay on list.

Spanos, Alexander Gus

Construction. Stockton, Calif. 74
His team lost the Super Bowl last year. Other assets didn't keep pace.

Speer, Roy Merrill

Home Shopping Network. Bahamas. 64
Stocks were flat. Maybe Barry Diller can breathe new life into Silver King.

Steinberg, Saul Phillip

Financier. NYC. 57
His Reliance shares down since last year; art collection overvalued.

Tate, Jack P.

Baby SuperStore. Greenville, S.C. 52
His Baby SuperStore stock now worth less than $200 million.

Tyson, Barbara

Tyson Foods. Fayetteville, Ark. 47
New information over control of trust removes her from list.

Wagner, Cyril Jr.

Oil. Midland, Tex. 62
Oil assets not enough this year.

NEAR
MISSES

These people didn't make The Forbes Four Hundred this year, but they were very close. But close counts only in horseshoes and hand grenades.

Howard Brighton Keck

$415 million
Inheritance. Los Angeles. 83.
Married, 4 children

Keck ended 30-year tenure as president of Keck Foundation this year; succeeded by nephew Robert Day *(see p. 220)*. Also ends 14-year run as member of The Forbes Four Hundred. Son of William Sr., renowned wildcatter who taste-tested core samples; founded Superior Oil 1921. Among first to drill offshore Venezuela, Louisiana. Became leading independent; huge reserves. Sons Howard and William Jr. feuded over control. William Sr. (d. 1964) tried to sell 1959, failed; chose Howard over namesake, who died 1982. Diversified unprofitably into mining, timber, farming; back to oil 1976. Avoids limelight. Directors forced him off board in 1983 proxy battle. Mobil bought Superior for $5.7 billion 1984. Keck Foundation has given away $500 million so far, including financing for two 10-meter Keck telescopes atop Hawaiian volcano. Keck staying on as chairman, president emeritus.

Frederick W. Smith

$415 million
Federal Express. Memphis, Tenn. 52.
Divorced, remarried; 10 children

Faced with stiff competition, Federal Express struggling to guard its position in the U.S. freight market. Global expansion: launched AsiaOne, an intra-regional express delivery service 1995. Son of Greyhound bus system builder. Outlined FedEx concept in Yale senior thesis: received gentleman's C. Started company with $4 million from family and $80 million venture capital 1973. No overnight success: lost $27 million first two years. Also lost $300 million on Zapmail, satellite document delivery service 1986, over $100 million on intra-European delivery 1992. Despite heavy losses, remains world leader in package delivery market. Today, 2.4 million packages delivered daily to 210 countries. FedEx is now a verb.

Laszlo Nandor Tauber

$410 million
Real estate. Potomac, Md. 81.
Divorced, remarried; 2 children

On the up-and-up with new financing and a reinvigorated real estate market. Born Budapest; champion gymnast, medical school. Escaped Nazi labor camp on second try: "I just walked away one day." To U.S. 1947, set up medical practice. Dreamed of building hospital, surgeon's income not enough; built apartment project instead. Switched to offices, primarily for government; became Uncle Sam's biggest landlord. Plan to float public REIT collapsed, but holdings thought to be worth $500 million before debt.

Michael D. Eisner

$405 million
Walt Disney Co. Los Angeles. 54.
Married, 3 children

Mickey Mouse empire now cleaning up NYC's porn-riddled 42nd Street. Eisner son of successful entrepreneur, grew up NYC. Denison U. grad, NBC page. Coordinator CBS children's programming, headed ABC West Coast programming under Barry Diller. Followed Diller to Paramount Pictures 1976. Selected to head troubled Disney by Bass Group and Roy Disney 1984. Jump-started animation unit, turned Magic Kingdom into entertainment powerhouse. "We have a good brand and we know how to manage it." Staged $19 billion acquisition of Capital Cities/ABC 1995 after major heart surgery previous year. Lost longtime Disney studio chief Jeffrey Katzenberg (see p. 305) who's now suing for $250 million. Film unit to halve annual output to 20 films; entered decade-long cross-promotional agreement with McDonald's. Much of Eisner's worth tied up in Disney stock options.

Jeffrey Katzenberg

$400 million
Hollywood. Los Angeles. 45.
Married, 2 children

Hollywood pals Steven Spielberg and David Geffen *(see both)* brought in the former Disney studio chief as 22% partner in startup studio DreamWorks SKG. Investments by Paul Allen and the Ziff brothers *(see all)* suggest a market cap of $2.7 billion, but so far little to show for all its hype, so we haircut implied value. Katzenberg's pending termination lawsuit against Disney seeks $250 million; victory there would elevate Katzenberg to The Forbes Four Hundred. As Disney film chief, greenlighted many of the studio's recent animated hits: *The Lion King, The Little Mermaid, Aladdin, Who Framed Roger Rabbit?* Onetime friend, now bitter rival of Disney head Michael Eisner.

Russell Solomon

$400 million
Tower Records. Sacramento, Calif. 71.
Separated, 2 sons

Big expansion abroad, domestic music market getting squeezed by discounters, but still the best chain in the business. "A hippie who learned to run a business," opened first record shop in father's drugstore 1941, age 16; went broke. Thrown out of high school; quit junior college for Army. Tried record store again 1960; had better luck. Opened the biggest record store in the U.S. 1968 in San Francisco. Concept: huge store, huge selection; let managers select merchandise to please local tastes. Now over 170 stores around the world, 33 in Japan alone. U.S. sales over $1 billion, but margins under pressure. Solution: expand overseas where the discounters aren't. New stores in Israel, Buenos Aires, Philippines, Korea. Also Tower Video and Tower Books. Son Michael, 48, Tower general manager; son David, 34, handles company finances.

Anne Hendricks Bass

$400 million
Divorce. Fort Worth; NYC. 55.
Single, 2 daughters

Split with Sid Bass *(see p. 135)* after 23 years marriage 1989. Reported $200 million settlement: Disney stock; $5 million Fifth Avenue apartment; Degas, Rothkos, Monets. "Sharing beauty with family and friends is, in part, a responsibility. I hope that doesn't sound too Midwest." Father Indianapolis surgeon, mother golf champ. Vassar 1963. Contributing editor *Vogue*. Supports NYC ballet, has studied ballet since childhood. Fort Worth, NYC social whirls. "She can do whatever she wants now. She really enjoys the freedom—and it shows." Mom and daughters have $280 million nest eggs each. If there were a First Wives Club, she'd be a great member.

George Yohn and family

$400 million
Airwalk. Altoona, Pa. 69.
Married, 3 children

40-year veteran of the shoe business struck gold repositioning small but growing sneaker company as the anti-Nike: "I thought there was a sea change coming—an opportunity for something different." Made sneakers out of wacky materials: neon-colored suede, snakeskin, fuzzy yellow tennis balls. Airwalk now the current rage among teenagers. Claims above industry average net profit margins, expects 1996 sales to reach $300 million.

Jay Stein

$400 million
Stein Mart Inc. Jacksonville, Fla. 51.
Married, 2 daughters

Grandfather Sam founded discount clothing store in Greenville, Miss. 1908. Jay spent every Saturday in store from age 12: "I ran the cash register. I did everything." Joined company after NYU 1966. Opened first branch store in Memphis 1977; others followed. Sells "upscale fashions at discount prices." Two public offerings since 1992. With wife owns 14 million shares. "[Joining The Forbes Four Hundred is the] one and only downside to IPO." Should be happier now: shares up since last year, but not enough to keep him on list.

John Jay Moores

$400 million
Software. Sugarland, Tex. 52.
Married, 2 children

Married high school sweetheart at 19; together attended University of Houston. Held programming and marketing jobs at IBM. Got law degree University of Houston, again with wife, but "I learned I didn't want to be a lawyer." Started BMC software firm 1980 to write faster program for IBM mainframe. Lured elite programmers with above-average royalties. Went public 1988; retired 1992. "My ego didn't require that I be CEO of a public company." Bought San Diego (baseball) Padres 1994. Collects Corvettes, Ferraris, Mercedes, Rolls-Royces. Has given nearly $75 million to University of Houston. Still actively invests: has stakes in over one dozen software companies.

ACKNOWLEDGMENTS

Tom Adams, Adams Media Research, Carmel, Calif.
Nick Allen, data storage analyst, The Gartner Group, Stamford, Conn.
Sharon Armbrust, Paul Kagan Associates, Carmel, Calif.
Jan Barenholtz, Barenholtz & Farrell, real estate consultants, New York, N.Y.
Connie Batchelder, senior analyst, In-Stat, Scottsdale, Ariz.
Beer Marketers Insights, Nanuet, N.Y.
Donald Bergenty, Musicland, New York, N.Y.
Beverage World, Great Neck, N.Y.
CDA/Investnet, Fort Lauderdale, Fla.
Ed Christman, retail editor, *Billboard Magazine*, New York, N.Y.
Wendy Close, software analyst, The Gartner Group, Stamford, Conn.
Editor & Publisher Yearbook, The Editor & Publisher Co., New York, N.Y.
Marc S. Ganis, Sportscorp Ltd., Chicago, Ill.
Joan Geoghegan, Geoghegan Associates, Boston, Mass.
Richard Gilbert, investment banker, Bulkley Capital, Chicago, Ill.
Jack Harvey, Blackburn & Co., Inc., Alexandria, Va.
John R. Hass, Brown Brothers Harriman & Co., Philadelphia, Pa.
Judy Hodges, software analyst, IDC, Framingham, Mass.
Ron Johnson, chief operating officer, Ashworth Card Clothing, Greenville, S.C.
Tom Lahive, data storage analyst, IDC, Framingham, Mass.
Perrin H. Long Jr., independent securities consultant, New Canaan, Conn.
Keith McCarthy, Sony Music Entertainment, New York, N.Y.
Stephen McClellan, securities analyst, Merrill Lynch, San Francisco, Calif.
Roger B. McNamee, general partner, Integral Capital Partners, Menlo Park, Calif.
Vincent Mierlak, vice president, Schroder Wertheim, New York, N.Y.
Marjorie L. Pendergast, Roach Wheeler Realtors, Rosemont, Pa.
Steven Pendergast, Smith Barney, New York, N.Y.
John Powell, general partner, Integral Capital Partners, Menlo Park, Calif.
Randy Prouty, president, Bristol Realty Corp., West Palm Beach, Fla.
Peter Redebaugh, private investments, Bloomfield Hills, Mich.
Gerald E. Reilly, newspaper broker and consultant, Greenwich, Conn.

Bruce M. Richardson, vice president–research strategy, Advanced Manufacturing Research, Boston, Mass.

Scott H. Roberts, partner, The Genesis Group, San Francisco, Calif.

Grace Salafia, PolyGram Distribution Group, New York, N.Y.

Donald Schnabel, vice chairman, Julian J. Studley, Inc. New York, N.Y.

M.R. Schweitzer, president, Schweitzer Galleries, New York, N.Y.

SoundScan, Hartsdale, N.Y.

SportsValue Newsletter, New York, N.Y.

Gary Stevens, Gary Stevens & Co., New Canaan, Conn.

Television & Cable Factbook, Warren Publishing, Inc., Washington, D.C.

A. Gordon Tunstall, Tunstall Consulting, Inc., Tampa, Fla.

James M. Todd, NBC, New York, N.Y.

Norb Vander Zanden, executive vice president, Associated Investment Services, Green Bay, Wis.

Jaime Weiss, president, Weiss Realty, Lyndhurst, N.J.

The Highest-Paid Entertainers: The Top 40

Show biz celebrities are making far more money than they used to make. Why?

ROBERT LA FRANCO

Data compiled September, 1996

Forbes has been tracking incomes of the world's top-paid stars since 1987, and it's been an impressive bull market: The price of celebrity has never been higher. Is it because the stars are handsomer, sing louder, act more impressively or crack funnier jokes? Of course not. It's the technology, stupid. When the VCR came along, it almost doubled the potential revenue from a movie. With satellite dishes now in the most remote Asian villages, the potential audience swells enormously. The outlets for popular entertainment include CDs, multichannel cable systems, digital videodisks, enhanced CDs that offer viewers video clips and interviews with stars—and, now, Web sites.

The demand for content to fill the proliferating distribution channels grows almost exponentially.

"There aren't many names available to fill a lot of competing slots," says James Wiatt, president and co-chief executive at Beverly Hills-based ICM.

A decade ago the top salary for a Hollywood actor was about $5 million. Today it's more like $20 million. A hot new rock band at the center of a bidding war can fetch $600,000 for delivery of a record—four times what it would have gotten in 1987. Top television writers have seen their pay jump more than 250% since the late Eighties.

One day, perhaps, the supply of popular entertainment may overwhelm demand, but it hasn't happened yet. "It's a trend that has not ended," adds Richard Lovett, president of CAA, Hollywood's leading talent agency. "There is such a hunger for movie stars."

Bruce Willis' $20 million salary for 1995's *Die Hard with a Vengeance* was quadruple what he was paid to do the original in 1988. He got that much more in good part because the worldwide box office gross grew as well, from $137 million for the first *Die Hard* film to $310 million for the third. You guessed it: *Die Hard IV* is in discussion.

New to our list this year: heavy metal band Metallica, whose current 88-city international tour will assure that everything the band has ever released remains on at least one of Billboard's charts.

Demi Moore slides off in part because her movie *Striptease* didn't match its hype. Off-peak merchandising sales knocked off Barney, the purple dinosaur. Pink Floyd, Elton John, Billy Joel, Aerosmith, Boyz II Men and Bon Jovi are gone—presumably to rest up from the grueling tours and albums that put them on last year.

1. *Oprah Winfrey*
'95: $74 million '96: $97 million Total: $171 million

The reigning queen of talk television, Oprah just keeps on going, despite a temporary dip in ratings two years ago. Her uplifting chatter grossed $212 million this year, up from $196 million last year. A fitness book, co-written with trainer Bob Greene, adds to the take.

2. *Steven Spielberg*
'95: $120 million '96: $30 million Total: $150 million

He hasn't been behind the camera since *Schindler's List,* but his Amblin Entertainment has a producer credit on the blockbuster *Twister,* as well as on the popular love story *The Bridges of Madison County.* Now he's preparing for the sequel to *Jurassic Park.* Here we go again.

3. *The Beatles*
'95: $100 million '96: $30 million Total: $130 million

They don't really exist anymore—except as a profit machine. Last year they pocketed $20 million for the U.S. airing of their self-produced, six-hour documentary. This year they will release a ten-hour version on home video for $150. Add sales of their three-volume *Anthology* CD set.

4. *Michael Jackson*
'95: $45 million '96: $45 million Total: $90 million

Losing fans in the U.S., the gloved one still has friends overseas. Saudi Arabian Prince Al-Waleed is sponsoring Jackson's latest international tour. The Sultan of Brunei paid him seven figures to play at his birthday. But Hyundai has bailed out as a sponsor due to public pressure.

5. *Rolling Stones*
'95: $71 million '96: $6 million Total: $77 million

Rock's most efficient corporation rolls on, thanks to the profits the band hauled in from its $300 million *Voodoo Lounge* tour. The Stones sell more than 2 million CDs a year in the U.S. Last year they pocketed $4 million for use of their *Start Me Up* to roll out Windows 95.

6. *Eagles*
'95: $43 million '96: $32 million Total: $75 million

"The Eagles aren't just a band, they're an industry," says manager Irving Azoff. Bitterly split apart 16 years ago, the Eagles reunited in 1994 as part of the wave of retread rock groups that are raking in profits with warmed-over acts .

7. *Arnold Schwarzenegger*
'95: $22 million '96: $52 million Total: $74 million

In *Eraser*, Arnold takes down a jet plane with a handgun while dangling from a parachute. His role in the Christmas comedy *Jingle All the Way* isn't nearly as exciting, but it's just as profitable, bringing him a rock-solid $20 million—plus a cut of the gross.

8. *David Copperfield*
'95: $52 million '96: $22 million Total: $74 million

The grand illusionist lands another top ten spot this year with his greatest trick: making money disappear from fans' pockets. He cashed in big in 1995 with a groundbreaking tour of Germany that cost up to $150 a seat. His U.S. tour this year sold tickets at one-third the price.

9. *Jim Carrey*
'95: $29 million '96: $34 million Total: $63 million

After his dark role as *The Cable Guy* took a big hit from critics, some in Tinseltown are already talking about the end. Don't count on it. Carrey gets $20 million for the upcoming *Liar, Liar* and will add to that a slightly smaller payday for his next film, *The Truman Show*.

10. *Michael Crichton*
'95: $22 million   '96: $37 million Total: $59 million

The first writer to make it to the top ten, Crichton has the blockbuster film *Twister*, the hit TV series *ER* and the upcoming novel *Air Frame* all to his credit. Next year look for a lucrative piece of the *Jurassic Park* sequel *The Lost World* to boost him even higher.

11. *Jerry Seinfeld*
'95: $31 million '96: $28 million Total: $59 million

The huge success of *Seinfeld,* a struggling show six years ago, has helped create a slew of programs centered on stand-up comics. NBC reportedly pays him $1 million for every episode, each of which brings the network triple that in prime time.

12. *Stephen King*
'95: $22 million '96: $34 million Total: $56 million

No writer's block here: This year King published a six-part series of paperbacks. Two more books came out in fall, 1996—one under his own name, one under his nom de plume, Richard Bachman. "He doesn't want to confuse consumers," says agent Arthur Greene. Who's confused?

13. *Garth Brooks*
'95: $22 million '96: $29 million Total: $51 million

Purists argue he's no Merle Haggard, but you can't argue with success. Brooks' commercial approach sells not only concert tickets but also CDs—42 million of them since 1991, according to SoundScan. Country music may be losing some appeal, but Brooks clearly isn't.

14. *Andrew Lloyd Webber*
'95: $24 million '96: $26 million Total: $50 million

No sign of slowdown here. *Phantom of the Opera* was ten years old in 1996; *Evita* is coming out as a movie starring Madonna; there is a new version of *Jesus Christ Superstar* in England; and *Sunset Boulevard* is finding new homes in Germany, Canada and Australia.

15. *Tom Hanks*
'95: $36 million '96: $14 million Total: $50 million

Life for Forrest Gump has been less lucrative this year. Hanks pulled down a slim $1 million for writing, directing and acting in *That Thing You Do*, down from some $35 million *Forbes* figures he'll get for *Apollo 13*. But he's opting for a big chunk of the box office for his next film, *Saving Private Ryan*.

16. *Siegfried & Roy*
'95: $23 million '96: $25 million Total: $48 million

The Teutonic tricksters carouse onstage with white tigers and white lions, and their fans eat it up. Their illusion show in Las Vegas grossed $60 million last year. An animated TV show may soon be syndicated. Their fee just for showing up to open a German theme park: $2 million.

17. *Tom Cruise*
'95: $19 million '96: $27 million Total: $46 million

The summer blockbuster *Mission: Impossible* will earn Viacom's Paramount Pictures up to $100 million, while Cruise could take home up to $60 million from his lucrative participation deal. Look for Sumner Redstone to flog the studio chiefs to produce a sequel.

18. *Harrison Ford*
'95: $19 million '96: $25 million Total: $44 million

One of the few who can command a $20 million acting salary. His *Sabrina* remake was disappointing, but his next action film, *The Devil's Own*, is a better bet. As is the following project, an action movie in which he plays the U.S. President. He could easily return to the top ten next year.

19. *Clint Eastwood*
'95: $18 million '96: $26 million Total: $44 million

He cried as an aging Secret Service agent in *In the Line of Fire* and played an even more sensitive role in *The Bridges of Madison County*. The fans loved it. But his next film, *Absolute Power*, is more of the old Clint: a story about murder and the excess of ego.

20. *R.E.M.*
'95: $24 million '96: $20 million Total: $44 million

The band signed a new deal this year that has brought it a healthy upfront bonus and a guaranteed home for its next five albums. R.E.M.'s North American tour last year was beset with troubles but still grossed $39 million, and its last album sold 6 million copies.

21. *Sylvester Stallone*
'95: $34 million '96: $10 million Total: $44 million

Sagging a bit from last year, Stallone hasn't started cashing in on the deal he signed with MCA's Universal Pictures that pays him $20 million for each of his three upcoming MCA pictures. *Assassins*, a box office disappointment, grossed $30 million in the U.S. His next role: the art film *Copland.*

22. *John Grisham*
'95: $13 million '96: $30 million Total: $43 million

Grisham recently became the highest-paid author in Hollywood, snagging $8 million for the film rights to his novel *Runaway Jury.* Yes, you guessed it, another one of Hollywood's glossy, overly dramatic legal thrillers. Hey, why mess with a good thing?

23. *Robin Williams*
'95: $15 million '96: $27 million Total: $42 million

After the success of *Mrs. Doubtfire, Jumanji* and *The Birdcage,* Williams has secured his place as one of the most bankable Hollywood stars. Nothing funny about that—and a long way from his days as Mork from Ork and the manic stand-up comedy routines he once did for a living.

24. *Robert Zemeckis*
'95: $32 million '96: $10 million Total: $42 million

Back to the Future was good, but *Forrest Gump* was a real bonanza. Zemeckis is now solidly among the ranks of moviedom's top directors and among its highest paid. His next directing effort: *Contact,* for Warner Bros., starring Matthew McConaughey and Jodie Foster.

25. *Roseanne*
'95: $19 million '96: $21 million   Total: $40 million

ABC's *Roseanne* may be slipping in ratings, but it still ranks among the top draws in television. Discovered in a nightclub doing stand-up comedy almost 11 years ago, the rude comic will collect a large cut of the program's initial syndication sales.

26. *Michael Douglas*
'95: $20 million '96: $20 million   Total: $40 million

Never mind that nobody much cared about *The American President.* Douglas is still one of the biggest box office draws and one of the best producers. His next film, *The Ghost and the Darkness,* may help him reclaim the box office power he had with 1994's *Disclosure.*

27. *Bruce Willis*
'95: $16 million '96: $20 million   Total: $36 million

Solid roles in *Pulp Fiction* and *12 Monkeys* aside, Willis makes his fortune from gunslinging, with *Forbes* estimating almost $20 million coming from participation profits on *Die Hard with a Vengeance* and nearly all the rest coming from his role as a gangster in *Last Man Standing.*

28. *Luciano Pavarotti*
'95: $11 million '96: $25 million   Total: $36 million

Without a doubt the world's most marketable voice, Pavarotti boosts his normally hefty intake with a run as one of the "Three Tenors". Add some $10 million for that to his record sales and solo gigs, and it amounts to a lot of pasta.

29. *KISS*
'95: $8 million '96: $27 million   Total: $35 million

After a 17-year hiatus, bandleader Gene Simmons and partner Paul Stanley reunited their aging former colleagues and dragged their blood-spitting, fire-breathing rock 'n' roll circus back on tour. As KISS and other groups are proving, old is new as never before.

30. *Charles Schulz*
'95: $18 million   '96: $15 million   Total: $33 million

"Peanuts" royalty payments dipped a bit for Schulz this year. But "Peanuts" remains one of the most comforting security blankets in the Scripps Howard licensing roster. Schulz got a chunk of that company's $33 million in royalty payments last year.

31. *Bill Cosby*
'95: $15 million   '96: $18 million   Total: $33 million

The original *Cosby Show* is still a big seller, having taken in more than $1 billion in syndication revenue. Now Cosby's earning a hefty salary per episode for his new television show, *Cosby*, from CBS, which has guaranteed 44 episodes.

32. *John Travolta*
'95: $11 million   '96: $22 million   Total: $33 million

Saturday Night Fever made him a movie star in 1977, but his role as a slimy thug in *Pulp Fiction* gave him a huge boost in salary power. He was offered $17 million for a movie called *The Double*, but settled for $11 million to do *Michael* instead.

33. *Mariah Carey*
'95: $8 million   '96: $24 million   Total: $32 million

She may be the boss' wife at Sony Music Entertainment, but to fans Mrs. Thomas D. Mottola is simply one of the hottest singers on the planet. Carey is the second-highest-selling artist in the U.S., behind Garth Brooks, according to SoundScan, with 26 million CDs sold since 1991.

34. *Tom Clancy*
'95: $15 million   '96: $16 million   Total: $31 million

In his 1994 novel *Debt of Honor,* an angry Japanese pilot wipes out the government with a 747 flown into the Capitol Building. Then in this year's follow-up novel, *Executive Orders,* dapper hero Jack Ryan takes over the presidency.

35. *Kevin Costner*
'95: $9 million   '96: $22 million   Total: $31 million

Waterworld wasn't quite the disaster for him or Universal Pictures everyone said it was. But Costner gave up a chunk of his usual deal to get the near $175 million (cost) film made. That held him back this year. Positive reviews for *Tin Cup,* and the $15 million he was paid to do it, will help him recoup.

36. *Denzel Washington*
'95: $10 million   '96: $20 million   Total: $30 million

With rap groups and the movie press raving about his handsome face, Washington hit success with Twentieth Century Fox's *Courage Under Fire.* He also snagged a fat $12 million payday for *Fallen,* a thriller due out in 1997. A man on a roll with an agent who knows when to push.

37. *David Letterman*
'95: $14 million '96: $14 million   Total: $28 million

Jay Leno is giving the New Yorker a good fight for the top rank in late-night TV, but Dave's fat contract from CBS keeps him in better suits. His production company, Worldwide Pants, is also working hard, with a new program, *Everybody Loves Raymond*, a situation comedy hitting CBS in fall, 1996.

38. *Metallica*
'95: $14 million   '96: $14 million   Total: $28 million

Seeing this band live is like sticking your head in a cannon just before it fires. Machine gun melodies and gothic ballads are a winner with the kids. Everything the band has ever released has been glued to one Billboard chart or another since hitting the market.

39. *Mel Gibson*
'95: $11 million   '96: $17 million   Total: $28 million

The audience loves to see him as the good-hearted hero doing battle with one-dimensional bad guys, playing a variation of the *Braveheart* theme. He's taking home nearly a $20 million paycheck for *Ransom,* and he doesn't have to wear that silly blue paint on his face.

40. *Sandra Bullock*

'95: $10 million   '96: $15 million   Total: $25 million

A surprise entry this year, Bullock, for the sequel to *Speed*, matched Top 40 dropoff Demi Moore's $12.5 million *Striptease* salary. Sorry, Demi, but momentum is momentum after all. Bullock's roles in *A Time to Kill* and *In Love and War* are accounted for here as well.

The Highest-Paid Athletes: The Super 40

No strikes, big fights, burgeoning TV rights—all add up to a half-billion-dollar haul for the world's Super 40 highest-paid athletes.

RANDALL LANE AND PETER SPIEGEL

The year 1996 was one for the sports-money record books. German auto racer Michael Schumacher was paid $25 million to drive for Ferrari's Formula One team—the highest salary in sports history. It was a short-lived honor. Another Michael, basketball's Michael Jordan, re-upped with the Chicago Bulls for $30 million over the 1996-97 season. Then yet another Mike—Tyson—eclipsed them both, pocketing purses totaling $75 million for three fights. In doing so Tyson made more money in one year than any other athlete in history.

Those three Michaels go a long way toward explaining how the total take of the Forbes Super 40 highest-paid athletes surged 13% last year, from $490 million to $556 million. Average per athlete: $14 million. And it wasn't just the top guys bringing up the average. Players at every rank got more. Even 40th-ranked Formula One driver Gerhard Berger took in $7.5 million, 21% more than last year's last-place Super 40 athlete.

To gauge the authenticity of any number of sports "trends," it's usually telling to follow the money. Example: Many sports promoters are forecasting a golden era in professional women's sports. There are two new women's basketball leagues, two gymnastics tours—and figure skating continues to gain in popularity—but that hasn't yet translated into the really big money. For the first time in the seven years Forbes has been following the dollars in the sports world, there are no women on our list. Top-ranked women's earners Monica Seles and Steffi Graf aren't starving—at $7 million apiece—but they didn't make the Super 40 this year.

Since Forbes began tracking the earnings of the world's top athletes in 1990, 3 have pulled in over $100 million, with a handful more than likely to do so in the next year or two. Notice the importance of endorsement income for nice-guy athletes Michael Jordan and Shaquille O'Neal. Note: Ayrton Senna died at the 1994 San Marino Grand Prix.

For all the hype coming out of the Atlanta Olympics, no Olympic stars made the list. Even gymnast Kerri Strug and sprinter Michael Johnson, the Olympics' two media darlings, will be lucky to make more than $2 million this year. Quadrennial fame does not wow the sponsors as much as the weekly, or even nightly, attention paid to a Shaquille O'Neal or a Steve Young.

Our list also confirms some trends we've noted before. The national pastime is struggling: As recently as 1992 there were ten baseball players on our list—versus four this year. Another struggling sport, tennis, has seen the number of players on our list drop from nine to three during the same time frame.

By contrast, football—fueled by a $1-billion-a-year television contract—is ascending. There are seven footballers among the Super 40 this year, up from two in 1992. Basketball has fared even better recently, both on TV and with the fans, and its Super 40 representation has zoomed from four to nine. Next year, when many of the recent NBA megacontracts kick in, there very well could be a dozen hoopsters on the list.

In compiling our numbers, Forbes counts only sports earnings and endorsements. We don't count outside business interests. But as athletes develop as business people, those lines are getting more and more blurred. Stock car legend Dale Earnhardt sold his $44 million (sales) licensing company last month for $30 million in cash and stock. Jack Nicklaus took several of his business interests public this year; still the majority shareholder in Golden Bear Golf, he owns stock worth $20 million.

Andre Agassi took stock options as part of his deal with Nike; that stock roughly quadrupled in the ensuing year, giving him a multimillion-dollar paper windfall.

Meanwhile, golfing phenom Tiger Woods is expected to join fellow Super 40 members Agassi, O'Neal, Wayne Gretzky and Ken Griffey Jr. in ownership of the Official All Star Cafe restaurant chain, which, as a sister company to Planet Hollywood, will likely make these athletes even richer. Top athletes—encouraged by their agents—are becoming richer still by sharing the rewards derived from their celebrity. Michael Jordan scored coveted "gross points" for his Warner Bros. film *Space Jam*. That means he'll get a share of the revenues from box office and video sales, TV rights, even merchandise.

It's slippery on this slope; the Super 40 has 12 new members this year—a 30% annual turnover. These newcomers include Woods, basketball bad boy Dennis Rodman, football teammates Emmitt Smith and Troy Aikman, and up-and-coming boxers Roy Jones Jr. and Oscar De La Hoya. Drop-offs from the rankings include Deion Sanders, Drew Bledsoe, Boris Becker, Pernell Whitaker, Greg Maddux and Mark Messier. Some have a decent shot at returning next year. Others are down for the count. Such is sport.

RULES OF THE GAME

All figures are Forbes estimates for the 1996 calendar year. The Salary/Winnings figure includes direct salary, prize money and signing and incentive bonuses. The Endorsements figure includes traditional endorsement income, licensing royalties, exhibition and appearance fees and money from celebrity-related activities such as autograph signings and speeches. Money made from private businesses or equity partnerships is not counted.

1. Mike Tyson, 30

Boxing
1995 rank: 2

Salary/Winnings:	$75,000,000
Endorsements:	$ 0
Total:	$75,000,000

One for the record books: With just three fights—wins over Frank Bruno and Bruce Seldon, followed by last month's shocking loss to Evander Holyfield—Tyson made more money in one year than any other athlete in sports history. A Holyfield rematch should bring Tyson $30 million more. But while the public's curiosity scores on pay-per-view, it doesn't get the convicted rapist any endorsements.

2. Michael Jordan, 33

Chicago Bulls
1995 rank: 1

Salary/Winnings:	$12,600,000
Endorsements:	$40,000,000
Total:	$52,600,000

His one-year, $30 million contract—the largest one-year salary in sports history—will factor in more during 1997. But potentially just as lucrative, Jordan got coveted "gross points" for starring (with Bugs Bunny) in the movie *Space Jam*—he'll get a cut off the top of revenues from box office, merchandise, videos, etc. The take could rival his basketball salary. Nice Guy Mike's blue-chip sponsors include Nike, of course, as well as Sara Lee, McDonald's, Wilson and Gatorade. Three newer endorsement deals:

Rayovac, WorldCom and Bijan (Michael Jordan cologne). Between salary, movie and endorsements, Jordan's gross could push $100 million in 1997.

3. Michael Schumacher, 27

Auto racing
1995 rank: 9

Salary/Winnings:	$25,000,000
Endorsements:	$ 8,000,000
Total:	$33,000,000

A new contract from Ferrari kicked in this year, paying this top Formula One driver $25 million. Starting in 1998, Schumacher will make $30 million annually. The German's popularity across Europe has led to a Schumacher collection of apparel and automobile accessories. Longtime endorsement deal from Germany's Dekra (pollution control) is his favorite. Nike pays him over $3 million to push the pedal to the metal with their shoes.

4. Shaquille O'Neal, 24

Los Angeles Lakers
1995 rank: 5

Salary/Winnings:	$ 7,400,000
Endorsements:	$17,000,000
Total:	$24,400,000

The Los Angeles Lakers wooed him with a seven-year, $120 million contract, and with proximity to Tinseltown. Movies and music now dominate Shaq's off-season. He earned about $3 million for starring in *Steel* this summer. A joint venture with Interscope Records yielded his third rap record (which includes a duet with Notorius B.I.G.). His label, Twism (The World Is Mine), also debuted other rappers. Twism Industries produces hip-hop apparel. Huge endorsement deals at Reebok and PepsiCo alone may bring him $10 million.

5. Emmitt Smith, 27

Dallas Cowboys
1995 rank: Not ranked

Salary/Winnings:	$13,000,000
Endorsements:	$ 3,500,000
Total:	$16,500,000

The Dallas Cowboys' star running back—and last year's NFL most valuable player—became the latest of owner Jerry Jones' bonus babies when he inked a contract with a $10.5 million signing bonus in August. But he's been hobbled by injuries this year, and so unlikely to regain NFL rushing crown. Big endorsement deals from Reebok, Starter, Quarterback Club.

6. Evander Holyfield, 34

Boxing
1995 rank: 14

Salary/Winnings:	$15,000,000
Endorsements:	$ 500,000
Total:	$15,500,000

As with George Foreman two years ago, one fight can make all the difference. Underdog Holyfield was guaranteed $11 million to fight Tyson (*see above*) in November and got some $2 million extra on brisk pay-per-view sales. Beating Tyson gives him leverage—at least $30 million for a rematch. Endorsements for the Atlanta native, once scarce, now abound.

7. Andre Agassi, 26

Tennis
1995 rank: 7

Salary/Winnings:	$ 2,200,000
Endorsements:	$13,000,000
Total:	$15,200,000

The second-best-paid endorser in the Nike stable, behind Michael Jordan. The Super 40 doesn't count equity stakes, which is too bad for Andre, since he was smart enough to insist on Nike stock options as well as salary for the deal he cut last year. Nike has quadrupled, and Andre has pocketed a paper profit of several million on the options. He plans to marry actress Brooke Shields, or will it be a merger?

8. Arnold Palmer, 67

Golf
1995 rank: 11

Salary/Winnings:	$ 100,000
Endorsements:	$15,000,000
Total:	$15,100,000

Has few endorsement deals for less than $1 million a year. Lots of takers: Cadillac, Rolex, Pennzoil, GTE, Rayovac, Office Depot. New deal from Cooper Tire. Like Jack Nicklaus, Arnie now looks to do more licensing, which requires less time and offers greater long-term potential. Lexington Furniture to make "Palmer Home Collection." Some 200 mahogany pieces, including "Palmer Carved Pineapple Tester Bed."

9. Dennis Rodman, 33

Chicago Bulls
1995 rank: Not ranked

Salary/Winnings:	$ 3,900,000
Endorsements:	$ 9,000,000
Total:	$12,900,000

Between his tattoos, cross-dressing and an affair with Madonna, Rodman knows how to manipulate the press. He made over $2 million from his tell-all book, *Bad As I Wanna Be,* and pocketed more than $2 million in advances for his next two tomes. Also $2 million to star opposite Jean Claude Van Damme in an upcoming movie; MTV show; etc. Yet compared with teammate Michael Jordan, these are small figures. Rodman gets about $2 million in endorsements. He casts the wrong image for most consumer brand companies—but not for Victoria's Secret and Oakley sunglasses.

10. Patrick Ewing, 34

New York Knicks
1995 rank: 19

Salary/Winnings:	$11,900,000
Endorsements:	$ 1,000,000
Total:	$12,900,000

Ewing has earned the second part of his $18.7 million paycheck for the 1995-96 season. But this season he makes a piddling $3 million. In 1997 he will be a free agent and seek well over $10 million a year. New endorsements by Discover Card and Warner Bros. helped with income.

11. Cal Ripken Jr., 36

Baltimore Orioles
1995 rank: 16

Salary/Winnings:	$ 6,000,000
Endorsements:	$ 6,000,000
Total:	$12,000,000

As good as gold, as solid as a rock. Baseball's iron man—he broke Lou Gehrig's cherished consecutive-game record last year—evokes an image of baseball as most fans think the game should be. Some endorsements, but Ripken makes most of his off-the-field loot by marketing his likeness to his fans, through licensed lithographs, minted coins and the like.

12. Roy Jones Jr., 26

Boxing
1995 rank: Not ranked

Salary/Winnings:	$12,000,000
Endorsements:	$0
Total:	$12,000,000

With about $70 million committed to boxing a year, through its Home Box Office and TVKO pay-per-view arms, Time Warner is the biggest bank in boxing. The suits at Time Warner have identified supermiddleweight Roy Jones Jr. as a comer. He fought on HBO four times last year, winning the fight—and about $3 million—each time.

13. Dan Marino, 35

Miami Dolphins
1995 rank: 40

Salary/Winnings:	$ 9,200,000
Endorsements:	$ 2,500,000
Total:	$11,700,000

With a new contract (including a hefty $5.8 million signing bonus) and a new coach (former Dallas Cowboys chief Jimmy Johnson), Marino hoped his 14th NFL season would bring him his first Super Bowl ring. But early in the season he broke his ankle, and his Miami Dolphins swooned. Endorsements from Nike, Logo Athletic, Sprint, McDonald's, many more.

14. Wayne Gretzky, 35

New York Rangers
1995 rank: 10

Salary/Winnings:	$ 6,000,000
Endorsements:	$ 5,500,000
Total:	$11,500,000

To fit under the National Hockey League's team salary cap, "The Great One" had to take a pay cut to join the New York Rangers (and former teammate Mark Messier). No problem: Cablevision and ITT, the team's owners, made it up to him with a $1-million-a-year contract for "off-ice projects." Many endorsements, but this year might mark his most impressive score: He's the first person to have his face on labels of Campbell's Soup cans—50 million of them.

15. Riddick Bowe, 29

Boxing
1995 rank: 4

Salary/Winnings:	$11,500,000
Endorsements:	$0
Total:	$11,500,000

Bowe got $5 million to fight Poland's Andrew Golota in June at Madison Square Garden. A postfight melee shamed even the boxing world. Bad news for Bowe's manager, Rock Newman, who was suspended for a year from fights in New York State, and several Bowe hangers-on, who faced criminal charges. Nevertheless, this month's rematch should get Bowe $6.5 million.

16. Pete Sampras, 25

Tennis
1995 rank: 15

Salary/Winnings:	$ 3,300,000
Endorsements:	$ 8,000,000
Total:	$11,300,000

He's a robot on the court, but advertisers like this soft-spoken winner. Fat endorsement contracts from Nike, Wilson, Movado watches, videogames, business aircraft, MBNA credit card, RCA. He scores huge appearance fees at major tournaments and pulls in $150,000 for one-day exhibitions. Hurt a bit by Andre Agassi's mediocre play this year—the Andre-Pete rivalry rang the cash register for both of them in 1995.

17. Oscar De La Hoya, 23

Boxing
1995 rank: Not ranked

Salary/Winnings:	$10,800,000
Endorsements:	$ 500,000
Total:	$11,300,000

The Golden Boy has the potential to be the most marketable nonheavy-weight since Sugar Ray Leonard. Assets: movie star looks, an "aw shucks" demeanor and amazing boxing skills. Already good endorsements for a boxer: Mennen, John Henry clothing, Anheuser-Busch. Fought twice this year, including a June victory over Mexico's legendary Julio Cesar Chavez, which earned him $8.75 million. Expect an even more lucrative rematch next summer.

18. Grant Hill, 24

Detroit Pistons
1995 rank: 24

Salary/Winnings:	$ 4,300,000
Endorsements:	$ 6,500,000
Total:	$10,800,000

Hill has almost single-handedly revitalized Fila's sneaker line. His shoes are outsold only by Nike's Air (Michael) Jordans. Other endorsements: Sprite, GMC trucks, Kellogg's, McDonald's, etc.

19. Ken Griffey Jr., 27

Seattle Mariners
1995 rank: 23

Salary/Winnings:	$ 8,000,000
Endorsements:	$ 2,800,000
Total:	$10,800,000

For the third year in a row, "Junior" had to sit out part of the season—this time due to a broken bone in his hand—but the slugger still hit 49 homers, making him one of the youngest players in baseball history to reach 200 home runs in a career. He is also one of the few endorsement superstars in baseball, with sizable deals from Nike, Nintendo, Upper Deck and Wheaties.

20. Dale Earnhardt, 45

Auto racing
1995 rank: 20

Salary/Winnings:	$ 2,500,000
Endorsements:	$ 8,000,000
Total:	$10,500,000

"The Intimidator" hasn't won the Winston Cup championship—the World Series of the Nascar circuit—since 1994, but the seven-time champ remains stock car racing's most popular driver. This year he sold the company responsible for his souvenir licensing for $30 million, but will retain royalties for at least the next 15 years. Worst year on track, however: 27 races without a win (longest in his career), and he broke his sternum and collarbone in a spectacular crash in July.

21. David Robinson, 31

San Antonio Spurs
1995 rank: 18

Salary/Winnings:	$7,400,000
Endorsements:	$2,000,000
Total:	$9,400,000

This is the last year of the Admiral's automatically escalating contract—which guarantees to make him one of the two highest-paid players in the league. He begins a more traditional four-year extension next year. Total damage: about $50 million. New endorsements: Doritos, AT&T and Old Spice, to go with Nike, Casio and Franklin sporting equipment.

22. Hakeem Olajuwon, 33

Houston Rockets
1995 rank: 27

Salary/Winnings:	$6,800,000
Endorsements:	$2,500,000
Total:	$9,300,000

The soft-spoken, Nigerian-born Olajuwon has long been the NBA's "international ambassador." The NBA now uses him as its chief promoter of consumer products; that deal pays him $250,000. Clothing line and a line of low-priced sneakers with Spalding, plus other endorsements.

23. Clyde Drexler, 35

Houston Rockets
1995 rank: Not ranked

Salary/Winnings:	$8,900,000
Endorsements:	$ 300,000
Total:	$9,200,000

Clyde the Glide makes the Super 40 for the first—and likely the last—time, courtesy of a $9.7 million one-time salary earned during the 1995-96 season. (Until modified this year, NBA's salary cap rules allowed players to get large one-year salaries to compensate for below-market salaries in previous years.) But playing with fellow Super 40 entrants Hakeem Olajuwon and Charles Barkley should keep him in the spotlight for the entire basketball season.

24. Michael Chang, 24

Tennis
1995 rank: 28

Salary/Winnings:	$2,500,000
Endorsements:	$6,500,000
Total:	$9,000,000

The most popular athlete in Asia, he's now the number two player in the world. His modest, good guy routine plays well globally. Gets $300,000 from some Asian tournaments just to show up. But his biggest money comes from Reebok and Prince: The Michael Chang frame is the top-seller in the world. Inked two new deals—Discover Card in U.S., and Tiger Balm, a Singapore-based Ben-Gay competitor.

25. Julio Cesar Chavez, 34

Boxing
1995 rank: Not ranked

Salary/Winnings:	$9,000,000
Endorsements:	$0
Total:	$9,000,000

Chavez made $7 million losing to Oscar De La Hoya. But the Mexican, considered at one time to be the best pound-for-pound fighter in the world, has more trouble outside the ring. An arrest warrant for Chavez was issued in his hometown of Culiacán. The charge: failure to pay $1.3 million in taxes. Chavez has dedicated most of the earnings from his October fight against Joey Gamache to the Mexican government.

26. Tiger Woods, 20

Golf
1995 rank: Not ranked

Salary/Winnings:	$ 800,000
Endorsements:	$8,000,000
Total:	$8,800,000

Woods debuts at number 26; expect him to crack the top 10 next year and stay there for a long, long time. Since turning pro four months ago, Woods has singlehandedly rekindled interest in golf, winning two tournaments and kudos galore for poise and manner. Nike (shoes and apparel) and Titleist both gave him five-year deals that should yield Woods $60 million. (Signing bonuses from those contracts propel him onto the list this year.) He also got $2.2 million from Warner Books. Expected to join other Super 40s at Official All Star Cafe. Could do a dozen other deals, but, says agent Hughes Norton: "He's got so much time—why rush it?"

27. John Elway, 36

Denver Broncos
1995 rank: Not ranked

Salary/Winnings:	$6,800,000
Endorsements:	$2,000,000
Total:	$8,800,000

Elway is the oldest football player on the Super 40, but he and the Denver Broncos are having one of their best seasons ever. Elway gets a boost from a new contract (with a sizable signing bonus) and income from the Quarterback Club, a group of star players—including fellow Forbes All-Stars Marino, Smith, Aikman and O'Donnell—that rake in extra cash by licensing jersey replicas, posters and jackets.

28. Neil O'Donnell, 30

New York Jets
1995 rank: Not ranked

Salary/Winnings:	$8,500,000
Endorsements:	$ 300,000
Total:	$8,800,000

After leading the Pittsburgh Steelers to the Super Bowl last season, O'Donnell jumped ship for New York, where Jets owner Leon Hess inked him to a contract with a $7 million signing bonus. Then Hess hired two top offensive linemen to protect his new star. Oops. The hapless Jets lost their first eight games.

29. Steve Young, 35

San Francisco 49ers
1995 rank: 35

Salary/Winnings:	$4,500,000
Endorsements:	$4,000,000
Total:	$8,500,000

Young has become the endorser for all seasons, pitching everything from shoes (Nike) and sports drinks (Pepsi's All Sport) to computers (Sun Microsystems), shampoo (Pert Plus) and even magazines (*Forbes*). So what's Young's secret? An all-American image that attracts companies in droves.

30. Frank Thomas, 28

Chicago White Sox
1995 rank: 25

Salary/Winnings:	$7,200,000
Endorsements:	$1,200,000
Total:	$8,400,000

"The Big Hurt" got hurt for the first time in his career in July, but when he played, the linebacker-size first baseman had arguably his best season yet, hitting 40 home runs for the third time in four seasons. But he has yet to develop an endorsement-friendly image.

31. Mario Lemieux, 31

Pittsburgh Penguins
1995 rank: Not ranked

Salary/Winnings:	$7,500,000
Endorsements:	$ 800,000
Total:	$8,300,000

A wasted asset. Lemieux should be a hero: he overcame cancer and chronic back pain to win the NHL's most valuable player award last season and take his Pittsburgh Penguins to within one game of the Stanley Cup finals. Yet by his own choosing he does little to promote himself, and his off-ice income suffers accordingly.

32. Barry Bonds, 32

San Francisco Giants
1995 rank: 29

Salary/Winnings:	$8,000,000
Endorsements:	$ 300,000
Total:	$8,300,000

On the field, Bonds was baseball's highest-paid player in 1996; off the field, his surly reputation cost him endorsement deals. Bonds publicly said he wanted to be traded after the San Francisco Giants demoted his father, Bobby, the team's batting coach. No deal emerged. But Bonds earns his large paycheck. In 1996 he became only the second man in baseball history to hit 40 home runs and steal 40 bases in one season.

33. Jack Nicklaus, 56

Golf
1995 rank: 8

Salary/Winnings:	$ 400,000
Endorsements:	$7,800,000
Total:	$8,200,000

A bad year for Jack's annual income; a great year for his net worth. Nicklaus folded his golf schools, golf course construction company, driving ranges and a 30-year master licensing arrangement into Golden Bear Golf Inc. and took it public in August. He owns 58%, worth about $20 million. Since the Forbes Super 40 list doesn't count equity stakes, Jack falls quite a bit on the income scale, but he retains his stellar endorsement portfolio and receives an $800,000 salary from the public company.

34. Damon Hill, 36

Auto racing
1995 rank: Not ranked

Salary/Winnings:	$7,500,000
Endorsements:	$ 700,000
Total:	$8,200,000

The Rodney Dangerfield of Formula One, Hill was the Grand Prix circuit champion this year, but most credit his car (a Williams-Renault), not his abilities. He makes far less than number three Michael Schumacher, and was even dumped by highly regarded Williams team at the end of the year. He'll race for less prestigious TWR-Arrows squad next year. But don't cry for this Brit: He makes another $700,000 pitching watches and Cellnet phones.

35. Troy Aikman, 30

Dallas Cowboys
1995 rank: Not ranked

Salary/Winnings:	$4,900,000
Endorsements:	$3,200,000
Total:	$8,100,000

After leading the Cowboys to three Super Bowl victories in the last four years, Aikman makes the Super 40 list for the first time. Aikman pitches for Coke and jumped from Nike to Adidas, but his biggest deal, worth about $1.5 million, is with Logo Athletics, a sports apparel company.

36. George Foreman, 47

Boxing
1995 rank: 6

Salary/Winnings:	$3,000,000
Endorsements:	$5,000,000
Total:	$8,000,000

He fought just once, beating up a mediocre former kickboxer in Japan in November. But Time Warner pays him $1.5 million for boxing commentary and promoting HBO. More pay from Meineke, Thompson Water Seal, videogames, Motorola, a cookbook, and tons of speaking engagements.

37. Charles Barkley, 33

Houston Rockets
1995 rank: 32

Salary/Winnings:	$4,500,000
Endorsements:	$3,500,000
Total:	$8,000,000

Traded from the Phoenix Suns to highly regarded Houston, which should aid his exposure. Needs it: Basketball's bad boy remains in Nike stable, but no national ad campaigns currently. McDonald's deal, but since it's an official league sponsor, it can get away with paying him and other NBA players less. Long-term deal with Right Guard deodorant.

38. Greg Norman, 41

Golf
1995 rank: 17

Salary/Winnings:	$ 900,000
Endorsements:	$7,000,000
Total:	$7,900,000

He choked in the Masters and was eclipsed by golfing phenom Tiger Woods in the endorsement department. But the Great White Shark gets lots of green from Reebok, Maxfli, Chevrolet. Can get up to $250,000 just for playing in some European tournaments.

39. Cecil Fielder, 33

New York Yankees
1995 rank: 39

Salary/Winnings:	$7,300,000
Endorsements:	$ 200,000
Total:	$7,500,000

A late-season trade brought this beefy banger to the Bronx Bombers, where he helped the Yankees win their first World Series since 1978. His share of the victory bonus was enough to nudge him back on the list.

40. Gerhard Berger, 37

Auto racing
1995 rank: 13

Salary/Winnings:	$7,000,000
Endorsements:	$ 500,000
Total:	$7,500,000

Replaced by Michael Schumacher on Formula One's Ferrari team, Berger and teammate Jean Alesi subsequently replaced Schumacher on the Benetton squad. Both took pay cuts: Alesi falls off the list, while Berger squeaks on. The Austrian retains some minor endorsements in his homeland. Even so, Berger pocketed over $1 million more than last year's 40th-ranked member of the Super 40 (Dan Marino, see number 13, p. 325).

Name Index

Subject Index